PURSUING
JUSTICE

PURSUING JUSTICE

An Introduction to Justice Studies

Second edition

Edited by

MARGOT A. HURLBERT

FERNWOOD PUBLISHING
HALIFAX & WINNIPEG

Editing: Jessica Antony
Cover design: John van der Woude Design
Printed and bound in Canada

Published by Fernwood Publishing
32 Oceanvista Lane, Black Point, Nova Scotia, B0J 1B0
and 748 Broadway Avenue, Winnipeg, Manitoba, R3G 0X3
www.fernwoodpublishing.ca

Fernwood Publishing Company Limited gratefully acknowledges the financial support of the Government of Canada, the Canada Council for the Arts, the Manitoba Department of Culture, Heritage and Tourism under the Manitoba Publishers Marketing Assistance Program and the Province of Manitoba, through the Book Publishing Tax Credit, for our publishing program. We are pleased to work in partnership with the Province of Nova Scotia to develop and promote our creative industries for the benefit of all Nova Scotians.

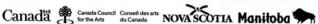

Library and Archives Canada Cataloguing in Publication

Pursuing justice: an introduction to justice studies /
edited by Margot A. Hurlbert. — Second edition.

Includes bibliographical references and index.
ISBN 978-1-77363-011-3 (softcover)

1. Justice. 2. Social justice—Canada. 3. Restorative justice—Canada.
I. Hurlbert, Margot Ann, 1964-, editor

KE444.P87 2018   349.71   C2018-903792-X   KF385.P87 2018

CONTENTS

ACKNOWLEDGEMENTS

Thank you to all the authors in this book for their insight, commitment and expertise in contributing to this project.

Thank you to our publisher, Wayne Antony, as well as development editor Tanya Andrusieczko, without whose guidance, reviews and comments this book would have never come together. Thank you as well to the other people who worked in the book: Beverley Rach, Debbie Mathers and Brenda Conroy for production, Jessica Antony for copy editing and John van der Woude for the cover design.

Many thanks to the anonymous reviewers who have provided detailed commentary and helpful suggestions.

Thanks as well to my colleagues, friends and family for their support. Special thanks to my husband for his continuous and steadfast encouragement and support. Without him I most certainly would still be practising law. Thank you to my mother for teaching me I could do whatever I set my mind to and giving me the confidence to do it. For my ability to write, and my ability to write a book, I owe my father a debt of gratitude.

ABOUT THE AUTHORS

GILLIAN BALFOUR is an associate professor of socio-legal studies and feminist criminology at Trent University. She has published widely in the areas of sentencing law reform impacts on Indigenous women and the implications of restorative justice in the context of gender-based violence. Her research examines victimization, criminalization and incarceration, as well as rape and legal narratives in sexual assault sentencing decisions, the role of victim impact statements in sentencing and the lived experiences of incarceration. She is member of Canada's Walls to Bridges collective that provides prison-based learning for incarcerated and non-incarcerated students.

SARAH BRITTO is a professor in the Department of Justice Studies at the University of Regina. Her primary research interests include understanding crime-related public perceptions, restorative justice and capital crimes and gender inequality and violent crime.

SELOM CHAPMAN-NYAHO is a PhD candidate in the sociology department at York University. His research focuses on youth regulation, race and policing. Selom teaches courses in the criminology program at York University and the Department of Humanities and Social Sciences at Centennial College.

GLORIA DeSANTIS is an assistant professor in the Department of Justice Studies at the University of Regina. Her interests include the non-profit sector, social justice, public policy advocacy, participatory action research and facilitating sustainable community development. She has more than thirty years experience working and volunteering with homeless youth, isolated seniors, immigrants/refugees and people living in poverty. She is the founder of the Voluntary Sector Studies Network at the University of Regina and a new undergraduate certificate in non- profit leadership.

HADLEY FRIEDLAND is an assistant professor in the Faculty of Law at the University of Alberta. She was the first Research Director of the University of Victoria Indigenous Law Research Unit. Hadley teaches and researches in the areas of Indigenous legal traditions, Aboriginal law, family law, child welfare and therapeutic jurisprudence. She is a married-in member of the Aseniwuche Winewak Nation. Her most recent book is *The Wetiko (Windigo) Legal Principles: Cree and Anishinabek Responses to Violence and Victimization.*

HIRSCH GREENBERG is the practicum coordinator for the Department of Justice Studies at the University of Regina. He worked for community-based organizations and First Nation communities for thirty years prior to his career at the University. His research focuses on homelessness, substance abuse, policing, specialized courts, inter-professional collaboration, circles of support and accountability and mental health. Hirsch is the past president of the Canadian Criminal Justice Association and a board member with the Regina Alternative Measures Program.

MARGOT A. HURLBERT is a professor jointly appointed to the Department of Justice Studies and the Department of Sociology and Social Studies, as well as the Johnson Shoyama Graduate School of Public Policy at the University of Regina. Her research interests include sustainability, climate change, energy, water and marginalized people. Margot became a full-time faculty member at the University after practising law for eighteen years.

CARL E. JAMES is a professor in the Faculty of Education and holds cross appointments in the graduate programs in Sociology and Social Work at York University where he is currently the Jean Augustine Chair in Education, Community and Diaspora. Using a framework of social justice, Carl teaches, does research and writes about institutional policies, programs and practices that afford accessible and equitable opportunities in schooling, education and employment for marginalized and racialized youth — particularly Black youth.

NICHOLAS (NICK) A. JONES is an associate professor in the Department of Justice Studies at the University of Regina. His research interests include restorative justice, transitional justice, genocide, policing and Indigenous justice issues. Prior to his academic career, he worked as a counsellor at a halfway house and a youth correctional worker and received training as a facilitator of family group conferencing.

JAMES MCNINCH is an emeritus professor and former dean of the Faculty of Education at the University of Regina. His writing and editing have focused on gender and sexual diversity (*I Could Not Speak My Heart*), racism and white heterosexual privilege (*I Thought Pochahontas was a Movie)*, the social construction of masculinity (*Queering Canadian Manhood*) and a critique of the audit culture of higher education (*Dissident Knowledge*). He was instrumental in bringing Camp fYrefly, an annual leadership and resiliency experience for queer youth, to Saskatchewan ten years ago, which expanded into fYrefly in Schools — programs and in-services to raise awareness of LGBTTQ2 issues and homophobic/transphobic bullying.

MARILOU MCPHEDRAN is an Independent Senator (for Manitoba) in the Parliament of Canada, a human rights lawyer and a professor with the University of Winnipeg Global College. She is a co-founder of the Ad Hoc Committee of Canadian Women and the Constitution(1981) as well as LEAF, the Women's Legal Education and Action Fund (1984).

JAMES P. MULVALE is an associate professor in social work and an associate member of St. Paul's College at the University of Manitoba, where he recently completed a term as Dean of Social Work. He also served at the University of Regina for fourteen years in the Department of Justice Studies and Faculty of Social Work. His research is focused on basic income and on social work theory, and especially on how justice and environmental sustainability pertain to both of these topics. He has previous professional experience in community development in the fields of developmental disability and mental health.

VAL NAPOLEON is the Law Foundation Chair of Aboriginal Justice and Governance, Director of the Indigenous Law Research Unit and Director of the Indigenous Law Degree (JID/JD) in the Faculty of Law at the University of Victoria. Val's current research focuses on Indigenous legal traditions, legal theories, feminisms, citizenship, self-determination and governance. She works with Indigenous community partners across Canada and with several national and international Indigenous law research initiatives. She is from Saulteau First Nation (BC Treaty 8) and an adopted member of the House of Luuxhon, Ganada, from Gitanyow (northern Gitksan).

AKWASI OWUSU-BEMPAH is an assistant professor in the Department of Sociology at the University of Toronto, Mississauga. His work focuses on the intersections of race, crime and criminal justice, with a particular interest in the area of policing.

RICK RUDDELL is a professor and Law Foundation of Saskatchewan Chair in Police Studies at the University of Regina. He has published extensively on crime, community perceptions of law enforcement, policing in remote communities and the economics of policing. His recently published books include: *Oil, Gas, and Crime: The Dark Side of the Boomtown*; *Policing Rural Canada*; *Exploring Criminal Justice in Canada*; and the third edition of *Making Sense of Criminal Justice*.

MICHELLE STEWART is an associate professor in the Department of Justice Studies and Director of the Community Research Unit at the University of Regina. She holds multiple appointments on research teams including the Strategic Research Lead for Justice Interventions with Canada FASD Research Network. Michelle is an applied political anthropologist with research focused on cognitive disabilities, mental health and racialized inequalities as they present in the criminal justice system.

PREFACE

I entered the practice of law with a passion and commitment for justice. While Canadian laws and institutions strive to achieve justice, I very soon learned that often the lived reality, or the experience of people within the justice system and other interconnected social systems, is not perceived by them or by their families, friends or any of us as just. This disconnect in peoples' lived reality is not a simple question of differing perceptions, but a complex question. It is difficult to fully define justice, to draw boundaries around what is or isn't just and to know what we can do to advance or achieve justice. This begs the question of where to start. Starting from the proposition of what is "fair" and what is not "fair" is one strategy for thinking about justice. Thinking about what is unfair and how to address it is another strategy. The authors in this book, in various ways and in various contexts, explore fairness, unfairness and justice.

Every day we make decisions that reflect our own individualized practice of justice. These individual decisions include whether to pollute by driving cars, shop at local farmers' markets or global food chains, purchase luxury goods contributing to our materialistic lifestyle (which will someday end up in our community landfill) or provide assistance to the poor. Decisions are also made in respect of social relations, occupations or volunteering activities. A career in helping people or a career in business might be chosen. Donations to charity, resistance to racial prejudice, jokes and behaviours or social activism through participating in local community non-profits or organizations are all activities that contribute to the practice of community justice. The summation of these individualized decisions and practices represents the justice practices of our community.

The primary objective of this book is to assist your thinking about what justice is and what it could be. By exploring justice in many different social and political contexts, we can critically reflect upon our own individual practices and how they impact justice in our community. New ways of thinking about justice can affect our perspectives, opinions and relationships.

Another important objective of this book is to enhance critical thinking. Critical thinking is not about criticizing and arguing, but rather the ability to conceptualize, apply, analyze, synthesize and evaluate the world around us and our relationships within it. Most importantly, the aim of this book is to help you undertake these activities while recognizing your own preconceived opinions and biases and seeking to understand those of others.

In Chapter 1 the foundations of pursuing justice are introduced. The components of justice are not mutually exclusive categories, but rather are interrelated. The key components of justice include formal justice, substantive justice and ethical practice. Formal justice recognizes equality, fairness, treating equals equally and following procedural justice. Substantive justice recognizes that sometimes equals have to be treated unequally in order to arrive at a just solution and includes distributive and redistributive justice. Ethical practice seeks to achieve justice through altruistic practice and being allies with the less fortunate or those without power to change the power relations in society

Each chapter of this book explores these foundational components in differing contexts. Formal justice, for example, is espoused by the explanation of the criminal justice system in Chapter 13 and parts of Chapter 10 that explain the legal system and its procedures. Substantive or distributive justice is explored in Chapter 3. The requirements of ethical practice are revealed in Chapters 7 and 8. These chapters do cover other aspects of the foundations of pursuing justice, but these ones predominate; as well, other authors set their contexts in formal and substantive justice and ethical practice.

Theoretical perspectives of justice are introduced in Chapter 2. There are significant distinctions between these theoretical perspectives that result in quite different frameworks for inquiry about justice. Often the theoretical perspective we feel most comfortable using reflects how we see the world. Structural functionalism aligns well with formal justice or treating equals equally. Structural functionalists represent the view of a predominately just world where institutions such as our criminal justice system function well. Chapters that align with the theoretical perspective of structural functionalism include Chapter 12 (and its explanation of the justice system) and Chapter 13. These chapters presume that formal equality achieves justice and treating equals equally advances justice. The presumption of our legal system is that everyone is not only subject to the rule of law, but also equal before the law.

On the other hand, in achieving justice, considering what is unjust or unfair in our society sometimes involves more than formal rules. Other approaches to justice such as post-structuralism, conflict theory and feminism are highlighted in chapters wherein the dominant purpose is to help us understand how power structures marginalize groups of people. For these perspectives and authors, it is seeing how power is distributed that helps us understand what is unfair. Post structuralists and feminists see a world influenced by structures of power, preventing some people from all the opportunities that life has to offer. Feminism is the underlying theoretical perspective of Chapter 6 and a closely related theoretical perspective surrounding the discussions in Chapter 8.

Recognizing and admitting our colonial past, present and (potentially) future are fundamental steps necessary to achieving justice in Canada and changing our future. Chapters 5 and 7 are important starting points in understanding and then being able to address our colonial past. Understanding the racism and oppression described in other chapters (such as Chapter 4 and Chapter 9) deepens our understanding of oppression in Canadian society. Understanding oppression allows us to find our personal ethical practices through which we can affect our circle of interactions, our jobs and our future jobs that will make Canada a little more just in the future.

This change is required both at a societal level, and in our own individual practices. In pursuing justice we must consider our actions (and even inactions) in our personal and work relations in achieving substantive justice and a fair distribution of access to societal resources. It is in Chapter 14 that we find answers to what constitutes ethical practice. Ethical practice includes moral righteousness, individual virtue and altruistic conduct. Ethical practice is the mechanism by which to achieve substantive justice; it is the act of recognizing, valuing and facilitating diversity. It is through the theme of ethical practice that social change is envisioned and oppressed minorities can be freed from exploitation by the most powerful in society, or the tyranny of the majority. Restorative justice is the culmination of how to achieve justice, how to implement our ethical practice and make real substantive justice changes in our path toward achieving formal justice. Chapter 14, on restorative justice, is more than a chapter about diversion of minor offences out of a criminal justice system. It is a chapter about embracing conflict, healing discord and making change in our own relationships.

The three themes — formal justice, substantive justice and ethical practice — are not independent, unrelated or mutually exclusive. Often they interconnect and overlap and can be envisioned as three interconnected circles. To pursue justice, each of these three foundations of justice need to be present.

—Margot Hurlbert

1

DEFINING JUSTICE

Margot A. Hurlbert

OBJECTIVES

At the end of this chapter, you will be able to:

- Define and discuss justice

- List the different disciplines that comprise of the study of justice, and describe how each discipline contributes to the multidisciplinary study of justice

- Discuss how law fits into the study of justice

- Understand the framing of justice underpinning this book

This book is about justice: its definition, its boundaries, its contradictions, its nuances. It is also about pursuing justice and the mechanisms and practices that enable this pursuit. But justice is tricky — just defining it is daunting. There are diverse and competing philosophies about what justice is, as well as several theoretical approaches to justice studies. Adding to the complication, justice is played out within many social contexts and issues: the Canadian justice system, the environment (including climate change), from the perspective of women (including their contact with the criminal justice system), the law surrounding equality, paid labour, poverty, the marginalization and colonization of Indigenous people, the oppression of racial minorities and the racial profiling practices conducted by the police, just to name a few. *Pursuing Justice* problematizes the notion of justice through an exploration of these contexts and issues, all while defining and pursuing the illusive notion of justice in Canadian society.

Justice is a term often used in everyday speech, but what is "justice"? Defining justice requires considering what justice is and the various approaches to studying it. As we will see, justice includes some key aspects: "desert"; "fairness"; "equality"; and "moral righteousness." A framework underpinning this study of justice includes formal justice, substantive justice and ethical practice. Underlying all this is philosophical theorizing about justice. Law is often thought of as the ultimate expression of justice in society. But, justice is surely more than just the law.

First, some "rules" of justice studies need to be reviewed. These rules should be kept in mind when reading all chapters in this book. These rules are meant to challenge our thinking and, by opening and broadening our perspectives, prepare us for learning. Thinking of these rules when confronted with challenging and perhaps uncomfortable material within this book may prove helpful.

STUDYING JUSTICE

Often when people think of the study of justice they think immediately of crime, perhaps a particular crime, the arrest of a person by the police, the court process and the eventual incarceration of an offender in jail and their rehabilitation. Another common theme is to describe justice in terms of laws and rules of society. Crime and laws are part of the study of justice, but only one part. Studying how these processes work together is the study of the criminal justice system. However, the study of justice entails more than just the operation of our criminal justice system and how to respond to a particular crime by passing a law to make another activity a crime.

The study of justice is also concerned with how a person came to be in trouble with the law in the first place. Factors contributing to behaviour in contravention to society's laws from both an individual perspective and also on a broader societal level expand justice analysis. Studying this behaviour in relation to social factors such as poverty, racism and education can significantly inform our understanding of law making and perhaps preventing crime. Trying to understand why poor and marginalized people in our society fill our jails and also our hospitals (because of poor health) and have higher suicide rates than the rest of the population is also a part of the study of justice.

Related to studying justice is determining what is or is not labelled as crime in our society. Historically, being drunk or using recreational drugs was not a crime. In some countries prostitution is a legal activity. In many countries, and even in Canada, many workplace deaths and injuries completely preventable with proper safety equipment but are labelled "accidents" not "crimes" (Rajan 2001: 385). Further, industrial discharges, which have polluted drinking water and resulted in deaths and illnesses, are not considered crimes (Nikiforuk 2008: 83). What is or is not a crime and who is and isn't prosecuted for crime in our society is part of the study of justice.

Studying justice also involves many other aspects of our society. In fact the study of justice by such people as Plato and Aristotle pre-existed modern notions of law and crime. How people are rewarded for their efforts in working, farming, creating and inventing, and who profits from these activities, such as corporations, retail stores and governments, are also justice concerns. Is the distribution of social, political and economic resources and rewards fair? Are developing countries in other parts of the world paid a just price for their goods and services, or are their people employed in sweatshops, working long hours for very little compensation? Justice studies asks how the environment of some of these developing countries supplying oil, rubber and other natural resources is affected and what the impacts of climate change are on these countries and their people in exchange for the exploitation of their resources. How this distribution is influenced by international human rights is also a paramount concern of justice studies.

RULES FOR THE STUDY OF JUSTICE

In respect of the entire multitude of issues and topics pursued in justice studies, a few common rules exist, regardless of the topic. The first rule is that our ethnocentrism (that is, preferences for practices and values reflective of our own culture) must be recognized. The potential of justice studies can only be achieved if we are able to break from our particular cultural background to take into account broader considerations that can affect the outcomes that we want to change. Recognition that we are ethnocentric and we think normatively (within the confines of our own values, norms, experiences and perspectives) is a key first step in pursuing the study of justice. If we are considering the destruction of the environment in a developing country supplying North America with oil and gas, we need to consider the perspective of people living in this developing country. Similarly, if considering the appropriateness of a woman to wear a head scarf while riding a bus we would have to approach the issue from the woman's perspective. To disregard her perspective, and consider only the thoughts, feelings and views of people where head scarves are not common, is not pursuing the study of justice. We must disengage from our personal emotions and recognize that we are products of our own cultural, religious and class background and, like most people, have a tendency to regard our own norms, values and standpoint as superior to all others.

The second rule in justice studies is recognizing that often the dominant viewpoint or the views of the majority are not the same as "justice." The idea of justice can't be captured by any single morality or standpoint but only emerges from the interaction among contending perspectives. Regard must be given to the perspectives of the marginalized, the poor and other "minorities." Justice requires recognition that sometimes minorities and the oppressed must receive what may be regarded as "special status" and privileges to prevent what otherwise would be tyranny of the majority or tyranny of the most powerful groups or people in society. To only think within one viewpoint and morality, especially when that perspective is the dominant standpoint or the majority of the population, limits meaningful contribution to broader issues of justice (Crank 2003: 2).

To fully understand the issues identified above, each of us must set aside our normative thinking. We have to be able to recognize when we are thinking normatively and understand that other viewpoints exist. Pursuing a full understanding of these viewpoints, even if it is held by a minority or only a few people, helps us to expand our understanding of a justice issue and approach it from more angles than our own thinking. In the example of the crime of drug possession, we can expand our understanding of the issues if we consider that in some countries the use of recreational drugs is not illegal (and at the time of writing Prime

Minister Trudeau is moving to legalize cannabis). This exercise expands our consideration of this topic outside of the norms, values and culture that have determined that the use of and therefore possession of recreational drugs is illegal. We are able to recognize our own thought patterns, biases and perhaps prejudices. When we expand our thinking and begin to consider thoughtfully and respectfully the position, viewpoints, thoughts and opinions of the "other," we approach the study of justice not as a "debate" between two viewpoints, but as a problematic. This approach challenges our traditional thinking and makes us embrace a plurality of positions.

THE INTERDISCIPLINARY NATURE OF THE STUDY OF JUSTICE

The study of justice is also multidisciplinary as it combines several usually separate branches of learning or fields of expertise. In this way, no one profession, be it law, philosophy, history or sociology has an exclusive claim to the study of justice. Each of these disciplines, and several more, play an important role in the study of justice. Knowing about the contributions of each discipline to the study of justice provides an important base to understanding justice.

Philosophers have wrestled with defining justice for centuries, dating as far back as 600 B.C. and the ancient philosophers Plato and Aristotle. The study of philosophy is the study of general and fundamental problems concerning matters of existence, truth, beauty, law, validity and justice. It is an approach to these matters that is critical, generally systematic (or all encompassing and not individualized) and relies on reasoned argument. It does not only rely on empirical or statistical methods or evidence but also on the pursuit of wisdom through rational and logical argument. Philosophy offers a meaningful starting point for defining justice as it has long history in struggling with the concept of justice.

More recently the philosophers' abstract speculation has been complemented by the empirical ways of knowing of the social studies (such as psychology or sociology). Social scientists developed many disciplines in their efforts to understand human behaviour. Each discipline contributes to the field in its own way. History contributes by providing information on the past record of human social development with useful insights into patterns, regularities and irregularities. For instance the historic treatment of people of Japanese ancestry during World War II, or the historic treatment of people enslaved several centuries ago from Africa has important implications for understanding human behaviour and our own and others' conceptions of justice or fairness. Not only does this history still have impacts in our society today, but it illustrates how society's conception of justice has changed over time.

Similarly, political science and the study of the organization, structure, operation and administration of government is crucial for understanding the justice system, the role of courts and corrections and the development of laws. Often the media will portray a particular court decision as "outrageous" and blame either the judge or perhaps the lawyer. However, closer analysis often reveals that the government was responsible for writing and passing the law that the court and the judge simply applied. Ultimately, the people elected the government.

Lastly, sociology, the systematic study of social structure, is crucial when studying justice or fairness within society. Law and the justice system of a society is a social structure that is influenced by other social structures in society. As an example, the laws surrounding marriage and divorce are influenced, at least in part, by the structure of the family (or families). Changing norms and patterns of the family, or the definition of what a family is, have had symbiotic effects on the laws surrounding the family. The heterosexual nuclear family was historically the only recognized family unit with the status to receive the benefits accruing to a family unit such as insurance payments and matrimonial support. This nuclear family consisted of a father, mother and child/ren. Now, however, benefits may accrue to same-sex couples, effectively giving a same-sex couple the status of a "family." Sociology focuses study on social structures and how human beings produce, reproduce and change social structures such as families and laws (Knuttila 2002: 21). The application of the principles of sociology to the study of law and the justice system improves and informs our understanding of justice.

Criminology makes an important contribution to the study of justice. Criminology is concerned with the study of the etiology or cause of crime. It looks at the role of the social setting and the interactions of various social groups in the cause of crime, as well as biosocial and psychological causes of crime, which tend to focus on the individual and their free will.

MULTIPLE AND CHANGING DEFINITIONS OF JUSTICE

Just as society changes over time and geography, so too does the definition of justice. Defining justice is an ever-changing, subjective process of determining whether the relations between individuals are fair, righteous and equitable. As illustrated in the last two sections of this chapter, philosophies and perspectives of justice are different for different people and different times. Justice has been of concern to society since its beginning. As stated by Bronowski:

> Justice is a universal of all cultures. It is a tightrope that man [sic] walks between his desire to fulfil his [sic] wishes, and his acknowledgement of social responsibility. No animal is faced with this dilemma: an animal is either social or solitary. Man [sic] alone aspires to be both, a social solitary. (Bronowski 1973: 41)

Justice is constructed individually as well as in groups and societies as a whole; it may be completely different between individuals whether a certain result is "just" or not. These individuals may use the same arguments based on fairness, equality, desert and moral righteousness to argue very different perspectives.

Consider two examples: divorce and law enforcement. One's views of divorce and its effects has an impact on one's views on the justice of divorce laws. Unique backgrounds and experiences affect viewpoints on the issue of justice and divorce. People perceive divorce laws in an individual manner based on their own views and life experiences. Those with a good relationship with both their parents might view the law granting each parent joint custody and 50 percent access to their children as just. Those with a poor relationship with one parent might perceive this same law as unjust.

Another example is one's relationship with law enforcement, or the legitimacy of the role of police officers in advancing justice. Those with a family member in law enforcement or a history of only good interactions with police may view the role of the police officer as important and facilitative of justice. However, those who have had consistently negative experiences with the police, such is the case with many Indigenous people, may perceive the role of police officers in the justice system somewhat differently or negatively. Education, reading and exploring others' perceptions can change these perceptions. Certain police practices result in the over-policing of minority groups and are very "unjust." Not being a member of a minority group, this knowledge and view is gained from exploring others' perceptions, reading and researching.

SO HOW DOES THE LAW FIT INTO THE STUDY OF JUSTICE?

People studying justice often expect the content to include much about the law. It does not. The law is a skeleton or framework for justice. It sets out certain attributes of the justice system but it is only one social institution in the study of justice. Other institutions have significant influence over the law and are important in our assessment of justice including the government, the economy, our education system, the family, marriage and religion, to name a few.

The law is often not the same thing as justice. Often when the two words are in the same sentence it is by way of contrast. A law may be unjust, immoral or not inclusive of all moral concerns. Syncrude's legal response to its killing of 1,606 birds in its tailing ponds was that it "had a permit" (Henton 2010). These same tailing ponds have poisoned many people (Nikiforuk 2008). Syncrude was found guilty and paid a $3 million fine and introduced a waterfowl protection plan to prevent a similar event happening in the future. However, a similar event occurred in 2015 and at the time of writing this matter has not yet been heard by a court (McDermott 2018). This illustrates another problem in conceiving the institution of law as the same as or synonymous with justice.

In court, there is always a winner and a loser and often even the winner does not feel they have achieved justice after thousands of dollars in legal bills and years of waiting for a court determination. There is a perpetual tension in each particular legal case between stability, certainty and predictability on the one hand and equity, fairness and justice on the other. Many people believe Canadian society should reinstate the death penalty for murder. This, they believe, would discourage "would-be" murderers from committing the crime, as they would realize that they would lose their life if they commit the crime. Enforcing the death penalty for murder would be done consistently and therefore contribute to the stability, certainty and predictably of the law and criminal justice system. However, what of the fairness for a women who is battered, abused and confined to her home and eventually gains the courage to use her spouse's gun in the middle of the night to murder him in order to free herself from her confinement? Is this a case where the certainty of the death penalty would be exacted, or should the criminal justice system recognize her dire circumstance? These questions illustrate the tension between the certainty of applying legal "rules" and imparting justice. Lastly, law as an institution or social structure in society often represents the interests of the powerful, dominant interests and groups in society.

TYPES OF JUSTICE STUDIES

Often we categorize the application of justice in a particular field as a special type of justice. For example, in respect to the environment, the area of environmental justice has developed. This area seeks to understand how the environment impacts our justice system and what aspects of the environment should be included in or protected by our justice system. Should sentient beings (entities with the ability to feel) have rights? Do horses or burrowing owls have rights? If we do grant them rights, are they the same as or different from the rights of humans? If their rights are less, how are their rights weighted against each other? Do we need to protect burrowing owls — an endangered species with fewer than 1,000 pairs in the wild (Wildlife Preservation Canada 2018) — from being trampled by horses? How do activities of development such as oil drilling, mining or manufacturing affect the environment and the people in the environment? Do these affected people determine what development is allowed to occur? How does carbon emissions contributing to climate change impact global justice? These are all questions of environmental justice.

When people commit crimes, or offend the norms and morals of our society important enough to have been labelled by our society as a "criminal" act, we state that they and their victims deserve criminal justice. In justice studies, we examine the demarcation in society between acts that are deemed "criminal" and those that are not and how this changes over time. Up until 1969 the *Criminal Code of Canada* contained an offence relating to homosexuality by prohibiting two men to have sex. Now, human rights statutes attempt to protect homosexuals from being discriminated against. In 2004, crimes in relation to occupational workplace safety appeared in the Criminal Code in s. 217.1 of Bill C-45, An Act to

Amend the Criminal Code (Criminal Liability of Corporations). The criminal justice system will be studied, and how it operates and achieves the parallel of corrective justice, the goals of rehabilitation of offenders and retribution or making one pay for their crime.

When we study compensation, monetary and otherwise, for a victim after a crime or injustice has been committed, we are speaking of the principle of restorative justice. Restorative justice also applies to more than just the victim. Restorative justice applies to offenders and the community. It can include reconciling harm done to a victim, restoring a compassionate, trustful relationship of offenders and victim after a criminal act, rebuilding a sound relationship between offender, victim and entire community after a criminal act and also the restoration of two disputing parties (committing a wrong or several wrongs against each other that are not necessarily criminal). Defining restorative justice is a difficult task. Narrow definitions focusing on crime and resolving crime exist to broaden definitions focusing on restoring community relationships (Marshall 1999; Zehr 2004; Braithwaite 2002).

Social justice is the broadest form of justice and relates to whether society as a whole is just. The remainder of this chapter will expand on ideas, concepts and issues that can help determine if society is just and provide a definition of social justice.

SEARCHING FOR A DEFINITION OF JUSTICE

Indigenous cultures each have a rich exploration of justice. Many Indigenous cultures use a combination of stories and elder teachings. One formulation of justice from an Indigenous perspective is offered on the website of the Federation of Sovereign Indigenous Nations — they define justice as:

> Strengthening First Nation communities by establishing peaceful and harmonious relationships through the restoration of our traditional justice and governance processes, and community based strategies that provide healing and community safety.
>
> Healthy, safe, self-determined First Nations who have the capacity to govern themselves according to their ancestral laws, spiritual beliefs, values, customs and traditions in accordance with their Inherent and Treaty rights. (FSIN 2017)

This is but one example of a worldview of Indigenous justice and should not be mistaken for being representative of all Indigenous worldviews. Yet, it shows that Indigenous worldviews respecting justice are inherently complex and multifaceted.

Moral prescriptions of 'justice' are key elements in major world religions. In the teachings of the Jewish faith in the Old Testament, the Hebrew word *mishpat* refers to the correct decision or ruling of a wise judge and *tzedak* refers to both righteousness and charity (Raphael 2001: 11). Major world religions also emphasize the importance of sharing our wealth and helping others as a requirement of religious belief and as a foundation of a just and virtuous society. In Islam, one of the pillars of belief is *zakat*, the giving of alms to the needy.

One of the first written definitions of justice is that of the philosopher Aristotle who lived approximately 2300 years ago (384–322 B.C.E.). In this book, we use some of the first principles of justice that Artistotle developed, with modern additions and adaptations, to build a foundation and framework of social justice that informs the remainder of the book. The foundational conceptual framework of justice consists of three interconnecting themes: formal justice, substantive justice and ethical practice.

Formal Justice

Aristotle stated that justice consists of righteousness, or complete virtue in relation to one's neighbour. He also espoused the idea of justice as a state of character — a cultivated set of dispositions, attitudes and good habits. Aristotle wrote about two types of justice: "rectificatory" justice and "distributive" justice (Artistotle 1985). Rectificatory justice in part lays the foundation for the first theme of justice — formal justice. Rectificatory justice was also referred to as "corrective justice" and focused on trying to restore to equality an unjust situation between people. For instance, restoring a victim of theft to the position they had been in prior to the act of theft by returning their money. Formal justice seeks to treat similarly situated people similarly, or treat equals equally. For instance, all people, no matter who they are, who pay money for goods that a store or vendor fails to deliver, have their money returned. In this way formal justice embodies laws and rules of procedure (often court processes) aimed at achieving a fair trial (sometimes referred to as "procedural justice"). Formal justice is also characterized by just deserts, fairness and equality.

Just Deserts

This is the idea of "getting what one deserves." On the positive side, we may bestow an award or social recognition on someone for a good deed or unselfish behaviour (for example, a medal for bravery for risking one's life to save a drowning person or designation as "Volunteer of the Year" for providing valuable help without pay in a community service organization). Awards and honours may also be a way to recognize extraordinary talent (first prize in the music festival; the gold medal at the Olympics) or great effort (designation as "the Most Improved Student"; award for "the Best Pie" at a baking fair).

There is also a negative side to "just deserts" — punishment or bad consequences for harmful or immoral actions, laziness or incompetence. Sentencing in the courts through the use of fines, imprisonment and community service orders certainly fits this category — although there are numerous ongoing debates about the balance that should be struck in criminal sentencing in regard to retribution, restoration and rehabilitation and about whether in fact the "punishment fits the crime" (more on this question later). Other examples of getting what one deserves through negative consequences include children losing privileges for misbehaving, lazy students getting poor or failing grades and employees without the necessary skills for a job being demoted or dismissed.

Sometimes consequences are perceived to be genuinely deserved — for example, a repeat offender drunk driver who has his driver's license taken away, or the athlete who avoids performance enhancing drugs and still wins the gold medal. However, sometimes credit or blame is ascribed in ways that are not "deserved" or fair. For instance, in regard to the distribution of wealth in society, sometimes people who are rich due to inherited wealth are highly regarded, and people who are poor due to circumstances beyond their control are seen as "lazy" or "stupid." In the latter regard, it is a common trend to distinguish between the "deserving" and "undeserving" poor in ways that reinforce invalid and negative stereotypes and that prevent us from adopting good policies and programs to combat poverty. Consider the case study of economic power.

CASE STUDY:
ECONOMIC POWER

Many social observers claim that some level of inequality is necessary in society (Davis and Moore 1945). Certain positions (jobs) in a given modern society are more important to the functioning of society than others are, and only a limited number of people can be trained, or have the talent, to do these jobs. Usually, those who succeed must sacrifice to do so (in terms of spending long years in educational pursuits) and therefore in order to induce the most talented members of society into those jobs, we must provide differential access to the rewards of society, which are already limited. Key jobs are those that are functionally important and take training or talent to achieve. Rewards for jobs are based on compensation in monetary terms, status (or ego expansion), and humour or diversion. Therefore, we have no choice but to live in a society that accepts some level of inequality.

In Canada an "economic elite" exists. A study of families raising children in Ontario (2000–2015) found the bottom half of families raising children in Ontario saw its share of earnings fall to 19 percent of total labour market income, down three percentage points, while the top half of families increased its share by three percentage points earning 81 percent of the total income pie (Block 2017). A study of Canada's one hundred highest paid Chief Executive Officers of companies concluded that their salaries in 2016 were 209 times the average income of $49,738, up from 193 times more in 2015 (Macdonald 2018).

This elite is increasingly a unified and class-conscious group. This is a result of the elite's solid organizational unity and coordinated lobbying efforts (Brownlee, 2005: 8). Corporate power has taken hold of the state and public spheres, influencing decisions about who governs and how, the production process, distribution of resources, nature and generosity of social programs, quality and quantity of jobs, and extent of environmental pollution (2005: 8). Two classes make up the economic elite: the capitalist class of large shareholders in major corporations and senior executives of business management (2005: 10). Sources of organizational unification include policy organizations, advocacy think tanks, and free-enterprise foundations. Mechanisms of unity of the elite include social class backgrounds, connections to major political parties, and interlocking directorships of companies (Brownlee 2005; Carroll 2005).

The public is not willing to have this continue in the future. In an Ipsos Global Public Affairs survey in 2009, 80 percent of Canada's citizens stated large companies have too much influence over government decisions (Barrera 2009).

Fairness

Fairness is the idea of "treating equals equally." For example, two people doing the same job competently with the same amount of experience and training should get the same pay. Under fairness, there should not be distinctions in rates of pay based on gender, age, racial or ethnic background, or any other factor not related to performance on the job. "Fairness," however, also means, in certain circumstances, treating people unequally in order to recognize and correct past injustices. For instance, if women or members of racial minorities have been historically excluded from certain (relatively well-paid and desirable) occupations, there may be a justifiable case for "employment equity" measures — giving suitable candidates from the disadvantaged group preference in hiring. Hence, there can sometimes be a distinction (and perhaps tension) between what is "fair" at the individual and collective levels. Consider the fairness represented in the following case study of social stratification and how it relates to economic power.

This concept of justice also denotes "procedural fairness" — ensuring that everyone receives a fair hearing and due process (for example, their case follows all the requirements of knowing the case against them, having enough time to prepare, having an impartial judge, and so forth) in courts, tribunals, appeal boards, and other formal decision-making bodies. For example, people who cannot afford legal fees should not be denied competent representation in court by a lawyer if they are charged with a serious criminal offence. Legal aid schemes, in principle, are supposed to ensure such legal representation for all. Procedural fairness also demands a transparent process for decision making that can be clearly

CASE STUDY:
SOCIAL STRATIFICATION

In addition to and in conjunction with economic stratification, social stratification exists in Canadian society. Social stratification refers to the systematic process by which individuals, groups, and places are categorized and ranked on a scale of social worth. This results in a hierarchy of individuals and groups and a resultant inequality of social relationships that determines who gets different rewards and burdens in society and why (Kerbo 2006). Social stratification is institutionalized (and backed by norms) and is based on statuses rather than personal attributes. Unfortunately, some people view specific racial populations to have more social worth than others. The same can be said of gender, whereby men tend to be ranked as more valuable, evidenced by pay inequities in Canada. Athletes, musicians, and writers are viewed as valued members of society. High school drop outs, criminals, and the unemployed are not. Finally, senior citizens seem to have less value and we provide fewer resources and pay less attention to their needs and contributions than we do to their other adult counterparts.

There is a correlation in North America between socio-economic status and social stratification (Kerbo 2006). Those who are represented by "upper" classes as denoted by occupation, property ownership (wealth), and access to power and other resources fare better in regards to access to society's distribution of rewards and benefits (Kerbo 2006). This has very real effects on people's lives in respect of many other aspects, including health. Canada spends 10.4 percent of its gross domestic product, or $142 billion dollars, on health care (Veenstra 2002: 364), and most of this is spent on reactive health costs responding to degenerative diseases. Degenerative diseases are predominantly experienced by lower socio-economic groups. Indicators of mortality and morbidity (including heart diseases, cancers, and cardiovascular diseases) strongly relate to socio-economic status. The poorer one is, the poorer their health (Segall and Chappell 2000). Preventative health care measures are not easily aimed at changing health expenditures given the significant time delay from their implementation and the effects of degenerative diseases like cancer and cardiovascular diseases (which take up a large proportion of health care dollars). So, health care funds are ultimately reactive, not preventative dollars.

Other examples where socio-economic status impacts social stratification can be seen in the interaction of people with the criminal justice system. Stratification results in social inequality and the reduction of the life chances of those people who occupy the lower echelons of stratification that are less valued.

understood by all, ready access to practical help to make one's case, and the right to appeal a decision to a higher body if one feels that one has been unjustly treated.

Equality

This common understanding of justice is embodied in equal citizenship rights for all persons (for example, the right of all to vote in elections and run for political office and equal entitlement to universal public programs such as health insurance and education). Equality also demands that there be an equitable sharing of civic burdens, such as paying taxes (although "progressive" taxation schemes may require the wealthy to pay proportionately more) or performing compulsory military service for a set period of time (in countries where this is required).

Equality also has economic and social dimensions. Does everyone enjoy adequate economic security through some combination of labour market earnings and income security programs provided by the government? Do all people in society have ready access to adequate and affordable housing, sufficient, safe and nutritious food, and other public goods such as transportation and green space?

Substantive Justice

Aristotle expands on justice by stating it consists of treating "unequals" unequally, in proportion to their inequality. This is also known as both substantive and distributive justice (Aristotle 1985). This pillar of justice is different than formal justice as it recognizes that individuals may need to be treated differently in order to achieve justice. Sometimes special considerations must be taken into account for groups who have been historically disadvantaged and marginalized. Examples of special treatment to alleviate historical inequality are affirmative action in hiring decisions and special sentencing considerations in criminal procedures. That is, procedural justice may demand that everyone be treated exactly the same, but substantive justice implies that not all are treated the same in order to achieve fairness.

Although this first appears simple, its application becomes somewhat problematic. Are women and men different, therefore, "unequal" and to be treated unequally? Are people of different skin colour different, unequal, or equal? Although most people today would say, "of course these people are all equal. These are categories of difference that we should not take into account to exclude from privileges in society like voting or riding at the front of the bus." This, however, was not always the case. In the first part of the twentieth century women could not vote and Black people could not ride at the front of the bus in the United States. Several years earlier in Canada, Viola Desmond protested the Canadian restriction preventing her from siting in the front of a movie theatre because of the colour of her skin and was convicted of a minor violation. In 2010 she was granted a pardon and in 2018 commemorated on the Canadian $10 bill and named a National Historic Person (Goffin 2016; Parks Canada 2018).

Normative thinking, beliefs, and value judgments form the basis for the determination of our categories of "equal" and "unequal." When we answer questions about equality, we answer them based on beliefs and biases, which we learned from parents, teachers, peers, and other subtle influences like the media, television, and books. It is these influences that form internalized beliefs and values, and a person's conception of "justice" and beliefs of what is fair and equal. Many people fifty years ago did not think of themselves as racist, although they supported the laws of racial segregation (the denial of full privileges of club membership, riding at the front of the bus, or swimming in a swimming pool to Black people); today we would consider these people and the laws segregating people on the basis of race as racist. Today, racist practices still occur. Until recently, police officers in Saskatoon, SK would routinely pick up Indigenous people in the winter and take them out of the city, leaving them to walk home in dangerously cold weather without proper clothing. Several died (Wright 2004). Although this practice is clearly racist, many would not consider Saskatoon police officers racist. The challenge for justice studies today is to ascertain what practices in today's society are unequal and unfair but are regarded as "normal."

These aspects of economic and social rights do not necessarily demand treating everyone exactly the same, or giving people exactly equivalent shares of a social good. It can be acceptable to have differences in income levels, house prices, and the consumption of goods and services. Such differences may in fact provide incentives that benefit individuals and society. For example, physicians tend to be well paid in order to encourage people to complete long years of medical training, and to provide this valuable service that benefits others. Economic and social differences also allow for individual preferences. For example, a person may decide to live in low-cost housing in order to save money for extensive travel. However, formal justice demands equality of access for everyone to adequate income, decent and affordable housing, food security, and the other necessities of a modest but dignified life. However, sometimes equality isn't enough. Substantive justice, or treating people differently, is required. A disabled person may require more resources than an able-bodied person for such things as transportation, communication, or housing.

Substantive justice brings up questions of "distributive justice" — how resources (such as money, health care, political power) and opportunities (such as placements in the best educational institutions, access to the best jobs, and access to the most lucrative business opportunities) are divided up across everyone in society. Unjust distributions may require corrective measures, in other words "redistributive justice." For example, wealthy people may be required to pay more taxes than those with modest or low incomes so that government can fund a reasonable level of public services for all. Educational institutions may have to take steps to recruit students and faculty members from groups whom they have historically excluded, such as women, racial minorities, or people with disabilities. Once again, treating every individual exactly the same may not be possible or even desirable, if we are to realize a collectively just distribution of money, social recognition, and political power. Such a redistribution of economic resources, positive social status, and representation in decision-making bodies may serve the collective good of society by creating a fairer, more inclusive, and more harmonious social order, even if some privileged individuals end up with a bit less than they started with. However, consider the problem of the growing gap of rich and poor where instead of redistributing resources to the more needy, the opposite is happening:

CASE STUDY:
THE GROWING GAP

The "growing gap" refers to the growing economic gap between the rich and the poor, which in recent years has reached unprecedented levels. Globally and nationally, the top income earners continue to earn increasingly more, while the lowest income earners are experiencing equally rapid decreases in their income (Mooney et al. 2008). According to the World Bank, the average income of the richest twenty countries was thirty-seven times that of the poorest twenty countries and this gap has doubled from 1960 to 2000 (Mooney et al. 2008).

Closer to home, David Macdonald found in a 2015 study that Canada's wealth gap is big and growing. "The wealthiest 10 percent of families enjoy a net worth that's millions more than families in the middle of the income spectrum" (Macdonald 2015: 5). In respect of the middle class, this advantage is disproportionately enjoyed by older middle-class families, rather than younger ones. For instance, middle-class families in their sixties and seventies saw wealth increases of close to 80 percent from 1999 to 2012 whereas middle-class families in their thirties have slightly less wealth in 2015.

For Canada's wealthiest families, all age groups have experienced breathtaking increases in net worth. Although affluent families in their thirties have only experienced a 33 percent real growth since 1999, the other age groups have experienced a doubling in the amount of wealth in real terms (Macdonald 2015). Canada's affluent twenty-somethings today have twice as much wealth as this group had in 1999, even after adjusting for inflation. Today their net worth is $540,000 up from $280,000 in 1999 (Macdonald 2015).

the rich are getting richer and more powerful and the poor are getting poorer and less powerful.

Rawls (1971) proposed we rethink what a just society is from the ground up, putting aside our individual interests. He felt that is was possible to commit to equality and freedom, while at the same time recognizing that there were unavoidable differences in individuals' talents, resources, and preferences. Working with both the "equality" and "difference" principles, Rawls argued that it was possible to design social arrangements and institutions in a way that would maximize fairness and welfare for all. We should start with no presuppositions about how society should be structured or how it should operate, but should understand that as human beings we are rational creatures and can act in cooperative ways to serve our own individual interests. This is what Rawls called the "original position." He also argued that in designing a just society, we should put ourselves behind the "veil of ignorance" — we should suspend knowledge of our own individual characteristics and talents (like our gender, age, and level of intelligence and talents), and design social arrangements that benefit all (including the worst off) as much as possible. This is called the "maximin" principle. In this way we would be sure to set aside our ethnocentrism and imagine a fair distribution of goods in society.

Ethical Practice

This final meaning of "justice" encompasses the ideal of individual virtue and ethical conduct. Inequality is acceptable if everyone has the same opportunity and if inequality is arranged to the greatest benefit of the least advantaged member of society (Miller 2003). In order to arrange distribution for the greatest benefit of the least advantaged, an ethical practice must inform our actions. Rawls' conception of justice assured the protection of equal access to liberties, rights, and opportunities, as well as taking care of the least advantaged members of society (Robinson 2010). Individuals are thought to be "just" when they engage in altruistic behaviour to help others or make society a better place, and set an example of altruistic conduct in both their personal responsibilities (as a spouse, parent, friend) as well as civic and public roles (as an employee, professional service provider, elected politician, business person, club president). One important theme of this book is that ethical practice entails ending oppression.

By invoking Rawl's mental exercise of putting oneself in an "original position" and invoking a "veil of ignorance," a philosophical foundation for ethical practice can be found.

However, there are other mechanisms of ethical practice. The process of redistribution, or more specifically arriving at a fair redistribution, entails social and economic participation. Redistribution entails a societal

CASE STUDY:
OPPRESSION

Oppression refers to the unjust or cruel exercise of authority or power by a majority group over a minority group. Oppression is an important concept as it informs ethical practice; by understanding oppression one can understand who the least favoured and marginalized in society are — they are the oppressed. Oppression can occur through the use of physical, psychological, social, cultural, or economic force (Henry and Tator 2006). People can experience oppression at many different levels simultaneously. Indigenous people experience oppression in Canada as evidenced by the processes of colonization and their contemporary inequalities. However, there is also evidence that women experience oppression. Thus, an Indigenous woman will have different experiences with oppression than will Indigenous men or non-Indigenous women. People may experience oppression at many levels and where these levels intersect the oppression can be particularly noteworthy. This is an important consideration when studying social justice issues as we are required to understand that stratification will result in different life experiences for different people in any given society.

decision mechanism or process that allows meaningful participation of all people in society with recognition, mutual respect, and an ethic of making decisions taking into account the position of the least favoured or neediest in society. Meaningful participation ensures that the voices of young people who are unable to vote are heard, and, similarly, older people in long-term care receive special attention in order to be heard. This is especially true in relation to matters that impact these people, such as legalizing marijuana or changing pharmaceutical drug plans.

INTERCONNECTIONS OF JUSTICE COMPONENTS

The components of justice described include formal justice, substantive justice, and ethical practice. Formal justice recognizes equality, fairness, treating equals equally, and following procedural justice. Substantive justice recognizes that sometimes equals have to be treated unequally in order to arrive at a just solution and includes distributive and redistributive justice. Ethical practice seeks to achieve justice through altruistic practice and helping the less fortunate, those without power and resources. These components are not mutually exclusive categories, and often piggy-back onto one another. For instance, it is ethical practice to volunteer to assist people who can't work because of disability, illness, or age. Volunteer activities might include assistance with day-to-day tasks or organizing outings to a museum or special event. Ensuring these people a dignified life through income assistance is a form of substantive distributional justice

It is also true that these components of justice may sometimes compete or run contradictory to one another. For example, advocates of social justice as equality often call for broad and generous social programs, and are willing to accept relatively high taxes so that we can afford such programs. On the other hand, those who advocate for "just deserts" in the marketplace tend to favour low taxes and highly differentiated rates of pay, in order to provide financial incentives for the talented and hard working and to "punish" those who are seen as lacking in skills or effort. These two different camps will likely disagree on many aspects of how to distribute resources justly, and on what a "just society" should look like.

Similarly, people in the "just deserts" frame of mind often believe that criminals deserve retribution and harsh treatment. On the other hand, people who equate justice with equality or fairness may see the roots of criminal behaviour in social and economic marginalization and a lack of rehabilitative services for individuals in trouble with the law. These two sides call for very different kinds of policies and programs in the criminal justice field.

DEFINING JUSTICE

We have only scratched the surface in defining justice, but we can make some tentative conclusions about it. The notion that the law is justice has been challenged. The law is one social institution that mediates relations between people and has an influence on the actions and choices of people. Whether the outcome of these choices and actions are just is sometimes a matter of one's norms, values, and perceptions. A verdict of not guilty of murder is felt by many people as allowing a criminal to walk free and a travesty of justice for the deceased. However, for most prosecutors, defence lawyers, and judges, the legal outcome is regarded as justice, albeit of formal, procedural justice.

Social institutions such as courts, governments, or police forces also impact the justice equation when making determinations, which affect the lives of individual people. Whether one is arrested for an offence and then convicted of that offence, and whether there is a criminal law making something an offence are all determined by these institutions. Governments are also one institution affecting how much minimum-wage earners make, whether unions are allowed to form, and how much corporations are taxed (money that contributes to social welfare programs). The study of justice entails a study of all these institutions and how they impact social relations.

The multiplicity of social institutions and relations impacting justice, or just relations between people, necessitates a multidisciplinary approach to studying justice. No one discipline has an advantage. Many approaches and perspectives must be pursued in studying justice and no simple solitary definition of justice exists.

The study of justice must be pursued with two rules in mind. First, recognition of one's own norms and prejudices must be made. Any justice issues should be analyzed with an acknowledgement of our own ethnocentrism. As well, it must be recognized that often the perspective of marginalized people must be seriously considered, explored, and given voice if unjust social arrangements are to be uncovered and challenged.

Even though we cannot develop a single universal concept of justice, we can study it with a framework of justice: of formal justice that includes just deserts, fairness, and equality; of substantive justice that addresses inequality and distributional justice; and of ethical practice that combats oppression. The study of justice entails using this framework, or parts of it, to examine the justness of a variety of social situations. Looking at more specific social arrangements — poverty, racialization, gender relations, policing, sexual minorities, the environment, human rights, and the criminal justice system (and there could be others), as is done in the rest of this book — also helps us refine how we see and understand justice.

DISCUSSION QUESTIONS

1. What are the differences between the understandings of justice (formal, substantive, and ethical practice)?
2. What are the two key differences between formal and substantive justice?
3. What are some forms of individual and group or collective ethical practice?
4. Is the law the same thing as justice?
5. What is the weakness of this chapter's representation of Aboriginal views on justice?

GLOSSARY

Distributive justice: The fair division of resources and opportunities within society.

Equality: Treating people the same. For example, all people receive equal rights of citizenship such as rights of voting and being free from unreasonable search and seizure.

Ethical practice: The altruistic practice of helping those that are less fortunate, without power, or without resources.

Ethnocentrism: The tendency to view one's own ethnic group or culture as superior to other ethnic groups or cultures.

Fairness: Treating equals equally, and unequals unequally; fairness achieves the correct balance in this formula.

Formal justice: Attaining fairness and just deserts and employing procedural justice.

Just deserts: The idea that one should be rewarded or punished based on the desirability (or undesirability) of their behaviour.

Multidisciplinary: Composed of or combining several usually separate disciplines at once.

Normative: Conforming to a standard of perceived correctness by adhering to rules of behaviour.

Procedural justice: Ensuring that all procedures are fair and carried out in a similar fashion for people in similar circumstances. This might include receiving notice of being charged with a crime, having one's rights read, having an opportunity to speak with a lawyer, and so forth.

Redistributive justice: Achieving fairness through redistributing resources in society to assist people living in poverty.

Substantive justice: Achieving fairness when it requires treating equals unequally as well as having fair distribution of the goods, resources, and "bads" in society, and redistributing resources if necessary.

REFERENCES

Aristotle. 1985. *Nicomachean Ethics: The Various Types of Justice.* (H. Hachett, trans.) Indianapolis, IN: Terence Irwin.

Barrera, J. 2009. "Big Companies Wield Too Much Power, Says Poll." *Leader Post*, January 2: A8.

Block, S. 2017. "Losing Ground: Income Inequality in Ontario 2000–2015." August 15. Toronto, ON: Canadian Centre for Policy Alternatives.

Braithwaite, J. 2002. *Restorative Justice and Responsive Regulation.* New York: Oxford University Press.

Bronowski, J. 1973. *The Ascent of Man.* Boston MA: Little Brown.

Brownlee, J. 2005. *Ruling Canada: Corporate Cohesion and Democracy.* Halifax, NS: Fernwood Publishing.

Carroll, W.K. 2005. *Corporate Power in a Globalizing World.* Don Mills, ON: Oxford University Press.

Crank, J.P. 2003. *Imagining Justice.* Cincinnati, OH: Anderson.

Davis, K., and W. Moore. 1945. "Some Principles of Stratification." *American Sociological Review,* 10 (April): 242–249.

FSIN (Federation of Sovereign Indian Nations). (n.d.). "Justice." <www.fsin.com/justice/>.

Goffin, P. 2016. "Civil Rights Pioneer Viola Desmond Will Appear on New Canadian $10 Bill." *Toronto Star,* December 8. Torstar.

Henry, F., and C. Tator. 2006. *The Colour of Democracy: Racism in Canadian Society,* third ed. Toronto, ON: Nelson Thomson Learning.

Henton, D. 2010. "Oilsands 'Doomed' if Duck Charges Stick, Syncrude Tells Court." *Leader Post*, April 28.

Kerbo, H.R. 2006. *Social Stratification and Inequality: Class Conflict in Historical, Comparative, and Global Perspective.* New York: McGraw Hill Higher Education.

Knuttila, M. 2002. *Introducing Sociology: A Critical Perspective.* Don Mills, ON: Oxford University Press.

Macdonald, D. 2015. *The Wealth Advantage: The Growing Wealth Gap Between Canada's Affluent and the Middle Class.* Canadian Centre for Policy Alternatives. Ottawa, Ontario.

___. 2018. *Climbing Up and Kicking Down. Executive Pay in Canada.* Canadian Centre for Policy Alternatives. Ottawa, Ontario.

Marshall, T.F. 1999. *Restorative Justice: An Overview.* London, UK: Home Office, Research

McDermott, V. 2018. "July summary disposition set after Syncrude 2015 bird deaths." *Edmonton Journal*, January 27. <dmontonjournal.com/news/ local-news/july-summary-disposition-scheduled-following-syncrude-bird-deaths-in-2015>.

Miller, D. 2003. *Principles of Social Justice*. Boston, MA: Harvard University Press.

Mooney, L.A., D. Knox, C. Schacht and M.M. Holmes. 2008. *Understanding Social Problems,* third ed. Canadian. Toronto, ON: Nelson Thomson Learning.

Nikiforuk, A. 2008. *Tar Sands: Dirty Oil and the Future of the Continent.* Vancouver, BC: Greystone Books.

Parks Canada. 2018. "Government of Canada Announces New National Historic Designations." Parks Canada news release, January 12.

Rajan, S.R. 2001. "Towards a Metaphysics of Environmental Violence: The Case of the Bhopal Gas Disaster." In N.L. Peluso and M. Watts (eds.), *Violent Environments*. Ithaca, NY: Cornell University Press.

Raphael, D.D. 2001. *Concepts of Justice*. Oxford: Clarendon Press.

Rawls, J. 1971. *A Theory of Justice*. Cambridge: Harvard University Press.

Robinson, M. 2010. "Assessing Criminal Justice Practice Using Social Justice Theory." *Soc Just Res.*, 23: 77–97.

Segall, A., and N. Chappell. 2000. *Health and Health Care in Canada*. Toronto, ON: Prentice-Hall.

Veenstra, G. 2002. "Social Inequality and Health." In E.G. Grabb (2002), *Theories of Social Inequality,* fourth ed. Scarborough, ON: Nelson Thomson Learning.

Wildlife Preservation Canada. 2018. "Burrowing Owl Recovery." <wildlifepreservation.ca/burrowing-owl-recovery/>.

Wright, D.H. 2004. "Report of the Commission of inquiry into Matters Relating to the Death of Neil Stonechild." <www.cbc.ca/news/background/stonechild/stonechild_report.pdf>.

Zehr, H. 2004. "Commentary: Restorative Justice: Beyond Victim-Offender Mediation." *Conflict Resolution Quarterly,* 22, 1–2: 305–315.

2

THEORIZING JUSTICE

Margot A. Hurlbert

OBJECTIVES

At the end of this chapter, you will be able to:

- Compare, contrast and link social and personal problems and view them in a context of neo-liberalism

- Identify individual problems in the context of social problems

- Discuss and evaluate several perspectives used in analyzing social problems

- Understand the method of discourse analysis

Justice studies is intriguing and challenging because it involves multiple social dimensions. Moreover, comprehending the social problems coincident with justice issues helps to develop a broad, nuanced, and contextualized analysis. A criminal act, for example, may be viewed as an unfortunate decision of an individual and often people wish to focus on that individual's decision and a sentence that will deter such decisions in the future. However, a broader understanding of justice is always necessary, including understanding how a person came before the justice system, why a particular act is a "crime" punishable by the state, what the victim's interests might be, and how society might prevent re-offending. These issues are broader than just considering crime as an individual's choice, and justice theory is bigger than just "crime."

A further example of this broader approach to thinking about justice problems and theory is to explore the social nature of an illness. A person diagnosed with tuberculosis is often viewed as having bad luck or the misfortunate of poor health. This viewpoint changes when reconsidered with more information. For example, Aboriginal people have a tuberculosis rate 26.4 times the rate of Canadian-born non-Aboriginal people (Public Health Agency of Canada 2007). They are also four times as likely to suffer from Type 2 diabetes and are more likely to experience health complications related to the disease than non-Aboriginal Canadians (Thommasen et al. 2004). This information illustrates that what is too often seen as a personal problem of illness is really a social health and justice problem. In Canada can it be said that such a significantly higher rate of illness is fair or just?

Understanding this broader ambit of justice wherein social problems are linked to personal problems is necessary for effectively eliminating injustice in society and achieving substantive justice. Substantive justice might require implementing measures and approaches contextualized for a particular person in a particular situation, which may not be the same for another person because of the social problems surrounding a particular person and their actions. Justice studies link the social problem of poverty and inequality to both personal health issues and the issues of individuals and their involvement with the criminal justice system. Both health issues and committing crime tend to be thought of as dependent on an individual and their personal choices, not dependent on the fact someone is poor. These are but two examples of society's justice issues; many more exist, such as homelessness, the treatment of disabled people and minority groups, and barriers to immigrants and refugees in Canada.

Recognition of the social problems contributing to an individual's problems allows understanding that all people are not similarly situated; the contextualization of a person's problems within social problems informs how people situated differently should be treated differently. Recognizing social problems informs the application of formal justice and the identification of what is a dissimilar situation because of social context. For instance, young children in foster care often have difficulty with learning at school because of the trauma they are experiencing in their lives, which includes not living with their parents as well as the causal circumstances. These young children often need special supports and programs in order to advance their learning. Recognition of when people are situated differently and when justice requires a different solution is foundational to achieving more substantive justice by recognizing and respecting an individual's human dignity through understanding that an individual's problems are not created solely due to bad luck and poor personal decisions. Identifying social problems as being social in origin allows us to move toward changing social conditions that assist in the goal of achieving justice.

In the last few decades there has been a trend to increasingly view problems as individual problems and not social problems. This is due to the increasing pervasiveness of the political ideology of neo-liberalism, which emerged in the 1980s (Ross and Trachte 1990). Neo-liberalism is both an ideology (a set of beliefs, attitudes, or opinions) of how modern society should operate and the foundation of a political strategy and platform about how society should be structured. The neo-liberal ideology is one that supports the self-regulation of the market economy; minimal involvement of the state in social programs, expenditures, and regulation; privatization of government-owned industry (of currently public services like water, power, or insurance); "free" global trade; predominance and protection of individual property rights; and replacing the concept and practices of "the public good" or "community" with that of individual responsibility. This last element pressures individuals and poor people to find solutions for their lack of health care, education, and security by blaming themselves if they are unsuccessful and having others label them as "lazy" (Martinez and Garcia 2007). This ideology is reflected in mainstream politics and the strategies of many powerful financial institutions like the World Bank and International Monetary Fund (IMF). Because of its predominance as both an ideology and a strategy of political parties for the last several decades, neo-liberalism may contribute to the difficulty we have in thinking of issues and problems in today's society as "social" problems and not just personal problems.

SOCIAL PROBLEMS

Cases going through the criminal justice system are (most) often seen as representing individuals with problems. This isn't inaccurate as particular individuals (accused, victims, and others) proceeding through the criminal justice system do have an individualized problem (whether it is an assault, a theft, or a murder). In an analytical sense, viewing criminal cases as personal problems suggests that "crime" can be explained in terms of the qualities of the individual involved — the "offender" has poor anger control, has ego issues, has had a poor moral upbringing, and the like. From that it is a small step to conclude that solutions to crime lie within the immediate environment of an individual.

In justice studies, we study not only the individual case proceeding through the justice system, but also how the individual case represents a wider social issue. In this way, not only is the individual circumstance studied, but also how it is connected to a "social problem." In a domestic assault, for example, the individual case is about the particular spouses who have engaged in physically violent behaviour. There are particular details about the abused, the abuser, the history of the relationship, the level of violence, the number of previous violent incidents, and previous criminal charges for assault. This is the individual problem or criminal justice case. However, the individual case does not occur in a social vacuum; it is connected to the larger social problem of violence in our societies, gender inequality and stereotypes, female economic dependency, child care obligations and inequalities, and a pattern of familial abuse. These factors represent the social structures that contribute to domestic violence on a global and individual basis. A social problem is one in which the causes and solutions lie outside of the individual and that individual's immediate environment; it is one rooted in our society's social structures and institutions.

The same analysis can be made with respect to health and illness. The significant link of poor health to poverty is well documented (World Health Organization 2014). Yet, the ill are most often conceptualized and treated as individuals with the misfortune to be "ill" and in need of a cure. Good health is no longer supported in significant policy or programs (of nutrition and exercise) because of both the reduction of government programs and spending over the last few decades and the neo-liberal belief that individual life choices determine individual health.

Studying and analyzing individualized "problems" as social problems involves the concept and method of the "sociological imagination." This term was developed by the American sociologist, C. Wright Mills, in his book, *The Sociological Imagination* (1959). For Mills, in order to understand ourselves, our behaviour, and the behaviour of others around us, both near and far, we need to have a sociological imagination. The relationship between (social) history and (personal) biography enhances seeing ourselves and others within the wider context of the social structures that have influenced us. This is a broader context than just thinking about parents and friends and their influence on people (although this is part of our social history). In order to truly understand individual lives, lives within society and within the historical processes that have shaped, structured, and moulded that society need to be considered. In this way, personal biography and the biographies of others that have been affected by these wider social and historical processes are connected to one another. Utilizing the sociological imagination is seeing the relationship between an individual's experiences and the larger society in which the experiences are contextualized, that is, relating private troubles of individual people to the public issues of a society in a particular time and place.

Issues in society often appear as personal problems and not as social problems to both non-participants (bystanders or observers) and to people experiencing problems. One reason is that people tend to take responsibility for their actions and what happens to them, instead of connecting that to other events, people, or circumstances. This, however, is a somewhat misguided reaction, albeit not completely erroneous. The object of thinking in broader societal terms is not to create "excuses" for things such as being let go from a job or committing a criminal act. The object is to be able to assess how social structures contributed to a particular circumstance and how to change life chances or opportunities in the future. Perhaps it is the social structure that needs to be assessed, not (just) the individual.

By defining unemployment as a social problem, the appropriate ways to deal with the problem are different. Consider the statistics in the Case Study of Unemployment and Banks that illustrate the level of unemployment in Canada over time. The rate of unemployment varies depending on the state of the economy, global competition, and many other factors. When considering these statistics, the individual loss of a job is clearly part of a much bigger social picture. In the individualized analysis and

CASE STUDY:
UNEMPLOYMENT AND BANKS

In 2008 the unemployment rate was 6.1 percent, hovering close to the record lowest rate of unemployment experienced in Canada in the mid-1970s of 6 percent (Statistics Canada 2009a). By July of 2009 unemployment jumped to just over 8.5 percent of Canadians, with thousands losing employment (Statistics Canada 2010; Statistics Canada 2009b). The unemployment rate reached its highest levels in 1983 (12.0 percent) and 1993 (11.4 percent), following two major recessions in Canada (Statistics Canada 2009a).

The 2008–09 recession, the "sub-prime mortgage economic downturn" was initiated when banks and mortgage companies (often fraudulently) enticed people who could not afford them to buy mortgages. The situation worsened when banks and mortgage companies resold these sub-prime mortgages to other financial institutions. Financial markets began to collapse when it became clear the mortgages could not be repaid.

When the conflicts of interest and fraudulent practices were exposed, the mortgages were devalued, resulting in the devaluing of house prices. Many people, especially in the United States, ended up with mortgage loans well in excess of the value of their houses. People lost their houses and banks began to fail (Guard et al. 2009).

The recession then cascaded through the whole economy. Many in the mortgage and banking industry lost their jobs and people lost their savings; as people couldn't get loans they stopped buying cars and houses, stopped making their mortgage payments, and many in the automobile and housing industries lost their jobs; because these people didn't have jobs and stopped spending generally, many in the retail industry lost their jobs as well.

As a result, unemployment around the world has skyrocketed. In 2009, the United States unemployment rate was 9.4 percent and in Spain unemployment reached 20 percent (Visual Economics 2010). This widespread problem was created by powerful financial firms who were more interested in making money than in helping house people. Thus, for an individual, losing a job was clearly situated in the context of a wider economic/social problem, not the result of individual shortcomings.

view, only the individual feels the consequences and is left to deal with the problem. However, if we view the issue as a social problem it is possible to identify causes other than personal shortcomings and identify appropriate solutions such as unemployment insurance or family-friendly workplaces that provide subsidized, affordable daycare services for mothers in the workplace. In order to make effective change in our society in the pursuit of social justice, it is important to analyze problems as social in nature.

In 2013, the police-reported crime rate was at its lowest point since 1969. However, it remains a central focus in our media every day and provided the basis for the federal government's campaign in 2008 to "get tough on crime" (McCulloch 2008). Media reporting of crime makes it sensationalized and readers' attention is drawn to individual incidents several times in each day's newspaper. This media context allows political parties to build platforms calling for tougher response to crime.

When a newspaper reports on an individual in a community committing a crime, many people immediately personalize the offender's

Figure 2-1: Crime Rates in Canada

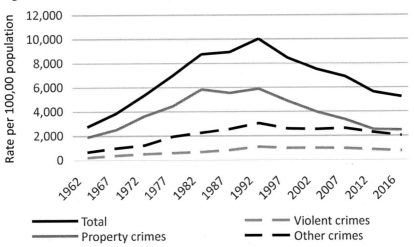

Source: Keighley 2017

problem. The person is thought of as having made a bad decision. They may even be thought of as a "criminal" or a bad person. They may carry this stigma for the rest of their life. But committing a criminal act, just like our example of being fired, may be reflective of social problems as well as personal problems. When we individualize crimes we focus on the people committing them as bad people. This allows us to feel good about declaring a "war on crime." War, when carried out against "bad" people, tends to be legitimized. This allows focus on ensuring retributive justice, which is a particularly individualized response to justice.

When crime is thought of as a social problem, then peoples' roles as members of society in both contributing to the crime rate and in helping to redress crime are considered. An example might be neighbourhood kids spray painting graffiti on a garage. If it is thought of as an individualized problem, the kids are seen as "bad" and needing some significant consequences in order to have their behaviour brought into line in the future. Often people want these kids to suffer a consequence, perhaps out of revenge or to satisfy a sense of "justice." If instead the youth are regarded as part of the community with not enough to do, or with parents who are forced to work long hours at minimum-wage jobs to get by and can't afford child care, we start to think of how the community contributed to the problem of painting graffiti. Why are minimum wages so low that people can't afford day care? Why is child care so expensive? Why are these children ignored in the community? Why do people not volunteer at schools and community centers to help run after-school programs? Pursuing this line of thought and inquiry allows crime to be viewed as a social problem. In order to restore communities to a state of health and vibrancy, the actions and roles of individual actors or people (other than the youth painting graffiti) must be included in the analysis and discussion. Recognizing the place of people in the community in the justice equation, after a "crime" like the appearance of graffiti on our garage, moves the analysis from individualized retributive justice to restoring, repairing, and rebuilding communities.

When answers start being provided to questions such as these, theory is actually being used. When the questions about why kids engage in graffiti, and why the low level of minimum wage and lack of affordability of child care exists, conclusions are being made based on observations, readings, and perhaps even research. In this way, working assumptions are being developed based on various forms of generalization from experience and knowledge that will be used to guide situations in the future. By undertaking these exercises, we are engaging in theoretical thinking (Sears 2005).

As with all learning, a certain amount is drawn from personal experience. However, using the theorizing of others can help to develop analytical capacity. Already developed theories help by, in large part, suggesting the kinds of questions that need to be asked in trying to understand individual behaviour resulting in problematic situations and identifying surrounding social issues. Understanding the social issues surrounding these problematic situations is a necessary component in pursuing the study of justice by utilizing a broad definition of justice, which includes social justice. If problems are only seen as "personal," then the most vulnerable groups of individuals in society who need assistance in order to achieve a just society can't be identified.

THEORETICAL PERSPECTIVES ON SOCIAL PROBLEMS

Every day, decisions are made by people from the simplest things like what to eat and what to wear to more enduring issues such as what program of study to embark on or which career to pursue. These decisions are based on understandings and beliefs about possible benefits and costs of these decisions and an additional amount of embedded theory that is possessed about the potential consequences of these decisions. For instance, a career as a police officer may be chosen because a person theorizes that it is a career providing interesting work (whether it be working on the streets to control crime or in the school to ensure our youth embarks on a proper path, and even perhaps managing and mentoring young officers).

Formal theories, developed through social movement activism or scholarly studies, tend to reflect a broader view than theories based on personal experience. These academic theories are developed through interchange over time and a more rigorous set of requirements for internal consistency and fit with the world. An example of a theory is Darwin's theory of evolution. Many people (including his grandfather) had the idea of evolution prior to Darwin. However, Darwin developed a theoretical account explaining how and why evolution occurred over time, referring to broader scientific frameworks used for understanding life forms (Sears 2005).

A theory provides an explanation of a phenomenon using some sort of broader framework of understanding and is not simply describing the phenomenon, but explaining it.

In the social sciences, social theories generally will not hold without qualification for all time, all conditions, and all cases, for at least two reasons:

1. The probabilistic nature of social inquiry: When predicting a social phenomenon (someone's future occupation, health, and educational outcomes, for example) it is impossible to do so with complete certainty. We can assign probabilities based on social class, education of parents, and other factors.

2. The inherent pluralism in social causation: One is unable to say that a child who suffers child abuse and is raised in a home of criminal gang members will become a criminal. This is partly due to the inherent pluralism in social causation — that is, many factors contribute to social outcomes. The abused child of criminals will have many other influences that may be positive and prevent that child from growing up to a life of crime. Perhaps the child will excel in school because of thoughtful caring teachers or will benefit from a particularly close relationship with grandparents. (Grabb 2002)

There are many theoretical perspectives for studying social problems. Five will be discussed here: structural functionalism, conflict theory, symbolic interactionism, feminism, and post-structuralism. These perspectives are widely accepted as the basic general approaches and a representative sampling of possible approaches. Each represents a different lens or analytic framework for approaching a social problem, and is based on different values and different assumptions about how society functions. They are more accurately described as "schools of thought" than justice theories because not all theorists agree on all the component principles. This makes it difficult to precisely define each theory and describe it in a manner all of its proponents will accept (Grabb 2002). No one perspective is necessarily superior to the others; no perspective is wrong. Much can be learned from all of the perspectives, but they should be evaluated on how well they can explain what happens in the world.

CLASSIC THEORIES OF SOCIETY AND JUSTICE

Structural Functionalism

Structural functionalism is characterized by a particular strategy of inquiry. This strategy investigates society as if it were a system of parts (or structures) that are interconnected, each of which perform various functions for the system (Durkheim 1893). Often the analogy of an organism is used: society is envisioned as a living (human) organism, with particular parts to fulfill particular functions and maintain a state of balance and social equilibrium. Just as a human body has organs such as a heart or liver performing different functions, so too does society have parts or structures performing functions. For example, the family is a structure that reproduces society through performing the function of having children and socializing them; politics is a structure within which members of society are governed; education is a structure that transmits society's skills and knowledge (Parsons 1937).

In analyzing society, structural functionalists often study "norms" (shared expectations about behaviour), "roles" (behaviour associated with a particular position in the social structure), "institutions" (collective means of dealing with basic social functions such as government, the economy, the family, education) and "values" (things preferred because they are defined as having worth) (Parsons 1951: 327; Williams 1960). All of these parts of society interrelate and work, according to structural functionalists, to maintain society as a functioning system (Parsons 1951). There are two types of function: manifest functions are those that society intends and are often formally set out as institutional goals; latent functions differ as they are functions that are unintended and almost always informal (Merton 1968). For example, a manifest function is performed by our educational institutions in educating and training youth. However, when we incarcerate people in our justice system to make society safer and rehabilitate offenders, a latent effect occurs in establishing, developing, and expanding gangs inside our jails that eventually are present outside the jail. The presence of these gangs results in our society being less safe.

Functionalism maintains that the ideal condition of any system is balance and stability, just like any living organism. Social problems arise when social institutions do not fulfill their functions; thus, dysfunction occurs.

Dysfunctions are undesirable consequences of an activity or social process that inhibit a society's ability to maintain balance and stability, to adapt or adjust (Merton 1968). Social disorganization in the entire society is caused by dysfunctions in social institutions. Social problems are a result of rapid social change from things such as technology advancement, which causes stress on institutions.

Illness is seen from a functionalist perspective as a dysfunction or a threat to social institutions operating as they should. This is easily analogous to the organism metaphor as illness is counterproductive to a healthy, thriving organism, causing an imbalance. People who are ill cannot fulfill their appropriate social roles, their responsibilities to family, employers, and larger society. According to Talcott Parsons (1951), a founder of this perspective, illness is a form of deviance that must be controlled. Sick individuals are seen as not responsible for their incapacity, exempted from their usual role and task obligation, expected to "get well" and obligated to seek and comply with the directions of a medical professional. In this way physicians are agents of social control by certifying a person is physically or mentally ill and specifying how they are to behave and treatment they are to undergo.

Structural functionalism would view crime as a social problem resulting from rapid change in society that has weakened social solidarity and social institutions like the family so that insufficient order is maintained. Our correctional and penitentiary institutions have become breeding grounds for criminality such as gangs. This is a latent function (arguably a dysfunction) as it is unintended and not a formal function of these correctional and penitentiary institutions. The manifest function is to retrain and rehabilitate offenders, punish and remove offenders to keep society safe.

Structural functionalists have two main theories of crime. The first is that deviance functions to maintain society (Erikson 1966). By criminalizing behaviour that is inconsistent with social norms, social cohesion and stability is endorsed and is expressed when those who do not conform are stigmatized. This view was expressed as early as 1927 when studying social problems of immigration (Thomas et al. 1927) and again in the 1960s when relating crime to the disintegration of traditional institutional authorities like the church, family, legal system, and community (Nisbet 1969). The reality is that crime is often committed in moments of passion or desperation with very little thought as to criminal consequences. As such, having a law against a certain act does not provide an incentive to a person to hold off in performing the act in that particular moment of passion.

A second functionalist theory of crime focuses on norm violation as a disruption of natural order and equilibrium. This perspective sees this disruption as a natural occurrence and an indication of social change. Philip Hauser (1969) argued that observable social problems — such as lack of housing, pollution, crimes of violence, protest, and war — are all related to "social morphological revolutions" or the transition of the smaller intimate community life of the past to a mass society. This change, he believed, was due in part to increased population, increased diversity of cultures in populations, and increased urbanization (such that more diverse people live in close proximity to one another).

One of the founding structural functionalists, Emile Durkheim (1858–1917) studied the social cohesion of industrial society. Durkheim referred to industrial society as being in a state of "anomie" — a condition where an absence of social regulation results in a state of normlessness. He considered this to be a pathological state characterized by a breakdown in social order and solidarity. In a healthy society people know exactly what goals are appropriate for their particular social positions and precisely how they are supposed to realize those goals. A state of anomie is a state of confusion about the legitimacy of various social aspirations and the propriety of certain ways of pursuing those aspirations (Durkheim 1895). For example, studying hard and doing well at school to pursue one's choice of career makes a healthy contribution to society; however, in a society that is in a state of anomie, being a member of a gang and pursuing economic reward through selling drugs occurs widely because the social processes that steer young people to school are not strong.

Durkheim distinguished physical needs from social needs. Physical needs are regulated by nature such as when one eats until one's hunger is satisfied; social needs are not so regulated. A person may have an unlimited desire for wealth, power, and prestige if they are not checked by external and social constraints. Unregulated, they escalate until they are unattainable. Unsatisfied social desires without social norms results in disappointment, unhappiness, and frustration. This increases stress and, for example, the individual propensity to commit suicide. In times of rapid economic change such as an economic decline, recession, or depression, the suicide rates escalate (Durkheim 1897). Although Durkheim studied suicide, Merton (1938) borrowed the concept of anomie to explain deviance in the United States.

Durkheim's theory of anomie and suicide has been revised to a more general theory of social deviance and crime in more recent times (Yablonsky and Haskell 1988). In North American society youth are taught the value of being successful, making money, and acquiring material wealth. The media assists with this materialism and the embracement of this lifestyle. However, the reality is that our society does not provide equality of opportunity to all to attain this sought-after lifestyle. In fact, a differential opportunity exists depending on one's social status, ethnicity, and background.

The overemphasis on ends (being wealthy) and under emphasis on means (ensuring equality of opportunity) produces anomie. With the overemphasis on the end goal of winning, the way people "play the game" is less important and inattention to the rules results in their becoming imprecise and less explicit. This mal-integration or anomie in turn produces strain, which is most acutely felt by lower status individuals. Society encourages these individuals to aspire but denies them equal access to legitimate avenues of opportunity to attain these goals through education and work. These individuals experience frustration, differential opportunity, and strain and this encourages deviance as a way of adapting to the gap separating social goals and the means of attaining them (Merton 1938).

The structural functionalist perspective allows us to fully consider formal justice. The overarching goal is to have a harmonious society where all people have equal opportunity to society's resources and opportunities and meaningfully participate in society.

Conflict Theory

Conflict theory evolved from the work of Karl Marx and focuses on power, oppression, and exclusion. Whereas structural functionalists view society as different parts working together, the conflict perspective views society as a struggle between particular groups and interests competing for power and resources. Karl Marx viewed society as having progressed through a series of class/power struggles: the slave with the master; the serfs with the lords; and finally the worker with the owner (capitalist) (Marx and Engels 1848). At the time Karl Marx was writing, in the nineteenth century, industrialization was rapidly occurring and capitalism had emerged as a dominant economic form. Capitalism is an economic system characterized by private ownership of the "means of production," — the elements that contribute to production such as buildings, machines, labour, raw materials, and so forth. From this private ownership, profits, which are actually created by the labour of workers, accrue disproportionately to capitalists — the owners of businesses (Marx and Engels 1848).

Karl Marx saw society as divided, fundamentally but not completely, into the two broad and unequal "classes": the workers (the "proletariat") and the business/corporate owners (the "bourgeoisie") (Marx and Engels 1848: 58). This division benefited the capitalists in two main ways. First, by paying workers wages that were less than the value of the goods they produced, owners had access to many resources not available to workers. Their goal was to amass surplus value or profit, not meet society's needs. But, their ownership and control of the surplus value and the means of production (the economy) gave capitalists control of not only the economy (the central institution of society) but also of the other institutions of society (such as the state, the media, and so on) to their advantage (Marx and Engels 1848). An example of this is the laws against vagrancy, or loitering in public places (Chambliss 1994), which penalized unemployed people as not contributing to the capitalist system of work and consumerism while they were unemployed through no fault of their own. For Marx, capitalism is fundamentally, at its very core, an unjust society.

Neo-Marxist conflict theorists today have further developed the ideas of class inequality inherent to capitalism and the rise to dominance of the ideology of neo-liberalism and the social problems linked to poverty; others focus on "race"/ethnicity or gender. An example of this is corporate crime or wrongs committed in the pursuit of profits without regard to other considerations such as worker or consumer safety. In a neo-Marxist analysis, worker and product hazards are inherent in capitalism because the fundamental goal is profit making.

The resolution of these issues is the creation of a classless society, changing work to make it safer and more fulfilling for everyone, applying stronger controls over corporations to ensure the economy serves society rather than social life existing to serve the economy. In relation to justice, the conflict approach would argue that powerful groups in society — particularly the economically powerful — have at their their disposal the means to if not define, then disproportionately influence, the kind of behaviour that is considered criminal. Most often, socially harmful behaviours that are key to profit-making will not likely be criminalized. In an inequitable society such as that under capitalism, they would argue, much crime results from the lack of opportunities for the poor and for racial or ethnic minorities. Again, a classless society would not define crime in a manner detrimental to those who are poor or not meeting the needs or interests of the powerful capitalist class in society.

In respect of health, for example, the conflict perspective concludes that the medical/industrial complex of a societal health care system rooted in the capitalist economy creates social problems. Not only do the poor all over the world experience poor health because of their highly stress-filled lives (where potentially being homeless is a paycheque away, but so too is their lack of access to resources for good health care such as medicine and doctors). In another example, pharmaceutical companies are well known to put profits before health. Pharmaceutical companies have been exposed for behaviour advancing profit making at the expense of the health of society in general. For instance:

- In the non-Western world, some pharmaceutical companies investigate Indigenous knowledge of traditional healing. Upon making a discovery, the pharmaceutical company will patent the discovery and prevent even the original Indigenous peoples from practising their own form of healing. Then, the pharmaceutical company will sell their patented "discovery" for a profit not shared with those Indigenous peoples (Shiva 1997). Take for example Catharanthus roseus, also known as Madagascar periwinkle, used by Indigenous groups in the Philippines and beyond as an appetite suppressant and a medication against leukemia as it reduces white blood cells. It is a component today of many medications patented and sold by pharmaceutical companies earning large profits (Baig 2013).
- Some pharmaceutical companies have actively prevented the publication of research exposing harmful effects of their patented drugs (Lexchin 2002; Thompson, Baird and Downie 2001). Cohen (2018) found that studies of the effects of pharmaceutical products in animals (a tuberculous drug specifically) were deliberately overstated in order to obtain funding to test the drugs on humans.

Other conflict theorists focus less on social classes and more on conflict arising from groups with opposing values and interests. Value conflicts occur between diverse categories of people including non-whites versus whites, heterosexuals versus homosexuals, environmentalists versus industrialists, and young versus old. These conflict theorists sometimes term their theory as "oppression theory." Oppression entails the domination of subordinate groups by more powerful groups and their exclusion from full participation in society. An example of this is the treatment of Indigenous peoples in Canadian society after centuries of colonialism (Alfred 2009).

Conflict theory is again, like structural functionalism, concerned with the social world at an aggregate, "big picture," or macro level. Broad aspects of society, such as institutions and large social groups, are studied. Structural functionalists focus on the achievement of formal equality, but this equality centers on equality of opportunity.

Symbolic Interactionism

Symbolic interactionism focuses on the individual in society. It examines the individual and how the individual, particularly identity, is shaped and influenced by the society he or she is living in. An individual's identity is shaped by symbolic interaction — social behaviour based on the meanings that are created and attached to behaviour. In other words, actual behaviour is less important than the meaning attached to behaviour. Max Weber (1864–1920) asserted that to understand individual and group behaviour one needs to see the world from the eyes of that individual or group. When conducting social science research, scientists must try to understand others' views of reality and the subjective aspects of their experiences, including the symbols, values, attitudes, and beliefs they use to express what reality means to them (Mead 1934). When trying to understand the individual who is being studied, the researcher is trying to understand that individual's "construction" of social life, or how that individual perceives the world and themselves. The influence of social structures on this perception or individual construction is the paramount object of study (Cooley 1902). Social problems are studied and analyzed from the aspect of how certain behaviours come to be defined as social problems and how individuals and groups come to engage in activities that a significant number of people, or a number of significant people, view as major social concerns (Becker 1963).

For symbolic interactionists, the way that people conceive of themselves, their society, and their specific situations, affects their behaviour. The labelling perspective is the classic symbolic interactionist perspective on deviance. From this point of view, a social group or a behaviour is problematic if it is viewed or labelled as such. Symbolic interactionists argue that mental illness, for example, is most importantly a label (a social construction) conferred on individuals who are "different" and who don't conform to particular definitions of appropriate behaviour. A growing number of behaviours and conditions are being labelled as medical problems, such as hyperactivity, attention deficit disorder, and learning disabilities. Even some natural aspects of life such as aging, menopause, and birth have been transformed into — that is socially constructed as — medical events.

In respect of crime, two questions are important. First, how do crime and deviance come to be defined as such or, more specifically, how are some behaviours "labelled" as crime? Second, what are the effects of being labelled as criminal or deviant? With respect to the former, Becker (1963) explains that deviance can often be in the eye of the beholder because various groups have different conceptions of what is right and proper in certain situations. That is, deviance is discovered by a dominant group that does not share a belief in the appropriateness of another group's behaviour. In his classic statement, Becker (1963: 9) explains:

> Social groups create deviance by making the rules whose infraction constitutes deviance, and by applying those rules to particular people and labeling them as outsiders. From this point of view, deviance is not a quality of the act the person commits, but rather a consequence of the application by others of rules and sanctions to an "offender." The deviant is one to whom that label has successfully been applied; deviant behavior is behavior that people so label.

For example, during the first half of the twentieth century, the potlatch tradition of some First Nations was illegal. This was a traditional ceremony and practice of sharing one's worldly goods and wealth with others.

With respect to the impact of being "labelled" as criminal and the creation of further deviant behaviour, two paths were identified. First, the label catches the attention of the labelling audience causing the audience to watch and continue to label the individual, and second, the label may be internalized by the individual leading to an acceptance of a deviant self-concept (Wilkins 1965). After an individual commits a criminal act and is caught and convicted, that person is stigmatized as a criminal. This deviant label then dominates that person's social identity and is thus the primary basis on which the person is defined by others. Being labelled deviant may then deny that person opportunities for engaging in non-deviant behaviour and causes the person to develop a deviant self-concept and act accordingly (Wilkins 1965; Schwartz 1962).

The labelling perspective can be seen in youth involved in crime. Teenagers who commit regrettable acts of crime are often expelled from school or placed in custody. This causes them to be denied opportunities to participate in sports and activities that regular students are able to participate in and affects their self-image as being a "druggie" or "gang member." Resolving social problems sometimes involves changing meaning and definitions attributed to people and situations (Goffman 1963).

Symbolic interactionism expands our understanding of an individual's problem in relation to the social problems that may have created it; as a result, it advances substantive justice because we understand the different circumstances that contributed to one's misfortune. If we condone neo-liberalism discussed at the beginning of the chapter, we believe that all individuals are responsible for their own behaviour and formal justice would categorize these individuals as having made bad choices, thereby responsible for the consequences. Understanding the contributing social context situates the individual circumstance in a broader setting, opening the door for an ethical practice of addressing this broader setting in addition to the individual circumstance.

These are the three "classic" perspectives, mainly from sociology. Each has their strengths and weaknesses. Although scholars often are drawn to one particular theory and reject others, it should be noted that there are scholars who study and apply each of these theories. No one theory has been endorsed as the superior theory; it would be impossible for a consensus such as this to be achieved. All three, though, have come under heavy criticism in recent years. Feminists have shown that all three ignore a fundamental fact about all societies — their division into two genders and the almost universal inequality between the genders. Post-structuralism criticizes the structural functionalist and conflict theories for "over-totalizing" society and social behaviour — that is, for over-emphasizing large institutions — and in the process ignoring the individual variation in behaviour and attitudes within society. Symbolic interactionism is criticized for being too focused on a psychological analysis at the individual level.

RECENT THEORIES OF SOCIETY AND JUSTICE

Feminism

Feminists aim at making what appears "natural" questionable. Dominant Western beliefs are that capitalism is the best economic institutional arrangement; the neo-Marxist conflict perspective seeks to denaturalize and question this. Feminism aims at "denaturalizing" beliefs and thought and behaviour patterns about gender. For all feminists/feminist theories, gender relations are patriarchal — those that give males privileged access to society's resources and social attitudes that see males and masculinity as superior to females and femininity. A patriarchal belief would be akin to the belief, started in the nineteenth century Victorian upper class, that a women's place was in a home having and caring for children (rationalized by the fact women have children, not men). Feminists seek to denaturalize this belief and the current parallel beliefs in today's era, for example, that certain occupations like engineering are better suited to men. The task of defining feminism is controversial and difficult because of its depth and breadth, but understanding its goals and methods is illuminating (Beasley 1999). At its most general, feminism can be understood as both a body of knowledge and a political movement aimed at understanding and alleviating the inequality of women (Comack 2006). Put simply, feminists argue that male-dominated societies are fundamentally unjust. There is both formal injustice in women not being treated the same way as or accessing the same privilege as men, and substantive injustice as women are paid $0.87 for every dollar earned by men (StatsCan 2017).

European and male perspectives, such as all three classical social theories, are valid, but only partially. Feminists were pioneers in exposing this. For example, the Marxist conflict perspective centers on the class struggle between workers and capitalists. This theorizing did not reflect the perspective of women in the workforce and the economy. Women's issues of maternity leave, gender equality in pay and promotion, and the capitalists' benefitting from unpaid labour in the home were all omitted. Theoretical frameworks of feminism were able to analyze these issues.

However, feminist theorizing shares with the conflict perspectives its insistence on analyzing power within relationships (both interpersonal relations and societal relations). The feminist focus is on gendered power and patriarchy. Patriarchy is the domination of women by men; the power of men over women. This domination occurs in two key and inter-related ways. Men dominate through their privileged access to the public institutions of social power — men occupy the key positions in the economy and politics. Men also dominate through the attitudes that privilege masculinity — that is, the attributes of men (strength, aggressiveness, and so on) are seen to be superior to those of women (relational, cooperative, and so on). The privileging of masculinity leads many of societies' institutions to have a male character.

Because there are many women, in many areas of the world, with many perspectives, there is no one feminist theoretical perspective. As well, there is no feminist issue per se. Feminists analyze all issues from a feminist, gendered power analysis. Sometimes this perspective is termed "reflexive." This means that the feminist perspective is constantly evolving through the process of reflection and a working and reworking of the personal biographies of women in relation to the dominant social structures of patriarchy.

This constant reflection and re-evaluation is a common feature of theoretical perspectives that reject the view that all knowledge rests on scientific method that holds the key to truth about human behaviour. Physical science, medicine, and psychology are some of the disciplines that rely heavily on positivism. Positivism is the idea that society can be studied objectively and rationally — without values, beliefs, feelings, and opinions. Feminism is a worldview that challenges these all-knowing claims to truth based on totalizing structures formulated on aggregated statistical data, for example, theories of structural functionalism. In the view of feminists, structural functionalism and conflict theory often make totalizing claims, such as women are responsible for the function of reproduction. While it is true many women have and raise children, not all do, and many men raise children. Feminism instead tends to focus on the standpoint of the individual woman and attempts to deconstruct totalizing claims exposing their socially constructed and patriarchal claims of truth.

To take one example. Within the health field, a concern of feminists has historically been the relatively small numbers of and treatment of women within the medical profession. Until only very recently it has been very difficult for women to enroll in medical faculties to become doctors and it still is somewhat difficult for women to attain the lucrative professional specialties of doctors. In addition, the majority of nurses are women fulfilling the caring, less well-paid positions in the health care field. Many of the traditional functions of midwifes in labour and delivery have been taken over by doctors, reducing their work load and paid compensation (Van Teijlingen et al. 2000). This was done, not because the practice of midwifery wasn't a safe medical practice, but because it didn't medicalize birth, or require the institution of a hospital and work of a doctor. These issues could be analyzed both from a feminist perspective and a conflict perspective. From a feminist perspective the place of women within the field of health and practices of health care is marginalized (in order to achieve formal justice in that all women have the same opportunity as men so are treated equality in the health field); from a conflict perspective the medical profession now controls, directs, and profits from what used to be a natural maternal process of giving birth. Advancing midwifery would advance substantive justice in allowing different medical practice for those women desiring a different medical treatment. An ethical practice of justice would make available this different medical treatment for those so desiring it.

Post-Structuralism

Post-structural theorists (of which feminism is one) reject the grandiose macro theories of structural functionalism, conflict theory, and symbolic interactionism based on totalizing structures that examine all of society, such as capitalism.

According to post-structuralists, privilege is a key element of society. It is embedded and replicated in all our social structures and social interactions through the exercise of power, which is everywhere (Foucault 1979). Instead of focusing on power itself and who holds the power (as some neo-Marxist conflict theorists do), post-structuralists employ Michel Foucault's focus on the mechanisms of power (Comack 2006). For example, regulation (control of people's behaviour) exists outside the formal purview of the "state" or government. This power over people exists in all aspects of our lives.

According to Foucault, often heralded as the founder of post-modernism, a new social mentality of regulation emerged in the sixteenth century, which contrasted and eventually replaced regulation by absolute submission to a sovereign King or Queen (Foucault 1978). The new mentality exerted a much less visible, more internalized, and less physically coercive influence and comprehensive regulation of behaviour without the sovereign's very overt and coercive mechanisms of control. This change in how society is ruled, from sovereign monarch to government, was characterized by an increase in individual liberty. Foucault saw current neo-liberalism as a mentality of rule, a method of rationalizing the exercise of power ("governing") through techniques for leading and controlling individuals without being responsible for them (Foucault 1997). By increasing individual liberties and freedoms and freeing individuals from subjugation by a monarch, societal norms and expectations of individual behaviour conforming to these norms became more widespread. Many new mechanisms of control rely heavily on individual perception and ideas of reality.

New mechanisms of control are part and parcel of neo-liberal ideology. Social risks such as illness, unemployment, and poverty are viewed not as the responsibility of the state, but as lying in the domain of the individual (Lemke 2001). Long gone were the days of absolute monarchy and feudalism wherein everyone had an unchanging (and unchangeable) role (such as serf or lord). Individual freedom brought individual choice and individual responsibility. An individual is seen as having a responsibility to obtain an occupation for financial support to be free from poverty and unemployment; an individual is also seen as having responsibility to eat healthy and be physically active to remain free from illness.

Mechanisms of control can be exposed through what post-structuralists call "deconstruction." What they see as "modernist" thinking relies on binary oppositions (for example, men versus women, workers against capitalists, black versus white). Deconstruction of everyday practices and interactions shows how a particular category such as whiteness is socially constructed. In doing this, the various privileges that being white is accorded are explored and how these privileges are embedded in between people is uncovered. Deconstruction also criticizes the forces of hierarchy that are present in such binary constructions or boundary formations implicit in social structures and language.

Post-structuralists often use "discourse analysis" to deconstruct social interactions. Discourses are forms of language use or ways of making sense of the world and its social practices (Phillips and Hardy 2002). Discourses are reflected in all manner of forms, whether they be letters, newspaper articles, trial transcripts, laws, art, or even music — what discourse analysts call (social) "texts." Discourse methodology assumes that the meaning making of a speaker or writer is both structured by and expressed in language. Post-structuralists assume that everyone has their own subjective experience of social life and, thus, what language means. Consequently, each of us constructs texts differently; but, those experiences and meanings take place within our own particular time, place, and community. The authors of this book have constructed the language used from their particular historical place and time. For example, most texts written prior to the 1970s used the term "he" to refer to an individual, a gendered practice whereby privilege was expressed subtly through a preference for the "he." Another construct is the term "Black" when describing a person. "The very notion of a black Torontonian conflates hundreds of different languages, histories traditions and stories. It could mean dark-skinned people who were born here or elsewhere, who might speak Arabic or Patois or Portuguese" (Cole 2015: n.p.). The term Black is the only classification that identifies a skin colour rather than a nation or region.

Through a process of examining and analyzing the discourses found in various texts from a standpoint or place of the "other" or the marginalized, the structures of power and influence are made visible. Specific forms of discourse that claim to speak the truth and thus exercise power in a society are shown to reflect the "truth" of the writer or speaker, but do not reflect the truth of all people. It is through this exposure of power and oppression that substantive justice (treating people differently) can be achieved. For example, many schools still teach that North America was "discovered" by various European explorers. This may reflect the fact Europeans discovered a land across the ocean of which they were previously unaware. But, to say they discovered North America reflects a white Eurocentric belief (and power) very different from the reality of all of the Indigenous peoples whose ancestors had lived and known North America since time immemorial. Just as importantly, using the language of "discovery" is an exercise of power and oppression, if only in that this language continually supports the idea for white people that they have a right to the land their ancestors "discovered."

The deconstruction of discourses reveals the various "centrisms" embedded and naturalized so as to not be questioned. These centrisms may be many and include ethnocentrism (belief in the superiority of one's own culture and ethnicity), anthropocentrism (the superiority of humans), or theocentrism (the superiority of a particular religion). The deconstruction of discourse can also reveal various myths that mainstream society like to believe, but are inaccurate. These myths are also termed "discourses of denial."

Residential schools operated by churches and government in Canada for many years provide another example of the discourses of denial. It can only be assumed that a discourse of denial was in existence at the time that these schools were described and thought of as "educating" Indigenous peoples. Now, decades later, the discourse of denial has been exposed as a "myth." A Truth and Reconciliation Commission has exposed the lived experience of oppression and horror that many of these students faced in acts of violence against them that were perpetuated within these schools (Sinclair 2009). The Truth and Reconciliation Commission calls to action provide many "discourses of another truth."

By critically engaging and deconstructing structures in society, post-structuralists expose mechanisms of power through which groups of people are oppressed. Often, these mechanisms are thought of as "natural" to many and not questioned. When this occurs, the "discourse of denial" is at work, making structures of oppression and domination appear quite natural. Without exposure, these structures of oppression would continue to oppress and marginalize. In order to assist the marginalized and least well off in society and achieve social justice, discourses of denial have to be questioned and replaced with practices that can achieve justice. This questioning and exposure of structures of oppressions is an ethical practice of justice. It is the altruistic practice of helping those less fortunate, or without the power or resources to live life to its fullest and participate equally in society. The ethical practice of exposing inequality and power illustrates the distributive injustice of our society, which can then be addressed through redistributive justice. In this way, the ethical practice aims to achieve formal justice or equality where equal representation in well-paid occupations — doctors, university professors, chief executive officers — all represent the gender, race, ethnicity, and Indigenous population of their community.

Often we assume that people are in the same circumstances and

Table 2-1 Comparison of Theoretical Perspectives

	Structural Functionalism	Conflict Theory	Symbolic Interactionism	Feminism	Post-Structuralism
Representative Theorists	Emile Durkheim Robert Merton	Karl Marx C. Wright Mills	George H. Mead and Erving Goffman	Dorothy Smith	Michael Foucault
Society	Society is a set of interrelated parts; cultural consensus exists and leads to social order; natural state of society is balance and harmony.	Society is marked by power struggles over scarce resources; inequities result in conflict; social change is inevitable; the fundamental inequality of capitalist society results in a constant state of imbalance.	Society is a network of interlocking roles; social order is constructed through interaction as individuals, through shared meaning, make sense out of their social world.	Rejection and questioning of totalizing societal models; focus is on the beliefs, practices, and institutions that create and recreate male privilege.	Rejection and questioning of totalizing societal models; focus is on exposing the structure of power and privilege that oppress people.
Individuals	Society's institutions socialize individuals; socialization is the process by which social control is exerted; people need society and its institutions.	People are inherently good, but societies based on capitalism and patriarchy institutionalize and reward negative aspects of humans such as materialism and wealth accumulation.	Humans are interpretative and interactive; they are constantly changing as their "social beings" emerge and are moulded by changing circumstances.	Men and women are products of social structures that privilege men, but also agents that can change these social structures	Individuals exist in a world where dominant powerful actors influence their decisions through subtle mechanisms of social control

	Structural Functional-ism	Conflict Theory	Symbolic Interaction-ism	Feminism	Post-Struc-turalism
Cause of Social Prob-lems	Rapid social change: social disor-ganization that disrupts the harmony and balance; inadequate socializa-tion, weak institutions, or a com-bination of these.	Inequality; the dominance of groups of peo-ple over other groups of peo-ple; oppression and exploita-tion; competi-tion between groups.	Different interpreta-tions of roles; labelling of individuals, groups, or behaviours as deviant; definition of an objective condition as a social problem.	Men have privileged access to institutions and power and mas-culinity is privileged.	Individu-als may be unaware of the structures of power and privilege and recreate them in their everyday ac-tions.
Social Policy Solu-tions	Repair weak institu-tions; assure proper so-cialization; cultivate a strong col-lective sense of right and wrong.	Minimize com-petition; create an equitable system for the distribution of resources.	Reduce impact of labelling and associ-ated stigma-tization; alter definitions of what is defined as a social prob-lem.	By recogniz-ing male privilege, it can be chal-lenged and changed.	By exposing structures of power and oppression the practices of oppres-sion can be changed.
Criti-cisms	Called "sunshine sociology"; supports the mainte-nance of the status quo; needs to ask "functional for whom?" Does not deal with issues of power and conflict; incorrectly assumes a consensus.	Utopian and simplistic model; Marxist states have failed; denies existence of cooperation and equitable exchange. Can't explain cohesion and harmony.	Concentrates on micro issues only; fails to link micro issues to macro-lev-el concerns; too psycho-logical in its approach; assumes label amplifies problem.	While drawing attention to women and denaturaliz-ing total-izing claims, the breadth, depth, and difference of women are hard to define and often total-ized.	As with feminism, making gen-eralizations about social structures suffers from over-gen-eralization, reducing credibility.

Source: Adapted from Mooney, Knox, and Schacht 2008: 16

CASE STUDY:
DISCOURSE OF DENIAL — RACIAL PROFILING EXPOSED

In October 2002 Police Chief Julian Fantino was quoted in the *Toronto Star*: "We do not do racial profiling ... there's no racism" (quoted in Henry and Tator 2006: 157). These sentiments were reiterated in the media by the President of the Ontario Association of Chiefs of Police, the Toronto Police Association, the Toronto Police Services Board and the Mayor of Toronto (Henry and Tator 2006). However, the *Toronto Star* had studied data (based on arrests, tickets, and detentions) confirming racial profiling, and the Ontario Human Right Commission conducted an inquiry (2003) and reported on the costs and impacts of racial profiling. Two other reports also confirmed systemic racial profiling (Henry and Tator 2006). This narrative continues today. In fact, it is experienced in the realms of education, retail, and child welfare (Shahzad 2017). One woman recounts, "I was at my workplace and we have swipe cards to get into rooms. I went into my office and immediately security knocked at the door. They said they wanted to check who had gone in. I am pretty sure they got alarmed because all they could see was someone wearing hijab walking into an office" (Shahzad 2017: n.p.). Despite evidence from courts and human rights tribunals of racial profiling occurring on a daily basis, the report said that many people and institutions deny it and say it is a normal and effective tool for gathering information, assessing risk, and ensuring safety. Consider the case of Cole, who documents being continuously stopped, interrogated, and followed at least fifty times by the police because of the Black colour of his skin (Cole 2015). While this has profound impacts on him, the police maintain a "discourse of denial" that racial profiling does not occur. This is the story that many Canadians like to hear and believe.

should be treated equally (formal justice). However, by understanding that Indigenous peoples and minority people are exposed to structures of power and marginalization we can understand that different practices are required in order to achieve justice. Chapter 4: Social Justice and Racism will expand on these practices and this area of justice. Once we understand this oppression and the requirement for different practices, we can invoke the ethical practice of justice in ensuring our exchanges with people reflect this new understanding. An understanding of these marginalized groups advances the ethical practice of eliminating the oppression in order to achieve substantive justice (the treatment of a group appropriately to allow for full participation in society).

NEO-LIBERALISM AND JUSTICE

At the outset of this chapter the concept of neo-liberalism was introduced. This is the view of the world as predominantly driven by a market economy, with minimal government intervention, and that individuals are responsible for life choices and life chances. This view of the world is contrary to the initial view of problems as social problems, and the analysis of the social problems covered in this chapter. Neo-liberalism focuses on the individual and themes of individual freedom, liberty, and personal responsibility; it is used mostly in a political economy sense, proclaiming the competitive, free market as capable of acting as a guide to all human action, thereby eliminating the public sector (Antony, Antony, and Samuelson 2017). Markets would govern in all areas, including health care, social security, water, and education, with individuals paying directly for all of the costs of these services because the public sector is viewed as inefficient, costly, and a waste of taxpayers' money (Antony, Antony, and Samuelson 2017).

The ideology of neo-liberalism is pervasive in our society in our time. In some important ways it is almost invisible, being so taken for granted by many in Canada. This ideology (this discourse) insists that our troubles of poor health, loss of employment, and crime are problems of the individual. However, this chapter argues that these individual problems also have social dimensions and implications. This is confirmed when acknowledging the statistics that poor people predominantly have problems of illness, crime, and unemployment. Illness, crime, and unemployment are but three illustrations; many other social problems exist in respect of many other social structures. The inequity built into these social structures casts doubt on the social justness of our society. Viewing problems as social problems allows for a richer policy response to assist people in alleviating them and also focuses the discussion on strengthening community or social cohesion, making our society more socially just.

Applying a theoretical perspective to a social problem allows a deeper analysis of both the causes and the potential remedies of a social problem. When analyzing problems as social problems, the societal factors contributing to a problem are part of the mix, not just the individual and their personal choices contributing to the problem. This chapter introduced five theoretical perspectives. It should be kept in mind that there are many theoretical perspectives applied by many people in many contexts, not just these five. No one theoretical perspective is the only correct theoretical perspective. Our knowledge of our society and of the people in it is expanded by understanding all theoretical perspectives. We will not have the diverse, multicultural, non-racist and non-sexist society we wish for without first acknowledging feminist and anti-racist theoretical perspectives. Obviously acknowledgment is a first step and much more beyond that is needed.

Discourse analysis is one method employed to expose and de-center the privilege embedded in the meaning of the language we use represented in texts. Often this privilege is subtle, hidden, and not even fully understood (especially by those with privilege) until exposed through the standpoint of another perspective. This method allows the many facets of power relations in society to be revealed and various "centrisms" to be uncovered.

DISCUSSION QUESTIONS

1. What is the difference between an individual's problem and an associated social problem? What are the similarities and differences?
2. Prior to reading this chapter did you think crime was increasing in your community and Canada, or decreasing? Why do you think crime is decreasing in Canada and as shown in Figure 2?
3. In the introduction, statistics outlined the disproportionate rate of poor health suffered by Indigenous peoples. Which theoretical framework best explains this situation?
4. How is power dealt with in each theoretical framework?
5. How does discourse represent power? Give an example.
6. Neo-liberalism is explained at the beginning of this chapter and referred to again in its ending. Will neo-liberalism continue to be as informative and as persuasive an ideology given the changes that are happening in Canadian society? For example, these changes might include the transforming accountability of individuals in

the new information technology communication practices, or the declining accountability in the "post-truth" era.

GLOSSARY

Anomie: A state of normlessness.

Conflict perspective: A theory of society that views society as an aggregate, focusing on power dynamics between groups in society.

Deconstruction: The exposure of centrism and embedded power structures through analysis.

Discourse: Forms of language that reflect ways of making sense of the world and social practices.

Feminism: A theoretical framework that exposes the way society privileges men and masculinity.

Ideology: A set of beliefs, attitudes, or opinions organized around certain values in respect of anything from religion, economics, or scientific knowledge, regardless whether it is accurate or not.

Modernity: This is the term commonly used to describe the time period ushered in by intellectual changes associated with the Enlightenment, rise of science, emergence and expansion of capitalism, and expansion of western Europe. The central political and analytical assumption of modernity included the notion that knowledge is progressive, cumulative, holistic, universal, and rational (Knutilla 2002).

Neo-liberalism: The view that the world is predominantly driven by a market economy with minimal government intervention, and that individuals are responsible for life choices and life chances.

Oppression: Powerful groups' domination of subordinate groups and their exclusion from full participation in society.

Personal problem: A problem explained in terms of an individual's choices.

Positivism: The idea that society can be studied objectively and rationally without values., beliefs, feelings, and opinions.

Post-structuralism: A theoretical perspective that exposes the mechanisms and operation of power and privilege in society through deconstruction and exposure.

Social problem: A problem explained not in terms of an individual's choices, but in terms of social structures, societal dynamics or occurrences such as war, famine, extreme events such as drought, hurricanes or tsunamis, that impact an individual and their life chances.

Social structure: Patterns of relationships or interaction among the various components of society that are relatively enduring.

Structural functionalism: A theory of society wherein each aspect of society has a purpose and function contributing to the whole.

Symbolic interactionism: A theory of society wherein an individual and their perceptions of themselves are shaped by their social interaction with others.

REFERENCES

Alfred, T. 2009. P*eace, Power, Righteousness: An Indigenous Manifesto,* second ed. Oxford University Press.

Antony, W.A., J. Antony and L. Samuelson (eds.). 2017. *Power and Resistance: Critical Thinking about Canadian Social Issues,* sixth ed. Halifax & Winnipeg: Fernwood Publishing.

Baig, R. 2013. "Biopiracy Rips off Native Medical Knowledge." October 14. *DW (Made for Minds)* <p.dw.com/p/18Clg>.

Beasley, C. 1999. *What Is Feminism? An Introduction to Feminist Theory.* London: Sage.

Becker, H.S. 1963. *Outsiders: Studies in the Sociology of Deviance.* New York: Free Press.

Chambliss, W.J. 1994. "Policing the Ghetto Underlclass: The Politics of Law and Law Enforcement." *Social Problems,* 41, 2: 177–194.

Cohen, D. 2018. "Oxford TB Vaccine Study Calls into Question Selective Use of Animal Data." *British Medical Journal,* 360:j5845 <doi.org/10.1136/bmj.j5845>.

Cole, D. 2015. "The Skin I'm In: I've Been Interrogated by Police More Than 50 Times – All Because I'm Black." *Toronto Life,* April 21.

Comack, E. 2006. *Locating Law: Race Class Gender Sexuality Connections,* second ed. Halifax, NS: Fernwood Publishing.

Cooley, C.H. 1902. *Human Nature and the Social Order.* New York: Scribner's.

Durkheim, E. 1951 [1897]. *Suicide.* New York: Free Press.

___. 1964 [1893]. *The Division of Labour in Society.* New York: Free Press.

___. 1965 [1895]. "The Rules of the Sociological Method." (S.A. Soloway and J.H. Mueller, trans.). New York: Free Press.

Erikson, K.T. 1966. *Wayward Puritans.* New York: Willey.

Foucault, M. 1978. *The History of Sexuality, Volume I* (R. Hurley, trans.). New York: Pantheon Books.

___. 1979. "Governmentality." *Ideology & Consciousness,* 6: 5–21.

___. 1997. *Ethics: Subjectivity and Truth.* In P. Rabinow (ed.). New York: New Press.

Goffman, E. 1963. *Stigma: Notes on the Management of Spoiled Identity.* Englewood Cliffs, NJ: Prentice Hall.

Grabb, E. 2002. *Theories of Social Inequality,* fourth ed. Toronto, ON: Thomson

Nelson.

Guard, J., and W. Antony (eds.). 2009. *Bankruptcies & Bailouts*. Halifax, NS: Fernwood Publishing.

Hauser, P.J.M. 1969. "The Chaotic Society: Product of the Social Morphological Revolution." *American Sociological Review*, 34, 1 (February 1): 1–19.

Henry, F., and C. Tator. 2006. *The Colour of Democracy: Racism in Canadian Society*, third ed. Toronto, ON: Nelson Thomson Learning.

Knuttila, M. 2002. *Introducing Sociology: A Critical Perspective*. Don Mills, ON: Oxford University Press.

Lemke, T. 2001. "The Birth of Bio-Politics: Michael Foucault's Lectures at the College De France on Neo-Liberal Governmentality." *Economy and Society*, 30, 2: 190–207.

Lexchin, J. 2002. "Profits First: The Pharmaceutical Industry in Canada." In B.S. Bolaria and H.D. Dickinson (eds.), *Health, Illness and Health Care in Canada*, third ed. Scarborough, ON: Nelson.

Martinez, E., and A. Garcia. 2007. "What Is Neo-Liberalism? Global Economy 101, Global Exchange." <http://www.globalexchange.org/campaigns/econ101/neoliberalDefined.html> (accessed June 29, 2009).

Marx, K., and E. Fredrick. 1846. "The German Ideology." In *Marx Engels Collected Works* (Vol. 5) (1976). New York: International Publishers.

____. 1848. *The Communist Manifesto*. New York: Washington Square Press.

McCulloch, B. 2008. "Harper Pledges to Get Tough on Crime." Newstalk 650 CKOM, September 23 <http://www.newstalk650.com/story/20080923/6126>.

Mead, G.H. 1934. *Mind, Self And Society*. C.W. Morris (ed.). Chicago, IL: University of Chicago Press.

Merton, R.K. 1938. "Social Structure and Anomie." *American Sociological Review*, 3: 672–682.

____. 1968. *Social Theory and Social Structure*. New York: Free Press.

Mills, C.W. 1959. *The Sociological Imagination*. New York: Oxford University Press.

Mooney, L.A., D. Knox, C. Schacht and M.M. Holmes. 2008. *Understanding Social Problems*, third ed., Canadian. Toronto, ON: Nelson Thomson Learning.

Nisbet, R.A. 1969. "The Twilight of Authority." *The Public Interest*, 15 (Spring): 3–9.

Ontario Human Rights Commission. 2003. *Paying the Price: The Human Cost of Racial Profiling*. October 21. Toronto, ON: Human Rights Commission.

Parsons, T. 1937. *The Structure of Social Action* (Vol. 1). New York: Free Press.

____. 1951. *The Social System*. New York: Free Press.

Phillips, N., and C. Hardy. 2002. *Discourse Analysis: Investigating Processes of Social Construction*. Thousand Oaks, CA: Sage.

Public Health Agency of Canada. 2007. "Special Report of the Canadian Tuberculosis Committee: Tuberculosis among Aboriginal Peoples of Canada, 2000–2004." Ottawa: Public Health Agency of Canada.

Ross, R.J.S., and K.C. Trachte. 1990. *Global Capitalism: The New Leviathan*.

Albany, NY: SUNY Press.

Schwartz, H., R.D. Jerone and S.K. Olnick. 1962. "Two Studies of Legal Stigma." *Social Problems,* 10: 133–38.

Sears, A. 2005. *A Good Book in Theory: A Guide to Theoretical Thinking.* Peterborough, ON: Broadview Press.

Shazad, R. 2017. "Racial Profiling Is Daily Reality for Many Ontarians: Ont. Human Rights Commission Report." Participants from Indigenous, racialized and Muslim communities shared daily experiences in report. CBC News, May 3. <cbc.ca/news/canada/toronto/ohrc-racial-profiling-1.4096977>.

Shiva, V. 1997. *Biopiracy: The Plunder of Nature and Knowledge.* Cambridge, MA: South End Press.

Sinclair, M. 2009. Chairperson, Truth and Reconciliation Commission of Canada (TRC), speaking to Assembly of First Nations annual general meeting in Calgary, July 22. <http://www.trc.ca/websites/trcinstitution/index.php?p=3> (accessed August 25, 2010).

Statistics Canada. 2009a. "Labour Force Historical Review 2008 (Table Cd1T46an)." Ottawa, ON: Statistics Canada (Cat. No. 71F004XCB). <http://www4.hrsdc.gc.ca/.3ndic.1t.4r@-eng.jsp?preview=1&iid=16> (accessed September 15, 2009).

___. 2009b. "Latest Release from the Labour Force Survey, Ottawa, ON." September 4. <http://www.statcan.gc.ca/subjects-sujets/labour-travail/lfs-epa/lfs-epa-eng.htm> (accessed September 15, 2009).

___. 2010. "Latest Release from the Labour Force Survey." July 9. *The Daily.* <http://www.statcan.gc.ca/cgi-bin/af-fdr.cgi?l=eng&loc=/subjects-sujets/labour-travail/lfs-epa/lfs-epa-eng.pdf> (accessed August, 10 2010).

___. 2015. "Police-Reported Crime Statistics in Canada, 2015." Juristat, 85-002-X. <http://www.statcan.gc.ca/pub/85-002-x/2016001/article/14642/tbl/tbl01a-eng.htm>.

___. 2017. "Women in Canada: A Gender-based Statistical Report. Women and Paid Work." 89-503-X <statcan.gc.ca/pub/89-503-x/2015001/article/14694-eng.htm>.

Thomas, W.I., and F. Zraniedi. 1927. *The Polish Peasant in Europe and America.* New York: Alfred A. Knopf.

Thompson, J., P. Baird and J. Downie. 2001. *The Olivieri Report: The Complete Text of the Report of the Independent Inquiry Commissioned by the Canadian Association of University Teachers.* Toronto, ON: Lorimer.

Van Teijlingen, E.R., G.W. Louis, P.G. McCaffery and M. Porter. 2000. *Midwifery and the Medicalization of Childbirth: Comparative Perspectives.* Hauppauge, NY: Nova Science.

Visual Economics. 2010. "Unemployment Rates Around the World." <http://www.visualeconomics.com/unemployment-rates-around-the-world/>.

Wilkins, L.T. 1965. *Social Deviance: Social Policy, Action, and Research.* Englewood Cliffs, NJ: Prentice Hall.

Williams, R.M. 1960. *American Society: A Sociological Interpretation.* New York:

Knopf.
World Health Organization. 2014. "Health Topics: Poverty" <www.who.int/topics/poverty/en/>.
Yablonsky, L., and M.R. Haskell. 1988. *Juvenile Delinquency,* fourth ed. New York: Harper & Row.

3

POVERTY, ECONOMIC SECURITY AND JUSTICE

James P. Mulvale

OBJECTIVES

At the end of this chapter, you will be able to:

- Explain the concepts of economic security and redistributive justice, and apply these concepts to the questions of poverty and social inequality in Canada

- Give examples of policies and programs in Canada designed to reduce poverty, decrease inequality, and enhance redistributive justice

- Outline differing approaches to measuring poverty in Canada

- Engage in critical thinking about additional and more effective pathways to economic security and environmental sustainability

WHAT'S JUSTICE GOT TO DO WITH ECONOMICS?

If justice incorporates the concepts of fairness and equality, then these concepts must be applied to the economic realm. Is "fairness" realized when some members of society are not able to adequately meet their basic economic needs for food, clothing, shelter, and the other necessities of life, while others have much more income and wealth than they need for a decent material standard of living? Does "equality" demand some sharing of the collective economic resources of society?

This sharing of social wealth (a form of "redistributive justice") is brought about in large measure through the state, usually at the national or sub-national level (for example, the provincial level). The state can bring about a greater degree of redistributive justice in two essential ways. First of all, it can provide income support for those who are unable to earn a living in the paid labour market. This inability may be the result of individual circumstances such as illness, disability, old age, or family care responsibilities. This inability may also be the result, of course, of an insufficient number of jobs available to those looking for work in the labour market. A related issue is whether the jobs on hand are good jobs — full-time, ongoing, and decently paid. In recent years in Canada, much of our job growth has been in the "bad" job sector — part-time, contractual or contingent, and at low rates of pay.

An additional form of indirect income support is labour legislation at the federal and provincial levels that promotes redistributive justice. Such laws include those that set an adequate minimum wage level for workers at the low end of wage-salary continuum; that enable workers to organize themselves into unions that can collectively bargain for better pay, benefits and working conditions; and that ensure safe and healthy workplaces to prevent work-related injury and illness (and subsequent loss of earning power). Labour law in any given jurisdiction will be an indication of how committed a government is to redistributive justice — how it balances its support for working people (who are in a relatively weak economic position) with its support for employers (who have more political clout as the owners of businesses and the holders of wealth).

The second major way for achieving redistributive justice through the state is the provision of public goods at low or no cost on a universal basis to all members of society. Public goods include education, health care (incorporating physical and mental health), childcare, good quality and affordable housing, food security and recreation. Public goods also encompass "non-social" services such as public transportation, parks and natural spaces, and affordable public utilities such as water, waste water treatment, electricity and home heating options.

Direct forms of income support as a means of alleviating poverty and increasing economic security is the primary focus of this chapter. But it is important to recognize that public goods affect the level of economic security for all in a society. They "decommodify" services that we all need (such as health care and education) by taking them out of the marketplace where the drive for profit is the most important imperative. Public goods are funded through taxes, which can be paid in proportion to ability to pay, with high income earners, wealthy individuals and profitable corporations paying proportionately more. Through the provision of public funding from taxes, public goods are available to everyone at low or no direct, out-of-pocket cost. If such services had to be purchased in the marketplace, they would be very expensive. Public goods that are decommodified lower costs for everyone, and these reduced costs are especially important to people with moderate or low incomes. While income support directly provides monetary benefits to individuals and families who struggle economically, public goods indirectly contribute to those at lower income levels by keeping necessary social supports affordable.

SOCIAL INSURANCE, SOCIAL ENTITLEMENTS AND SOCIAL ASSISTANCE

Income support programs in Canada take three general forms. The first is "social insurance" for people in the paid labour force. Employees pay a small proportion of their paycheques and employers pay a small proportion of their total payroll into a publicly administered social insurance fund that protects employees against common economic risks, such as loss of income due to lay off or retirement. When workers experience such a loss of income, they can collect benefits in a predetermined amount from the social insurance fund.

The two large social insurance programs offered by the federal government in Canada are Employment Insurance (EI) and the Canada Pension Plan (CPP). EI benefits can be claimed when a contributing worker becomes unemployed due to various circumstances, or when a contributor takes time off due to the birth or adoption of a child. EI benefits are paid out at a lower rate than a claimant's regular pay, but can provide valuable financial relief until the claimant is called back to work, finds another job, or returns to work after the arrival of a new child. CPP benefits are paid to older people who have contributed and who retire from the paid labour force. CPP benefits can also be claimed by contributors who are unable to work due to disability but who have not yet reached retirement age, and by surviving family members of a deceased contributor.

The second form of income support are entitlements based on family status or age which are "income-tested" — that is, the less one's total income level, the larger the benefit. Two important programs of the federal government that fall into this category are the Canada Child Benefit (CCB) for families with children, and the Old Age Security/Guaranteed Income Supplement (OAS/GIS) program for seniors. Unlike social insurance programs, recipients do not have to contribute in advance in order to receive these benefits. Income levels as reported on income tax returns are used to determine the benefit amounts to those who qualify for the CCB or OAS/GIS. Above a certain level of income, people are not eligible to receive any benefits from these programs.

Both of these two forms of income support — social insurance and benefits based on age or family status — are generally perceived in Canadian society as programs to which recipients are entitled, with no negative value judgment made against them. This is not the case with the third type of income support that prevails in Canada, the "social assistance" programs offered by the provincial and territorial governments. Social assistance programs are broadly perceived as the "last resort" form of income support for those who do not earn enough to support themselves in the labour market, and who do not qualify for social insurance or for age- or family-related benefits. Social assistance recipients are often perceived as somehow to blame for their plight; they are seen as being in financial need due to their laziness or moral failings. These perceptions and judgements of social assistance recipients are false and grossly unfair, and are not held by all people in Canadian society. But the stigmatization of those who receive social assistance is pervasive, and is a long-standing pattern going back over four centuries to the Elizabethan Poor Law in England (Finkel 2006).

Our already stigmatized, difficult-to-navigate and inadequate social assistance programs in Canada have become even more unwelcoming and punitive in recent years (Lightman and Lightman 2017). "Workfare" programs have been introduced in many provinces, whereby applicants who are judged to be "ready to work" must accept menial jobs or take part in demeaning "job readiness" programs as a condition of receiving benefits.

THE STATE AND REDISTRIBUTIVE JUSTICE

A state with a weak commitment to redistributive justice will not place a strong emphasis on income support generally, and will depend more on last resort programs such as social assistance in order to force its citizens into the paid labour market. A state with a stronger commitment to redistributive justice and income support will place more emphasis on social insurance and entitlement programs, and relatively less on social assistance.

It is also a question of redistributive justice as to how a state allocates the burden of paying taxes across different income levels. States with a strong commitment to redistributive justice will rely to a greater degree on "progressive taxation" that imposes progressively higher rates of taxation on individuals with higher levels of income and wealth. The opposite of progressive taxation is "flat taxation," whereby all pay the same amount or rate of taxation regardless of their ability to pay. Progressive taxation is the more just and redistributive method to raise the necessary public revenue to pay for public programs, including income support and public goods — it does not place an unfair tax burden on people at lower income levels, and mandates that the wealthy pay proportionately more.

So, a society with a strong commitment to redistributive justice is characterized by adequate income support programs and readily available, good quality public goods funded through progressive taxation. Such a set of programs, policies and laws can and will go a long way towards closing the economic gap between the rich and the poor. Such redistributive justice measures can work together to ensure substantive justice — treating people in unequal economic circumstances (who may be wealthy, just getting by economically or living in poverty) differently. Redistributive justice entails using the tax and transfer system to move economic resources from those with more than they need to those who are economically insecure or who are living in poverty. A given society's set of redistributive justice measures do not typically comprise a coherent and "neat and tidy" set of programs. They may not even be identified as having the objective of redistributing wealth. But collectively they can significantly raise the level of substantive equality and help us to achieve "equality of outcomes" — not just "equality of opportunities."

Equality of opportunities refers to everyone starting out with the same chances to succeed in life and follow their dreams, in various aspects of life, such as education, career advancement and the development of individual talents. It is analogous to everyone beginning a running race at the same starting line. Equality of outcomes refers to everyone achieving or possessing what is necessary for a decent and fulfilling life — an adequate income, a decent place to live, a nutritious diet, meaningful and fulfilling work and the emotional support of family and friends. Equality of outcomes is analogous to everyone finishing the running race, even if we take somewhat different routes and some take longer than others to complete the distance. The goal is successful completion of the course by all, not that there is a rank-ordered list of "winners" in the top spots and a lot of "losers."

Redistributive justice measures to achieve equality of outcomes often run up against the just deserts principle that is also part of a broad conception of justice. This principle posits the notion that what individuals earn for themselves is theirs to keep. An argument based on just deserts would be that earnings through wages, salaries, production of commodities, business dealings or investment should be retained by the earner, and should not be taken away through taxes. In the other words, the just deserts principle is used to support the argument that I deserve to keep what I earn and to amass as much wealth as I wish, through the exercise of my talents and my willingness to work.

On the other hand, we can question the just deserts principle and debate the extent to which individuals are solely and personally responsible for their economic success. All of us — regardless of our degree of talent or motivation to exert ourselves — depend on a huge social infrastructure that we inhabit and benefit from, but that we did not create through our own initiative. This infrastructure includes existing and accumulated knowledge and technology, the education system that transmits this knowledge and expertise and the social institutions that provide instrumental support and emotional nurturance to all of us (such as one's family, fellow workers, public services and so on). So, our common reliance on this shared social infrastructure weakens the "rugged individualist" claim that it is primarily through our own talent and motivation that we achieve success, wealth or other desirable outcomes as members of society.

In pursuing justice, there is also the question of how redistributive justice and substantive equality can be ensured for those with fewer talents and abilities, or who live with conditions of individual disability or in social circumstances that hamper their ability to be economically "successful." Along this line, one modest improvement in income support programs for persons with disabilities has been made in certain Canadian provinces in recent years. This has been the separation out of benefits for disabled persons from generic social assistance benefits. These income support programs for disabled persons pay slightly higher benefits than the general social assistance rates, and are intended to be non-stigmatizing and non-punitive. Disabled persons are spared some of the unpleasant and judgmental aspects of applying for benefits, compared to those applying for generic social assistance benefits.

But of course this distinction between the two groups of finanical assistance recipients does not address the injustice of regular social assistance. In fact, it may entrench the popular perception that we can and should differentiate between those who are "deserving" of support (having a disability is not your fault) and those who are "undeserving" (you are an "able-bodied" claimant who is asking for support due to personal failings).

In thinking specifically about income support for disabled persons, frequently there is an oversimplified and misleading distinction made between "dependence" and "independence." According to this line of reasoning, our goal should be to have everyone who is labelled as disabled to live "independently" despite their personal or social limitations. But a better way to think about this question, and perhaps what justice requires, is that we strive to enhance both personal autonomy (the ability to make one's own choices and realize one's freely chosen goals) and the level of support to which we are all entitled as socially interdependent members of society. This way of thinking focuses on the need to remove the social barriers to autonomy and interdependence, rather than on physical impairments as such, and guards against the tendency to have low expectations of disabled persons or to label them in negative ways.

Persons with low income or who live in poverty, and those who face particular challenges related to disability or social background, may require more resources of the state than those who have more advantages or who face fewer obstacles. This is the ethical demand of equity (providing to everyone what they need) and is a precondition of the achievement of formal and substantive equality.

To achieve such equity and equality, the state (which in a democracy is empowered to act on behalf of its citizens) can use the tax and transfer system to ensure an adequate income for all, provide universal public goods, and ensure that we all have what we need in order to live our lives within an inclusive web of social interdependence. This is a precondition to ensuring freedom and dignity for all. As the English poet John Donne (1623: XVII) wrote almost four hundred years ago, "no man is an island." Redistributive justice is based on this premise.

In considering the economic dimensions of justice, we can also think about "distributive justice" (the relative fairness of how income and wealth are distributed among everyone in society in the first place) as the departure point for the consideration of "redistributive justice" (the economic wealth and resources that need to be transferred from the well off to those who do not have enough for a decent life). We must ask: how are the rules of economic distribution set? For instance, why do bond and currency traders make huge amounts of money, and those who work in childcare centres looking after small children earn very low wages? Do the exorbitant earnings of popular entertainers and sport superstars generally reflect their actual value to society? Is it right that care work in the family (still performed mostly by women) is given very minimal recognition in our tax and transfer system?

It can be difficult to pose such questions of fundamental distributive justice when so much of public discourse is dominated by economic elites — particularly large corporations devoted to maximizing their own profits — who are invested in the status quo. Those with economic power and privilege do not usually want a more redistributive tax and transfer system, as they would be expected to bear most of the cost of improved income support programs and public goods. However, if we are as deeply committed to democracy in Canada as we say we are, it is possible for the majority of citizens who are at low and middle income levels to elect and hold accountable governments that are committed to strong measures for redistributive justice.

HOW SHOULD WE DEFINE "POVERTY"?

The most obvious way to define "poverty" is in monetary terms. If one's access to money from all sources — including wages or salaried income, earnings through self-employment, income from social benefits, investment income and accumulated or inherited wealth — falls below a pre-determined threshold, then one is "poor" or (as Statistics Canada prefers to say) has a "low income."

The determination of poverty or low-income thresholds takes two general approaches. One method is the "absolute" approach, in which the actual cost of the goods and services necessary for an economically adequate and decent life is calculated; those who do not have sufficient income to pay these costs are judged to be poor. The other method of calculating the poverty rate is the "relative" approach, in which a specific level of income is compared to all others in a given community or society; if one's income falls below a pre-determined threshold of adequacy relative to all other levels, then one is considered to be poor.

Canada, unlike many other countries, does not have one official poverty or low-income line.[1] Rather, the government agency Statistics Canada uses three different measurements of low income. One of them, the Market Basket Measure (MBM), uses the absolute approach to setting a low income line. Two of them, the Low Income Cut-Off (LICO) and the Low Income Measure (LIM), take a relative approach to defining a line below which people are classified as low income or poor.

The Market Basket Measure of Poverty

The MBM is:

> based on the cost of a specific basket of goods and services representing a modest, basic standard of living. It includes the costs of food, clothing, footwear, transportation, shelter and other expenses for a reference family of two adults aged 25 to 49 and two children (aged 9 and 13). (Statistics Canada 2015a)

The MBM adjusts for community size (which affects the cost of this basket of goods and services) across each of the ten provinces. To measure poverty, "these thresholds are compared to disposable income of families to determine low income status." In the MBM, "disposable income" is the amount remaining after all non-discretionary expenditures are deducted, including income tax, employee premiums for Employment Insurance and the Canada Pension Plan, deductions for workplace pension and benefit plans, childcare expenses, child support and alimony payments and "non-insured but medically prescribed health-related expenses such as dental and vision care, prescription drugs, and aids for persons with disabilities" (Statistics Canada 2015a).

As two illustrative examples, the MBM in 2013 for a family of four was determined to be $35,584 for Regina and $39,084 for Toronto.

The Low Income Cut-Off

LICOs are "income thresholds below which a family will likely devote a larger share of its income on the necessities of food, shelter and clothing than the average family" (Statistics Canada 2015b). LICOs are based on the benchmark that "the average family spent 43% of its after-tax income on food, shelter and clothing." The LICO method assumes that any family that has to commit 63 percent (that is, 43 percent + 20 percent) or more of its after-tax income on food, shelter and clothing would be in "straitened circumstances" and should be defined as low income. The LICO adjusts for family size and area of residence, and is a "made-in-Canada" measurement developed in 1959 that has been used extensively and developed since then (Statistics Canada 2015d).

As one example of this benchmark, the LICO (after taxes) in 2016 for a family of four living in a community with a population between 100,000 and 500,000 was calculated to be $33,060. The figure for a single individual was $17,485.

The Low Income Measure

The LIM is a fixed percentage (50 percent) of median household income adjusted to size of the household, given that costs are greater for larger households (Statistics Canada, 2015c). The "median" amount of household income is the income level that falls exactly in the middle of a distribution of all incomes from the lowest to the highest. Any household with an income below this 50 percent threshold of the median is categorized as low income. For example, the LIM (after taxes) for a household of four persons in 2013 was $41,866 — meaning that the median income level for that year was double that, or $83,732. The LIM is a method that is used in many other countries, and (unlike LICO) makes comparisons between Canada and other countries easier to make. The LIM (similar to LICO) can be calculated before and after taxes are paid.

WHICH POVERTY LINE SHOULD WE USE?

These various poverty thresholds lead to differing measures of the amount of poverty in Canada. For instance, the LIM after tax for a family of four in 2016 was set at $ 45,314. The LICO after tax for this family of four in 2016 varied between $25,571 in a rural community and $39,092 in communities with more 500,000 people, rising as the size of the population rose. The MBM is broken out by provinces and size of the community. To give two examples, the MBM in 2016 in Ontario for a family of four varied between $34,565 in small cities to $41,287 in Toronto; the MBM in Saskatchewan varied less than that of Ontario, with the cheapest communities being those with a population of 30,000–99,999 (at $35,892), and the most expensive communities being those non-rural centres with a population under 30,000 (at $38,120). Saskatoon was close behind as the second most expensive place to life in Saskatchewan, according to the MBM, at $38,032 (Statistics Canada 2018a, 2018b, 2018c).

As these figures illustrate, the LIM sets a poverty threshold that is much higher than the LICO or MBM amounts. So the LIM identifies a higher proportion of people living in poverty in all of Canada than does LICO and MBM. The LIM after tax and LICO after tax figures for 2015 were 14.2 percent and 9.2 percent respectively.[2] The MBM measure of low income (for 2016) fell in between these two figures, at 12.9 percent nationally.[3] In this way, poverty rates can be calculated in different ways to serve varying political agendas, although the daily hardships of those living through the multiple and diverse effects of poverty do not change at all!

Murphy, Zhang and Dionne (2012: 6) make the case for "using a number of different low-income thresholds [that] can facilitate a more complete picture of the low-income population." On the other hand, anti-poverty organizations such as Campaign 2000 (2016: 3), argue for the "adoption of the internationally comparable Low Income Measure–After Tax as Canada's official income poverty line to track progress or lack thereof against poverty."

It is sometimes a controversial topic as to what should or should not be included on the list of "necessities" when calculating the cost of living in absolute or market basket approaches to setting poverty lines. Should the list of necessities include such items as the cost of an annual vacation? Or high-speed internet in one's home? Or life insurance premiums? Social justice advocates and people working in the social welfare field tend to argue for a relatively broad and inclusive list of items to include as necessary for a minimal but adequate standard of living.

The total cost of this list of necessities is affected by the extent to which governments provide their citizens with some of these items as public goods at reduced or no cost. Public goods include, as discussed above, universal, publicly funded health care and education; government investment in the housing market with the goal of ensuring that everyone has an adequate and affordable place to live; and readily available and cheap public transportation. A specific modest amount of income in a society with readily available public goods might be adequate. The same income in a society with few public goods — in which one has to pay out of one's own pockets for health care, education, and other services — may mean that one lives in poverty.

If you are unable to afford elements of a decent life due to lack of income, it can be said that you are living in a state of deprivation. One method of capturing this is in a "deprivation index," an example of which was developed by The Daily Bread Food Bank in Toronto and the Caledon Institute of Social Policy (Matern et al. 2009). This index was developed to include ten indicators that, if lacking in a person's life, would indicate deprivation associated with poverty:

1. Being able to get dental care if needed.
2. Replace or repair broken electrical goods such as a stove or toaster.
3. Being able to buy modest presents for family/friends at least once per year.
4. Appropriate clothes for job interviews.
5. Having friends or family over for a meal at least once a month.
6. Fresh fruit and vegetables every day.
7. Being able to get around your community, either by having a car or in a larger centre a monthly bus pass or equivalent.
8. Hobby or leisure activity.
9. Meat, fish or vegetarian equivalent at least every other day.

10. Having a home or apartment free of pests, such as cockroaches, bedbugs and mice.

According to Matern et al. (2009: 24), these ten items were "strongly associated with one or more themes that were seen as representing a poverty level standard of living" — social isolation, lack of economic security and lack of personal agency. This deprivation index was applied to residents of Ontario in 2009. It was found that 19.9 percent of Ontario residents were experiencing one or more deprivations, 9.9 percent were experiencing two or more and 5.7 percent were experiencing three or more. In the lowest income quintile (the bottom fifth of the income distribution), 22.5 percent experienced two or more deprivations, including a high incidence of not being able to afford dental care if needed (23 percent within the quintile) and not being able to afford to replace or repair broken/damaged appliances (15.8 percent within the quintile).

BROADER DEFINITIONS OF POVERTY

While most efforts to define and measure poverty deal with cash income and the monetary cost of the material necessities of life, there are also calls for a deeper understanding of the social dimensions of "involuntary poverty." There are, to be sure, some instances of "voluntary poverty." Some individuals and communities embrace a lifestyle of minimum consumption and forgo the accumulation of wealth or excess goods, based on their religious beliefs, political commitments or values based in social justice. Those choosing voluntary poverty often have communal living arrangements such as a convent or monastery, or a rural self-sustaining commune committed to radical ecological values.

But instances of voluntary poverty are relatively rare. The vast majority of poor people do not choose this condition. For them, poverty is certainly about the lack of access to the material necessities of life, but it also has negative emotional, psychological, behavioural and health-related consequences for individuals, families and communities. Poverty is usually accompanied by the lack of opportunities for positive social interactions and relationships, exclusion from participation in political decision making, and the disparagement of one's social (and perhaps cultural) identity. Reducing or eliminating poverty involves not just ensuring people have an adequate income, but also that they are connected with supportive communities and benefit from inclusion in society as a whole.

One such broader definition of poverty (that has been especially influential in conceptualizing poverty in developing countries) is Amartya Sen's "capability approach" (U.N. OHCHR 2004: 6–8). It takes a "multidimensional view of poverty" that goes beyond lack of income and focuses on "the non-fulfillment of human rights." Sen is concerned with "how well a person can do or be the things she has reasons to value." For this to be achieved, "the goodness of social arrangements [must] be judged in terms of the flourishing of human freedoms" — which includes being free of "hunger, disease and illiteracy."

Freedom from poverty defined in this broader way goes beyond "low income [to include] the broader concept of inadequate command over economic resources" such as "publicly provided goods and services," "communally owned and managed resources" and "resources that are made available through formal and informal networks of mutual support" (U.N. OHCHR 2004: 6–8). Poverty may result from "non-economic factors" such as discrimination against women, ethnic minorities or other groups.

The capability approach to understanding poverty as the non-fulfillment of human rights also avoids the adoption of "a uniformly low level of command over economic resources" as its minimum criterion. The capability approach also seeks to account for individual differences in needs (such as for food or health care) and for cultural variation (such as in the amount of clothing considered normal).

THE DIMENSIONS OF POVERTY

The focus in this chapter and this entire book is primarily on Canada. However, poverty and economic (in)justice are also global issues, and it is important to consider whether or not we are making progress towards the reduction of poverty — especially deep poverty — around the world. The World Bank (2016) states that "there has been marked progress on reducing poverty over the past decades," pointing out that the global poverty rate was cut in half between 1990 and 2010. Nonetheless, the World Bank also indicates that "the number of people living in extreme poverty globally remains unacceptably high." There was a reduction of the rate of people living in extreme poverty (defined as living on less than

$1.90 USD per day) during the period between 1990 and 2013 from 35 percent to 10.7 percent. However, this still left leaves 767 million people around the globe living in desperate circumstances. Most of the reduction in extreme poverty during this period occurred in Eastern and Southern Asian countries such as China, Indonesia and India. The area where extreme poverty is not being rolled back is in Sub-Saharan Africa, which now accounts for half of people in this category globally. Additionally, the World Bank (2016) notes that "a vast majority of the global poor live in rural areas and are poorly educated, mostly employed in the agricultural sector, and over half are under 18 years of age."

It is clear that global poverty is still a huge problem. Countries such as Canada that possess high aggregate wealth have a special moral and political obligation to redistribute a portion of their wealth to alleviate — and eventually eliminate — poverty in all parts of the globe. Canada must face the dual challenges of ending poverty within its own borders, and doing its share to reach the same goal on the international level.

The Dimensions of Poverty in Canada

Understanding poverty is first and foremost a question of knowing and feeling the lived experience of people who are living in poverty — their daily struggles and privations, and the emotional and physical toll that they experience by not being able to provide the necessities of life for themselves and their loved ones. Many groups that advocate for poverty reduction are committed to tell the stories of people living in poverty through "first voices" — that is, by having people with lived experiences of poverty talk about its effects and their ways of coping and trying to overcome these challenges. These first voice perspectives give us insight into the subjective and existential dimensions of poverty, elements that are missing from statistical analysis. One way in which the first voices of people living in poverty has been captured is in "Photovoice" projects. These accounts of poverty combine real stories of individuals and families who are poor with photographic or video images drawn from their lives. Two examples are the Regina PhotoVoice Project (2007) and a video production called "Photovoice: A Youth Lens on Poverty in Winnipeg" of the Canadian Centre on Policy Alternatives (2013).

Due largely to the efforts of an organization called Campaign 2000, there has been considerable attention paid in Canada over recent years to the problem of child poverty — that is, children who live in households that fall below the poverty line. The organization got its name from a resolution passed unanimously in the House of Commons in 1989 to eliminate child poverty in Canada by the new millennium. This goal was not attained — in fact, the rate of child poverty rose between 1989 and 2000 from 15.8 percent to 22.3 percent. In 2015 the nationwide child poverty rate in Canada (using the LIM-AT method) was at the obscenely high level of 17.4 percent; for First Nations children, this rate more than doubles to 37.9 percent (Campaign 2000 2017: 6). Across the provinces and territories in 2015, the lowest child poverty rate was in Quebec, at 14.4 percent. The highest rate among the provinces was in Manitoba (27.5 percent), and the worst rate among the territories was in Nunavut (36.1 percent) (2017: 7).

The problem of child poverty is particularly acute in Indigenous communities — 40 percent of all Indigenous children live in poverty, with the rate rising to 60 percent for children living on First Nations reserves (Campaign 2000 2016: 17). Poverty among Indigenous peoples of Canada is related to our history of colonialism and racist assumptions and practices (now often subtle and systemic, rather than blatant and explicit). This poverty has had very serious negative social outcomes for the first inhabitants of the land that we share; these outcomes include poorer health status, lower educational attainment and grossly inadequate housing in many Indigenous communities.

Canada Without Poverty (2017) points out additional aspects of contemporary poverty in Canada. Disabled persons are twice as likely as the non-disabled to live below the poverty line; single mothers have a 21 percent poverty rate, compared to 7 percent for single fathers; racialized families have a 20 percent poverty rate, compared to 5 percent for non-racialized families; and elderly single individuals have a poverty rate of almost 15 percent despite the existing income security programs for seniors.

There is also evidence that income advantages and disadvantages are transmitted from one generation to the next, and that good outcomes for children (such as normal physical and cognitive development, success in school and good mental health) are related to higher income levels of parents (Raphael 2007: 122).

Poverty and the Work Ethic

There is a widespread belief in Canadian society that everyone needs to "work for a living" — that it is morally objectionable for healthy adults to be furnished with the material necessities of life without expending efforts on their own behalf to provide for themselves and for those who depend upon them, such as their children. This belief is related to what is called the "reciprocity" norm — if we receive benefits from others (be they family members, friends, groups to which we belong or our government), we should also contribute something in return. This is a belief that lines up with the Golden Rule of "do unto others as you would have them do unto you."

While we value work and reciprocity in contemporary Canadian society, we also consider it to be right and just to pay taxes to government so that it can provide services that we cannot reasonably be expected to provide for ourselves. Our tax money is invested in schools for our children, health care for when we are ill, roads and highways that take us where we want to go and public media (such as the Canadian Broadcasting Corporation) that help us communicate with one another and define ourselves as Canadians.

Widely held beliefs in the work ethic and the reciprocity norm are also sometimes expressed, unfortunately, in negative and inaccurate attitudes towards individuals and groups who receive specific types of income support from the government. This is especially true when it comes to social assistance. There is a tendency in public opinion and media coverage to draw lines between the "deserving" and "undeserving" poor (Proudfoot 2011; Redden 2011). For instance, senior citizens are thought to deserve a public pension after a lifetime of work, or children with life-threatening illnesses are thought to deserve expensive medical treatment paid for with public funds. Other categories of people, however, such as single mothers on social assistance or seasonal workers in fishing or forestry, are often suspected of taking unfair advantage of benefit programs, being "lazy" or making poor life choices.

Such moral judgments, based on negative stereotypes and untested assumptions, are inaccurate and unfair. To be sure, all of us have moral obligations to contribute to our families, communities and places of employment, and to act as citizens who have responsibilities as well as rights. However, the construction in the public's mind of broad categories of the "undeserving poor" completely submerges individual differences in circumstances and fails to take into account the complexities of people's lives. Is the woman with young children who applies for social assistance because she must leave an abusive husband not deserving of financial support? On the other hand, do wealthy people who make use of tax write-offs and tax shelters (which are also "benefits" granted by the government) deserve these advantages? Negative judgements about those thought to be non-deserving are often aimed at groups of people who are already victims of inequality and marginalization, such as women, Indigenous peoples and people of non-European ancestry.

THE COMPONENTS OF ECONOMIC SECURITY

Given the injustice of poverty and its various dimensions, what are some key components of universal and stable economic security for all people in Canada? These components include an adequate cash income obtained through wages or a salary earned in the labour market, earnings from business activities or investment, and income support programs of the state. They also include various public goods that should be available to all of us at no or affordable cost.

Five key components of economic security include basic income (the first component) and a set of public goods (the last four components). Taken together, they will go a long way towards ensuring economic security for all in Canadian society, and towards realizing (through the redistribution of resources) formal and substantive economic justice.

Income Security: A Model of Universal Basic Income

A new model for economic security that is gaining currency around the world is "basic income" (Van Parijs and Vanderborght 2017), which is sometimes referred to as "guaranteed annual income" in Canada. Basic income is "a periodic cash payment unconditionally delivered to all on an individual basis, without means-test or work requirement." It is delivered to individuals (not to households), is universal (paid to all, regardless of their income) and is unconditional ("paid without a requirement to work or to demonstrate willingness-to-work") (Basic Income Earth Network n.d.).

Interest in basic income has been on the rise in Canada in recent years

(Mulvale and Frankel 2016). Most of this attention has been on possible versions of basic income that would target lower income people, rather than a universal version of basic income that is paid to everyone regardless of their income. Current income support programs at the federal level in fact approximate this approach to basic income — they "top up" the earnings of those making lower incomes through a mechanism known as "negative income tax" or "refundable tax credit." These programs include the Canada Child Benefit (CCB) paid to families with young children; the Guaranteed Income Supplement (GIS) that is paired with the Old Age Security (OAS) benefit and is paid to low income seniors; the Working Income Tax Benefit (WITB) for the working poor; and the GST/HST credit available to all low-income people. None of these programs pay benefits at a high enough rate to ensure an escape from poverty. But they can provide income support to segments of the population in ways that lower the extent and depth of poverty in Canadian society.

The Canadian Association of Social Workers (Drover et al. 2014) has argued for the creation of "basic income architecture" in Canada, building from these existing federal programs that deliver refundable tax credits. The CCB, OAS/GIS, WITB and the GST/HST credit could have their benefit levels increased, and could be expanded in scope and "stitched together" to create a comprehensive and seamless set of basic income entitlements for individuals in all age ranges and family circumstances.

There is also interest in the negative income tax approach to basic income at the provincial level in Canada. Some provinces are exploring this model as an alternative to our current last resort social assistance programs, which tend to be stigmatizing, punitive and inadequate. Notably, the province of Ontario (2017) has launched basic income pilot projects in three different communities to test out this type of income support as an alternative to the Ontario Works (OW) program (social assistance) and the Ontario Disability Support Program (ODSP, income support for disabled persons). Features of these basic income pilots include benefit levels more generous than OW and ODSP, the ability of recipients to retain 50 percent of any earned income, the ability to pursue training and education and the removal of any requirement to work for benefits or dispose of assets such as one's house or car. Basic income advocates are watching the development of the Ontario pilot projects with great interest.[4]

One advantage of the basic income model is that it can expand our definition of "work" beyond activities in the paid labour market. Basic income can be a way of recognizing the many forms of socially necessary and useful work that people do that is not paid. Such non-remunerated forms of work include: care work within the family, such as looking after children and other dependent family members; volunteer work in community organizations; and subsistence work to grow or gather our food, make clothing or produce other domestic necessities. If we take as our departure point this more expansive understanding of work, we can begin to think of economic security in broader terms. We can ask ourselves fundamental questions about what is "just" compensation for unpaid care work, and what we "owe" to one another for the socially valuable contributions that we all make to our families and communities.

Food Security

Food security includes having cash in one's pocket to buy groceries. As such, food security is directly tied to questions of income security and support. But taking food security seriously also demands that we take a critical look at other issues, such as the supply and ready availability of nutritious food to everyone in our community at a price that all can afford. Food security can also encompass public education on topics such as food preparation and storage, healthy eating choices, environmentally sustainable food production and the importance of food as an aspect of cultural identity and community building.

The goal of food security leads us to ask specific, practical questions such as: why do school children often have easier access to junk food than to fresh fruits and vegetables in the school cafeteria? Are there ways to distribute nutritious and natural foods in ways that bypass large corporations, and follow a much shorter and more direct route from the farm gate to the kitchen table? Do chemical additives and genetically modified ingredients in food products threaten our health? Why have we become so reliant on food banks, when they barely existed and were not considered necessary in Canada before 1980?

Food Secure Canada (n.d.a.) presents "five big ideas" on how to ensure a better food system based on social justice:

- Realize the human right to food: Under the United Nations International Covenant on Economic, Social and Cultural Rights, our government is legally obliged to "guarantee its citizens the right to adequate food."

- Champion healthy and sustainable diets: The government must take steps to support more healthy diets for all Canadians. Measures could include taxing food products that are high in sugar and salt, requiring warnings on food packaging about unhealthy components and additives to processed food, and providing healthy meals and food education in schools.
- Support sustainable food systems: Ensure environmentally sustainable farming and fishing practices and cut down on the amount of food waste in Canada, which is at a level of about 40 percent. We must recognize that "our current food system is a leading contributor to climate change," and that we must address how food production and distribution systems contribute to "water and air pollution, soil contamination, and loss of biodiversity."
- Make food a part of reconciliation: A national food policy must respect Treaty rights, including the right to hunt and fish. It must also support the development of strong Indigenous food systems, including traditional foods, and address the "epidemic of diet-related disease and food insecurity among Indigenous populations."
- Invite more voices to the table: Involve players other than the food industry and government in determining food security policy and programs. Such additional voices should include "eaters, cooks, community groups, producers, workers, [and] food entrepreneurs."

Food Secure Canada (n.d.b.) in fact calls for a move beyond food security to "food sovereignty." This goal is adopted from La Via Campesina, an international organization that is composed of small farmers from around the globe. Food sovereignty is "the right of peoples to healthy and culturally appropriate food produced through ecologically sound and sustainable methods, and their right to define their own food and agriculture systems" (Food Secure Canada). While food security calls for improvements in the existing food production and distribution system, food sovereignty has the more fundamental goals of bringing food production under democratic control, and restructuring the food system to be truly environmentally sustainable and oriented to the needs of communities rather than to the profit margins of large agri-business.

Adequate and Affordable Housing

The Canadian Housing and Renewal Association (CHRA) is a key advocate for adequate and affordable housing for everyone in Canada. The CHRA (n.d.) points out that with rising rents and stagnant wages, "12.5% of Canadian families are in core housing need, making it difficult to afford other life necessities such as healthy food, clothing, transportation, and medication." The CHRA (n.d.) also notes:

> Canada has invested very little in building and renewing social housing infrastructure in the last 25 years. As a result, there are tens of thousands of households on city [social housing] waiting lists — and tens of thousands of units needing urgent repairs to be livable.

This situation was brought about in no small way by the complete withdrawal of the federal government from the funding of social housing in the mid-1990s, as part of government cost cutting. Since then there has been some government reinvestment in social housing, but it has not matched the level of the earlier cuts. CHRA calls upon the federal government, in partnership with provincial governments, to reinvest significant funding in new social housing stock and the repair and maintenance of existing units. It also calls for "supporting people with rent subsidies" so that they can obtain suitable accommodation in social housing or on the general housing market.

An adequate supply of publicly funded social housing can have both direct and indirect benefits. It can provide more rental units that are decent places to live at affordable levels of rent, which directly benefits low-income people. An adequate supply of social housing can also moderate the rapidly inflating cost of renting or buying accommodation in the private marketplace, by providing more units at affordable prices.

Social housing is a public good that is an essential piece of a broad commitment to redistributive justice. All levels of government in Canada must renew their commitment to this public good, if we are to ensure economic security for all in our changing economy.

Accessible, Affordable and Relevant Education

Our education system is a public good that plays essential roles in building an inclusive and just society. It equips young people and adult learners with the necessary skills that they need to succeed in the labour market, including basic literacy and numeracy, social and technical skills and knowledge and credentials to pursue various careers. In a liberal democratic society such as Canada, the education system also plays a vital function in shaping informed, tolerant and critically thinking citizens. Such citizens are well equipped to contribute to political decision making, economic innovation and the social and cultural life of our neighbourhoods, communities and voluntary organizations.

Canada has one of the more highly developed K-12 and post-secondary education systems in the world. Keeping post-secondary education affordable has been a concern of many social justice advocates, as tuition levels have risen with the contraction of government spending and tax cuts, and levels of student debt have greatly increased (Harden 2017). At the other end of the age continuum, our provision of early childcare and development programs here in Canada lags behind many other advanced industrial countries (Alexander et al. 2017). Our commitment to education as a public good needs to be strengthened in Canada, if it is to retain and extend its many essential functions in building a democratic and just society.

Accessible and Affordable Health Care

Our system of universal and readily accessible health care in Canada is a vital element of our economic security arrangements and our commitment to redistributive justice. The cost of physician and hospital care is very high, and can devastate the finances of those who experience serious or prolonged ill health — which is a condition that affects just about everyone at some point in their life.

Our "medicare" system in Canada was pioneered in Saskatchewan in the 1940s and 1950s, and was established as a national program across Canada in the 1960s. It provides medical and hospital care at no direct cost to the person requiring care, through a "single-payer," government-administered insurance plan that covers all Canadians and reimburses a wide range of direct-care providers. Medicare is not a perfect system, and faces challenges such as the rising cost of serving an aging population, over-crowded emergency rooms in hospitals and long wait lists for certain types of medical specialists and surgery. Nonetheless, medicare has been a remarkable success story (Campbell and Marchildon 2007) and is very strongly supported by Canadians.

It is common sense that we should spend wisely and strive for efficiency in the health care system, given the very large amounts of public funds that are spent on it. The reduction of poverty (through better income support programs and the more generous provision of public goods) will in fact save money in health care. There is a very strong link between living in poverty, being in ill health and (as a result) placing more demand on the relatively expensive health care system. In other words, poverty quite literally makes us sick. Lightman et al. (2008: 2) point out:

> the poorest one-fifth of Canadians, when compared to the richest twenty percent, have:
>
> - more than double the rate of diabetes and heart disease;
> - a sixty percent greater rate of two or more chronic health conditions;
> - more than three times the rate of bronchitis;
> - nearly double the rate of arthritis or rheumatism.
>
> The poorest fifth of our population face a staggering 358 percent higher rate of disability compared to the richest fifth. The poor experience major health inequality in many other areas, including 128 percent more mental and behavioural disorders; 95 percent more ulcers; 63 percent more chronic conditions; and 33 percent more circulatory conditions.

While Canadians are strongly supportive of our universal health care system, there are significant gaps in the system that have to be addressed. The report of the Commission on the Future of Health Care in Canada (Romanow 2002) called for extending our national health insurance system beyond physician and hospital care to include the cost of prescription drugs and home care (such as nursing and homemaking) for those with chronic health problems who are not in hospital. The Canadian Health Coalition (n.d.) warns against "increased privatization of our public system focusing on profits rather than patient care." It also calls for "the expansion of the public system to include a universal drug plan, a system of home and community care, long-term care, and a strategy for mental health."

The Canadian Health Coalition (n.d.) points to other necessary reforms and improvements in health care. It calls for action on the health status of Indigenous peoples through collaboration between the federal and Indigenous governments. It also points to a "community-based, multi-disciplinary team approach to the management, organization and delivery of services, especially in primary care" as a more responsive and cost-effective way to deliver health care. Finally, as a key element of social justice, the Canadian Health Coalition underlines the importance of the five principles found in the Canada Health Act that governs federal funding for provincially delivered health services. These principles are public administration, universality, comprehensiveness, accessibility and portability. These principles prohibit practices such as extra billing of patients by physicians, user fees charged to patients by other professionals or hospitals, and queue-jumping in wait lists for services by those who are willing to pay extra.

Economic Security and Environmental Sustainability

In Canada and on the global level we face immediate and grave problems posed by our abuse and destruction of the natural environment. These problems include global climate change caused by the emission of greenhouse gases, depletion of natural resources, loss of natural habitat and species extinction and threats to our health caused by pollution and environmental toxins.

It is therefore essential to link any discussion of economic security to the question of environmental sustainability of the planet. Social justice and ecological justice are now inextricably linked, both in moral and material terms. Economic security will only be achievable if there is wide and deep economic redistribution that provides everyone with what they need, and at the same time lowers overall levels of consumption, resource extraction and environmental damage. Environmental sustainability and social equality can be mutually reinforcing goals, and both are essential in building a more just society.

Our traditional approach to extending prosperity in Canadian society has been to rely on economic growth to increase wealth, thereby enabling those with less to take a relatively bigger slice of the economic pie. But we have now reached critical environmental limits, and open-ended, indiscriminate economic growth is no longer viable. The rules of the economic "game" must change. We now need to regulate and reduce consumption through measures such as green taxes (on fossil fuels, for example) and restrictions on non-essential activities that leave a big environmental footprint (such as the recreational use of snowmobiles or ATVs, or the constant replacement of electronic devices as a result of marketing by companies that manufacture these devices). In particular, we must ensure that economic elites roll back their standard of living and accept lower profit margins through such measures as large tax increases on the wealthy, limits on corporate profit taking and calling a halt to economic investment or production that causes environmental destruction.

Our focus must shift from economic growth to acting as careful stewards of economic resources. We must find ways to provide people with the material necessities of life in the context of a "steady state" economy that maximizes emotional and social well-being (Mulvale 2007). All of us (especially the wealthy, but also those with low income and the working and middle classes) need to adjust our lifestyles and consumption patterns in order to minimize our environmental footprint. Of course, the "well

---

CASE STUDY:
CHALLENGING INJUSTICE AND INEQUALITY:
A GENERATIONAL CHANGE

A key underlying issue in regard to poverty and economic justice in Canada is the large and expanding gap between those with the highest incomes and those with the lowest incomes. Heisz (2015: 80) point out that "the top 20 percent of income earners [in Canada] earned 39.0 percent of all income between 2000 and 2011, up from 36.7 percent between 1976 and 1995." Heisz also documents that the share of total income among the top 1 percent is increasing. This trend is the highest in Calgary and Toronto, where the top 1 percent earn 17.5 percent and 16.5 percent of total income respectively. Another way to understand this income inequality is to measure the pay of CEOs (chief executive officers of large corporations) in relation to the pay of average workers. Macdonald (2018: 6) points out that "in 2016, Canada's 100 highest-paid CEOs made on average $10.4 million —

209 times the average income of $49,738 that year." Expressed in a different way, workers earning the minimum wage (which varied by province, ranging from $10.85 per hour in Nova Scotia to $14.00 per hour in Ontario on January 1, 2018) would have to work between 1.1 and 1.4 *months* to earn the average *hourly* wage of the top 100 CEOs based on a standard work week (Macdonald, 2018: 9).

One can think of how this income gap has affected successive generations. The author of this chapter is part of the baby boomers — the generation born during the period of roughly 1945 to 1960. As boomers in Canada, we grew up in a time of economic growth and relative prosperity. There was a large gap between the richest and poorest, but there was also a general expectation (even if it was imperfectly realized) that children from working-class and middle-class backgrounds would have the chance to pursue an advanced education and find a well-remunerated and secure job.

The millennial generation (born in the 1980s and 1990s) face very different economic circumstances and career prospects. The current labour market has a large and increasing proportion of precarious jobs that are short term and part-time, and that have low pay and no benefits (such as a pension plan, or drug and dental coverage). In many cases, jobs — both bad and good ones — are completely disappearing due to automation driven by information technology. At the same time, the level of economic inequality (measured by share of income of those at the top, or by CEO compensation packages) is growing. Where is the justice in all of this?

But there is also evidence that many millennials are becoming mobilized and are taking action to achieve economic and social justice. Their activism is expressed in diverse ways — through student organizations, labour unions, women opposing sexual aggression, Indigenous young people reclaiming their cultures and rallying against racism and LGBTT2Q groups challenging heteronormativity. The struggle for economic and social justice is being taken up by the younger generation.

off" might have more to give up in this regard, as they tend to be the ones who own monster homes and summer cottages, travel to far-off destinations for their vacations and live generally more extravagant lifestyles.

STRATEGIES FOR THE ELIMINATION OF POVERTY AND ECONOMIC SECURITY FOR ALL

The components of universal economic security call for fundamental changes in Canadian society and on the broader international level. Many social movements (such as organized labour, feminists, environmental activists and anti-racism groups) and advocacy organizations (such as anti-poverty groups, faith-based social justice bodies, peace and international development groups, human rights watchdogs and fair-trade advocates) continue to struggle for the various aspects of economic security here in Canada and internationally. These movements and organizations must continue and increase their struggles — working in concert with one another whenever possible, and using new research data and innovative campaigning strategies as they become available.

It is interesting to look at two specific examples of practical organizing to address poverty and increase economic security in Canada that have had a positive impact in recent years. One is the nationwide (and indeed worldwide) campaign to make basic income a fundamental aspect of our income security system and the broader redistributive state. At the national level, the Basic Income Canada Network[5] and its provincial and local allies are dedicated to changing the conversation about income support, and to ensuring that all of us have the economic means that we require to live with dignity and choices. At the international level, the Basic Income Earth Network[6] has been promoting discussion and research on basic income for over thirty years.

Another notable example of strategic activity to reduce poverty in Canada, and to bring about a greater degree of redistributive justice, has been the work of Campaign 2000. As discussed above, this organization is dedicated to end child and family poverty in Canada. Campaign 2000 continues to monitor the federal and provincial governments and to press them to take effective steps to redistribute resources in ways that will eliminate the scandal of children living in poverty in our very wealthy country of Canada. In particular, its annual "report cards" (Campaign 2000 2017) on governments' progress (or lack thereof) in lowering rates of poverty among children and families have had considerable success in focussing the attention of Canadians on steps that we still must take if we are to make progress on economic equality and redistributive justice.

Canada has set in place some significant measures to reduce poverty and redistribute economic resources. These measures, such as income support programs of the federal government and public goods such as health care, take us some steps toward a just and redistributive society. But we have much, much more to do to achieve deep social justice in an ecologically sustainable economy that will endure for our children and grandchildren.

DISCUSSION QUESTIONS

1. In your opinion, which of the existing social programs in Canada are likely to be most effective in reducing poverty and enhancing equality? Which of these programs are likely to be the least effective in this regard? Why?
2. What are the advantages and disadvantages of the different approaches to measuring poverty in Canada (LICO, LIM, MBM)? If Canada were to adopt one "official" poverty measurement, should it be one of these three approaches? Why or why not?
3. You have been asked to make three recommendations to the federal government about what it can do to enhance redistributive justice in Canada. What would your recommendations be?
4. What would be the best ways for governments at the federal, provincial, and local levels to facilitate progress towards the goal of environmental sustainability? Can these activities or policies be pursued in ways that simultaneously contribute to social justice?

GLOSSARY

Basic income: A periodic cash payment unconditionally delivered to all on an individual basis, without a means test or work requirement. It is delivered to individuals (not to households), is universal (paid to all, regardless of their income) and is unconditional (paid without a requirement to work or to demonstrate willingness to work).

Economic security: The availability to an individual or family of sufficient cash income (earned in the labour market or available through government income support programs) *and* adequate public goods (health care, education, affordable housing and so on) to ensure a life free of want and with opportunities for dignity and emotional satisfaction.

Environmental sustainability: The ability of our natural environments and global biosphere to support, maintain and reproduce human and other forms of life. It implies that human beings (both individually and collectively) have a moral and practical obligation to behave in ways that minimize our negative impacts on the natural environment and all forms of life on planet earth, and that promote the well-being and thriving of all species (including non-human animals, plants, micro-organisms). It also implies that human beings and societies in the here and now must act in ways that will enable future generations to gain an adequate livelihood (in regard to food production, availability of clean water and access to essential natural resources) and to benefit from healthy and enriching natural environments.

Income support programs: Government programs that provide cash income on a regular (usually monthly) basis to individuals or families. These programs may be set up as social insurance, entitlements or social assistance.

Income support programs — Entitlements: A social support program based on factors such as having young children at home, being elderly or earning a very low income in the labour market (where the benefit supplements earned income).

Income support programs — Social assistance: An income support program that is a "last resort" measure to support those in financial hardship who have no other income.

Income support programs — Social insurance: A fund into which paid workers and their employers contribute and from which workers receive cash benefits when they lose their jobs, retire or are unable to work due to injury or illness.

Just deserts: The principle that what persons earn for themselves should be theirs to keep. This idea supports the argument that earnings through wages, salaries, production of commodities, business dealings or investment should be retained by the earner, and should be subject to no or low taxation.

Poverty: A condition in which an individual or family lacks the means (cash income, goods and services) required to secure the material requirements of life (adequate and nutritious food, a decent place to live, personal necessities, services such as health care and education and so on). The state of material poverty is often accompanied by the lack of positive social interactions and relationships, exclusion from community life and political decision making and the devaluing of one's social (and perhaps cultural) identity.

Poverty line: The level of income that divides those who are poor (those whose income falls below this level) and those who are not poor (those whose income is above this level). Poverty lines can take into account family size and composition, the relative costs of living in specific localities and income before and after taxes and cash transfers from government.

Poverty line, Absolute poverty line: Based on the income necessary for a decent and secure life, taking into account all the essential costs of living (food, housing, utilities, clothing, personal necessities, transportation and so on).

Poverty line, Relative poverty line: Based on the overall range of incomes from the richest to the poorest, with those whose income falls below a certain point on the continuum defined as poor.

Public goods: Supports and services that are made available to all members of society at no or relatively low cost through programs and policies of the state (such as education, health care, social services, childcare, affordable housing, public transportation, parks and natural spaces and public utilities).

Redistributive justice: An aspect of justice as fairness that calls for state action to transfer resources from those with more than they need to those who have insufficient resources. This transfer of resources may be applied to income, accomplished through the payment of taxes by those with high incomes to fund income security programs for those at low income levels. This same redistributive approach can be applied to the provision of universal public goods (such as education and health care) to ensure equitable access for all.

NOTES

1. In August 2018 the federal government announced that it is adopting an official poverty line, which is a market-basket measurement. See Opportunity for All – Canada's First Poverty Reduction Strategy [available on-line].
2. See Statistics Canada, Income Highlight Tables, 2016 Census.
3. See Statistics Canada, Data Tables, 2016 Census.
4. Unfortunately, the Ontario Basic Income Pilot was cancelled by the newly elected Conservative provincial government on 31 July 2018.
5. See Basic Income Canada Network <https://www.basicincomecanada.org/>.
6. See Basic Income Earth Network <http://basicincome.org/>.

REFERENCES

Alexander, C., K. Beckman, A. Macdonald, C. Renner, and M. Stewart. 2017. *Ready for Life: A Socio-Economic Analysis of Early Childhood Education and Care.* Ottawa: Conference Board of Canada. <http://www.conferenceboard. ca/e-library/abstract.aspx?did=9231>.

Basic Income Earth Network. n.d. "About Basic Income." Louvain-la-Neuve, Belgium: BIEN. <http://basicincome.org/basic-income/>.

Campaign 2000. 2016. "A Road Map to Eradicate Child and Family Poverty." 2016 Report card on child & family poverty in Canada. Toronto: Campaign 2000. <http://campaign2000.ca/wp-content/uploads/2016/11/ Campaign2000NationalReportCard2016Eng.pdf>.

___. 2017. "A Poverty-Free Canada Requires Federal Leadership." [The 2017 report card on child and family poverty in Canada.] Toronto: Campaign 2000. <https://campaign2000.ca/wp-content/uploads/2017/11/ EnglishNationalC2000ReportNov212017.pdf>.

Campbell, B., and G, Marchildon (eds.). 2007. *Medicare: Facts, Myths, Problems, Promise.* Toronto: James Lorimer.

Canada Without Poverty. 2017. "Just the Facts." Ottawa: Canada Without Poverty. <http://www.cwp-csp.ca/poverty/just-the-facts/>.

Canadian Centre for Policy Alternative (Manitoba Office). 2013. *Photovoice: A Youth Lens on Poverty in Winnipeg.* Winnipeg: CCPA Manitoba. <https://www. policyalternatives.ca/multimedia/photovoice-youth-lens-poverty-winnipeg>.

Canadian Health Coalition. n.d.. "What We Do." Ottawa: Canadian Health Coalition. <http://www.healthcoalition.ca/about-us/what-we-do/>.

Canadian Housing and Renewal Association. n.d. "Housing for All One-Pager." Ottawa: CHRA. <http://housing4all.ca/housing-for-all-one-pager>.

Donne, J. 1623. *Devotions upon Emergent Occasions.*

Drover, G., A. Moscovitch, and J. Mulvale. 2014. "Promoting Equity for a Stronger Canada: The Future of Canadian Social Policy." Ottawa: Canadian Association of Social Workers. <https://casw-acts.ca/en/ promoting-equity-stronger-canada-future-canadian-social-policy>.

Finkel, A. 2006. *Social Policy and Practice in Canada: A History.* Waterloo, ON: Wilfred Laurier University Press.

Food Secure Canada. n.d. a. "Five Big Ideas For A Better Food System." Montreal: Food Secure Canada. <https://foodsecurecanada.org/policy-advocacy/ five-big-ideas-better-food-system>.

Food Secure Canada. n.d.b. "What Is Food Sovereignty?" Montreal: Food Secure Canada. <https://foodsecurecanada.org/who-we-are/what-food-sovereignty>.

Harden, J. 2017. "The Case for Renewal in Post-Secondary Education." [Alternative Federal Budget Technical Paper, March 2017.] Ottawa: Canadian Centre on Policy Alternatives. <https://www.policyalternatives.ca/publications/reports/ case-renewal-post-secondary-education>.

Heisz, A. 2015. "Trends in Income Inequality in Canada and Elsewhere." Montreal:

Institute for Research on Public Policy. <http://irpp.org/research-studies/aots5-heisz/>.

Lightman, E., and N. Lightman. 2017. *Social Policy in Canada,* 2nd. ed. Don Mills ON: Oxford University Press.

Lightman, E., A. Mitchell, and B. Wilson. 2008. *Poverty Is Making Us Sick: A Comprehensive Survey of Income and Health in Canada*. December. Toronto: Wellesley Institute and Community Social Planning Council of Toronto. <http://www.wellesleyinstitute.com/wp-content/uploads/2011/11/povertyismakingussick.pdf>.

Macdonald, D. 2018. *Climbing Up and Kicking Down: Executive Pay in Canada*. Ottawa: Canadian Centre for Policy Alternatives. <https://www.policyalternatives.ca/sites/default/files/uploads/publications/National%20Office/2018/01/Climbing%20Up%20and%20Kicking%20Down.pdf>.

Matern, R., M. Mendelson, and M. Oliphant. 2009. "Developing a Deprivation Index: The Research Process." Toronto: Daily Bread Food Bank and the Caledon Institute of Social Policy. <http://www.dailybread.ca/wp-content/uploads/2010/12/DevelopingaDeprivationIndexFINAL.pdf>.

Mulvale, Jim. 2007. "Enough to Live On: The Case for Guaranteed Income and the End of the Growth Economy." *Briarpatch*, 36, 7 (November): 29–33. <https://briarpatchmagazine.com/articles/view/enough-to-live-on>.

Mulvale, J., and S. Frankel. 2016. "Next Steps on the Road to Basic Income in Canada." *Journal of Sociology and Social Welfare,* 43, 3: 27–50.

Murphy, B., X. Zhang and C. Dionne. 2012. *Low Income in Canada - A Multi-Line and Multi-Index Perspective*. Ottawa: Statistics Canada, Income Research Paper Series, March. <http://www.statcan.gc.ca/pub/75f0002m/75f0002m2012001-eng.htm>.

Ontario. 2017. "Ontario Basic Income Pilot." Toronto: Ministry of Community and Social Services. <https://www.ontario.ca/page/ontario-basic-income-pilot>.

PhotoVoice Regina Committee. 2007. *PhotoVoice: Freedom from Poverty*. Regina SK: Prairie Women's Health Centre of Excellence. <http://www.pwhce.ca/photovoice/regina_intro.html>.

Proudfoot, S. 2011. "Survey Finds Many Canadians Believe Poor Are 'Part of the Problem.'" *National Post*, March 1. <http://www.nationalpost.com/Survey+finds+many+Canadians+believe+poor+part+problem/4365289/story.html>.

Raphael, D. 2007. *Poverty and Policy in Canada: Implications for Health and Quality of Life*. Toronto, ON: Canadian Scholars' Press.

Redden, J. 2011. "Poverty in the News: A Framing Analysis of Coverage in Canada and the UK." *Information, Communication & Society,* 14, 6. <https://doi.org/10.1080/1369118X.2011.586432>.

Romanow, R. 2002. *Building on Values: The Future of Health Care in Canada – Final Report*. Ottawa: Government of Canada. <http://publications.gc.ca/collections/Collection/CP32-85-2002E.pdf>.

Statistics Canada. 2015a. "Market Basket Measure (2008 base)." Ottawa: Statistics Canada. <http://www.statcan.gc.ca/pub/75f0002m/2012002/mbm-mpc-eng.htm>.

___. 2015b. "Low Income Cut-Offs." Ottawa: Statistics Canada. <http://www.statcan.gc.ca/pub/75f0002m/2012002/lico-sfr-eng.htm>.

___. 2015c. "Low Income Measures." Ottawa: Statistics Canada. <http://www.statcan.gc.ca/pub/75f0002m/2012002/lim-mfr-eng.htm>.

___. 2015d. "Low Income Lines, 2013–2014: Update." Income Research Paper Series. Ottawa: Statistics Canada (Release date: 2015-12-17). <http://www.statcan.gc.ca/pub/75f0002m/75f0002m2015002-eng.htm>.

___. 2017. "Low Income Statistics by Age, Sex and Economic Family Type, Canada, Provinces and Selected Census Metropolitan Areas (CMAS)." Table: 206-0041. Ottawa: Statistics Canada (Release date: 2017-05-26). <http://www5.statcan.gc.ca/cansim/a26?lang=eng&retrLang=eng&id=2060041&&pattern=&stByVal=1&p1=1&p2=31&tabMode=dataTable&csid=>.

___. 2018a. "Low Income Measures (LIMs) by Income Source and Household Size in Current Dollars and 2016 Constant Dollars, Annual." Table 206-0091 CANSIM. <www5.statcan.gc.ca/cansim/a26?lang=eng&retrLang=eng&id=2060091&&pattern=&stByVal=1&p1=1&p2=31&tabMode=dataTable&csid=>.

___. 2018b. "Low Income Cut-Offs (LICOs) Before and After Tax by Community and Family Size in 2016 Constant Dollars, Occasional." Table 206-0092 CANSIM. <www5.statcan.gc.ca/cansim/a26?lang=eng&retrLang=eng&id=2060092&&pattern=&stByVal=1&p1=1&p2=31&tabMode=dataTable&csid=>.

___. 2018c. "Market Basket Measure (MBM) Thresholds (2011 Base) for Reference Family, by Market Basket Measure Region and Component, in Current Dollars and 2016 Constant Dollars, Annual." Table 206-0093, CANSIM. <http://www5.statcan.gc.ca/cansim/a26?lang=eng&retrLang=eng&id=2060093&&pattern=&stByVal=1&p1=1&p2=31&tabMode=dataTable&csid=>.

U.N. OHCHR (United Nations, Office of the High Commissioner for Human Rights). 2004. *Human Rights and Poverty Reduction: A Conceptual Framework*. New York and Geneva: United Nations.

Van Parijs, P., and Y. Vanderborght. 2017. *Basic Income: A Radical Proposal for a Free Society and a Sane Economy*. Cambridge, MA, and London, England: Harvard University Press.

World Bank. 2016. "Poverty: Overview." Washington DC: World Bank. <http://www.worldbank.org/en/topic/poverty/overview>.

4

RACISM AND JUSTICE IN CANADA

Selom Chapman-Nyaho, Carl E. James,

and Akwasi Owusu-Bempah

OBJECTIVES

At the end of this chapter you will be able to:

- Examine the nature and scope of racism and justice in Canada

- Define structural racism and its manifestations

- Understand the role of racialization in the creation of marginalized groups

- Outline the history of racialized exclusions that underlie the nation's formation

- Discuss Multiculturalism and its role as part of our national "mythology"

In February of 2017, a motion brought by Liberal MP Iqra Khalid calling for Canadians to condemn Islamophobia and for Parliament to study the issue was met with widespread protest and capitalized on by the opposition Conservatives. Prayer rooms in schools caused people who believed Canada's "values" were being infringed upon to disrupt school board meetings. Immigrants are welcome so long as they conform to "Canadian culture." On the surface, this notion is fairly benign. It's expected that when you travel to a new location you obey the laws and norms of that society as a sign of respect. But what is this Canadian culture? And how has it come to be defined as something to which non-white Canadians conform rather than contribute? And what does this all have to do with notions of justice? To explore these questions, we must problematize Canada's history and colonial past in order to understand that in its 150-year history, Canada was formed, sometimes explicitly, as a nation for white western Europeans. We must see how racism is part of our history and how its effects last to the present day. For all of Canada's successes and promises, we must grapple with this past and with these effects in order to become a society premised on notions of justice.

The fact is that, despite all the celebration of our diversity, Canada is still a country in which Indigenous and racialized peoples experience racism, discrimination and marginalization. Moreover, Canada is a country that was deliberately founded on principles of white supremacy. It was imagined as a white nation. This may sound controversial in a time where most of us have been taught to believe in principles of equality and "colour blindness," but our history reveals the nation to be one that diligently worked to manage, constrain and restrict non-white people for much of its past. A consequence of this colour blindness is that in a country that celebrates multiculturalism, inequalities in housing, education, employment and the criminal justice system are excused as an anomaly or reflective of an inability to adapt to the dominant norms of Canadian society. This effect is exacerbated by the well-intentioned tendency to promote colour blindness. Because "old-fashioned" or "redneck" racism has become increasingly socially unacceptable, individuals will often reject any notions of race, instead embracing abstract notions of justice and equality (Malhi and Boon 2008). This notion of colour blindness is considered polite and liberal, but too often leads to a refusal to examine or acknowledge power and systemic inequalities (Malhi and Boon 2008: 129). Multicultural discourses, perhaps unwittingly, feed into this colour blindness by promoting ideals of "tolerance, accommodation, harmony, and diversity," which in and of themselves prove "inadequate as measures taken to eradicate the deeply rooted problems of racism" (Malhi and Boon 2008: 129).

RACIAL INEQUALITY IN CANADA AND ITS RELATION TO SURVEILLANCE, CRIMINALIZATION AND EMPLOYMENT

Most people understand racism as an individual feeling or action of overt bigotry. According to Henry and Tator (2010), we think of physical assaults, slurs and offensive graffiti as actions that the vast majority of us would condemn. But this is a limited, and limiting, understanding of the role and effects of racism. Fleras (2016b: 65) also claims that we tend to think of racism as, "bad people with twisted attitudes inflicting abuse on those less fortunate." But racism does not only manifest itself within individuals; it operates at the level of groups, organizations and institutions. This is a structural or systemic view of racism. Of course, it is informed by racist ideologies, but these are often subtle. Racist ideologies can seep into how we understand and view the world. They feel like "common sense" (Henry and Tator 2010: 17–18). Like all ideologies, racism (both historical and contemporary) can come to shape how we understand our complex world. According to Henry and Tator (2010: 18):

> Recently unemployed people can easily blame the new immigrants who have taken their jobs away. People who are fearful in their homes and on the streets can now blame all those Black or Asian people who commit crimes. Teachers whose Black students are underachieving can believe that it has nothing to do with their racial attitudes or classroom practices. The corporate manager is able to justify a refusal to hire those who are racially "different" on the basis of not wanting to disrupt the harmony of the workforce ... Racist assumptions and beliefs provide a ready explanation for the stress experienced by people who live in a country undergoing rapid social and cultural change.

Structural, or systemic, racism is defined based on the recognition that, "society is *founded on* the principle of advancing a racialized and Eurocentric society; *grounded in* the exploitation and oppression of Aboriginal peoples and racialized minorities; and *bounded* by the need to preserve the prevailing and racialized distribution of power and privilege" (Fleras 2016b: 80). According to structural definitions of racism, society and its institutions reflect a set of values and practices that can disproportionately affect racialized groups in a negative way. "Racialized minorities find themselves disadvantaged within institutional contexts, not necessarily because of openly discriminatory barriers, but because mainstream institutions were neither designed to reflect their realities or experiences nor constructed to advance their interests or agendas" (Fleras 2016b: 95). It is also crucial to understand how race intersects with other social statuses like class, gender and immigrant status. Henry and Tator (2010: 16) explain that, "one of the most complex aspects of racism is its elusive and changing nature." For example, Fleras (2016a) claims that although attitudes towards racialized groups in Canada have changed, social and economic inequality remains stubbornly persistent. Too often, the problems that affect racialized groups are believed to be individual problems or secondary issues, rather than problems that confront the nation as a whole.

Framing inequality as a question of "'who gets what,' how, and why" (Fleras 2016b: 149), Fleras maintains that Canada is still marked by a high degree of social inequality. Social inequality is, "an umbrella term for a variety of social disadvantages related to powerlessness, discrimination, political participation, institutional involvement, health outcomes, and quality of life factors, as well as vulnerability to violence deprivation, and violation of people's rights" (Fleras 2016b: 149). Accordingly, racialized groups in Canada are still shown to have higher rates of poverty and dep-rivation, while being underrepresented in terms of the social and political power that can affect substantial change (Fleras 2016b).

One of the areas where we can see the persistence of racialized dis-crimination is in the criminal justice system. Research has consistently shown that marginalized social groups, and certain racialized groups in particular, are over-represented in official crime and criminal justice statistics across Western nations (Tonry 2011). Canada is not unique in this sense (Owusu-Bempah and Wortley 2014). Black and Indigenous peoples in particular face disproportionately high rates of criminal justice processing, long having been a focus of the states' social control efforts (Henry and Tator 2010; Walker 2010). However, given a lack of access to readily available criminal justice data, it is difficult to examine the full extent to which racialized Canadians are, or are not, over-represented in criminal offending and the criminal justice system.

Unlike the United States and the United Kingdom, the Canadian gov-ernment does not systematically collect and release criminal justice data that details the racial or ethnic background of people who are accused or convicted of crimes, nor how these groups are processed through the criminal justice system. The data that is available is generally limited in its scope and must be obtained through special request. It is not automatically released to the public. Supporters of racial data collection and dissemination argue that such information is necessary in order to monitor the processing of racial minorities through the criminal justice system; provide useful information that is necessary for the development of criminal justice and social policy; objectively determine if there is a relationship between race and crime; and provide transparency within the criminal justice system. But others fear that this data could further stigmatize already marginalized populations. The fear is that statistics that might show higher rates of offending among certain racialized groups without providing sufficient context about why they are over-represented — as a result of social or economic marginalization, for example — and would be used by some to justify racist stereotypes and discriminatory policies (Owusu-Bempah and Millar 2010).

In the absence of race-relevant criminal justice data, the Canadian public tends to over-estimate the extent to which racialized Canadians commit crimes. For example, a survey conducted in Ontario in 1995 found that nearly half of respondents felt that there was a relationship between race and crime, and that two-thirds of these respondents selected "West Indians" or "blacks" as being the most crime prone (Henry, Hastings and Freer 1996). In 2008, a *Toronto Star* poll asked members of the public to estimate what proportion of Canadians with a criminal record were from racialize groups. Respondents believed that over twice as many racialized group members had a criminal record than the police records showed (36.7 percent perceived vs. 16.7 perent actual). The official data illustrated that "visible minority" group members were in fact under-represented amongst Canadians who had a criminal record compared with their proportion of the population (16.7 percent with criminal record vs. 20.0 percent of population) (Rankin and Powell 2008). Such perceptions of minority criminality have important implications for how criminalized racial groups are treated by the criminal justice system and by society at large. Singh and Sprott (2017), for example, provided adult Canadians with a series of sentencing vignettes and asked them to rate the dangerousness and to hand down a sentence to offenders of different racial backgrounds. Their research found that adult Canadians rated the hypothetical Black offender as significantly more dangerous than the hypothetical white offender and gave the former a significantly harsher sentence than the latter (Singh and Sprott 2017). Essentially, people believed Black offenders were more dangerous and recommended harsher sentences than they did for white offenders who had the exact same criminal profile. This is concerning insofar as it suggests that people who sit on juries may not be as "colour blind" as we pretend to assume. As a result, Black Canadians may be more likely to be found guilty by judges and juries during criminal trials, or deemed more deserving of harsh punishments in the eyes of the public and justice officials alike.

Related to the public perceptions about crime are public perceptions about the fairness of the law and legal institutions. Available evidence suggests that a significant proportion of Canadians believe that bias exists in at least some sectors of the criminal justice system and that these perceptions vary according to race. Using data from the 1999 General Social Survey, O'Conner (2008), for example, found that "visible minorities" in Canada are more likely than are white people to perceive the police as biased. Sprott and Doob (2014) analyzed data from the 2009 General Social Survey and found that racial differences in attitudes towards the police existed and that these differences were complex and varied by province. Whereas Blacks in Quebec and Ontario were more negative in their appraisal of the extent to which the police were effective at fighting crime, Indigenous peoples in Alberta held more negative views than white and Chinese respondents with regards to police effectiveness and sensitivity towards dealing with members of the public. Similarly, Wortley and Owusu-Bempah (2009) found that perceptions of the justice system (the police and the courts) varied by length of time spent in the country for immigrant respondents, regardless of race: the longer immigrants had lived in Canada, the more negative their perceptions of the justice system tended to become.

Much of the public attention to and criticism about discrimination in the Canadian justice system has been directed at the police. Racialized Canadians have long complained that they are mistreated by federal, provincial and municipal law enforcement agencies (Tator and Henry 2006; Tanovich 2006). Recent attention to race and policing, in particular, has focused on the experiences of Black Canadians in Toronto (Owusu-Bempah 2014). Spurred first by police killings of unarmed Black men, activists, concerned citizens and politicians alike have also brought attention to police stop-and-search activities, and to the significant racial disproportion in police carding — the practice of stopping and questioning individuals who are under no suspicion of criminal activity and the compiling of their personal information in a database (Owusu-Bempah 2014). Indigenous groups have also frequently complained of disproportionately high rates of use of force, combined with a seeming lack of concern for Indigenous victims of crime — including the hundreds of missing and murdered Indigenous women and girls (Jiwani and Young 2006).

In the court system, too, concerns about racial disparities and discrimination have been raised. While little data is available, many have pointed out that there are few racialized Canadians serving as judges, which contributes to perceptions of bias amongst those accused and the lawyers that represent them. A study conducted for the Commission on Systemic Racism in the Ontario Criminal Justice System found that slightly over two-thirds of Ontario lawyers whose clientele was substantially non-white felt that their clients were treated unfairly because of their race (Commission 1995). Perceptions of racial bias are compounded by individual acts of racism exhibited in court by members of the judiciary and judges have been especially criticized for expressing "stereotypical attitudes, behaviours and views of racial minority members" (Henry and Tator 2005: 134). A judge in Manitoba, for example, made disparaging comments about some of the Indigenous offenders that came before his court, remarking that he would be "joyful if the residents of the Long Plaines Indian Reserve killed each other off" (Henry and Tator 2005: 134). Incidents like this feed perceptions that the criminal justice system is biased towards already marginalized groups. And these perceptions are supported by evidence that different suspects are treated differently by the courts. Over a six-month period, Kellough and Wortley (2002) tracked over 1,800 criminal cases from two Toronto bail courts. Their findings indicated that Black accused were more likely to be detained before trial than were accused from other racial backgrounds. Importantly, race remained a significant factor in this study even after controlling for relevant factors such as flight risk and danger to the public (Kellough and Wortley 2002).

Perhaps the best available data on race and criminal justice processing comes from Canada's federal correctional system. Each year Public Safety Canada produces a report on the state of corrections in the country that includes information on the racial make-up of the federal offender population (Public Safety Canada 2016). The data suggest that Indigenous and Black peoples are disproportionately confined to federal institutions and disproportionately under community supervision (Owusu-Bempah and Wortley 2014). Whereas Black Canadians are most over-represented in correctional facilities in the eastern and central regions of Canada, Indigenous peoples are most over-represented in the Prairie and western provinces and in the territories. There has been a dramatic increase of Black and Indigenous inmates (between 70 percent and 90 percent, depending of the population under examination) within the federal correctional system over the past decade. These high rates of incarceration are compounded by perceived racial injustices behind bars. Both Black and Indigenous inmates have complained that they experience overt and covert forms of discrimination behind bars, including name-calling, unequally applied disciplinary practices and lack of access to employment within correctional facilities (Wesley 2012; OCI 2013). It is important to distinguish between minority participation in crime and the criminalization of some racialized groups. Because there are social factors that are known to increase some offending behaviours, some socially marginalized groups reported to offend at higher rates than the general population. However, over-representation in police statistics, for example, can also result from the disproportionate levels of police attention or surveillance that particular groups are subject to. The latter results in what is often referred to as "criminalization," thereby acknowledging the role of justice agencies in producing these outcomes.

The notion of criminalization leads to increased surveillance (over-policing) of racialized populations at the same time that these groups remain under-protected (Jiwani 2011: 43–45). Race intersects with immigrant status and class, "to produce 'undesirable' subjects of criminalization, illegalization, marginalization, and exclusion" (Chan and Chunn 2014: 117). For example, South Asian, Arab and Muslim communities, in particular refugees, have found themselves subject to increasing levels of screening and surveillance and explicitly racialized debates over levels of immigration (Chan and Chunn 2014). But both the social factors that produce offending and the criminalization of marginalized groups are not confined to the criminal justice system. The child welfare system in Canada, for example, has also disproportionately affected certain racialized populations.

In Canada, Indigenous peoples have been disproportionately affected by state efforts to "protect" children. Following the systemic apprehension of five generations of Indigenous children with Canada's residential school system (a system intended to remove the "Indian" from the child), the child welfare system began to remove Indigenous children from their families at high rates in the 1950s, leading to the unprecedented overrepresentation of Indigenous young people in care (Sinclair 2017). The data indicate that by the 1970s, one-third of Indigenous children in Canada were separated from their families though adoption or foster care (Fourner and Crey 1997). Today, while Indigenous children make up just 7 percent of the child population in Canada, they represent 48 percent of children in foster care in the country (Fourner and Crey 1997). The reasons for such overrepresentation are multiple and compounding. Undoubtedly, a history of colonialism and marginalization has created conditions of poverty in which some Indigenous parents are unable to properly provide for their children. Likewise, the cultural genocide perpetuated by the residential school system has left deep scars in Indigenous communities, compounded by economic precarity that destabilizes families (Sinclair 2017; Trocmé, Knoke and Blackstock 2004). Continued racism in child welfare decision making, including assumptions about culture, language and spirituality, also leads to the overrepresentation of Indigenous children in care.

Racism and poverty have also been credited with fuelling the disproportionate representation of African-Canadian children in Ontario's welfare system. Although African Canadians comprise only 8.5 percent of the population of Toronto, 40.8 percent of children in care in Toronto are Black, according to data released by the Children's Aid Society of Toronto (Ontario Association of Children's Aid Societies 2016). Beyond the numbers, African Canadians report being treated more harshly than their white counterparts (Ontario Association of Children's Aid Societies 2016). King et al. (2017) analyzed data from Ontario's child welfare agencies, finding that Black children were more likely to be investigated than white children. They report that severe economic hardship, combined with assessments about the quality of the parent-child relationship, contributed substantially to the decision to provide child welfare services. As in the case with Indigenous peoples, it could be argued that assessments about parent-child relationships are based on white middle-class norms about family and parenting that are culturally biased against immigrant Black families. The practice of extended families caring for children, something common outside of the Western world, for example, may clash with Western notions of the nuclear family and ideas about who should have primary responsibility for raising children. These differences are compounded by the economic hardships facing many immigrant and racialized groups in Canada, which result in parents working long hours to support their families, while children are left in the care of grandparents, aunts and uncles. Structural and institutional forms of discrimination also produce injustices in Canada's employment sector. For example, Canadian census data demonstrates a persisting income gap between the racialized and Indigenous populations in Canada and their white counterparts. In fact, data from the 2016 census shows that the income gap for racialized Canadians actually increased between 2006 and 2016, with members of racialized groups earning on average 26 percent less than non-racialized group members (Monsebraaten 2017). Indigenous peoples, by comparison, earn on average 25 percent less than non-Indigenous people in Canada (Monsebraaten 2017). As noted, these differences are not new. Hou and Coulombe (2010) analyzed data from the 2006 census to examine the earning gaps between Canadian-born "visible minorities" and "non-visible minorities" working similar jobs in Canada's public and private sectors. Their research shows that while income was similar for members of racialized group members in comparison to whites working in the public sector, the data from the private sector told a different story. Racialized men and Black women in particular, earn significantly less than whites who have comparable educational attainment and years of experience working similar jobs in private industry. Hou and Coulombe (2010) attribute the income differences to differences in equality of opportunity; whereas the public sector is subject to employment equity regulations, the private sector faces less pressure, and small firms present more obstacles in this regard.

Other institutionalized practices also create injustices in Canada's employment sector. The lack of recognition for the foreign credentials or work experience of many immigrants, for example, blocks access to skilled jobs and results in under-employment, unemployment and vulnerability. A study of South Asian and Chinese immigrant professionals in Vancouver, for example, found that only 18.8 percent of those surveyed worked in the professional fields in which they were initially trained (as doctors, engineers, teachers and so forth) after moving to Canada (Basran and Zong 1998). Houle and Yssaad (2010) found that at the national level, only 28 percent of immigrants to Canada with foreign credentials had received recognition for these credentials, while 39 percent of those with foreign experience had that experience recognized within four years of arrival.

The structural and institutional bases of these inequalities are complex, but they are made more egregious because they come about within a discourse in which non-white Canadians are seen as somehow less Canadian than their white counterparts. Justice would demand that these issues be seen as Canadian issues, and yet too often they are hidden or explained away as if they have no bearing on the nation's self-image as a meritocratic society. Racialized bodies are made foreign within the nation, placing these issues outside of the realm of justice. Jiwani (2011) writes that the 2009 comments on "barbaric cultural practices" by then-minister of Citizenship, Immigration and Multiculturalism, Jason Kenney, served to reinforce stereotypes about the fundamental un-Canadianness of racialized immigrants. By "point[ing] the finger at racialized group members because of a small number of incidents involving specific acts of violence" the government representative served to "disregard the larger and prevalent patterns of violence that occur throughout Canadian society" (2011: 39). These acts of violence are positioned as a foreign problem. Like issues of police profiling and apathy over the large number murdered and missing Indigenous women and girls, because racialized Canadians are implicitly conceived as not fully a part of the nation, they too easily exist outside the realm of our notions of justice in Canada. As Jiwani writes, behaviours attributed to racialized subordinate groups are stripped of all historical and social context and naturalized "as being inherent to the individuals within that group" (2011: 40). Whiteness is the invisible normative background through which difference is judged.

IMAGINING "WHITE" CANADA

Sherene Razack (2002: 2) uses the term "white settler society" to describe Canada. A white settler society is a nation founded on a racial hierarchy and structured in such a way to support a national mythology that posits whites as those "most entitled to the fruits of citizenship." By mythology, Razack is referring to the stories nations construct about their origins and histories. "They enable citizens to think of themselves as part of a community, defining who belongs and who does not belong to the nation" (2002: 2). All nations construct these mythologies. In Canada it is one in which hard-working settlers developed a mostly empty land, bringing agriculture, industry and civilization to what would become a great nation. In this way, First Nations peoples are relegated to a pre-modern time while people of colour are considered new arrivals, entering a country that was already developed. "In this way, slavery, indentureship, and labour exploitation — for example, the Chinese who built the railway or the Sikhs who worked in the lumber industry in nineteenth-century Canada — are all handily forgotten in an official national story of European enterprise" (2002: 3). According to Stanley (2006), a central aspect of colonialism involved not just the appropriation of Indigenous land and suppression of Indigenous peoples, but a comprehensive organizing of the social, economic and political landscape of Canada based on a structured racial hierarchy. National mythologies, subsequently, render this process invisible.

The extent to which these national mythologies are true is not as important as how they shape certain cultures and a national consciousness. The rugged self-reliance and independence that characterizes the story of Canada links notions of space and race. Furthermore, it is necessary — and directly linked — to a more recent aspect of our national story: immigration and multiculturalism. Razack claims that much anti-immigration rhetoric draws from the story of an empty land "populated by hardy settlers" (2002: 4). Opposition to refugees and migrants that is based on notions of cultural incompatibility and government expenditure rely on the idea that Canada is a nation that provides equal opportunity to everyone and a nation in which people historically rose or fell based on their work ethic and commitment to the norms and values of their new home. But this narrative erases how the perceived "whiteness" of Canada was no accident. Canada was a nation that actively sought to confine the Indigenous inhabitants of the land and to restrict and exclude those who were deemed racially undesirable.

Drawing on the work of Peter Li (2003), Ismaili (2011) outlines four distinct phases of immigration/settlement to Canada. The first, from 1867 to approximately 1895, can be characterized as a *laissez-faire* period during which migration had few restrictions in order for Canada to acquire the labour required to build infrastructure, farm and expand settlement across the nation. The primary concern during this time was to limit the number of poor British subjects. But by the 1880s, those concerns shifted to alarm over the number of non-white immigrants originally brought over to labour, but who seemed intent on remaining. The Canadian government was explicit in its categorization of *preferred* and *non-preferred* immigrants (Ismaili 2011).

The second phase — from the early 1900s to the start of World War I — saw high levels of immigration to coincide with increasing industrialization. Many immigrants during this time came from Eastern and Southern Europe. While they were often viewed as culturally foreign and treated as undesirable, acute labour shortages necessitated their acceptance. But both formal and informal restrictions were placed on "racially undesirable" persons (Ismaili 2011: 91).

During the third phase, a preferred hierarchy of immigration was enforced. British and American immigrants were at the top of the hierarchy, with Central, Southern, and Eastern Europeans begrudgingly welcomed. But Jewish people and non-white immigrants were explicitly unwelcome. During this time, anti-immigrant sentiment was high with fears that Jewish people and Eastern Europeans were spreading communist and other subversive ideologies and contributing to labour unrest. Throughout World War II, over 22,000 Japanese Canadians had their property confiscated and were placed in internment camps and Canada accepted fewer than four thousand Jews fleeing Nazi persecution. Immigration overall slowed to a trickle between 1930 and 1945, with only 200,000 entrants compared to the nearly five million who came between 1900 and 1930 (Ismaili 2011).

In 1952 the Immigration Act changed to eliminate race and country of origin from its criteria for preferred and non-preferred immigrants, but "unsuitability with regard to Canada's climate, and perceived inability to become assimilated into Canadian society" (Ismaili 2011: 92) were still considered grounds for denial. However, with increasing pressure to accept global refugees, including pressure from the United Nations and the Commonwealth, and the need to attract skilled workers to the country, in 1967 Canada implemented a points system that prioritized immigrants who applied with desired languages, occupations, education and skills. This change dramatically increased the number of racialized immigrants from Asia, Africa, the Middle East and the Caribbean. And the resulting rapid increase in ethno-cultural diversity presented a need to reshape the nation from being explicitly grounded in concepts of white supremacy to being one that is able to accept and accommodate difference. At the heart of this effort was Canadian multiculturalism.

RACIALIZING CANADA

Canada, thus, is a country that came into being based on the explicit racialization of space. People were categorized into various groups and their desirability — their right to the nation — was based on these group memberships. To understand this it is important to appreciate the history of race. Social scientists use the term racialization to define the process of sorting individuals into particular ethnic or racial identities.

The idea of race is often taken for granted but nothing about it is as obvious as it seems. James (2010: 285) defines race as, "The socially constructed classification of human beings based on identified or perceived characteristics such as colour of skin and informed by historical and geographical context; it is not a biological classification. It is often the basis upon which groups are formed, agency is attained, social roles are assigned and status is conferred." Rather than legitimate biological categories, race is a set of "pseudological rationalizations based on a confusion of emotions, prejudiced judgements, and disordered values" (Montagu 1965: 6). This does not mean that there are not genetic and biological differences between individuals or that these differences tend to cluster around geographical locations of origin. Race as a social construct means that the categories were based on social and historical factors rather than objectively scientific criteria. But these classifications have been extremely influential in how we see ourselves, how others see us, and how we fit within social structures. According to James (2010: 50–51), race has become one of the most important "basis upon which groups are formed, agency is attained, social roles are assigned, and status is conferred."

Racialization is an exercise in power. Not only are our contemporary racial categories relatively recent concepts, dating primarily to the late 1700s, but they are the product of different sets of social relations (Gilroy 1987; Omi and Winant 1994; Comaroff 1996). Early racial classifications in the eighteenth century were arbitrary insofar as there were no clear lines where one race would end and another would begin (Montagu 1965) making it, "impossible to discuss the issue of race with any logic or consistency" (Hirschman 2004: 386). But the idea of race was very useful in the age of exploration to justify both colonization and the Trans-Atlantic African slave trade (Banton 1977). Of course, slavery existed prior to this and there had always been a notion of "outsiders" or different groups considered inferior to one's own. But according to Smedley (1998: 693):

What was absent from these different forms of human identity is what we today would perceive as classifications into "racial" groups, that is, the organization of all peoples into a limited number of unequal or ranked categories theoretically based on differences in their biophysical traits. There are no "racial" designations in the literature of the ancients and few references even to such human features as skin color.

But in the eighteenth century, a new understanding and interpretation of human differences came to justify attempts to claim and control land. This is a pattern found throughout history. Most of us today would not think of the Irish as a separate race, but the concept of race as we understand it today has historical precedence in attempts to define groups like the Irish, Southern Italians and Jews as separate and inferior in order to justify their cruel treatment. In the sixteenth and seventeenth centuries, for example, Irish people were frequently described as "human chimpanzees" and "squalid apes" in order to "prove that Ireland was such a degenerate place that only English domination would enable the inhabitants to become part of the human race" (Shanklin 1994: 3–5).

The image of human differences based on relative civilization and savagery combined with more recent scientific racial classifications served to structure colonialist thought in the New World. Expropriation and subjugation of Indigenous populations was justified on the basis of entitlement and of subjecting "inferior" races to the civilizing process (Smedley 1998: 694). These attitudes were the foundation for the early development of Canada. Ismaili (2011: 90) claims that, "since 1867, the Canadian government's decisions concerning who should be allowed into the country have been guided by two questions: 'Are certain immigrants better suited than others for certain kinds of jobs?' and 'Are certain immigrants better candidates than others for participation in Canadian social and political life?'" (p. 90).

Revisiting immigration, Canada's early policy was deliberately designed to control and/or exclude the settlement of particular immigrant groups. Race, ethnicity, nationality and social class were all factors considered in immigration. "This meant that white Europeans (specifically Western Europeans) were initially the preferred immigrants, after Americans and white citizens of Commonwealth countries" (James 2010: 173). In 1908 the minister responsible for immigration, Robert Borden, announced "the

Conservative Party stands for a white Canada." The successive Liberal government introduced a 1911 Order in Council designed to limit 1,300 Black American homesteaders migrating to Alberta from Oklahoma (James 2010: 174). Much the same sentiment was expressed by J.S. Woodsworth, one of the founders of the Co-operative Commonwealth Federation (CCF) which later became the New Democratic Party (NDP). In his 1909 book, *Strangers Within Our Gate*, Woodsworth wrote explicitly of preferring certain classes of European immigrants suited to the harsh North American climate. Notably, Woodsworth advocated the exclusion of Britain's poor because of their perceived criminal tendencies; Southern Italians due to their supposed low intelligence; and Syrians and Armenians because they were seen as too shrewd and parasitic (James 2010: 174).

The first people of African descent arrived in Canada as early as the 1620s. During the late 1700s, Jamaican Maroons — escaped slaves in Jamaica who fought a series of conflicts with the British colonial administration — were transported to Nova Scotia and employed building fortifications before most were eventually resettled in Freetown, Sierra Leone. The combined effect of the Underground Railroad, Black American migration during the American Revolution and War of 1812 and the labour force migration of a smaller number of people from the Caribbean who had come to work in mines or as domestic servants, was a population growth in the Black community: the 1901 census indicated that at least 17,437 Blacks resided in Canada. Yet, in 1955, the minister of immigration claimed that "coloured people" were not suitable for assimilation and could not adapt to Canada's climate (James 2010: 177–178). As McKittrick (2006) explains, the histories of the everyday realities of Black people in the diaspora are rendered invisible through a narrative that focuses on land ownership and questions of belonging. The presence of people of African descent in Canada since its inception matters less than elite political pronouncements on their suitability and adaptability.

In order to limit entry of South Asians to Canada, the Canadian government employed indirect measures of exclusion. The "Continuous Voyage" legislation of 1908 required immigrants to Canada to travel directly from their point of origin with a ticket purchased in that country. At the time, only the Canadian Pacific Railroad offered a continuous journey from India and Canada's governor had issued a directive that they should not sell through tickets to Canada. In 1914, this legislation was tested. An Indian businessman chartered the Komagata Maru, a Japanese ship that originated in Hong Kong and carried 376 South Asian passengers. As British subjects they were legally permitted to settle in Canada, but they were detained on-ship in Burrard Inlet for two months while government officials scrambled to find a way to prevent them from staying. Ultimately, the British Columbia Court of Appeal upheld the continuous passage legislation. The media at the time published headlines decrying the danger of "Hindu invaders." The ship, with 355 of the migrants on board, was escorted back to sea by a Canadian naval vessel and forced to return to India. The Court's ruling explicitly reaffirmed the sentiment that the migrants were not suitable immigrants to Canada (James 2010; Somani 2015).

Although often coded in Canadian discourse as recent arrivals, the Chinese presence in Canada is foundational to the country's development. "From its inception, the colonizing of British Columbia was linked to China and as a result also brought people from China to the area" (Stanley 2011: 53). In 1789 Chinese carpenters and shipbuilders were brought to Vancouver Island to work. Similarly, thousands came during the 1858 Fraser River gold rush. In fact, the British census in 1881 documented a Chinese population of 4,350 on Vancouver Island compared to 19,134 whites. Chinese people were a significant part of British Columbia's population, prompting concerns over property ownership; in response, the government enacted policies to severely restrict Asian access to land (Stanley 2006). In 1885, the government issued a $50 head tax on Chinese immigrants. In 1900, it was increased to $100 and to $500 in 1903 (James 2010). At the same time that Chinese people were actively excluded from Canada, their labour was exploited to build the Canada Pacific Railway (CPR). In the 1880s, over 1,500 Chinese labourers were recruited by the CPR to work for five to ten years; the company held their earnings and provided just enough compensation for food and shelter. Forced into the most dangerous work, many died in explosions and rock slides. After the railway was completed, Chinese labourers were recruited for work in mines, fisheries and sawmills, shut out from occupations like law and pharmacy, and excluded from labour unions. Many Chinese workers moved into service positions, opening laundromats and restaurants, but these were seen as a threat to white businesses. In 1907 large numbers of whites rioted in Victoria, smashing windows and destroying Asian properties in Chinatown. Saskatchewan passed laws forbidding Asian men from hiring white women (Henry and Tator 2005).

When Japanese Canadians first settled in British Columbia in the 1870s, they were paid lower wages than whites, electorally disenfranchised, and segregated in schools. In 1908, the Canadian government negotiated an agreement with Japan to limit the number of migrants allowed in Canada. Many worked as fishermen and the B.C. legislature pressured the federal government to limit the number of fishing licences that would be granted to Japanese Canadians in 1920 so as to limit competition with white fishermen. To the extent that Japanese people were permitted into the nation, their ability to become a part of it and to create for themselves the same opportunities granted for others was severely curtailed. But it was after Japan's bombing of Pearl Harbour in 1941 that anti-Japanese sentiment reached its peak. During WWII, over 22,000 Japanese Canadians were interred in British Columbia, Alberta and Manitoba, where they were forced to labour in work camps. Their property, including 1200 fishing boats, was confiscated and their houses and business were sold. Men were put in separate camps from their wives and children and forced to work on road construction and sugar-beet farms. Women and children performed farm labour and some women were hired out to perform domestic labour in private homes and institutions (Oikawa 2002; Henry and Tator 2005).

Earlier, we mentioned that racialization is an exercise in power. Throughout Canada's history, certain populations were systematically denied the same opportunities that other groups — who were themselves at one point immigrants — were granted to settle, establish economic opportunities and fully participate in the social and political spheres of Canadian society. As James (2010: 170) noted: "how and when immigrant groups are permitted to enter a country — and the ways in which they are accommodated and expected to participate economically, politically, socially, and culturally — sets the stage for how they come to be perceived and treated by members of the ruling elites of that society." Today, however, Canada and many Canadians tout our reputation for multiculturalism. The official policy of multiculturalism has been hailed as a successful framework for incorporating diversity, particularly when invoked in comparison to other societies where inter-ethnic conflict and/or coercive assimilation appear more frequent (Fleras 2016a). But, as Fleras and other writers point out, multiculturalism is, in part, another "mythology" by which Canada can imagine itself as a nation committed to justice and equality without addressing continuing processes of inequality and exclusion.

THE LIMITS OF OFFICIAL MULTICULTURALISM

While the increase of racialized immigrants to Canada following the introduction of the points system prompted discussions about multiculturalism, according to Eve Haque (2011), the primary push for the implementation of official state multiculturalism were the long-standing tensions between French and English Canadians. Established in 1963 in response to growing fears of French nationalist sentiment in Quebec, the government established the Bilingualism and Biculturalism Commission to inquire into the state of English-French relations and strengthen the notion of cooperation and an equal partnership between Canada's "two founding races" (2011: 5). As before, this was an endeavor in nation-building — one that would unite Canada through language and culture. But the commission faced significant pressure from Indigenous peoples and ethnic groups (significantly from Ukrainian Canadians, whose ancestors had come from regions of Europe outside England and France) such that the emphasis switched from notions of biculturalism to that of multicultural belonging (Haque 2011). Haque and Eva Mackey (2002) have shown that while change to an emphasis on multiculturalism in the Bilingual and Bicultural Commission appeared more inclusive, it also served a number of strategic purposes. First, it brought Indigenous groups under the umbrella of the "nation" in order to undermine more substantive claims to the land and self-governance, and it tempered Quebec's demands for special recognition by positioning it as one of many ethnic groups with a claim to Canada (Haque and Mackey 2002: 61–65). Whatever its political nuances, the move towards multiculturalism marked a significant shift in the way the nation understood itself and its values. Multiculturalism became a part of the narrative of the Canadian nation. It becomes another part of the mythology that allows us to imagine the country as open and benevolent towards those who wish to become a part of it.

In 1971, Prime Minster Pierre Elliott Trudeau announced Canada would move towards a policy of multiculturalism. The aim was to move towards recognizing diversity as a strength of the nation and the identity and resourcefulness of Canada would be improved by encouraging the kind of civic participation that encouraged immigrants and ethno-racial minorities to take pride in their ancestries and maintain their cultural identities (James 2010). In 1985, multiculturalism became official policy under Brian Mulroney with the Act for the Preservation and Enhancement of Multiculturalism. According to James (2010: 137), "The official policy, and later the Act, helped to promote a belief among Canadians that, in contrast to the policies and practices of assimilation in the United States, 'we are multicultural.'" The assumption was that the freedom to express multiple cultures and heritages under a broad definition of what it meant to be Canadian would allow us to develop respect and tolerance for our differences while working together for the benefit of the nation. The vision was that discriminatory attitudes would eventually be overcome and Canada would be able to avoid the tensions and conflicts seen in other ethnically diverse societies. James notes that it is important to keep in mind that Canada's multicultural policy was driven not only by the increase in workforce immigration from previously European colonies in the Caribbean, Asia and Africa and the need to accommodate the resulting diversity, but also by "the social justice and human rights movements of the 1960s and 1970s, which highlighted the demands of minority group members in North America and elsewhere: women's rights, civil rights, Red Power, Black Power, and anti-colonialism movements." (2010: 138). In other words, inclusion was not graciously granted to racialized and marginalized people in Canada; it was demanded.

The problem with multiculturalism, according to Mackey (2002: 2), is that it "implicitly constructs the idea of a core English-Canadian culture and that other cultures become 'multicultural' in relation to that unmarked, yet dominant, Anglo-Canadian core culture." The Canadian story of tolerance is premised on the notion that some groups who were more Canadian have decided to welcome and accept others who are less Canadian. This mythology of the nation "misrepresent(s) the messy and controversial reality of history" (Mackey 2002: 2). Canadian nationalism is thus construed as one in which some are multicultural while others can view themselves as, "'mainstream' or simply '*Canadian*-Canadians'" (Mackey 2002: 3, emphasis in original).

Himani Bannerji (2000) claims that one of the dangers with state-sponsored multiculturalism is that, in its celebratory guise, it can conceal issues of race and class. Culture is collectively celebrated while racism is relegated to individuals. It sometimes seems that contemporary Canadian society is driven by debates over racism. Whether police killings of unarmed Black men, questions about cultural appropriation, issues of freedom for offensive speech, or whether and/or how to recognize historic figures — like Sir John A. MacDonald and Edward Cornwallis, who today are understood to have had racist motives — there is often heated debate over how to recognize and deal with racism. Most people agree that overt expressions of racism are bad but it sometimes seems very few can agree on what exactly racism is. Unsettling the taken-for-granted nature of race allows us to see that racism is best understood not as some inherent property of certain individuals, but as a set of ideologies and understandings that can be used to maintain preferential access to specific groups of people. Thomas Holt (2000) maintains that rather than asking what racism is, it is more instructive to consider what racism does. According to Holt (2000: 199), "racism can be recognized by the work it does, by its effects" (119):

> By nature a changeling, it attaches itself to and draws sustenance from other social phenomena and from racist discourse itself, like one of those insidious monsters in late-night science-fiction movies. The historian is left to examine the carcass it once inhabited before moving on to another social body, while the sociologist busily constructs diagnostic questionnaires after the disease has already mutated. (Holt 2000: 21)

CONCLUSION

The persistence of inequalities based on race in Canada is an issue that should concern us all. It is fundamentally an issue of justice. While we publicly celebrate our multicultural identity and while egregious acts of racial violence and discrimination are condemned, we have yet to fully examine how the legacy of a country built upon explicit notions of white supremacy affect the social, economic and political lives of racialized people in Canada today. This recognition is especially important now because Canada is not immune to the sentiment increasing in many countries that diversity and immigration are somehow destroying the foundations of previously harmonious societies. History tells a different story. The history of Canada and its colonial past is one in which those deemed racially inferior were excluded, exploited and denied justice.

In this context, what would justice for racialized groups in Canada look like? Early in the chapter we mentioned the notion of colour blindness — the idea that people should be treated the same regardless of race, ethnicity or origin. While this may seem a laudable goal, it does nothing to reconcile the inequalities that exist due to the pattern of historical exclusions and contemporary structural inequalities that deny people living in Canada true equality of opportunity. How can we correct this? There are no easy answers. But we would suggest that we must begin by acknowledging the racist policies and practices behind Canada's foundation. This acknowledgement must carry with it the recognition that the experiences of racialized groups are at the very centre of what it means to be Canadian in terms of our history and our culture. Therefore, any conversations of justice in Canada must pay particular attention to those to whom it has too often been denied. We must recognize the systemic and institutionalized roots of contemporary inequality in order to conceive and create a nation based on a more substantial notion of justice.

DISCUSSION QUESTIONS

1. Can a person engage in social justice work and be colour blind? Why or why not?
2. It is generally accepted that inequality is woven into the fabric of Canadian society and maintained by racism and other forms of discrimination. Beyond simply targeting these things in individuals, where should we directing our efforts if we are to achieve the social justice we seek?
3. The federal government has a tradition of appointing judges to the Supreme Court who are from different regions in Canada. What is the idea behind this practice? Could an argument be made to similarly have representation of Indigenous peoples and other racialized judges on the bench in the administration of justice? What are the advantageous and/or disadvantages of this approach?
4. It is the case in Canada that collecting racial identity data is not common practice; and if and when done, the data groups significantly different populations under the label "visible minorities." Discuss how in the absence of such data affects efforts to address injustices in Canadian society. What are the potential concerns that could arise from producing more data that breaks populations down into individual racialized groups?

GLOSSARY

Colour blindness: The belief that all people should be treated the same regardless of race, ethnicity or origin that, while noble in principal, often leads to the masking and perpetuation of deep-rooted inequalities based on race, ethnicity and origin.

Criminalization: The process by which behaviours and/or individuals are labelled "criminal."

Multiculturalism: Canadian state policy that encourages the recognition, expression, and maintenance of the multiple heritages and cultural practices within the nation.

Racialization: The process of sorting individuals into distinct racial identities and through which ideas about race are developed.

Structural racism: A history and system of societal arrangements and/or a set of values and practices within an institution that serve to limit the participation and opportunities of marginalized groups, even without conscious intent.

White settler society: A nation founded on the displacement of the land's Indigenous inhabitants by European settlers and organized based on a racial hierarchy.

REFERENCES

Bannerji, H. 2000. *The Dark Side of the Nation*. Toronto: Canadian Scholars' Press.

Chan, W. and D. Chun. 201). *Racialization, Crime, and Criminal Justice in Canada*. Toronto: University of Toronto Press.

Commission on Systemic Racism in the Ontario Criminal Justice System. 1995. *Report of the Commission on Systemic Racism in the Ontario Criminal Justice System*. Toronto: Queen's Printer for Ontario.

Department of Justice Canada. 2005. *Employment Equity Act (1995)*, c. 44. <http://laws-lois.justice.gc.ca/PDF/E-5.401.pdf>.

Fleras, A. 2016a. "Theorizing Micro-aggressions as Racism 3.0: Shifting the Discourse." *Canadian Ethnic Studies*, 48, 2: 1–19.

___. 2016b. *Unequal Relations: A Critical Introduction to Race, Ethnic and Aboriginal Dynamics in Canada*, eighth ed. Toronto: Pearson.

Fournier, S., and E. Crey. 1997. *Stolen from Our Embrace: The Abduction of First Nations Children and the Restoration of Aboriginal Communities*. Vancouver: Douglas & McIntyre.

Guo, S. 2009. "Difference, Deficiency, and Devaluation: Tracing the Roots of Non-Recognition of Foreign Credentials for Immigrant Professionals in Canada." *Canadian Journal for the Study of Adult Education*, 22, 1: 37.

Haque, E. 2012. *Multiculturalism Within a Bilingual Framework*. Toronto:

University of Toronto Press.

Henry, F., P. Hastings and B. Freer. 1996. "Perceptions of Race and Crime in Ontario: Empirical Evidence from Toronto and the Durham Region." *Canadian Journal of Criminology*, 38: 469–476.

Henry, F., and C. Tator. 2005. *The Colour of Democracy: Racism in Canadian Society*, third ed. Toronto: Nelson.

Holt, T.C. 2000. *The Problem of Race in the 21st Century*. London: Harvard University Press.

Hou, F., and S. Coulombe. 2010. "Earnings Gaps for Canadian-Born Visible Minorities in the Public and Private Sectors." *Canadian Public Policy*, 36, 1: 29–43.

Houle, R., and L. Yssaad. 2010. "Recognition of Newcomers' Foreign Credentials and Work Experience." *Perspectives on Labour and Income*, 22, 4: 18.

Ismaili, K. 2011. "Immigration, Immigrants, and the Shifting Dynamics of Social Exclusion." In B. Perry (ed.), *Diversity, Crime, and Justice in Canada*. Don Mills, ON: Oxford University Press.

James, C.E. 2010. *Seeing Ourselves: Exploring Race, Ethnicity and Culture*, fourth ed. Toronto: Thompson Educational Publishing.

___. 2012. "Strategies of Engagement: How Racialized Faculty Negotiate the University System." *Canadian Ethnic Studies*, 44, 2: 133–152

Jiwani, Y. 2011. "Mediations of Race and Crime: Racializing Crime, Criminalizing Race." In B. Perry (ed.), *Diversity, Crime, and Justice in Canada*. Don Mills, ON: Oxford University Press.

Jiwani, Y., and M.L. Young. 2006. "Missing and Murdered Women: Reproducing Marginality in News Discourse." *Canadian Journal of Communication*, 31, 4: 895.

Kellough, G., and S. Wortley. 2002. "Remand for Plea. Bail decisions and Plea Bargaining as Commensurate Decisions." *British Journal of Criminology*, 42, 1: 186–210.

King, B., B. Fallon, R. Boyd, T. Black, K. Antwi-Boasiako, and C. O'Connor. 2017. "Factors Associated with Racial Differences in Child Welfare Investigative Decision-Making in Ontario, Canada." *Child Abuse & Neglect*, 73: 89–105.

Mackey, E. 2002. *The House of Difference: Cultural Poliics and National Identity in Canada*. Toronto: University of Toronto Press.

Malhi, R.L., and S.D. Boon. 2008. "Discourses of 'Democratic Racism' in the Talk of South Asian Canadian Women." *Canadian Ethnic Studie*, 39, 3: 125–150.

Monsebraaten, L. 2017. "Income Gap Persists for Recent Immigrants, Visible Minorities and Indigenous Canadians." *Toronto Star*, October 26. <https://www.thestar.com/news/gta/2017/10/25/income-gap-persists-for-recent-immigrants-visible-minorities-and-indigenous-canadians.html>.

O'Connor, C. 2008. "Citizen Attitudes Toward the Police in Canada." *Policing: An International Journal of Police Strategies and Management*, 31, 4: 578–595.

OCI (Office of the Correctional Investigator). 2013. "A Case Study of Diversity in Corrections: The Black Inmate Experience in Federal Penitentiaries." <http://

www.oci-bec.gc.ca/cnt/rpt/pdf/oth-aut/oth-aut20131126-eng.pdf>.

Ontario Association of Children's Aid Societies. 2016. *One Vision One Voice: Changing the Ontario Child Welfare System to Better Serve African Canadians.* Ontario: Ontario Association of Children's Aid Societies.

Owusu-Bempah, A. 2014. "Black Males' Perceptions of and Experiences with the Police in Toronto." Unpublished doctoral dissertation, Toronto, University of Toronto.

Owusu-Bempah, A., and P. Millar. 2010. "Research Note: Revisiting the Collection of 'Justice Statistics by Race' in Canada." *Canadian Journal of Law and Society,* 25, 1: 97–104.

Owusu-Bempah, A., and S. Wortley. 2014. "Race, Crime, and Criminal Justice in Canada." In S. Bucerius and M. Tonry (eds.), *The Oxford Handbook on Race, Ethnicity, Crime, and Immigration.* New York: Oxford University Press.

Perry, B. 2011. "Framing Difference." In B. Perry (ed.),, *Diversity, Crime, and Justice in Canada.* Don Mills, ON: Oxford University Press.

Public Safety Canada. 2016. *2015 Corrections and Conditional Release Statistical Overview.* Ottawa: Public Safety Canada.

Rankin, J., and B. Powell. 2008. "The Criminals Among Us: Not as Many Lawbreakers as Canadians Believe Are Members of Visible Minorities, Survey Shows." *Toronto Star,* July 21: A01.

Razack, S.H. 2002. "When Place Becomes Race." In S.H. Razack, *Race, Space, and the Law: Unmapping a White Settler Society.* Toronto: Between the Lines.

Sprott, J.B., and A.N. Doob. 2014. "Confidence in the Police: Variation across Groups Classified as Visible Minorities." *Canadian Journal of Criminology and Criminal Justice,* 56, 3: 367–379.

Stanley, T.J. 2011. *Contesting White Supremacy.* Vancouver: UBC Press.

Tanovich, D.M. 2006. *The Colour of Justice: Policing Race in Canada.* Toronto, ON: Irwin Law.

Tator, C., and F. Henry. 2006. *Racial Profiling in Canada: Challenging the Myth of "A Few Bad Apples."* Toronto: University of Toronto Press.

Tonry, M. 2011. *Punishing Race: A Continuing American Dilemma.* New York: Oxford University Press.

Trocmé, N., D. Knoke, and C. Blackstock. 2004. "Pathways to the Overrepresentation of Aboriginal Children in Canada's Child Welfare System." *Social Service Review,* 78, 4: 577–600.

Walker, B. 2010. *Race on Trial: Black Defendants in Ontario's Criminal Courts, 1858–1958.* Toronto: University of Toronto Press.

Wesley, M. 2012. *Marginalized: The Aboriginal Women's Experience in Federal Corrections.* Ottawa: Public Safety Canada.

Wortley, S., and A. Owusu-Bempah. 2009. "Unequal before the Law: Immigrant and Racial Minority Perceptions of the Canadian Criminal Justice System." *Journal of International Migration and Integration,* 10, 4: 447–473.

5

INDIGENOUS LEGAL TRADITIONS FROM ROOTS TO RENAISSANCE

Val Napoleon and Hadley Friedland[1]

OBJECTIVES

At the end of this chapter you will be able to:

- Place in context the journey of Indigenous peoples to recover pre-existing legal traditions as part of their decolonization and self-determination efforts

- Analyze one Indigenous legal concept, the wetiko, to illustrate Indigenous justice practices while keeping in mind the diversity of Indigenous legal tradition

- Understand the past repression, recovery and revitalization of Indigenous laws within the limited spaces afforded to them, and the current work of rebuilding Indigenous law so that it may be taught, practised and applied

"Now is the Time to Start Reconciliation, and We are the People to Do So": Contextualizing Indigenous Legal Traditions in the Components of Pursuing Justice

— *Note from editor, Margot A. Hurlbert*

In this chapter, the authors discuss their perspectives on the current Canadian justice system and Indigenous justice and law. As we read, it is important to set aside preconceived notions that privilege our Canadian justice system. One such notion might be that Indigenous peoples did not have legal traditions prior to colonization, or that the current Canadian justice or legal system is superior. It is also important to attempt to see this world through the eyes of the authors, in order to understand their perspective. If we can truly hear and try to understand, we will be on the first step to pursuing Indigenous justice.

Several years ago, the Saskatchewan Treaty Commissioner created an education package for Saskatchewan residents based on the understanding that "We are all Treaty People." This is true for all people living where treaties exist (which covers most of Canada, other than B.C. and the North). For me, this phrase reconfirmed the part I play as a descendent of white European settlers in continuing the knowledge and traditions of the treaties. After the report of the Truth and Reconciliation Commission (TRC), I search for the same understanding of my part in acknowledging and enhancing the change called for by the Commission: pursuing reconciliation.

Reconciliation can be understood, in the large societal sense, as a form of restorative justice, which in itself is important in advancing the ethical practice of justice. Now, in the twenty-first century, it is impossible to restore Canada to a previous era. In order to achieve restoration, all people affected must participate in a healing process with an open mind and an open heart. Perhaps it is not so much restoring as creating balance and justice in Indigenous-Canadian relations? I spend a lot of time reflecting on what I can do to advance truth, reconciliation and healing.

A good starting point is to do our utmost to listen and to really hear the experiences and legal thought of Indigenous peoples. Reading the TRC report is one starting point in the journey. Reviewing these truths and really hearing them involves invoking an ethical practice. Ethical practice requires, in large part, listening and setting aside judgement, preconceived biases and potential ethnocentrism.

The TRC's report is only one starting point. There is an evolving, diverse Indigenous conversation occurring in Canada, reflecting the dynamic process of reconciliation, healing and justice between Indigenous peoples and Canada. It is not unitary, it is not static and it is not for me, or Canada, to determine, only listen and support. As students and scholars of justice, hearing these voices and engaging in our ethical justice practice will allow us to find where we fit into the interconnected web of truth and reconciliation. This chapter on Indigenous legal traditions documents principles for and practices of resolving conflict and responding to crime in Indigenous communities. Chapters 10 (Law and Justice) and 14 (Restorative Justice) show that there is no clear demarcation of where restorative justice and the criminal justice and legal system start and end. What is critical is not to conflate Indigenous law with restorative justice. In this chapter, the authors consider Indigenous legal histories and principles, conflict resolution practices and Indigenous law and justice.

The path to healing entails significant substantive justice. However, it is for Indigenous peoples to determine their part of this path for themselves — with support from allies where possible. This chapter is a starting point in identifying what substantive justice might be. I am a supporter, an ally, walking beside people on this path — not standing in front or hiding behind — I am a part of the cheering crowd on the sidelines.

One day, Canada may achieve formal justice. This will be a world without oppression and discrimination; a world where everyone has the same opportunities and life chances. In this world, Indigenous peoples and visible minorities will not be over-incarcerated and under-represented in our most rewarding occupations. Indigenous governance and Indigenous justice is part of this future imaginary. It is this state of formal justice that I believe is the end goal of justice.

As Indigenous peoples, we are beautiful, and we are messed up.
—John Borrows, "Our Way"

This is one moment,
But know that another,
Shall pierce you with a sudden painful joy.
—T.S. Eliot, Murder in the Cathedral, 1935

INTRODUCTION TO INDIGENOUS LAW

The fundamental ability of any society to deal with the universal issue of human violence and vulnerability is central to its maintenance of peace, order, stability, civility and overall political governance. All societies experience the universality of the human condition, complete with the corresponding messiness, pain and joy that are generated when human beings live together. Each society has unique collective responses to these universal issues that are expressed through its legal traditions. This is no different for Indigenous societies. What is different for Indigenous societies is that colonialism has gutted, obscured and undermined this essential aspect of social order and good governance. Today, many Indigenous peoples are on an important journey, with uneven progress and ongoing challenges, to recover these legal traditions as part of their decolonization and self-determination efforts.

In this chapter we hope to place this journey in context. To do so we set out four phases or eras of the major past, present and future debates about Indigenous laws. First, as we can never capture the past of any tradition definitively, instead of speculation or guesswork, we set out a logical starting point from which to think about the roots of all Indigenous legal traditions. Secondly, we discuss both the repression of Indigenous legal traditions that occurred within early colonization and the resilience of these traditions through this dark era. Thirdly, we explore the contemporary recovery and revitalization of Indigenous laws within the limited spaces afforded to them in the larger frame of state justice systems. Finally, we describe the latest promising steps toward a renaissance or resurgence of Indigenous law, where it is treated seriously as *law*, not as isolated relics or artifacts of a fading past, nor merely as cultural customs or practices.

It can be challenging to talk broadly about Indigenous legal traditions without grossly oversimplifying them or resorting to sweeping pan-Indigenous generalities. Indigenous societies, and thus Indigenous legal traditions, are incredibly diverse. Across Canada alone, there are eleven major linguistic groups and within these, there are sixty distinct Indigenous peoples with numerous regional dialects.[2] It is simply impossible adequately to capture such diversity in the space of this chapter. For simplicity's sake, we will examine one example of a legal concept or category that we are familiar with and one that was common in

Algonquin groups across North America, including, particularly, Cree and Anishinabek societies — the *wetiko* (also known as *windigo*). The *wetiko* is sometimes roughly translated into "cannibal," but, upon closer analysis, is better understood as a legal concept that describes people who are harmful or destructive to others in socially prohibited ways within these societies.[3] When properly understood, the *wetiko* legal category shares commonalities with, or is even roughly comparable to what we currently characterize as criminal law.

We will follow the *wetiko* example through this chapter as an illustration of the broader issues all Indigenous legal traditions have had to grapple with, in one form or another, through the different eras described herein. Similarly, as we are most familiar with Canadian history and the Canadian criminal justice system, we will primarily follow Indigenous experiences in relation to Canada throughout this chapter. We encourage the reader to consider analogous categories in other Indigenous legal traditions, as well as the corresponding similarities in the historical and present interactions between other Indigenous legal traditions and state justice systems throughout the world.

ROOTS

A Logical Starting Point

We want firmly to root any discussion about Indigenous legal traditions in a logical starting point about the past. This starting point is broad enough to cover the diversity of Indigenous societies and does not require the reader to be Indigenous or to even have any knowledge about Indigenous peoples.

Prior to European contact or "effective control" (*R. v. Powley* [2003] SCR 207, 40), Indigenous peoples lived in the place that is now called Canada, in groups, for many thousands of years. We know that Indigenous peoples did not organize themselves in "state" models of governance. We know that when groups of human beings live together, they have ways to manage themselves and all their affairs.[4] This task of human coordination is "the most common of common denominators in law" (Webber 2009). Therefore, as a matter of logic alone, our starting point has to be that, for a very long time, all Indigenous groups had self-complete, non-state systems of social ordering that were successful enough for them to continue as societies for tens of thousands of years.

It is actually discomforting, and it should be, explicitly to have to identify this as a logical starting point. However, it is important to do so because the myth of Indigenous peoples as lawless has too often been used as a trope by European theorist and jurists (Webber 2009: 591). These writers' tropes have become so powerful and persuasive that they may still be unconsciously assumed as *a priori* knowledge or felt as plain common sense at this point in time. Their perpetuation imposes a continuing social reality with meanings that makes it appear normal, obvious, and therefore unquestionable. Dispensing with these very familiar, but illogical tropes does not lead us to subscribe to a utopian vision of Indigenous legal traditions of the past. However, we have no logical reason to think Indigenous laws did not work well enough for thousands of years (Napoleon 2009). We can logically assume that Indigenous legal traditions of the past, while not paragons of perfection (and no legal order is ever perfect), were reasonable legal orders managed by intelligent and reasoning people.[5] This is our logical starting point.

Minimal Content

Some of the laws in these legal orders had to address the unavoidable reality of human violence and destructiveness, and the aching reality of human vulnerability, because these factors are both present in all societies. Rules and prohibitions around violence, bodily harm and killing are part of the minimal content and some of the most characteristic provisions of any functional legal or moral order (Hart 1994: 194 ff.). If pre-contact Indigenous societies did not have such provisions, then, as H.L.A. Hart argues, they would have had social and legal orders akin to the social arrangements of a "suicide club" (Hart 1994), and would have all perished long before European contact. Indeed, North America would have truly been *terra nullius*. Since Indigenous societies functioned and persisted for thousands of years, their legal orders logically must have included this minimal content of law. In other words, we can safely assume that all Indigenous legal orders must have had some way to address the issues of human violence and vulnerability that we now characterize as "criminal law" matters.

The *Wetiko* Example

Again, there is a great diversity of Indigenous groups. While all Indigenous societies logically must have had some way of addressing what we characterize as criminal law matters, each society would have had different ways of organizing and articulating this category of law within their legal order. As mentioned previously, because it is impossible adequately to capture this diversity in the space of this chapter, we will study one example of such a characterization, which we will follow through the different eras of thinking about Indigenous laws: the *wetiko*, a concept that described people who are harmful or destructive to others in socially prohibited ways in Cree and Anishinabek societies.[6]

Like analogous criminal law concepts, the *wetiko* legal concept or category grappled with the "ordinariness of human monstrousness."[7] It triggered particular obligations, legitimate collective reasoning processes and legal principles for determining an appropriate response to human violence and harm in particular circumstances. These principles were balanced and implemented differently based on specific facts in each circumstance, but the overriding goals were preventing harm, protecting the vulnerable and ensuring group safety (Friedland 2009: 96). While we are not suggesting that these goals were accomplished with any less heartache or any more efficacy than in any other analogous "criminal" area of law, there is enough evidence, even from the written records of early Europeans, to support the logical inference that they worked well enough in their historic political and social context.

Just like people today theorize and philosophize about the causes of crime, and struggle to understand criminal behaviour, Cree and Anishinabek people had theories about the causes of *wetiko* behaviour.[8] These theories were often, but not always, spiritual in nature.[9] This made sense in the context of decentralized societies where there was no brutal history of oppression necessitating the wrenching of church from state, and where law was not associated with centralized, formal and hierarchal processes, but with people, as legal agents, make necessary decisions and conducting themselves in principled and predictable ways (Fuller 1969). In this non-hierarchal context, respected spiritual leaders and healers often contributed meaningfully to the collaborative reasoning through resolution of difficult issues. A crucial aspect of this historic social context is that the specific principles, practices and aspirations related to the *wetiko* legal category did not stand alone, just as those in the criminal law category do not stand alone in other legal traditions today. Rather, they were interconnected aspects of a "comprehensive whole," a broader, functioning Indigenous legal tradition: (1) that was large enough to avoid conflicts of interests and which ensured accountability; (2) that had collective processes to change law as necessary with changing times and changing norms; (3) that was able to deal with internal oppressions; (4) that was legitimate and the outcomes collectively owned; and (5) that had collective legal reasoning processes.[10]

The *wetiko* legal category and analogous categories in other Indigenous legal traditions were, like criminal law today, necessarily a core aspect of the wider legal orders they were part of because they addressed the unavoidable and critical issue of human vulnerability and violence. For a very long time, these laws served as legitimate responses and processes, and were a relatively effective means to protect the vulnerable, prevent harm, and ensure group safety. This contributed in an essential way to an overall functioning social order within Indigenous societies, just as it does in every society.

REPRESSION AND RESILIENCE

Repression on a Massive Scale

There have been devastating political and *legal* consequences for Indigenous societies and individuals based on illogical assumptions about an absence of law.[11] There are long dark eras in every commonwealth country where Indigenous legal traditions were suppressed and delegitimized in many different ways from many different angles. It is well documented that, as initial European contact and interaction gave way to European intrusion and control, Indigenous peoples found themselves faced with a loss of territory and essential resources, catastrophic disease, forced dislocation, externally imposed disruption and compulsory replacement of governance structures and practices, oppressive educational policies and entrenched poverty. While there is much diversity among Indigenous peoples, and there were various manifestations of and responses to these colonial factors, there was nonetheless a common experience in that Indigenous social, political and legal orders were undermined on a massive scale, at both a practical and symbolic level.

Legal traditions encompass far more than just rules for conduct. They include formal laws and informal laws, worldviews, aspirations, pedagogies, processes and practices (Napoleon 2009). The impact of the disintegration of so many aspects of Indigenous legal traditions, consequent to colonialism, would be difficult to overestimate. From our vantage point in history, ensconced in our familiar worlds where our state legal actors, laws and legal processes can be relied on, at least to do what they usually do, and accomplish what they usually aim to, such disintegration of the social ordering we take for granted is hard to conceive. We may question, criticize or dislike our state laws, but there are no powerful outsiders that are so blind to their existence and necessity that they use force to sweep them away as superstitious nonsense, or even criminalize them, as was done with Indigenous laws. One can only imagine the disorientation, chaos and fear that would result from the gradual but relentless loss of all our familiar normative signposts, from the most mundane to the most significant. For the purposes of this chapter, we focus on the impact of the state criminalizing the categories of law within Indigenous legal traditions that are analogous to criminal law and we continue with the example of the *wetiko* legal category.

A common issue facing almost all Indigenous laws of this nature is that legal responses to human violence and vulnerability are the most likely to require, not always, but certainly in the most acute or extreme circumstances, some recourse to force. Yet laws that require or authorize the use of force were exactly the ones first criminalized by colonial states, which monopolized the legitimate use of coercive force as part of the "civilizing" project. In this way, states actively delegitimized and belittled Indigenous people's categorization and responses to violence, harm, and group safety needs within their own societies. In Canada, within the nineteenth and early twentieth centuries, there are numerous documented court cases that led to the execution or imprisonment of Indigenous legal decision makers who had implemented a legitimate collective legal decision to execute someone in the *wetiko* legal category, in cases where they had determined that there were no other means left to prevent harm or keep the rest of the group safe.[12]

The fact that there were other principled and preferred responses to someone in the *wetiko* legal category, such as healing, supervision and temporary or permanent separation, which were required to be employed first, and which usually worked effectively to resolve most cases,[13] was rarely considered by state legal decision makers. Although in many of these cases, Cree or Anishinabek people extensively described their collective decision-making processes and principled reasoning leading to these tragic last resort decisions, these explanations were dismissed. Indigenous peoples were often described as "child-like" and incapable of reason. Their legal decisions to employ force were reduced to, at best, an "honestly held belief," but even this was weighted down by demeaning notions that Indigenous individuals or groups were only acting under the pernicious influence of "pagan" or "superstitious belief" or "a form of insanity to which the whole tribe is subjected," which had to be eradicated for their own good (Harring 1998). The unfortunate legal actors tasked with implementing the incapacitation of a dangerous *wetiko*, who were respected and trusted leaders within Indigenous groups, were not only executed or imprisoned, but also held up as examples of irrational barbarism, which no longer had any place within the state legal order.[14] Similar examples to the Canadian *wetiko* cases abound.

Let us reflect on what the analogous situation would be in current Canadian criminal law. While what is called "capital punishment" no longer exists in Canadian law, judges and juries make decisions that some people need to be incapacitated or removed from society. In turn, a justice bureaucracy of police, sheriffs and prison guards implement these decisions by imprisoning people who are deemed to be guilty of heinous offenses and dangerous to society. Imagine then, if one day another society's legal actors took the Canadian judge, the police officer or the prison guard into custody, tried and found them guilty of an offence, say, of kidnapping or forcible confinement, and then imprisoned or otherwise punished them for their actions. What, then, if it were announced to the community at large, through word of mouth, official notices and social media, that these respected people — the judges, police officers and prison guards — were backwards, superstitious and had to be stopped from doing what they had always done? As a Canadian people, for our protection, we would now have to rely entirely on the outside legal actors who had criminalized, ridiculed and debilitated our laws and justice system. Who would dare remain a police officer? What would we do when faced with a person suspected of committing grave harm or becoming dangerous to others?

Our current legal actors would be placed in an untenable position. So would we, as ordinary Canadian citizens. Those who trusted and turned to these legal actors when in need would suddenly no longer know what or who to rely on for protection from harm. We would know that our reliable, respected legal actors were punished according to the outsiders' rules for following the rules we knew. So whose rules should we trust? Neither would feel particularly solid or reliable. Not for nothing did Hart ask, "If there were not these rules then what point could there be for beings such as ourselves in having rules of *any* other kind?" (Hart 1994: 192 ff). Even if other aspects of our legal traditions were not disintegrating around us, the gutting of these core elements related to human violence and vulnerability would shatter the foundation of the entire legal order. This is what *happened*, everywhere, with Indigenous societies.

RESILIENCE AND PERSEVERANCE

Yet just as Indigenous societies have persevered, against all odds, so too the eradication of Indigenous legal traditions was never completely realized. Comprehensively denied, disregarded, and damaged through the concerted efforts and willful blindness of colonialism, they still did not wholly disappear. The legal concepts, processes and principles are as resilient as the people who reason through them and continue, in different ways, meaningfully to practise those they still can. As James Tully explains:

> No matter how relentlessly domineering governors try to implant and internalize ... role-related abilities without the active interplay of the patients, as if they are blank tablets, in behavioural modification experiments, repetitive advertising and total institutions of colonial and post-colonial discipline (such as internment camps and residential schools), they invariably fail to "construct" the other all the way down. They cannot eliminate completely the interactive and open-ended freedom *of* and *in* the relationship or the room to appear to conform to the public script while thinking and acting otherwise, without reducing the relationship to one of complete immobilization. (Tully (2008): 278 ff)

All Indigenous peoples have struggled with demoralization and constructed internalized shame, but no Indigenous people have ever been "constructed" all the way down.

When Potlatches and Sundances were made illegal by the Canadian state, Indigenous peoples continued to practise these important political and legal processes "underground." When entire communities realized that they had lost meaningful practices over time, they sought out other Indigenous communities to learn from and revive them. Medicine people and elders continued to help people who came to them from within their own communities, and from others, even as they hid these practices. If some legal concepts, such as the *wetiko*, were ridiculed, reduced to cultural remnants, fetishized oddities, individual pathology or manifestations of group hysteria by outsiders, they also continued to be widely recognized and used as the complex intellectual concepts they were when it made sense to do so within Indigenous groups (Friedland 2009: 31–32 ff.). If certain principled responses to people within the *wetiko* legal category were criminalized, some legal decision makers continued to implement others, such as healing, supervision or separation, when doing so was possible and useful. Where there are the spaces of freedom, however limited, to reason through and practice with their own legal traditions, Indigenous peoples have continued to do so.

Even through this era of forced social disintegration, dislocation and assimilation, a lack of state recognition, or even state and outsider reprobation, did not and could not completely repress Indigenous legal traditions. As John Borrows has argued, part of the strength and resiliency of Indigenous laws derive from them having been practised and passed down through "Elders, families, clans, and bodies within Indigenous societies" (Borrows 2010: 179 ff.). Indigenous laws continued to be recorded and promulgated in various forms, including in stories, songs, practices and customs (Borrows 2010: 139 ff.). The fact that many Indigenous peoples continue to use the meaning-making resources within their own legal traditions is sometimes most evident in unspoken or implicit ways, in the "commonsense" or preferred responses to crimes within Indigenous communities (Napoleon, Cameron, Arcand and Scott 2008). The passing down, practice and promulgation of Indigenous laws may have been significantly damaged and disrupted through the years of near totalizing repression, yet, however differently, quietly and unevenly, it still occurred.

RECOVERY AND REVITALIZATION

The Failure of State Criminal Justice Systems

There is no bright line between the phases of repression and resilience and of recovery and revitalization of Indigenous legal traditions. Dispossession, dislocation and social disintegration continue. At a certain point, though, in almost every country with an Indigenous population, there is some recognition that the state criminal justice system has failed and is failing Indigenous peoples. All over the world, the grim statistics are similar. Indigenous peoples face substantially higher rates of incarceration than their non-Indigenous counterpoints[15] and they also face disproportionately higher rates of violent crime, victimization, and death.[16] In Canada, between 1967 and 1993, when the Royal Commission of Aboriginal People's (RCAP) Report was written, over thirty government-commissioned justice studies had been undertaken to investigate the causes and possible solutions to this massive failure (Blackburn 1993: 15 ff.).[17] Since RCAP, several more studies have been commissioned and, by all accounts, despite hundreds and hundreds of recommendations, the statistics keep getting worse (Canada, Treasury Board of Canada Secretariat 2004). The sheer volume of literature on this phenomenon is noteworthy.

At the same time that we have statistics saying, for example, in Saskatchewan, a young Indigenous male has a better chance of going to jail than university (Judge Patricia Lynn and Representatives of Federation of Saskatchewan Indian Nations, *Report of the Saskatchewan Indian Justice Review Committee* 1992 as cited in Findley and Weir 2004: 74 ff.), an increasing number of Indigenous peoples, overcoming tremendous obstacles, and again attesting to the resilience within Indigenous societies, are seeking out and achieving higher formal education. There were many extraordinary people working within their own communities, determined to provide better opportunities and build better, healthier lives for everyone within those communities. There are also professionals within the justice system who see the human faces and senseless suffering behind the statistics and genuinely seek more humane, effective and just solutions. The confluence of the widely acknowledged failure of state criminal justice systems, an increasing cohort of strong, dedicated and formally educated Indigenous individuals, and sincere and compassionate justice system professionals has been the opening of spaces within the state justice system to allow for some recovery and revitalization of Indigenous laws.

Aboriginal Justice Initiatives

The spaces that open within a state's justice system for recovery or revitalization of Indigenous legal traditions are never very large. Yet they do exist. In partial response to the widely acknowledged failure of the criminal justice system related to Indigenous people, select aspects of certain Indigenous legal traditions have been adopted as pan-Indigenous "traditional" or "culturally appropriate" responses to crime, and subsumed within specific parts of the states' criminal justice processes, almost always in the sentencing phase. Importantly, these select aspects are rarely, if ever, described, recognized, argued or used as *law* in these spaces. Instead the language of "values" or "practices" is used, and the overall processes are considered "alternative" or "community" justice initiatives. In Canada, the argument for the inclusion of these select aspects is not a jurisdictional one. Rather, it is explicitly ameliorative, based first on the statistics on overrepresentation of Indigenous offenders and, secondly, on the premise that this overrepresentation is the result of cultural differences between Indigenous people and the rest of Canada (*R. v. Gladue* [1999] 1 SCR 688, 171 DLR (4th) 385 ff.).

Some of the most well known of justice initiatives that adopt select aspects of Indigenous legal traditions are Family Group Conferencing and Sentencing Circles. Family Group Conferencing emerged out of New Zealand, based on Maori and restorative justice principles and has been widely adopted and implemented in New Zealand, Australia and Canada. These typically involve family and extended family, as well as appropriate professionals, gathering to resolve issues, most often in child welfare or young offender matters. Sentencing Circles developed in Canada, and were actually first initiated by a non-Indigenous Yukon circuit court judge, Judge Barry Stuart, in the early 1990s, who was frustrated with the criminal justice system inadequacies in relation to Indigenous individuals he often saw before him (*R. v. Moses* [1992] 2 CNLR 116, 71 CCC (3d) 347 ff.). They essentially involve any number of people connected to the offender and possibly the victim, gathering in a circle to discuss the offense and the offender's circumstances, and then recommending what they consider to be an appropriate sentence to the presiding judge, who decides whether to follow the circle's recommendation. They have since been adopted and used in several U.S. states and in Australia. Over time, their use in Canada seems to have abated, although the reasons for this are complicated and unclear (Rudin 2005).

In Canada there are also some well-known and long-standing adapted Aboriginal court processes, such as the Cree circuit court in northern Saskatchewan, the First Nations Court in British Columbia, the Gladue Court in Toronto and the Tsuu T'ina Peacemaking Court in southern Alberta.[18] These innovative court processes operate within the mainstream justice system, conform to Canadian criminal procedure and apply the Criminal Code. The level of adaptation from the mainstream justice process varies greatly. The Cree court is a regular court, except that it operates entirely in Cree, with a Cree-speaking judge and lawyers. The First Nations Court and Gladue Court implement an adapted "culturally appropriate" process at the sentencing phase to understand the root causes of the criminal behaviour and develop a "healing" plan that aims to address these. The Tsuu T'ina Court begins with a court process, held on the Tsuu T'ina reserve but, with a guilty plea, the judge agrees to suspend sentencing and turns cases over to a peace-making process. Peacemakers selected from the community then facilitate a structured circle process. Conditions are imposed through this process, and the offender returns to court only once these are completed, at which time the judge sentences accordingly (Whonnok 2009).

The space these justice initiatives and court processes open up for the recovery and revitalization of Indigenous laws is real. This is so even though the language of "law" is not used, the actual amount of community control is usually minimal due to a lack of resources, and indirect government control and extensive reporting requirements and processes are either state procedures or rooted in ideas of pan-Indigenous restorative justice rather than in specific Indigenous legal traditions (Rudin 2005). Whenever Indigenous people have some input and control of the conversation over responses to crime in their communities, groups and individuals can reason with and through the intellectual legal resources from their own legal traditions. This occurs at an implicit or informal level, through people referring to, reasoning through, and acting on their legal obligations, whether or not they explicitly identify them as such (Napoleon et al. 2008). It also occurs at a discursive level, within the debates that are generated when Indigenous peoples' opinions and narratives about a particular case are brought into a public conversation about the appropriate legal response to that case (Richland 2008: 141 ff.). Even if the language of "values" or "customs" is used, rather than the language of law, the conversations and solutions generated within these spaces are the very "hard work" that continually recreates and sustains the legality and legitimacy of any law, and which is particularly relevant when legal orders are horizontal, without formalized enforcement mechanisms, as with most Indigenous legal orders (Brunnée and Toope 2011: 355 ff.).

How Justice Becomes Just Healing

Call it what you will, but to the extent that the work of law is happening in these spaces, the space for recovery and revitalization is real. However, its limits have led to certain distortions about Indigenous legal traditions. Because only select aspects of certain Indigenous legal traditions are acceptable within the Canadian state, specifically those aspects that do not require the use of coercive force or enforced separation from society, a peculiar set of assumptions develop regarding Indigenous laws related to what we broadly understand to be criminal behaviour. This narrative completely and problematically conflates "Aboriginal justice" with "restorative justice" or rallies around the singular description of justice as "healing."[19] All other aspects of Indigenous legal traditions are ignored, or described in whispers as "uncivilized" oddities or embarrassing cultural remnants. The *wetiko* legal concept has been relegated to these whispers for some time.

It is not that healing and restorative processes are not important, or even preferable, to other responses to crime within many Indigenous legal traditions. It is just that, when we start from the logical starting point that these legal traditions once had to have dealt with the whole spectrum of harms and violence human beings inflict upon one another, it is obvious that these could not have been the only available responses. Without question, healing was the predominant and preferred response to people fitting within the *wetiko* legal category (Brightman 1988: 358 ff.).[20] However, in any society there will always be a small minority of human beings, whether we call them *wetikos* or whether we call them criminals, who are beyond healing, either at a certain time or at all. For example, no one would argue that Jeffrey Dahmer or Charles Manson would have been an appropriate candidate for healing. They are rare, but not alone. Let them be and we are, once again, faced with Hart's suicide club.

The predominant narrative of "justice as healing" is not false, but it is dangerously incomplete. It flattens the complexity of Indigenous legal traditions and raises real questions about their utility effectively to respond to the "pressing reality" of the "unprecedented levels of violence experienced within Aboriginal families and com- munities in the current generation" (Turpel Lafond 2005: 295 ff.). It has disproportionate and chilling effects on the lives, bodily integrity and safety of Indigenous women and children.[21] Healing alone is not enough to prevent harm, protect the vulnerable, or ensure group safety in many situations, and at any rate, is a long-term process, not a panacea. It is not logical or accurate to say that healing is the only legal response to crime in Indigenous legal traditions. It is more accurate to say that healing is the only legal response permitted to Indigenous groups within most states, which monopolize the use of coercive force.[22]

The analogous situation in current Canadian society would be if powerful outsiders permitted us to operate parts of our criminal justice system but, regardless of the individual facts, our legal decision makers could only apply the sentencing principle of rehabilitation. It would be indicative of the limits of the permissible space for our law in the dominant society, not of the limits of our law itself, if we found that we could not safely or successfully manage every case on those terms. There are clear cases where, based on the facts, sentencing principles other than rehabilitation need to be prioritized in order to maintain individual and community safety. There are equally clear cases, within Indigenous communities, that require responses other than or in addition to healing. Returning these cases to the mainstream criminal justice system in order to access the state monopolized resources those responses require, should not be (but often is) seen as a failure of Aboriginal justice initiatives.

Idealized Values as State Critiques

Indigenous laws are often even further reduced to oversimplified, idealized foils to critique state criminal justice systems within academic literature. This creates two major problems. First and foremost, it creates an artificial dichotomy between Indigenous and state responses to harm and violence, one that is "fraught with stereotypes, generalizations, oversimplifications and reductionism" (LaRocque 1997: 78 ff.). This inhibits any productive discussion examining cultural differences *and* similarities between legal principles that grapple with the same universal human issues. It also obscures the range of normative choices available within and across diverse legal traditions. Secondly, highly idealized, even romanticized, Indigenous "values," with no grounding in current practices or real issues, are contrasted with state legal principles that are practised imperfectly in the chaos and messiness of everyday life, unavoidably carrying the historical and political baggage of the day, and applied to real-life cases. This purely oppositional space has the unintentional impact of reducing conversations about Indigenous laws to veiled critiques of current state laws. It does not allow us the intellectual room to imagine Indigenous laws beyond a symbolic resistance to colonialism (Napoleon et al. 2008). Once reduced down to cultural differences or ideals, narratives of incommensurability and fragility can inhibit critical and rigorous scholarship engaging with Indigenous laws, further obscuring their presence and inadvertently perpetuating the colonial myth of an absence of Indigenous legal thought (Christie 2009: 213 ff.).

THE RENAISSANCE

Engaging with Indigenous Laws Seriously as Laws

The recovery and revitalization of Indigenous legal traditions is well underway, but the limited spaces for this within colonial states has led to distortions and dangers at practical, political and intellectual levels. At this point in time, though, we are on the cusp of a new era: the renaissance or resurgence of Indigenous law, claimed, recognized and engaged with seriously as *law*.

On a general level, there has been increasing and sustained momentum toward a greater recognition and practical and public use of Indigenous legal traditions in Canada. This has been occurring within and across academic, legal, professional and Indigenous communities. For example, the Canadian Bar Association recently passed a resolution to recognize and advance Indigenous legal traditions in Canada (Canadian Bar Association Resolution 2013). This resolution was followed closely by a national Aboriginal Law section conference entitled, "Working with and within Indigenous Legal Traditions," which focused on the various ways lawyers are currently engaging with Indigenous laws in different areas of legal practice, including criminal justice initiatives (Canadian Bar Association, National Aboriginal Law Conference 2013).[23] The Chief

Justice of the British Columbia Court of Appeal, Lance Finch, C.J., stated clearly that Canadian courts have recognized preexisting Indigenous legal orders, and recommended that every Canadian law school should have a course, not only on Aboriginal law (Canadian state law about Aboriginal issues), but also on Indigenous legal traditions themselves (Continuing Legal Education Society of British Columbia Conference 2012).[24]

This is a crucial recommendation. When we imagine more public, explicit and integrated use of Indigenous legal traditions in Canada or other countries generally, there are many political, legal, practical and institutional issues to address.[25] But there are also real intellectual hurdles to overcome, as we have seen previously. Today, one of the big questions is how Indigenous laws and state laws will interact in the future, which includes questions about legitimacy, conflict of laws, harmonization efforts and, in the criminal justice field, how legitimate responses to human violence and vulnerability that require coercive force should or will be acted on today. These and more issues need to be seriously discussed and addressed. However, when they are discussed entirely in the abstract, relying on oversimplified pan-Indigenous stereotypes (negative or positive), or people's illogical assumptions about Indigenous legal traditions, rather than on grounded research about specific legal principles within specific legal traditions, they tend to operate as conversation stoppers, and are distorting in and of themselves. How well we are able to address the real political, legal, practical and institutional issues will depend on whether we actually address the intellectual ones, or whether we skip this step and assume we already know certain answers about the substantive content of Indigenous legal traditions. The renaissance of Indigenous legal traditions is not about a specific concrete outcome, but rather about rebuilding the intellectual resources and political space to have more symmetrical, reciprocal and respectful conversations within and between Indigenous and state legal traditions.

Recently, several North American law schools have started to develop and offer substantive courses on Indigenous legal traditions. These schools include the University of British Columbia, the University of Alberta, the University of Ottawa, Osgoode Hall and the University of Minnesota.[26] Perhaps the most innovative and ambitious academic initiative is the work toward developing a joint common law and Indigenous law degree program at the University of Victoria (*Juris Indigenarum Doctor* and *Juris Doctor*, otherwise known as the JID). This degree program would be the first of its kind in the world.[27]

This academic work is important for the renaissance of Indigenous laws, particularly because there are real challenges, at this point in history, to accessing, understanding and applying Indigenous legal principles, beyond finding the political and jurisdictional space to do so.[28] Indeed, even in American tribal courts, which do hold clear, if contested, jurisdiction and have for a relatively long and stable period, the actual use and application of Indigenous legal principles, as opposed to state or adapted state jurisprudence, is surprisingly sparse (Fletcher 2006). The deeply engrained but illogical starting points about Indigenous laws and the long periods of repression in colonial states, as well as the distortions born of limited spaces openly to recover and practice Indigenous laws, have all led to deep absences within legal scholarship and serious challenges to Indigenous peoples' own capacity to articulate, interpret and apply Indigenous laws to contemporary issues. However, that is changing.

Intellectual Shifts

Today there is a growing trend of legal scholarship that advocates for and has begun the robust and respectful engagement needed to work critically and usefully with Indigenous legal traditions. This type of scholarship begins by asking different questions *of* Indigenous legal traditions than are typically or were historically asked. Rather than focusing on broad generalities, or on using Indigenous laws as rhetorical tools to critique state legal systems, leading Indigenous scholars are starting to focus on the specifics of Indigenous laws themselves. This focus leads to the intellectual shifts from typical research questions about "Aboriginal justice" shown in Table 5.1.

Table 5.1 Analytical Shifts for Working with Indigenous Law

From	To
What is Aboriginal justice?	What are the legal concepts and categories within this Indigenous legal tradition?
What are the cultural values?	What are the legal principles?
What are the "culturally appropriate" or "traditional" dispute resolution forms?	What are the legitimate procedures for collective decision making?
Overall shift:	
What are the rules? What are the answers?	What are the legal principles and legal processes for reasoning through issues?

Source: Friedland 2013: 29 ff.

To illustrate the results of these shifts, we will focus in more detail on recent scholarly treatment of the *wetiko* legal concept. One of the first and clearest examples of an Indigenous legal scholar employing these shifts in his analysis is John Borrows's treatment of a *wetiko* or *windigo* case recorded in 1838 by the Superintendent of Indian Affairs, William Jarvis, which involved an Anishinabek group that had to urgently respond to, and ultimately execute, someone who had become increasingly dangerous to himself and to others (Borrows and Rotman 2003: 908–919 ff.). Rather than staying at the level of cultural "practices" or "values" in the account, Borrows identified several transferable legal principles. For example, he identified procedural principles, such as waiting, observing and collecting information before acting, and counseling with others around the person when it is clear something is wrong. He identified legal response principles, such as helping the person who is growing harmful and, "if the that person does not respond to help and becomes an imminent threat to individuals or the community, remove them so they do not harm others." In addition, he highlighted restorative principles that met the needs of the people closest to and most reliant on the person who had to be removed (Borrows and Rotman 2003). He argued that it is these underlying principles, not the specific practice or outcome, that would still be familiar to Anishinabek people today, and it is worth considering how they might apply in the contemporary context (Borrows and Rotman 2003). In treating the Anishinabek group's historical actions seriously as *legal* practices, Borrows was able to look seriously beyond just bare rules or historical practices, to the underlying legal principles as well as the legitimate processes of legal reasoning, deliberation, interpretation and application (Napoleon et al. 2008).

This refreshing intellectual shift frees up the discussion about Indigenous laws from distracting debates that perseverate on particular historic practices, to the detriment of serious contemporary analysis. This is particularly relevant when discussing the *wetiko* legal concept. No one is arguing that Cree or Anishinabek communities should be able to (or would even want to) execute someone becoming a *wetiko* today. In fact, the adaptability of how the particular legal principle of incapacitation or removal was applied in practice is demonstrated even historically. For example, when other resources for incapacitation or removal were accessible to Indigenous groups, such as police outposts or even missionaries, Indigenous groups often preferred to access these rather than having to execute a *wetiko* who was at risk of causing imminent harm to others.[29] This demonstrates that the underlying principle can be recognized and applied in different ways, and using the available resources, which today include access to and partnerships with state law enforcement and mental health professionals.[30] Focusing on the underlying principles, rather than just practices, helps others to understand the ongoing relevance and potential usefulness of the principles related to legal categories like the *wetiko* for responding to contemporary issues of violence and harm.

Research Examples: Indigenous Legal Principles

There is currently exciting collaborative research and work engaging with Indigenous legal traditions being carried out within and across professional, academic and Indigenous communities. The newly created Indigenous Law Research Unit (University of Victoria, Faculty of Law), the Indigenous Bar Association (IBA) and the Truth and Reconciliation Commission (TRC) have partnered, with funding from the Ontario Law Foundation, to undertake a national research project engaging with Indigenous legal traditions called the Accessing Justice and Reconciliation Project (AJR Project). The AJR project partnered with seven Indigenous communities and engaged with six distinct Indigenous legal traditions across Canada to identify responses and resolutions to harms and conflicts within Indigenous societies. From west to east, these were: Coast Salish (Snuneymuxw First Nation and Tsleil-Waututh Nation); Tsilhqot'in (Tsilhqot'en National Government); Northern Secwepemc; Cree (Aseniwuche Winewak Nation); Anishinabek (Chippewas of Nawash Unceded First Nation #27); and Mi'kmaq (Mi'kmaq Legal Services Network, Eskasoni).

The fundamental premise behind the AJR Project was that legal researchers would engage with Indigenous laws seriously as *laws*.[31] The results reveal a wide variety of principled legal responses and resolutions to harm and conflict available within each legal tradition. Both authors are involved in this project, and we want to give but one of many examples of the rich complexity that emerged out of pursuing this shift in approach to researching Indigenous laws regarding harms and conflicts. One clear finding of this project is that while there is often a strong emphasis on concepts such as healing, reconciliation and forgiveness in many Indigenous legal traditions, they are not idealized, simple or stand-alone responses to harms and conflicts. Every Indigenous legal tradition represented had nuanced and robust understandings of what implementation of these principles entail, *and* had a much broader repertoire of principled legal responses and resolutions to draw on where specific factual situations so warranted.

Carrying on with our example of the *wetiko* legal concept, in our engagement with the Cree legal tradition, respondents in our Cree partner community made it very clear that they see healing of the offender as the predominant and preferred legal response to even extreme harms. For example, when one researcher asked about published stories in which people who became *wetikos* were killed, one elder, who practices traditional medicine, exclaimed: "probably someone who didn't know nothing and had no compassion would just go kill someone." She went on to state emphatically that instead the proper response is to try to help and heal the person turning *wetiko*. She stressed that people turning *wetiko* should not be seen as faceless dangers, but rather, "these are our family members" (Draft Cree Legal Summary 2013: 26–27 ff.).

However, it was also made clear to researchers that while healing was a preferred response for Cree peoples, it was not implemented in isolation or blind to ongoing risks of harm. When someone was waiting for or not willing to accept healing, the principle of avoidance or separation was often employed in order to keep others safe. Avoidance or temporary separations were also principled ways of de-escalating conflict and expressing disagreement. Other Cree principles guiding responses to harm and conflict more generally included acknowledging responsibility as a remedy, reintegration, learning from natural or spiritual consequences and, historically, in published stories, incapacitation in cases of extreme and ongoing harm. Reintegration followed healing or taking responsibility. These responses were fact specific and decisions were made based on an extensive deliberative process, which included elders, family members, experts (medicine people) and the person causing harm when possible. The same elder quoted earlier pointed out that reintegration might require ongoing observation and monitoring, even for life where warranted, as in the case of someone helped from turning *wetiko*, as she explained that no one can be completely healed from this (Draft Cree Legal Summary 2013: 26–35 ff.).

This is just one small example of the kind of informative, nuanced and complex response principles we saw in research results from each Indigenous legal tradition that legal researchers approached seriously as law. The research results raise many practical and philosophical questions, and that is how it should be. The important point is that the level of detail and sophistication raises different questions, and creates different conversations, whether about responses to particular cases or about the wider legal, political and institutional issues that must be resolved, than previous ones based on illogical assumptions or on oversimplified or stereotypical pan-Indigenous values or practices related to responding to criminal behaviour.

It is this kind of serious and sustained engagement with Indigenous laws that is beginning to build a solid intellectual foundation for, as Navaho Court of Appeal Judge Raymond D. Austin puts it, bringing Indigenous legal traditions into their "rightful place among the world's dispute resolution systems" in the future.[32] Although people may be using new fora and methods to do so, Indigenous legal traditions are once again being publicly and explicitly recognized, explored and understood as the intellectual and normative resources they are. We can imagine many ways in which Indigenous peoples can draw out and draw on these resources collectively to manage their affairs and deal with the range of human and social issues that are part of being strong self-governing and interdependent peoples, including the reality that the core concerns of human violence and vulnerability will always be with us, in any society. There are also many ways that Canada and other countries can learn from, collaborate with and incorporate principles and practices from Indigenous legal traditions.

CONCLUSION

When we speak of criminal law matters related to Indigenous people, it is important not to underestimate the vast losses and damage from colonialism that Indigenous peoples have suffered. It is both naïve and dangerous to ignore the immense social suffering, the massive intergenerational trauma, the frightening level and intensity of violence and the ongoing conditions of vulnerability within many Indigenous communities today. Sadly, too often acknowledgment of these realities sinks into a tired and insulting "primitivist" discourse about Indigenous people in non-Indigenous circles or, within Indigenous circles, into narratives of demoralization and despair.

It is no wonder that many people, Indigenous and non-Indigenous alike, hope that Indigenous legal traditions have something positive to bring to these urgent and pressing issues. Yet these legal traditions do not survive in some pristine, untouched state, as if they were magically immune to the damages and devastation of colonialism. Searching to revive some imagined past utopia, or waiting for a future day of glorious transcendence will simply not do the job. At this point, we need robust and practical approaches to the pressing realities Indigenous people face on the ground, otherwise our work will be meaningless or, worse still, will inadvertently perpetuate the maintenance of the status quo.

In this chapter, we have set out four phases or eras to describe the changing state of debate regarding Indigenous legal traditions, in order realistically to contextualize the current challenges and potential of Indigenous laws, as applied to the universal issue of human violence and vulnerability. First, we posited not an imagined utopia or a free-for-all, but a logical starting point to talk about the roots of Indigenous legal traditions. Secondly, we acknowledged the long dark era of the almost totalizing repression of Indigenous laws, as well as their resilience through this period. Thirdly, we looked at the opportunities and distortions within the limited spaces for the recovery and revitalization of Indigenous laws in the wider frame of state justice systems. Finally, we discussed the recent movement toward a renaissance or resurgence of Indigenous legal traditions, where they are recognized and treated seriously as *law*.

Setting out these four phases explicitly acknowledges the deeply rooted nature, as well as the strength, resiliency and promise of Indigenous legal traditions, without underestimating the devastating and demoralizing impacts of colonialism, the difficult present reality and the huge amount of work required to be able to access, understand and apply Indigenous laws constructively today. It is both a challenging and exciting time to be engaging with Indigenous legal traditions. There is much work to be done, and there is much hope.

DISCUSSION QUESTIONS

1. What specific Indigenous legal traditions did you learn about in this chapter? Which Indigenous group(s) practised them?
2. Explain the legal concept or category of the wetiko (or windigo) and its goals. What are its similarities or differences with Canadian criminal law?
3. Explain what is meant by underlying Indigenous legal principles and why they are important for research, recovery and revitalization.

4. Why is it important not to talk about abstract practices of Indigenous legal traditions but to speak of actual principles underlying practices?
5. Why is it important not to conflate Indigenous law with restorative justice?

GLOSSARY

Aboriginal: The legal term used to give constitutional recognition and protection of the rights of Indigenous peoples in section 35 of the Constitution Act, 1982, which states, "(1) The existing Aboriginal and treaty rights of the Aboriginal peoples of Canada are hereby recognized and affirmed. (2) In this Act, 'Aboriginal peoples of Canada' includes the Indian, Inuit and Métis peoples of Canada."

Aboriginal justice initiatives: Spaces within a state's justice system for recovery or revitalization of Indigenous legal traditions that allow select aspects of certain Indigenous legal traditions, but are subsumed within specific parts of the states' criminal justice processes almost always in the sentencing phase.

Indigenous: People indigenous to Canada.

Indigenous laws: Rules, principles and practices present in Indigenous communities around problem solving, order, safety, violence, bodily harm and so forth that frame a functional legal or moral order.

Indigenous legal traditions: More than just rules for conduct, but include formal laws, informal laws, worldviews, aspirations, pedagogies, processes and practices.

Justice as healing: A narrative that conflates Aboriginal justice with restorative justice, ignoring all other aspects of Indigenous legal traditions.

Wetiko: A legal concept or category referring to someone causing severe harm to oneself or others. *Wetiko* legal principles refer to specific principles, practices and aspirations in Cree and Anishinabek societies that protected the vulnerable, prevented harm and ensured group safety in response to an identified *Wetiko*. These principles are one part of a larger comprehensive whole of those legal orders.

NOTES

1. Thanks to Emily Snyder for her helpful comments and suggestions, as well as the many generous community participants and diligent student researchers who contributed to the Accessing Justice and Reconciliation Project, our

partners, the Indigenous Bar Association and the Truth and Reconciliation Commission of Canada, and the project funder, the Ontario Law Foundation.

2. There are 500 distinct Indigenous societies in North America. See Canada, Royal Commission on Aboriginal Peoples 1996.

3. For a more in-depth discussion of this legal concept or category, see Friedland 2009: 35–40.

4. Fuller (1964: 130) describes law as "a direction of purposive human effort" consisting in "the enterprise of subjecting human conduct to the governance of rules."

5. Our use of "legal orders" may be understood as "the norms, rules and institutions formed by a society or group of people to ensure social stability. They usually describe what is right and how to act, and what is wrong and how not to act; and the remedies and consequences of such actions" (International Council on Human Rights 2009: 1).

6. For a more in-depth discussion of this legal concept or category, see Friedland 2009: 35–40.

7. This is Ruth Landes's description of the *wetiko* in her reply in Marano et al. 1982: 401.

8. For some examples, see Friedland 2009: 70–81.

9. See, e.g., Friedland 2009: 31 ff. For a good discussion of the context of these spiritual theories, see Brightman 1988: 363–367.

10. Napoleon (2009: 47–48), arguing it is reasonable, and crucial, to contextualize individual Indigenous legal concepts this way.

11. See, e.g., Tully 1995: 65 ff., and Asch and Macklem 1991.

12. See, e.g., *R. v. Machekequonabe* [1897] OJ No. 98, 2 CCC 138.

13. See Friedland 2009: 96–105 ff. See also Brightman 1988.

14. See the fictionalized demonstration of this in graphic novel form, based on a compilation of real cases, in Napoleon, Henshaw, Steacy, Johnston, and Simon Roy 2013.

15. "The justice system has failed … Aboriginal people on a massive scale" was the opening statement of the Manitoba Justice Inquiry. See Hamilton and Sinclair, Commissioners. See also MacPherson 1993: 4 ff.

16. For some of these statistics, see, e.g., Canada, Canadian Centre for Justice Statistics 2001: 6–7 ff.

17. Eight of these were reviewed for the Roundtable on Justice (16–38 ff.).

18. For a concise summary of these and other court processes, see Whonnok 2009.

19. e.g., see the Supreme Court's description of this in *R. v. Gladue* (n. 37), and *R. v. Wells* [2000] 1 SCR 207, 27 ff.

20. See also Friedland 2009: 97 ff.

21. See, e.g., LaRocque 1997: 75 ff.

22. The leading case affirming this is *Thomas v. Norris* [1992] 2 CNLR 139 (BCSC), where the British Columbia court found that any aspects of Spirit Dancing that would be contrary to the common or civil law, such as someone being forced to take part in an initiation ceremony against his or her will (as the plaintiff was in this

case), was not protected as an Aboriginal right under section 35 of the Constitution (89, 90 ff.). Hence, the defendants were liable for assault and battery in the case, despite arguing that they were acting in accordance with their responsibilities, after the plaintiff's common law wife requested their help, because of "marital and other problems" (32 ff.). The judge maintained the "supremacy of English law to the exclusion of all other" (104 ff.).

23. For a description and papers, see CBA Professional Development <http://www.cbapd.org/details_en.aspx?id=na_abl13>.

24. For a description and papers related to this conference, see <http://www.cle.bc.ca/onlinestore/productdetails.aspx?cid=648>.

25. Borrows (2010: chs. 4, 5, 7, and 8) explores many of these comprehensively.

26. Professors offering these focused courses include one of the authors (Val Napoleon), at UVic, Gordon Christie and Darlene Johnston at University of British Columbia, Larry Chartrand and Sarah Morales at University of Ottawa, Andree Boisselle at Osgoode Hall, and John Borrows at University of Minnesota.

27. The first proposal for the JID program was drafted by John Borrows in September 2005, following his study of Indigenous legal traditions entitled, "Justice Within," sponsored by the Law Commission of Canada. See Law Commission of Canada (2006). See also Borrows (2005: 153 ff.).

28. For a longer discussion of some of these challenges, see Friedland (2013: 8–17 ff.).

29. See Friedland (2009: 119–121 ff.).

30. See Borrows' stressing of this in Borrows (2010: 82–84 ff.).

31. For more on the method and outcomes of this project, see Napoleon and Friedland (2014) and Friedland and Napoleon (2015).

32. Williams (2009: xv ff.) points out that this aspiration is one goal for establishing a solid foundation for the Navajo courts.

REFERENCES

Aboriginal Peoples and the Justice System: Report of the National Round Table on Aboriginal Justice Issues. 1993. Ottawa, ON.

Asch, Michael, and Patrick Macklem. 1991. "Aboriginal Rights and Canadian Sovereignty: An Essay on *R v. Sparrow." Alberta LR,* 29: 507 ff.

Austin, Raymond D. 2009. *Navaho Courts and Navaho Common Law: A Tradition of Tribal Self-Governance.* Minneapolis, MN: University of Minnesota Press.

Blackburn, Carole. 1993. "Aboriginal Justice Inquiries, Task Forces and Commissions: An Update." [RCAP: Aboriginal Justice Inquiries Update.] In Jim MacPherson 1993: (n. 32) 15 ff.

Borrows, John. 2005. "Creating an Indigenous Legal Community." *McGill LJ,* 50: 153 ff.

___. 2010. *Canada's Indigenous Constitution:* 179 ff. University of Toronto Press.

___. 2012. "Our Way." Conference presentation, University of Saskatchewan (Mar. 23, 2012).

Borrows, John, and Leonard Rotman. 2003. *Aboriginal Legal Issues: Cases, Materials, and Commentary,* second ed.: 908–919 ff. Toronto: Butterworths.

Brightman, Robert. 1988. "The Windigo in the Material World." *Ethnohistory,* 35: 363–367 ff.

Brunnée, Jutta, and Stephen J. Toope. 2011. *Legitimacy and Legality in International Law: An Interactional Account:* 355 ff. New York: Cambridge University Press.

Canada, Canadian Centre for Justice Statistics. 2001. Profile Series 18, *Aboriginal Peoples in Canada.* <http://www.statcan.ca/english/research/85F0033MIE/ 85F0033MIE2001001.pdf>: 6–7 ff.

Canada, Royal Commission on Aboriginal Peoples. 1996. *Looking Forward, Looking Back,* 1, 12: 15–17 ff. Ottawa.

Canada, Treasury Board of Canada Secretariat. 2004. *Canada's Performance: Annual Report to Parliament.* Ottawa: Her Majesty the Queen in Right of Canada.

Canadian Bar Association Resolution. 2013. 13-03-M, carried by the Council of the Canadian Bar Association at the Mid-Winter Meeting held in Mont-Tremblant, QC, Feb. 16–17. <http://www. cba.org/CBA/resolutions/ pdf/13-03-M-ct.pdf>.

Canadian Bar Association, National Aboriginal Law Conference—Working with and within Indigenous Legal Traditions, Victoria, BC, Apr. 11–12, 2013. For a description and papers, see: CBA Professional Development. <http://www. cbapd.org/details_en.aspx?id=na_abl13>.

Christie, Gordon. 2009. "Indigenous Legal Theory: Some Initial Considerations." In Benjamin J. Richardson, Shin Imai, and Kent McNeil (eds.), *Indigenous Peoples and the Law: Comparative and Critical Perspectives:* 213 ff. Oregon: Hart Publishing.

Continuing Legal Education Society of British Columbia Conference. 2012. "Indigenous Legal Orders and the Common-Law," Nov. 12–13. For a description and papers related to this conference, see <http://www.cle.bc.ca/ onlinestore/productdetails.aspx?cid=648>.

Draft Cree Legal Summary. 2013. AJR Project (unpublished, on file with authors), 26–27 ff.

Fiddler, Chief Thomas, and James R. Stevens. 1991. *Killing the Shaman.* Moonbeam, ON: Penumbra Press.

Findley, Isobel, and Warren Weir. 2004. "Aboriginal Justice in Saskatchewan: 2002–2021—The Benefits of Change." In *First Nations and Métis Peoples and Justice Reform,* Vol. 1: 74 ff.

Fletcher, Mathew. 2006. "Rethinking Customary Law in Tribal Court Jurisprudence." Indigenous Law and Policy Centre Occasional Paper Series.

Friedland, Hadley. 2009. "The *Wetiko* (*Windigo*) Legal Principles." Unpublished LLM thesis: 35–40 ff.

___. 2013. "Reflective Frameworks: Methods for Accessing, Understanding and Applying Indigenous Laws." *Indigenous LJ,* 11: 8–17 ff.

Friedland, Hadley, and Val Napoleon. 2015. "Gathering the Threads: Developing a Methodology for Researching and Rebuilding Indigenous Legal Traditions." *Lakehead Law Journal*, 1, 1 (Special ed). <https://llj.lakeheadu.ca/article/view/1408/726>.

Fuller, Lon. 1964. *The Morality of Law:* 130 ff. New Haven and London: Yale University Press.

___. 1969. "Human Interaction and the Law." *American Journal of Jurisprudence*, 14: 2 ff.

Hamilton, A.C., and C.M. Sinclair, Commissioners. 2010. "The Justice System and Aboriginal People: Report of the Aboriginal Justice Inquiry of Manitoba." Winnipeg: Queen's Printer Manitoba. <http://www. ajic.mb.ca/volumel/chapter5.html#8>.

Harring, Sidney L. 1998. "The Enforcement of the Extreme Penalty: Canadian Law and the Ojibwa-Cree Spirit World." In Sidney L. Harring (ed.), *White Man's Law: Native People in Nineteenth-Century Canadian Jurisprudence:* 232 and 223 ff. University of Toronto Press.

Hart, H.L.A. 1994. *The Concept of Law,* second ed.: 194 ff. New York: Oxford University Press.

International Council on Human Rights. 2009. *When Legal Worlds Overlap; Human Rights, State and Non-State:* 19 ff. Geneva, Switzerland.

LaRocque, Emma. 1997. "Re-examining Culturally Appropriate Models of Criminal Justice." In Michael Asch (ed.), *Aboriginal and Treaty Rights in Canada: Essays on Law, Equity and Respect for Difference.* Vancouver, BC: UBC Press.

Law Commission of Canada. 2006. *Justice Within, Indigenous Legal Traditions,* DVD.

MacPherson, James C. 1993. "Report from the Round Table Rapporteur." In *Aboriginal People and the Justice System: National Round Table on Aboriginal Justice Issues:* 4 ff. Ottawa: Royal Commission on Aboriginal Peoples.

Marano, Lou, et al. 1982. "Windigo Psychosis: The Anatomy of an Emic-Etic Confusion [and Comments and Reply]." *Current Anthropology*, 23, 4: 385–412.

McCaslin, Wanda D. (ed.). 2005. *Justice as Healing: Indigenous Ways: Writing on Community Peacemaking and Restorative Justice from Native Law Centre.* St. Paul, MN: Living Justice Press.

McNamara, Luke. 2000. "The Locus of Decision-Making Authority in Circle Sentencing: The Significance of Criteria and Guideline." *Windsor Yearbook of Access to Justice*, 18.

Napoleon, Val. 2009. "Ayook: Gitksan Legal Order, Law, and Legal Theory." Unpublished Ph.D. dissertation.

Napoleon, Val, Angela Cameron, Colette Arcand, and Dahti Scott. 2008. "Where's the Law in Restorative Justice?" In Yale Belanger (ed.), *Aboriginal Self Government in Canada: Current Trends and Issues,* third ed. Saskatoon, SK: Purich Publishing.

Napoleon, Val, and Hadley Friedland. 2014. "The Inside Job: Engaging With Indigenous Legal Traditions Through Stories." In Tony Lucero and Dale Turner (eds.), *Oxford Handbook on Indigenous Peoples' Politics*. Oxford: Oxford University Press.

Napoleon, Val, Jim Henshaw, Ken Steacy, Janine Johnston, and Simon Roy. 2013. *Mikomosis and the Wetiko*. Victoria, BC: Indigenous Law Research Unit

R. v. Gladue [1999] 1 SCR 688, 171 DLR (4th) 385 ff.

R. v. Moses [1992] 2 CNLR 116, 71 CCC (3d) 347 ff.

R. v. Machekequonabe [1897] OJ No. 98, 2 CCC 138.

R. v. Powley [2003] SCR 207, 40.

R. v. Wells [2000] 1 SCR 207, 27 ff.

Richland, Justice B. 2008. *Arguing with Tradition: The Language of Law in Hopi Tribal Court:* 141 ff. Chicago, IL: University of Chicago Press.

Ross, Rupert. 1996. *Returning to the Teachings: Exploring Aboriginal Justice*. Toronto: Penguin Canada.

Rudin, Jonathan. 2005. "Aboriginal Justice and Restorative Justice." In Elizabeth Elliot and Robert Gordon (eds.), *New Directions in Restorative Justice: Issues, Practice, Evaluation*. Cullompton: Willan.

Sekaquaptewa, Pat. 2007–8. "Key Concepts in the Finding, Definition and Consideration of Custom Law in Tribal Lawmaking." *American Indian LR,* 32: 319.

Stewart, Wendy, Audrey Huntley, and Fay Blaney. 2001. *The Implications of Restorative Justice for Aboriginal Women and Children Survivors of Violence: A Comparative Overview of Five Communities in British Columbia*. Ottawa: Law Commission of Canada.

Thomas v. Norris [1992] 2 CNLR 139 (BCSC).

Tully, James. 1995. *Strange Multiplicity: Constitutionalism in an Age of Diversity:* 65 ff. Cambridge University Press.

___. 2008. *Public Philosophy in a New Key, Volume II: Imperialism and Civic Freedom:* 278 ff. Cambridge University Press.

Turpel-Lafond, Mary Ellen. 2005. "Some Thoughts on Inclusion and Innovation in the Saskatchewan Justice System." *Saskatchewan LR,* 68: 293

Webber, Jeremy. 2009. "The Grammar of Customary Law." *McGill LJ,* 54: 583 ff.

Whonnok, Karen. 2009. "Aboriginal Courts in Canada, Fact Sheet." <http://www.scowinstitute.ca/library/documents/Aboriginal_ Courts_Fact_Sheet.pdf>.

Whyte, John D. 2008. *Moving Toward Justice: Legal Traditions and Aboriginal Justice*. Vancouver. BC: UBC Press.

Williams, Robert A. Jr. 2009. "Foreword: The Tribal Law Revolution in Indian Country Today." In Raymond D. Austin, *Navajo Courts and Navajo Common Law: A Tradition of Tribal Self-Governance:* xv ff. Minneapolis, MN: University of Minnesota Press.

6

WOMEN AND (IN)JUSTICE

Gillian Balfour

OBJECTIVES

At the end of this chapter, you will be able to:

- Understand the key principles of feminist engagement with (criminal) justice

- Understand the limits of retributive justice for women

- Discuss the implications of restorative justice for victimized and criminalized women

Akey strategy for achieving social change and substantive equality for oppressed peoples has been to turn to law. The power of law is its presumed objectivity and impartiality, where facts and evidence of harms, needs and rights are heard before a court of highly trained lawyers and judges. The idealized aim of formal justice is to treat everyone the same, and to denounce discrimination. However, formal justice and its presumed procedural correctness does not allow for substantive justice because of its very intention: to be blind to difference. Social justice — the provision of resources and opportunities based on specific or different needs and experiences — can only be realized through a contextualized understanding of oppression. For example, feminist-inspired legal strategies have tried to address sexism in society (such as pay inequities for women workers or the invisibility of marital rape) through removing gender from law. The aim of this "liberal feminist" tactic has been to make men and women equal in law. "Radical feminists" countered that the "myth of liberation" (Firestone 1970) presupposed by liberal feminists would only buttress the patriarchal intention of law: to protect the rights and power of men by erasing the unique societal, cultural and economic realities of women's lives: their vulnerability to sexual violence, motherhood and the public/private spheres of paid and unpaid work. For example, the liberal feminist tactic of using formal justice to protect the privacy rights of rape victims have been successfully challenged as being a threat to the constitutional rights of men accused of rape. In this way the rights of men (who are almost always those accused of rape) are seen as more important than the rights of women (who are almost always the victims of rape). How then can feminists seize law to achieve substantive justice? Unfortunately, the recent history of feminist legal activism to address gendered violence and poverty has been to position women as victims in need of protection by the state. This has created institutions of surveillance and monitoring of women on social assistance and women who report domestic violence, and has done little to achieve substantive equality of women: access to a living wage, affordable housing and childcare. There have also been those women left behind and harmed by these feminist-inspired legal strategies: trans women, racialized women, women living with mental illness, women addicted to drugs, women in prison and women who use violence. For this group of the most marginalized women, legal and social exclusion has been wrought by how some feminists have engaged with law.

This chapter will focus on one site of law: the criminalization and punishment of women. Women are increasingly confined in immigration detention centres, psychiatric institutions, jails and penitentiaries (Sudbury 2005). For example, the World Female Imprisonment List, published by the Institute for Criminal Policy Research, reported in 2015 the global rate of women's imprisonment and detention had increased by 50 percent since 2000, whereas the rate of male imprisonment had increased by 18 percent. Of the 700,000 women incarcerated around the world, 200,000 are confined in the United States (Walmsley 2015). How do we make sense of this global trend towards greater punitive treatment of women? Have women become more dangerous? What can law do differently to address the trend of over-incarceration? In what follows we will explore women's social and criminal histories, theorize how Canadian sentencing laws have responded to women's lived experiences and consider the implications of restorative justice for criminalized and victimized women.

WHO ARE CRIMINALIZED AND IMPRISONED WOMEN?

Much of our common sense understanding of the social world comes to be defined through the narratives and images of movies, books and news media. Very few of us have been inside a courtroom or a prison. Instead, much of our awareness of criminalized and imprisoned women comes from dominant discourses that privilege certain explanations and solutions of social problems. Cultural stereotypes of criminalized women are reproduced in the media, but such images and narratives are also echoed in the administration of criminal justice in cases involving criminalized women.

Much of what we read in newspapers and watch on movie screens depicts women and girls as butch-like lesbians or prostitutes. Charlize Theron in the blockbuster movie *Monster* tells the story of Arlene Wournos, a lesbian woman who was violently raped as a young woman while she worked as a prostitute. She was eventually executed for killing several of her johns. In a similar genre, Ali Larter is featured as a vindictive sexualized stalker in *Obsessed*. Most of us are familiar with the wild popularity of young adult fiction series by Stephanie Meyers' *Twilight* and Sean Olin's *Killing Brittany*. In Twilight, Bella — a chaste young white woman — falls in love with a vampire and a werewolf. Both of these masculine characters pursue Bella, vying for her virginity. In *Killing Brittany*, a young woman kills her family and boyfriend amidst book cover images of blood-spattered lipstick kisses. The hit Netflix series, *Orange is the New Black* features a sometimes voyeuristic look into the private sexualized worlds of women prisoners, with a blonde bisexual protagonist serving a sentence for drug trafficking.

More recently and closer to home, a different story is told of how victimized women and girls are treated by the criminal justice system. For example, in a ground-breaking investigation by the *Globe and Mail* into police treatment of sexual assault cases, it was found that one in five cases are "unfounded" or "uncrimed" by police officers after interviewing the victim (Doolittle 2017). Victims of sexual assault — especially those who were intoxicated during their assault — who reported to police across Canada are oftentimes disbelieved due to the investigating police officer's view of her credibility (Benedet 2010; Gotell 2010; Sheehy 2015). Earlier this year, a judge acquitted three police officers charged with sexually assaulting a heavily intoxicated woman. Justice Malloy stated that the social media campaign that erupted during the trial, such as the Twitter hashtag #Ibelieveher, "has no place in the courts" (Fine 2017). Indeed, the judge suggested public reaction to the case on social media had jeopardized the accused's right to fair trial. This acquittal followed two high profile cases: Jian Ghomeshi — a popular CBC radio talk show host — was acquitted of several counts of sexual assault after the judge deemed the complainants (the legal term for a victim of a crime prior to conviction) to be unreliable in their testimony; and in Halifax a cab driver was acquitted in the sexual assault of a young woman who had passed out in the back of his taxi. In that case, the judge pronounced that the complainant has the capacity to consent to sex even while heavily intoxicated. As these media reports reveal, criminal law in Canada seldom denounces sexual violence.

The lines between popular consumer culture and newspaper crime reporting also blurs in the journalistic accounts of criminalized young women. Media coverage of the trial and conviction of a 15-year-old "puppet master" who directed her boyfriend to stab his former girlfriend to death abounded with claims of her sexual jealousy, body image problems and delayed toilet training. In one article, the accused is said to suffer from "borderline personality disorder and resemble Glenn Close's character in Fatal Attraction" (Hewitt 2009). Similarly, a 12-year-old girl in Medicine Hat, Alberta was convicted for convincing her 24-year-old "boyfriend" to kill her family in exchange for sex. In a *Globe and Mail* article, Christie Blatchford (2009) pities the male killer in this case as a product of an alcoholic mother and a series of her abusive partners and possibly a sufferer of fetal alcohol syndrome. Blatchford riles against "the seemingly studious, obedient, intelligent girls of good background who moved boys about like chess pieces."

Are criminalized and imprisoned women who they seem to be in these images and narratives — white, middle class, hypersexualized and dangerously capable of wielding control over older men for sex? Statistics Canada reported that in 2015, women and girls accounted for 22 percent of persons accused of violent crimes (most often for making threatening and harassing phone calls or common assault), 28 percent of all persons accused of property-related offences, such as theft under $5000 or fraud and 20 percent of persons accused of drug-related offences (Hotton-Mahony, Jacob and Hobson 2017). More recently, the Office of the Correctional Investigator recently reported that 45 percent of women prisoners are prescribed psychotropic medications, most often for depression, whereas 29 percent of male prisoners are prescribed these medications (Sapers 2016). These rates are four times the Canadian average (Sapers 2016).

For the most part, women in trouble in Canada bear little resemblance to those images and narratives that we consume on Netflix and elsewhere. Most are young Indigenous and Black women, living in poverty, many as single mothers, with little education, histories of profound victimization including childhood sexual abuse, rape, domestic violence and alcohol or drug dependency (Balfour and Comack 2014). While more than 80 percent of women in Canada have progressed beyond Grade 9, for women prisoners the figure is closer to 50 percent. The Canadian Association of Elizabeth Fry Societies — a feminist prisoner advocate network — reported two-thirds of federally sentenced women are mothers and they are more likely than men to have primary childcare responsibilities; there are about 25,000 children whose mothers are in either federal prisons or provincial jails in Canada each year (CAEFS 2009). So, how does criminal law make sense of women's lives?

WHAT'S LAW GOT TO DO WITH IT?

In Canada, persons can be charged and prosecuted for a summary offence and sentenced to a provincial prison for two years or less; or they can be charged and prosecuted for an indictable offence and sentenced to a federal penitentiary for a term of two years or more. Once charges are laid against a person, the court can decide to confine the accused to pre-trial custody in a remand centre, to release her on bail, or under an order to promise to appear before the court at a later date. According to the principles of fundamental justice, the deprivation of liberty (imprisonment) is to be administered only in the direst circumstances (the accused is a flight risk or presents an imminent threat to themselves or others). However, in Canada, the greatest increase in prisoner populations has been at the pre-trial level — prior to conviction when an accused is considered legally innocent. A disproportionate number of women are held in remand centres. In comparison to 2005–2006, the average number of adults in remand was 35 percent higher in 2015–2016 (Reitano 2017). It would seem that, despite the protections of legal rights under the Canadian Charter of Rights and Freedoms, courts are more likely to detain legally innocent people (those not yet convicted of a crime) than release them on bail. In August of 2017, the *Globe and Mail* reported on a study conducted by news agency Reuters. In their study of news stories, coroner's inquests and interviews with families, they reported that in Canada's provincial and territorial jails 174 people died while awaiting trial, compared to 80 who died while serving sentences. "Moreover, people awaiting trial comprised 56 per cent of all inmates in these provinces over that time period, but 65 per cent of the dead" (Mehler-Paperny 2017). Provincial and federal correctional data also show a pattern of gender inequality with regards to increases in the numbers of men and women sentenced to custody. In 2015–2016, the overrepresentation of Indigenous adults was more pronounced for females than males. Indigenous females accounted for 38 percent of female admissions to provincial- and territorial-sentenced custody, while the comparable figure for Indigenous males was 26 percent. In the federal correctional services, Indigenous females accounted for 31 percent of female admissions to sentenced custody, while the figure for Indigenous males was 23 percent (Reitano 2017).

What has contributed to the significant increase in the number of women in prison in Canada over the last decade? How can we begin to understand the paradox between the social histories of victimization and social exclusion and criminal histories of women in trouble, and the increasing rates of women's imprisonment? Shouldn't the courts take into consideration the unique circumstances of women in poverty and women who have been victims of sexual violence? Unfortunately, throughout most of Canada, liberal, conservative and social democratic provincial governments alike have introduced neo-liberal economic policies that prize market deregulation and lower taxes for corporate elites, and work to dismantle key public institutions created decades ago to address crime through reducing poverty, increasing education and providing preventative community mental health services. In addition, these economic policies are compounded by neo-conservative political rhetoric that touts the greater use of police and prisons to ensure public safety. Much of these significant changes have been strongly supported by white, middle-class voters who denounce rehabilitation of offenders as being soft on crime, harm reduction approaches to drug addiction as enabling drug dependency or welfare supports for the poor as fostering laziness rather than self-sufficiency. The "prison industrial complex" is an economic opportunity for rural and Indigenous communities as prisons are used as job-creation opportunities. Yet, these prisons are increasingly used to house persons who are homeless and/or unemployed, or living with mental health problems. As outlined earlier in this book, racialized women, immigrant women and single mothers comprise the largest proportion of the underclass in Canada. As neo-liberal reforms have restricted eligibility to welfare and increased levels of surveillance of those on welfare, women have been increasingly vulnerable to criminalization for welfare fraud (for example, failure to report additional income such as student loans or saving accounts). As well, zero-tolerance mandatory-charging practices in cases of domestic violence have resulted in dual charging of some women who call police to report being assaulted. Together, neo-liberal economic policies and neo-conservative law-and-order reforms have adversely impacted women in poverty and living with violence. As imprisonment is a form of punishment to be proscribed by the criminal justice system as proportionate to the seriousness of the offence and the moral blameworthiness of the offender, we should be greatly concerned about the use of prisons because of failed social policies.

What is the connection between race, class, gender and the criminal justice system? Conditions of social inequality and social exclusion heighten the likelihood of police charges, criminalization and imprisonment. The principles of fundamental justice that underpin the "official version of law" (Naffine 1990) (discussed in Chapter 10) are purported to ensure a rights-based adversarial system of justice to protect the accused's rights to security of the person and freedom from arbitrary detention by the state. Indeed, the image of the blindfolded maiden of justice suggests the sacred right to procedural fairness, thus, protecting against the influence of racial, class and gendered stereotypes in the administration of justice. Regardless of the constraints of due process proscribed in law, cultural stereotypes of race, class and gender appear to enable or shape the administration of justice.

As the case study on cocaine "mules" (Marsha Hamilton and Donna Mason) shows, attempts by the sentencing judge to contextualize women's

CASE STUDY:
COCAINE "MULES" AND FEMALE MARGINALIZATION –
EXCERPT FROM WRITTEN COURT DECISION:

Cocaine courier importation cases are, almost invariably, not about greed in the sense of an offender reaping profits to maintain a lavish lifestyle or to acquire luxuries. These individuals, highly dispensable throwaways of elusive overseers, live in the despair of poverty — single mothers and subjects of systemic racism. The reward for the risk taken pays rent, feeds children, and supports a subsistence level existence ... on ... the cocaine importation offence ... women constitute a third to one half of those charged. It is apparent that women, and especially African-Canadian women, like the offenders here and so many others, are virtue tested by drug operation overseers deliberately preying on their social and economic disadvantage ...

Each of the offenders in this case has three young children. Each is a single mother with no financial assistance from their children's fathers. Each requires welfare to survive. In Canada, the feminization of poverty is an entrenched social phenomenon with a multiplicity of economic barriers faced by women. Courts have long recognized the economic disadvantage of the female partner in a domestic relationship. The impact of childcare on women's financial ability and independence is equally well known. Offenders like those before the court are subject to both the systemic economic inequality of women caring on their own for young children and the compounding disadvantage of systemic racism securing their poverty status. These individuals, almost inevitably without a prior criminal record, are in turn conscripted by the drug distribution hierarchy targeting their vulnerability. Poor, then exploited in their poverty, these women when captured and convicted have been subjected to severe sentences perpetuating their position of disadvantage.

Source: *R. v. Hamilton and Mason* 2003

CASE STUDY:
SENTENCING AND GENDER MARGINALIZATION —
EXCERPT FROM WRITTEN COURT DECISION

Sentencing is not based on group characteristics, but on the facts relating to the specific offence and specific offender as revealed by the evidence adduced in the proceedings. A sentencing proceeding is also not the forum in which to right perceived societal wrongs, allocate responsibility for criminal conduct as between the offender and society, or "make up" for perceived social injustices by the imposition of sentences that do not reflect the seriousness of the crime ... The trial judge stepped outside of the proper role of a judge on sentencing and ultimately imposed sentences that were inconsistent with the statutory principles of sentencing. He rested his conclusion that conditional sentences were appropriate primarily on his finding that the [women] because of their race, gender, and poverty, were particularly vulnerable targets to those who sought out individuals to act as cocaine couriers. Ms. Hamilton received a conditional sentence of twenty months on terms that provided for partial house arrest in the first year of the sentence and a curfew for the remainder of the sentence. Ms. Mason received a conditional sentence of two years less a day on terms that provided for partial house arrest in the first fifteen months of the sentence and a curfew for the rest of the sentence. The trial judge lost his appearance of impartiality ... While no doubt well-intentioned, the trial judge effectively took on the combined role of advocate, witness, and judge, thereby losing the appearance of a neutral arbiter. The Crown submits that the women received conditional sentences because they were poor, black, and female, and that none of these factors diminish the seriousness of the offence or justify a conditional sentence. Counsel further argues that the imposition of conditional sentences based on the race and gender of the respondents will only reinforce the prevailing wisdom among drug overlords that young black women make ideal drug couriers, thereby perpetuating and exacerbating the vulnerability of the very group the trial judge sought to assist.

The trial judge's role as the arbiter of the respective merits of competing positions developed and put before the trial judge by the parties best ensures judicial impartiality and the appearance of judicial impartiality. Human nature is such that it is always easier to objectively assess the merits of someone else's argument. The relatively passive role assigned to the trial judge also recognizes that judges, by virtue of their very neutrality, are not in a position to make informed decisions as to which issues should be raised. It is also important that the trial judge limit the scope of his or her intervention into the role traditionally left to counsel. The trial judge should frame any issue that he or she introduces as precisely as possible and relate it to the case before the court. This will avoid turning the sentencing hearing into a *de facto* commission of inquiry.

Source: *R. v. Hamilton and Mason* 2004: 3, 7, 33–34, 68–70)

choices were overturned on appeal to uphold the retributive principles of deterrence and denunciation. To explore this question further, we should consider an earlier case in the sentencing of two women convicted of drug trafficking for couriering cocaine from Jamaica to Canada. This case reveals how women's lived experiences of structural inequality and racism are not recognized through law's method of objectivity and impartiality. In 2001, two women were arrested at Toronto's Pearson International Airport for trafficking and possession of cocaine. The provincial court judge in this case asserted that the women should not be sentenced to prison because gendered social conditions of poverty, single parenting, minimum-wage employment and lack of family support led to their offence.

The judge in this case decided upon a conditional sentence (a prison term to be served in the community) for the two women because of their remorse, the personal circumstances (poverty) that led to their crimes and the impact of imprisonment upon their children. In response to the judge's attempt to achieve substantive justice within the administration of formal justice, the province of Ontario appealed the sentence, seeking a term of imprisonment. The following case study is an excerpt from the appeal judge's written decision.

RETRIBUTIVE JUSTICE AND THE WOMAN OF LEGAL DISCOURSE

The cases of Marsha Hamilton and Donna Mason reveal the limits of law as a site of social justice, and the hegemony of the official version of law: the criminalization process is one that unfolds in a context of rationality and objectivity. In this view, the legal system is founded on a series of procedural requirements and technical exercises to protect the rights of the accused balanced off against the role of the state to denounce conduct that is not in the public interest. That is, according to the procedural requirements of law, persons are criminalized and condemned solely on the basis of their behaviour and its harmfulness. In this view of the law, gender is not and should not be considered.

Yet, the over-representation of marginalized groups in the criminalization process reveals a paradox between law and the administration of justice. The disconnection between "what the legal world would have us believe about itself" (Naffine 1990: 24) and law in practice raises the possibility that the criminalization process is influenced by gendered, racialized and class-based presuppositions. Smart (1992) argues that much of early liberal feminism saw the "law as sexist" or discriminatory towards women, and sought to engage with law through rights-based reforms to the black letter of the law to demand equality with men with regards to material resources and opportunities. Radical feminists rejected the equity argument and instead asserted the "law as male," drawing on the re-victimizing experiences of raped and battered women by the police and before the courts. Feminist lawyers and anti-violence activists have tackled law's sexist treatment of raped and battered women through appealing lower court rulings and filing constitutional challenges of such decisions before the Supreme Court of Canada.

FEMINIST-INSPIRED LAW REFORMS

Feminists have long argued that the laws concerning rape have been framed by mythologies that normalize women as liars and sexual temptresses (Busby 1999; Smart 1989). Drawn from wider patriarchal culture, these rape myths have played a significant role in Canadian jurisprudence. Rape myths that frame our everyday common sense include: "A woman who dresses in sexy clothes is asking for it"; "Rape is caused by men's natural impulses once a woman has turned him on"; "No means yes: when a woman flirts with a man, what does she expect?"; "If yes to one then yes to all"; "Women cannot be trusted, they make false accusations and blackmail ex-boyfriends"; "Real rape is when you have physical injuries" (Comack 2000: 139–142). In this way, law is male in that it protects men's sexual access to women and blames women for rape. Seen in the context of other behaviour, in cases of robbery for example, it is never suggested that the robbery victim is to blame because he left his door unlocked. Numerous reforms have been made in Canadian criminal law as a result of feminist legal activism to combat the place of rape mythologies in the strategies of lawyers and decisions of judges. For example, in 1983, feminist lawyers challenged the sexism of rape laws, and won changes to the legal category of rape. The offence was changed to sexual assault, husbands could be charged with sexually assaulting their wives, vaginal penetration was no longer required as corroborating evidence necessary for conviction and lawyers' ability to ask questions about a woman's sexual history was restricted.

These reforms were designed to acknowledge rape as a crime of violence not a crime of passion, and to shield women from humiliating experiences before the courts. Other changes to the form of law achieved by feminist lawyers included changes to protect child victims of sexual assault; clarification of when consent to sex can be obtained (for example, a woman cannot consent to sex if she is intoxicated). Finally, the defence of "mistaken belief in consent" based on a woman's sexual history, lifestyle or dress was struck down as discriminatory against women, although provisions were implemented to allow judges to consider some evidence under certain conditions. One of the key Supreme Court decisions in sexual assault case law is *R. v. Seaboyer and Gayme* (1991), as it is the first constitutional challenge of section 276, the rape shield provision. At issue is whether two men convicted of sexual assault should be allowed to cross-examine a victim as to her sexual history and to use a defence of mistaken belief in consent. The Supreme Court agreed with accused men and ruled the rape shield provision unconstitutional, but upheld the convictions. The dissenting opinion of Justice Claire L'Heureux-Dube, who argued strongly against the ruling to strike down the rape shield provision, is presented here in part:

Following this decision, feminist lawyers proposed a revised rape shield provision to ensure the protection of the accused's rights to a fair trial

CASE STUDY:
RAPE SHIELD?
— EXCERPT FROM WRITTEN COURT DECISION

Judges L'Heureux-Dubé and Gonthier wrote:

Sexual assault is not like any other crime. It is for the most part unreported and the prosecution and conviction rates are among the lowest for all violent crimes. These statistics indicate that prejudicial beliefs may distort our perception of what actually happens. Rape myths still present formidable obstacles for complainants in their dealings with the very system charged with discovering the truth. From the making of the initial complaint down to the determination of the issue at trial, stereotype and mythology are at work, lowering the number of reported cases, influencing police decisions to pursue the case, thereby decreasing the rates of arrest, and finally distorting the issues at trial and, necessarily, the results.

The concept of relevance has been imbued with stereotypical notions of female complainants and sexual assault. This is plain from the common law which held that evidence of "unchasteness" was relevant to both consent and credibility The irrelevance of most evidence of prior sexual history is clear once the mythical basis of relevancy determinations in this area of the law is revealed. Nevertheless, Parliament has provided broad avenues for its admissibility in setting out exceptions to the general rule in s. 276. Moreover, all evidence of the complainant's previous sexual history with the accused is prima facie admissible under those provisions. Evidence that is excluded by these provisions is simply irrelevant in a decision-making context free of myth and stereotype.

The exclusion of "pattern" evidence and "habit" evidence is not unconstitutional; the mythical basis of these arguments denies their relevance. "Pattern of conduct evidence" usually occurs where the complainant has had consensual sexual relations in circumstances that look much like those supporting the assault allegation. Such evidence is almost invariably irrelevant. Arguments in its favour depend for their vitality on the notion that women consent to sex based upon such extraneous considerations as the location of the act, the race, age or profession of the alleged assaulter and/or considerations of the nature of the sexual act engaged in. Consent is to a person and not to a circumstance.

Such arguments are implicitly based upon the notion that women will, in the right circumstances, consent to anyone and, more fundamentally, that "unchaste" women have a propensity to consent. Evidence characterized as habitual, as being more specific than character and as denoting one's regular response to a repeated situation, too, is inadmissible. Adopting such an argument here would lend support to the stereotypical proposition that "unchaste" women have a propensity to consent. No analogy can be drawn between this behaviour and volitional sexual conduct. The relevance of evidence of mistaken belief in consent in some cases does not conclusively demonstrate the infirmity of the provision. No relevant evidence regarding the defence of honest but mistaken belief in consent is excluded by the legislation under attack here. Evidence of prior acts of prostitution or allegations of prostitution are properly excluded by the provision. This evidence is never relevant and, moreover, is highly prejudicial. A prostitute is not generally more willing to consent to sexual intercourse and is no less credible as a witness because of that mode of life. There is no understandable reason for asking complainants in sexual assault cases if they are prostitutes.

The evidence excluded by s. 276 is simply irrelevant because it is based upon discriminatory beliefs about women and sexual assault. The importance of Parliament's objectives in the reform of the law of sexual assault is amplified by the nature of the harm done and by the fact that its legislative effort gives voice to values that are paramount in a free and democratic society.

Source: *R. v. Seaboyer; R. v. Gayme* 1991

and a woman's equality and privacy rights. However, despite feminist-inspired reforms to the form of sexual assault laws to constrain the place of rape myths in sexual assault trials, rates of self-reported sexual assault have not increased, suggesting women still do not believe they will be taken seriously by police or the risks of shame and humiliation are too great. Rates of successful prosecution have not increased, and rates of imprisonment for sexual assault remain the lowest of any violent crime. For example, according to a report by Mahony, Jacobs and Hobson (2017), the rate of self-reported sexual assault between 2004 and 2014, has remained relatively stable at 37 reported incidents per 1,000 women. For young women aged 15–24, the rate was much higher: 134 reported incidents per 1,000 young women. As discussed earlier in this chapter, one in five cases of sexual assault reported to police are uncrimed and not subject to criminal justice processing (Doolittle 2017). In cases that are considered by police to be founded — or could be substantiated through credible evidence — charges are laid in only 40 percent of those cases, demonstrating what Holly Johnson (2012) refers to as case attrition: the systematic removal of sexual assault cases from criminal justice processing. Johnson's study of Canadian criminal justice data reveals that of the 460,000 incidents of self-reported sexual assault, 2,800 cases are prosecuted and 1,500 are convicted. Upon sentencing, 70 percent of sexual assault perpetrators are likely to receive a sentence of probation, whereas 50 percent will be sentenced to a period of incarceration (Johnson 2012: 653). Furthermore, a series of formidable challenges by the defence bar against these reforms have resulted in a reassertion of the accused's right to make a full defence to the charge of rape over women's equality and privacy rights. For example, defence lawyers rely upon third-party evidence aimed at discrediting the victim (personal diaries, therapeutic counselling records and school records).

In 1999, such anti-feminist backlash reappeared with a vengeance in *R. v. Ewanchuk* (1999). A provincial court judge ruled that the perpetrator accused of sexually assaulting a young woman he was interviewing for a job, was entitled to the defence of implied consent — although no such defence existed in law — because the victim did not actively resist the attack. The victim claimed she was terrified of the perpetrator and said no repeatedly but did not physically resist. The Supreme Court of Canada overturned the lower court's acquittal of the accused. The Court threw out the defence of implied consent and expressed in its decision a feminist analysis of "sexual violence as a matter of equality as it is an offence against human dignity and violation of human rights" (para 7). Although the Supreme Court of Canada recognized the importance of protecting women's constitutional rights, the lower court rulings in the Ewanchuk case reveal the contested terrain of rape law reform, and how the form of law can reproduce rather than remedy gender inequality. Why is the form of law not more effective in its denunciation of rape and recognition of raped women's rights? Is it perhaps that law is sexist or male in its treatment of victimized women? If understood in this way, does law also engender criminalized women?

THE PRACTICE OF LAW AS A GENDERING PROCESS

Feminist socio-legal theory needs to reconsider law's treatment of women as a gendering process (Smart 1992). That is, view it as a series of processes or strategies that weave together various cultural constructs of masculinity, femininity, dangerousness, blameworthy and victimization. Smart (1992) goes on to explain that women do not enter the criminal justice system already gendered or sexed, rather women's identities as rape victims or murderers are scripted according to dominant discourses of femininity. Kathleen Daly (1994: 433) goes further arguing that law is also "colour coded and class compounded." For example, prostitutes are rarely viewed by the courts as rape victims regardless of the brutality of the violence perpetrated against them. The rape and murder of a prostituted Indigenous woman, Pamela George, in Regina, Saskatchewan, helps us make sense of law as gendered and racialized (Razack 2000). Under law, Indigenous peoples are culturalized. For example, addiction and violence are understood to be a normative part of Indigenous relationships, culture and communities. Razack cites examples of lawyers' strategies at the trial of the two white, middle-class university students accused of the killing of George after she refused to get into the car with them. The site of the murder was described as "a romantic place where couples are often necking or petting in vehicles" (Razack 2000: 114). George herself was referred to as the "hooker" or the "Indian" whereas the accused men were referred to as "boys who did pretty darn stupid things" (2000: 117). Razack argues that these strategies constitute the identities of the men and Pamela George as well as where the death occurred in such a way that "no one could really be held accountable for her death, at least not to the extent that there would have been accountability had she been [white]" (Ibid.).

Through the analysis of the practice of law, we are able to see how Indigenous women are constituted as "drunken squaws" as such cultural presuppositions make up the ideological content of law. According to

Marlee Kline (1994: 458), these "squaw narratives" of Indigenous women developed out of colonialism (including the Indian Act, reserve system, residential schools) and have become "abstracted and indeterminate in law." Through law's appearance of neutrality, its power to naturalize and legitimize racist ideologies is obscured. Teresa Nahanee (1994) and Margo Nightingale (1991) have shown how stereotypes of the "drunken Indian" have influenced the courts to minimize the culpability of Indigenous men accused of sexual assault. Alcohol abuse is often raised as a mitigating factor when sentencing a man convicted of rape, "even as the root cause of violence against women" (Nahanee 1994: 198). Similarly, law as a gendering and racializing strategy comes into view when examining how Indigenous women's credibility is assessed according to the image of the "drunken Indian." Nightingale (1991) suggests that either an Indigenous woman is not likely to be believed by the police or band leaders when she alleges to have been raped because she was intoxicated, or her claim of being passed out during the rape is over-exaggerated to enable lawyers to argue that the rape was less traumatic. In more recent research on law's treatment of violence against Indigenous women in the context of sentencing circles, Emma Cunliffe and Angela Cameron (2007) point out how the procedural requirements of law for evidence and victim impact statements take control of women's victimization by deciding what is credible testimony and the necessary punishment. In their study of sentencing circles in cases of domestic violence, women's victimization narratives are often omitted from sentencing decisions, at best interpreted by judges as to their meaning and significance. So, despite efforts to take gender into account in the sentencing process, the context of women's experiences and needs for safety are overshadowed by the form of law.

LOOKING FORWARD: RESTORATIVE JUSTICE

Is it possible to engage with law to resolve the problem of women's increasing rates of imprisonment and the persistence of violence against women? Compulsory criminalization of domestic violence, for example, has had the unintended consequence of locking up women who call police for help (Snider 1994). Similarly, rape law reforms to protect women's rights and to challenge rape myths in the form and practice of law appear to have done little to stem the rate of sexual violence against women and improve conviction rates. Moreover, given the ethos of criminal justice is punishment not social justice, and its process is entrenched in a rights-based adversarial model, feminists have rightly reconsidered law as an effective means of resistance to patriarchy and social change.

For some socio-legal scholars and anti-violence activists, restorative justice offers a new paradigm of justice. Over the past two decades, restorative justice policies and practices have been implemented in most industrialized countries and many developing nations. Broadly speaking, a restorative justice framework holds that crime is "action that harms specific people and relationships, which in turn creates needs and obligation to be fulfilled through a model of justice that brings together victim, offenders, and communities" (Cheon and Regehr 2006) in reparation of harm. Throughout the process of reparation, the offender must accept responsibility for her actions and make amends, whereas the community is expected to ensure the safety and support of the victim and offender (Braithwaite 2001). Alison Morris (2002) asserts that in some countries such as New Zealand, restorative justice has come to emphasize a human rights perspective that seeks to restore the victim's security, self-respect, and dignity. She states:

> Restorative processes and practices, therefore, should empower offenders and victims by giving them a sense of inclusion in and satisfaction with these processes and practices; they should enable victims to feel better as a result of participating in them; and they should hold offenders accountable in meaningful ways by encouraging them to make amends to their victims. If all these occur, we might expect the restorative justice processes to impact on reoffending and reintegration and to heal victim's hurt. (Morris 2002: 600)

In Canada, the Indigenous community of Hollow Water responded to the high rate of intergenerational child sexual abuse with a holistic community centred strategy that addresses the trauma of abuse experienced by the victim, the victim's family and the needs of the victimizer. The aim is to restore the capacity of the community to care for the needs of its members, not vengeance or retribution through the incarceration of the perpetrator. Proponents of restorative justice in the violence against women context point to how retributive justice (mandatory charging, vigorous prosecution and minimum sentencing) has not addressed low reporting and prosecution rates and the re-victimization of women under vigorous cross-examination. Successful convictions and punitive sentences are achieved only in cases where women are viewed by the courts to be chaste, respectable, sober and physically injured in her resistance against the attacker (Balfour, Du Mont and White 2017). Women must adopt the identity of "victim" and relinquish their autonomy and self-determination (Lacey 1998). Moreover, the punitive sentencing of men may create conditions of endangerment for women as their abusers seek revenge upon women for calling the police or testifying in court (Snider 1998; Balfour, Du Mont and White 2017). Proponents further assert that the principles of restorative justice can address women's needs for safety and denunciation of the violence. "Restorative justice can empower a woman to define herself and the harm that has been done; she is at the centre of events, in control and telling her stories and in her own way" (Hulsman 1991 cited in Hudson 2002: 624).

In contrast, opponents of restorative justice for rape and domestic violence assert that such a criminal justice response is "cheap justice" (Coker 2006) that does not take seriously the impact and prevalence of gendered violence. Oftentimes, communities have a limited capacity or willingness to respond to the safety needs of women who have been victimized (Cameron 2006; Daly and Stubbs 2005; McGillvray and Comaskey 1999). Razack (1998) has argued that sentencing circles do not take into account complex historical, economic and political contexts of gendered violence perpetrated against women, especially those who are Indigenous. Such debates have questioned the safety of women who may feel pressure from the community to support the offender and the risk of trivializing gendered violence and returning to its place in the domestic sphere as a relationship problem (Coker 2006). In Canada, the response of women's organizations to the implementation of restorative justice in response to gendered violence has been mixed. Cameron (2006) calls for a moratorium in cases of domestic and sexualized violence, especially within the Indigenous community, as tradition is not always respectful of women's status in the community and in some instances can fail to protect women from their abusers. Overall, most feminist, Indigenous and critical race scholars are uncertain as to the potential of restorative justice practices to address the root causes of gendered violence (Balfour 2013).

One example of an alternative intended to lessen the rate of incarceration in Canada is conditional sentencing. In those cases where imprisonment for no more than two years is determined to be an appropriate sentence, judges can grant a conditional sentence wherein the offender serves their term in the community under various conditions. This sentencing option was created by Parliament in 1996 as part of sweeping reforms to the Criminal Code. Bill C-41 also codified sentencing purposes and principles to guide judges in their sentencing decisions. Judges were to consider a variety of mitigating and aggravating factors in their decision making. Mitigating factors, for example, include the "special consideration of Indigenous offenders" (section 718.2e) and aggravating factors include the nature of the relationship between the perpetrator and the victim — familial and intimate partner violence is to be taken more seriously by the courts. The failure of sentencing courts to apply section 718.2e and to utilize a conditional sentence in the case of a young Indigenous woman convicted of manslaughter in the death of her common-law husband, was challenged on appeal in 1997 and went to the Supreme Court of Canada in 1999. In that landmark ruling (*R. v. Gladue*), the Supreme Court directed lower court judges to abide by the wishes of Parliament in Bill C-41 to stem the rates of incarceration of Indigenous peoples, and to use incarceration as a last resort. As our prison data reveals, Bill C-41 and *R. v. Gladue* has done little to stop the over-incarceration of Indigenous peoples, especially women (Williams 2009).

As you can imagine, the law-and-order backlash against conditional sentences and *R v. Gladue* was swift. Victims' rights groups and conservative politicians alike challenged the "soft on crime" approach of the Supreme Court. Yet, the principles of *Gladue* (the recognition of the consequences of colonialism such as loss of one's culture, family breakdown, residential schools, substance abuse and high unemployment) began to be applied in various points of the legal system: bail courts as well as correctional institutions and parole hearings. Conditional sentencing raised some difficult challenges for feminist legal scholars and lawyers: on one hand, the gender disparity in the sentencing of Indigenous women and men was increasing, therefore conditional sentences could potentially address that problem and keep Indigenous women out of prison. However, it could also mean that Indigenous men convicted of domestic violence or sexual assault could be returned to their communities under the terms of conditional sentence, placing women at risk. Indeed, the Supreme Court of Canada has ruled that a conditional sentence is not precluded by the

---

CASE STUDY:
1996 SENTENCING OPTIONS

Statutes of Canada 1995 Chapter 22
An Act to amend the Criminal Code (sentencing) and other Acts in
consequence thereof
BILL C-41 Assented to 13th July, 1995

742.1 Where a person is convicted of an offence, except an offence that
is punishable by a minimum term of imprisonment, and the court

(a) imposes a sentence of imprisonment of less than two years, and

(b) is satisfied that serving the sentence in the community would
not endanger the safety of the community,

the court may, for the purpose of supervising the offender's behaviour
in the community, order that the offender serve the sentence in the
community, subject to the offender's complying with the conditions of
a conditional sentence order made under section 742.3.

---

seriousness of the offence, rather sentencing decisions should be based
on the offender's needs for treatment and successful reintegration into
the community (*R. v. Ipeelee* 2012). Regardless of the Supreme Court's
decision to recognize the over-incarceration of Indigenous peoples and
to provide opportunities for community-based non-carceral sentences, in
2012, section 742.1 of the Criminal Code was amended to disallow such
sentences in a variety of cases. As stated here by the Public Prosecution
Service of Canada:

Under the new regime, conditional sentences are now unavailable in
the following circumstances:

- In the case of all offences prosecuted by way of indictment for which
  the maximum term of imprisonment is either 14 years or life;
- Offences prosecuted by indictment for which the maximum term
  of imprisonment is 10 years, that:
  i. resulted in bodily harm;
  ii. involved the import, export, trafficking or production of drugs,
  or
  iii. involved the use of a weapon.

In addition, a list of eleven offences, when prosecuted by indict-ment, are expressly excluded from eligibility for conditional sentences. This list includes prison breach (s. 144 of the Code), criminal harassment (s. 264 of the Code), sexual assault (s. 271 of the Code), kidnapping (s. 279 of the Code), trafficking in persons-material benefit (s. 279.02 of the Code) and abduction of person under 14 (s. 281 of the Code), but also includes a number of property offences:

- motor vehicle theft (s. 333.1 of the Code);
- theft over 5,000 (s. 334 (a) of the Code);
- breaking and entering a place other than a dwelling house (s. 348 (1)(e) of the Code);
- being unlawfully in a dwelling-house (s. 349 of the Code); and
- arson for fraudulent purpose (s. 435 of the Code).[1]

The list of offences that are now excluded from conditional sentences appears to be a patchwork of crimes that serve conservative "tough on crime" political ends rather than public safety. As discussed earlier, sexual assault cases are seldom successfully prosecuted, therefore restricting section 742.1 in cases of violent crimes will do little to protect women from sexual violence or address the systemic barriers to prosecution. Preliminary research indicates that conditional sentences were sought by defence counsel in cases of intimate partner sexual violence (Balfour and Du Mont 2012), and Indigenous men and women were more likely to go to jail *following* the introduction of conditional sentences (Balfour 2008, 2013). By this I mean law reforms to denounce violence against women and sentencing reforms to slow the rate of incarceration have not ben-efited the population of women most likely to be victims and prisoners. Feminist socio-legal theory and anti-violence activists need to consider in their work those women whose lives are lived at the crossroads of punishment and victimization.

GETTING GENDER INTO JUSTICE

Despite popular cultural narratives of "bad girls" that depict young women in trouble as violent and manipulative, criminalized women are amongst the most marginalized and vulnerable people. Their criminal histories reveal the impact of poverty, addiction, mental illness and single parenting. Most women prisoners are convicted of non-violent crimes, such as fraud and drug- and prostitution-related offences, and are more likely to be imprisoned in pre-trial custody and sentenced to prison for a first offence than are male offenders. Moreover, women offenders are a very low risk to commit another offence. A disproportionate number of federally sentenced women are Indigenous or Black, convicted of serious crimes that resulted from impacts of social exclusion, sexual violence, addiction and mental illness. Despite these realities about women in trouble, we have witnessed a global lockdown of women. And, as we have seen here, feminist engagement with law has resulted in reforms to sexual assault laws, asserted the human rights of women prisoners, and challenged the sexism inherent in welfare reforms. Yet, the form and practice has yet to create real systemic changes to the criminal justice response to women in trouble. Such as in cases of restorative justice and sexual assault, victimized and criminalized women fall between the cracks. It appears, then, that law reforms are of little consequence or benefit to women and should not be the central strategy of feminist politics. Other feminists believe that while law remains sexist or male, law is a very important power resource to articulate and defend women's rights. It is important to broaden the site of struggle against gender oppression and to bring law to bear upon political and economic practices of injustice. Violence against women has been a key site of feminist legal activism, yet prisons are filled with women who have been criminalized for fighting back or surviving on streets because of poverty and mental illness. Perhaps it is time for feminists to consider economic oppression and political disenfranchisement as state violence against women, worthy of condemnation.

DISCUSSION QUESTIONS

1. Given the challenges of achieving substantive equality for women in conflict with the law both as victims and prisoners, should feminists continue to engage with law? If not, what other sites of social change would be effective in addressing gender-based violence and over-incarceration?
2. What do you think was the reason for the backlash against *R. v. Gladue*, and section 718.2e of the Criminal Code by a) Crown prosecutors and b) the general public?

3. What are some of the elements of a feminist critique of restorative justice, even though such alternatives to incarceration could reduce the rate of women's incarceration?

GLOSSARY

Anti-feminist backlash: Feminist-inspired victories to denounce gendered violence, achieve pay equity and mount significant legal challenges against the state to protect the rights of women have been met in response by (mostly male) critics who see feminist politics and policies as a threat to family values, as underestimating violence against men and the seriousness of women's own violence and undermining the rights of men before the law.

Canadian Association of Elizabeth Fry Societies: A network of feminist prisoner-advocacy and prison-abolition organizations who provide support to women and girls in conflict with the law, as well as challenging government policies with regards to the conditions of confinement in women's prisons.

Conditional sentence: A new sentencing option created by the federal government in 1996 to allow offenders receiving sentences of two years less a day to serve their sentences in the community under strict conditions. The intent was to decrease the high rate of incarceration, especially for non-violent offenders, and to encourage judges to be creative and flexible in their sentencing practices.

Hollow Water: An Indigenous community in Manitoba that has created a Community Holistic Circle Healing that seeks to address the intergenerational impact of sexual abuse through the combined power of community and law. An abuser may plead guilty and then to be sentenced to probation requiring full cooperation with the healing process, or be abandoned to the courts, with jail as the probable outcome.

Law as male: A perspective of radical feminists that law perpetuates patriarchal oppression by protecting men's entitlement to women's bodies by failing to criminalize men who sexually exploit women through prostitution, pornography and sexual violence.

Law as sexist: A viewpoint of liberal feminists that law can perpetuate discrimination against women by allowing for differential treatment on the basis of sex. Instead, liberal feminists believe women and men should be seen as individuals.

Legal innocence: When an individual is not proven guilty beyond a reasonable doubt with regards to both *mens rea* and *actus reus.*

Liberal feminism: A feminist perspective that formal equality can be achieved through law and policy reforms that are gender neutral and create individual opportunities.

Official version of law: This is how law sees itself — as rational, objective, impartial and unaffected by stereotypes or biases. The official version of law is best portrayed by the image of the blind-folded maiden of justice holding the scales of justice weighing the factual evidence put before her.

Prison industrial complex: A phrase coined by Angela Davis (1997) to describe the rapid expansion of the U.S inmate populations to the political influence of private prison companies and businesses that supply goods and services to government prison agencies, equalling the military industrial complex that emerged out of the Second World War. Activists have described the prison industrial complex as perpetuating a belief that imprisonment is a quick fix to underlying social problems such as homelessness, unemployment, drug addiction, mental illness and illiteracy.

Radical feminism: This feminist perspective claims that women are oppressed under patriarchy (a male-centered political and cultural system) through sexual violence and reproduction.

Rape shield: A legal provision in the Criminal Code that protects women from having to testify about their sexual history. This provision has been challenged by defence lawyers who claim a woman's sexual history can lead the man to believe she consented to sex, therefore violating a man's right to a fair trial.

Sentencing circles: A restorative justice sentencing practice that takes place in the community where the crime took place, and involves the victim and the victimizer. The community decides the nature of the sentence to be handed down. Circles are typically practised in small, rural Indigenous communities.

Victim impact statement: A legal provision created in 1987 to allow victims of crimes to formally document the impact of their victimization. However, impact statements are rarely taken into account in sentencing hearings, as judges are more likely to sentence according to principle of general deterrence and denunciation.

NOTE

1. Director of Public Prosecutions, March 1, 2014 (http://www.ppsc-sppc.gc.ca/eng/pub/fpsd-sfpg/fps-sfp/tpd/p6/ch03.html).

REFERENCES

Balfour, Gillian. 2008. "Falling Between the Cracks of Retributive and Restorative Justice: The Victimization and Punishment of Aboriginal Women." *Feminist Criminology*, 3, 2: 101–20.

___. 2013. "Do Law Reforms Matter? Exploring the Victimization-Criminalization Continuum in the Sentencing of Aboriginal Women in Canada." *International Review of Victimology*, 19, 1: 85–102.

Balfour, Gillian, and Elizabeth Comack (eds.). 2014. *Criminalizing Women*. Halifax and Winnipeg: Fernwood Publishing.

Balfour, Gillian, and Janice Du Mont. 2012. "Confronting Restorative Justice: Legal and Rape Narratives in Conditional Sentencing." In E. Sheehy (ed.), *Sexual Assault, Practice, Activism in a Post Jane Doe Era*. Ottawa: University of Ottawa Press.

Balfour, Gillian, Janice Du Mont, and Deborah White. 2017. "'To This Day She Continues to Struggle with the Terror Imposed upon Her': Rape Narratives in Victim Impact Statements." *Women & Criminal Justice*: 1–20. <http://dx.doi.org/10.1080/08974454.2017.1342744>.

Benedet, Janine. 2010. "The Sexual Assault of Intoxicated Women." *Canadian Journal of Women and the Law*, 22, 2: 435. <http://dx.doi.org/10.3138/cjwl.22.2.435>.

Blatchford, C. 2009. "What Are Little Girls Made Of These Days?" *Globe and Mail*, August 12.

Braithwaite, J. 2001. *Restorative Justice and Responsive Regulation*. Oxford: Oxford University Press.

Busby, K. 1999. "Not a Victim Until a Conviction Is Entered: Sexual Violence Prosecutions and Legal Truth." In E. Comack (ed.), *Locating law: Race/Class/Gender Connections*. Halifax, NS: Fernwood Publishing.

CAEFS (Canadian Association of Elizabeth Fry Societies). 2009. "Fact Sheet 2009." <http://www.elizabethfry.ca/eweek09/factsht.htm> (accessed August 15, 2009).

Cameron, A. 2006. "Stopping the Violence: Canadian Feminist Debates on Restorative Justice and Intimate Violence." *Theoretical Criminology*, 10, 1: 49–66.

Cheon, A., and C. Regehr. 2006. "Restorative Justice Models in Cases of Intimate Partner Violence: Reviewing the Evidence." *Victims and Offenders*, 1, 4: 369–394.

Coker, D. 2006. "Restorative Justice: Navajo Peacemaking and Domestic Violence." *Theoretical Criminology*, 10, 1: 67–85.

Comack, E. 2000. "Women and Crime." In R. Linden (ed.), *Criminology: A Canadian perspective*. Toronto, ON: Harcourt Brace.

Cunliffe, E., and A. Cameron. 2007. "Writing the Circle: Judicially Convened Sentencing Circles and the Textual Organization of Criminal Justice." *Canadian Journal of Women and the Law*, 19, 1: 1–35.

Daly, K. 1994. "Criminal Law and Justice System Practices as Racist, White, and Racialized." *Washington & Lee Law Review,* 51: 431.

Daly, K., and J. Stubbs. 2006. "Feminist Engagement with Restorative Justice." *Theoretical Criminology,* 10, 1: 9–28.

Doolittle, Robyn. 2017. "Unfounded: How Alcohol Complicated Sexual Assault Cases." *Globe and Mail,* March 3. <https://beta.theglobeandmail.com/news/investigations/unfounded-too-drunk-to-consent-how-alcohol-complicates-sex-assault-cases/article34338370/>.

Fine, Sean. 2017. "Believe the Victim Has No Place in Courts, Judge Says in Sexual Assault Ruling." *Globe and Mail,* August 9. <https://www.theglobeandmail.com/news/toronto/decision-expected-in-trial-of-three-toronto-officers-accused-of-sexual-assault/article35918734/>.

Firestone, S. 1970) *The Dialectic of Sex: The Case for Feminist Revolution.* New York: Morrow.

Gotell, Lise. 2010. "Canadian Sexual Assault Law: Neoliberalism and the Erosion of Feminist-Inspired Law Reform." In Clare McGlynn and Vanessa Munro (eds.), *Rethinking Rape Law: International And Comparative Perspectives.* London: Routledge.

Hewitt, P. 2009. "MR Likened to 'Fatal Attraction' Character." *Cnews,* July 15. <http://cnews.canoe.ca/CNEWS/Crime/2009/07/14/10125576-cp.html> (accessed September 29, 2009).

Hotton Mahony, Tina, Joana Jacob and Heather Hobson. 2017. "Women and the Criminal Justice System." Ottawa: Statistics Canada. <http://www.statcan.gc.ca/pub/89-503-x/2015001/article/14785-eng.htm> (accessed March 4, 2018).

Hudson, B. 2002. "Restorative Justice and Gendered Violence: Diversion or Effective Justice." *British Journal of Criminology,* 42: 616–34.

Johnson, Holly. 2012. "Limits of a Criminal Justice Response: Trends in Police and Court Processing of Sexual Assault." In E. Sheehy (ed.), *Sexual Assault, Practice, Activism in a Post Jane Doe Era.* Ottawa: University of Ottawa Press.

Kline, M. 1994. "The Colour of Law: Ideological Representations of First Nations in Legal Discourse." *Social and Legal Studies,* 3: 451–476.

Lacey, N. 1998. "Unspeakable Subjects: Impossible Rights: Sexuality, Integrity, and Criminal Law." *Canadian Journal of Law and Jurisprudence,* 11, 1: 47–68.

McGillivray, A., and B. Comaskey. 1999. *Black Eyes All the Time: Intimate Violence, Aboriginal Women and the Justice System.* Toronto, ON: University of Toronto Press.

Mehler-Paperny, Anna. 2017. "Canada's Jailhouse Secret: Legally Innocent Prisoners Are Dying." *Globe and Mail,* August 3. <https://www.theglobeandmail.com/news/national/canadas-jailhouse-secret-legally-innocent-prisoners-are-dying/article35871181/>.

Morris, A. 2002. "Critiquing the Critics: A Brief Response to Critics of Restorative Justice." *British Journal of Criminology,* 42: 596–615.

Naffine, N. 1990. *Law and the Sexes: Explorations in Feminist Jurisprudence.*

Sydney, Australia: Allen & Unwin.

Nahanee, T. 1994. "Sexual Assault of Inuit Females: A Comment on 'Cultural Bias.'" In J. Roberts and R.M. Mohr (eds.), *Confronting Sexual Assault: A Decade of Legal And Social Change*. Toronto, ON: University of Toronto Press.

Nightingale, M. 1991. "Judicial Attitudes and Differential Treatment: Native Women in Sexual Assault Cases." *Ottawa Law Review*, 23, 1: 71–86.

Razack, S. 1998. *Looking White People in the Eye: Gender, Race and Culture in Courtrooms and Classrooms*. Toronto, ON: University of Toronto Press.

___. 2000. "Gendered Racial Violence and Spatialized Justice: The Murder of Pamela George." *Canadian Journal of Law and Society*, 15, 2: 91–130.

Reitano, Julie. 2017. *Adult Correctional Statistics 2016/2016*. Ottawa: Statistics Canada.

Sapers, Howard. 2016. *Annual Report of the Office of the Correctional Investigator 2015–2016*. Ottawa: Correctional Investigator Canada.

Sheehy, Elizabeth A. 2012. *Sexual Assault in Canada: Law, Legal Practice and Women's Activism*. University of Ottawa Press/Les Presses de l'Université d'Ottawa.

Smart, C. 1989. *Feminism and the Power of Law*. London: Routledge.

___. 1992. "The Woman of Legal Discourse." *Social and Legal Studies*, 1: 29–44.

Snider, L. 1994. "Feminism, Punishment, and the Potential for Empowerment." *Canadian Journal of Law and Society*, 9, 1: 75–104.

___. 1998. "Understanding the Second Great Confinement." *Queen's Quarterly*, 105, 1: 29–46.

Sudbury, J. (ed.). 2005. *Global Lockdown: Race, Gender, and the Prison Industrial Complex*. New York: Routledge.

Walmsley, R. 2015. *World Female Imprisonment List: Women and Girls in Penal Institutions, Including Pre-Trial Detainees/Remand Prisoners,* third ed. World Prison Brief: Institute for Criminal Policy Research

Williams, Toni. 2009. "Intersectionality Analysis in the Sentencing of Aboriginal Women in Canada: What Difference Does It Make?" In E. Grabham, D. Cooper, J. Krishnadas, & D. Herman (eds.), *Intersectionality and Beyond: Law, Power, and the Politics of Location*. Abingdon: Routledge-Cavendish.

LEGAL CASES

R. v. Ewanchuk, [1999] 1 S.C.R. 330.

R. v. Gladue, [1999] 1. S.C.C. 688 (Q.L.).

R. v. Hamilton and Mason, 2003 Canadian Legal Information Institute 2862 (Ontario Superior Court), [191-198].

R. v. Ipeelee, 2012 SCC 13, [2012] 1 S.C.R. 433.

R. v. Seaboyer; R. v. Gayme, 1991 [1991] 2 Superior Court Report. 577.

7

RACIALIZED POLICING, SETTLER COLONIALISM AND JUSTICE

Michelle Stewart

OBJECTIVES

At the end of this chapter, you will be able to:

- Define racialized policing and settler colonialism

- Understand the links between racialized access to justice and settler colonialism

- Analyze historical and contemporary examples of racialized policing

- Identify how racialized policing is confronted — and the limits therein

In recent years, the Black Lives Matter movement has drawn attention to racialized policing practices in North America. The movement's founders describe Black Lives Matter as, "an ideological and political intervention in a world where Black lives are systematically and intentionally targeted for demise" (BLM n.d.); the guiding principles are an affirmation that "All Black Lives Matter" (BLM n.d.). The origin of the movement in the United States followed the death of 14-year-old Trayvon Martin at the hands of a "neighborhood watch" volunteer who was later acquitted of murder. The social unrest continued following a number of high-profile, police-involved killings, including the death of Mike Brown in 2014. Brown was killed by police and left in the streets for four hours; the charges laid on the officer did not lead to trial. Eric Garner's death at the hands of police was captured on video in which he repeatedly told police (and bystanders) "I can't breathe" as officers restrained him and he eventually lost consciousness and died. Again, no indictment in the case. Freddie Gray was seen being roughed up by police and later died after being subjected to a "rough ride" in which, during an eleven-minute police transport, Gray sustained mortal injuries such that his neck was effectively severed from his spine — the officers were later acquitted or had their charges dropped.

Civil unrest and protest were sustained during this time as protesters took to the streets with chants such as "Hands Up, Don't Shoot" and "Black Lives Matter" — the first to draw attention to the number of unarmed people that were being killed, the second to reinforce the racialized nature of these deaths. The movement includes drawing attention to the often less-discussed incidents of violence against Black women and transgender Black women. Matt Richardson notes that, while people appear to be "poised to notice violence against Black men, there are many other bodies that experience extreme violence and lethal force when encountering police … When will we put our time and energy into fighting for Black (trans)women?" (Richardson 2015: n.p).

The Black Lives Matter movement drew international attention. The scope and capacity of Black Lives Matter continues to grow with chapters across the United States and Canada. Black Lives Matter started as a Twitter hashtag and then grew into a sustained and transnational social movement — a movement mobilized in direct response to anti-Black police violence. For this reason, Black Lives Matter serves as a contemporary and well-known example of civil unrest and response to racialized policing, and the key intersecting issues this entails include racism, classism, sexism and heterosexism. However, racialized access and racialized encounters with the justice system are not unique to the United States.

Canada was thrust onto the international stage with a high-profile example of racialized policing in the early 2000s when inquiries and inquests were held into the deaths of several Indigenous people. One of these individuals was Neil Stonechild, a 17-year-old youth who froze to death in a field outside Saskatoon. He had been subject to what is called "the Starlight Tours." The Starlight Tours came to be known as a deadly police practice whereby police officers would drive Indigenous people to the outskirts of town or city, dropping them off, often in the dead of winter, to walk back. Sherene Razack (2015: 173) notes that having a popular descriptor of "Starlight Tours" "is testimony to the fact that it happened more than once." Given that the individuals who died were all Indigenous, this informal yet punitive practice appeared to be reserved exclusively for Indigenous peoples, thus raising the issue of the connections between racialized policing practices and settler colonialism.

This chapter focuses on one element of Canada's racialized policing by discussing the Starlight Tours and its ongoing legacy. In this context, racialized policing and systemic racism have a particular relationship to settler colonialism. By placing the issue of racialized policing within a broader context of settler colonialism, the chapter will demonstrate the need to think about the intersecting issues of racism and settler colonialism as it relates to justice. Given the fundamental nature of settler colonialism to what is Canada, broader systemic and structural issues must be changed in Canada to effectively address racialized policing. Nothing short of paradigm shifting change is required. Such deep change raises the question: do those in power have the capacity and willingness to make such a shift?

To better understand the substantive nature of this paradigm shift, let's return to the opening chapter and three framings of justice. Formal justice "seeks to treat similarly situated people similarly, or treat equals, equally ... In this way, formal justice embodies laws and rules of procedure (often court processes) aimed at achieving a fair trial (sometimes referred to as 'procedural justice'). Formal justice is also characterized by the concepts of just deserts, fairness and equality" (Chapter 1). However, when thinking about the justice system in a settler state, one is left to wonder how it is going to execute anything but further disparities. Specifically, formal justice is seeking to treat similar people similarly — Indigenous peoples in Canada are not treated similarly to non-Indigenous peoples. Period. Across all sectors there are disparities. Indigenous peoples are over-represented in the justice system and child welfare; Indigenous peoples experience higher rates of unemployment and lower rates of success in education; Indigenous peoples are most likely to experience food insecurity, housing overcrowding and violence (structural, lateral, sexual and physical). In the light of these facts, how could a justice system set up by a settler state execute anything less than what it is set out to do: subordinate Indigenous peoples through the same practices that are perpetuated outside the courts? When facing structural inequality in each sector, Indigenous peoples are not seen or treated as equals in Canada. Therefore, formal justice is not created or accessible by Indigenous peoples in its current configuration. Until there is redistributive justice we cannot and will not have a truly just system in Canada. Until then, we have a liberal idea of justice and liberal ideologies that are then executed within the justice system by particular justice actors — like police officers who have the right to use "legitimate force." Once again, who decides what is legitimate when the system itself is colonial in practice?

POLICING AND THE RIGHT TO USE FORCE

While it is generally taken for granted, we should ask, why do we have police? What is their particular role in society? Many believe that police maintain public order, plain and simple. But is it that simple? Political theorist Max Weber notes that the state has a unique set of powers within a territory. The state has a "monopoly of the legitimate use of physical force" and it is only the state that can endow institutions and individuals with the rights to use such force (Weber 2004: 34). Police agencies and officers are some of the institutions and individuals that are endowed with such rights. The agreement that only the state can hold such power, and thereby provide protection for citizens, is part of the broader social contract that Thomas Hobbes' spoke about a few centuries ago in *Leviathan*. Whether implicitly or explicitly, individuals give up (voluntarily or by force) a certain amount of freedom and agency in exchange for the safety of the state to protect them. Without such an exchange, Hobbes (2008: 78) famously noted, life is "solitary, poor, nasty, brutish, and short." And while this might seem like an antiquated way to understand the relationship that each of us has with the state in the twenty-first century — Hobbes was writing in the seventeenth century and Weber in the eighteenth and nineteenth centuries — we nevertheless find ourselves embroiled in this same dynamic. Specific freedoms have been surrendered to a state power that has the ultimate right to use legitimate force, and one such legitimate outlet is through police who are understood to maintain law and order or maintain the peace. And here we find ourselves in the early twenty-first century with the question of what type of law, order or peace is being maintained. For whom and at what cost?

The work of Michel Foucault (1977, 1991) is helpful to think about the ways in which we, as members of society, exchange our personal rights and freedoms for the security of the state, as well as the ways in which the rules and norms of the state permeate our individual behaviour. For example, the ways in which each of us perform our obedience to norms and rules so that we avoid detection or punishment by the state — we obey rules without having them explicitly explained to us. We are trained to accept that. David Schneider (1980) uses the example of a stoplight. Many of us, probably most of us, will stop at a stoplight because we are supposed to. Even when there is clearly no oncoming traffic, we will still stop and obey the law. There is no traffic so there is no threat of injury — but we will stop. There is not a police officer there, there is no direct threat of punishment — but we will stop. We stop because we have been conditioned — what Foucault calls "disciplined" — to adhere to the rules of the state and society even without the direct threat of the state. Yet, not every citizen experiences these rules and norms of the state in the same way. Thus, rules and expectations must be understood within broader contexts that necessarily include broader historical contexts and the ways in which power and race (for example) are determining factors.

RACIALIZED POLICING

Criminologist Elizabeth Comack, in her 2012 book, *Racialized Policing: Aboriginal Peoples' Encounters with Police*, delineates between individual acts of racism by police officers and the need for a broader, more systemic understanding of racialized practices. She argues:

> to fully appreciate the ways in which race and racism invade the practice of policing — in other words, to understand policing as *racialized* — we need to go beyond the individual or the interpersonal level and adopt a more macro or systemic perspective. While racial profiling and individual racism are significant issues and must receive attention, we need to broaden our gaze to include the ways in which race and racism play out in institutional practices and systemic processes. (Comack 2012: 15)

Racialized policing, then, is not about the individual police officer; it is not *just* about the individual moment of racial profiling (in which a racialized person is subject to particular practices associated with suspicion) resulting in being pulled over. Racialized policing is the term used to describe broader, system-wide practices. In this way, Comack points out, racialization can become part of formal and informal practices. When carried into the world of policing, however, there is also the matter of overall policing culture. Police can cultivate a shared set of traits and beliefs that can then result in particular practices and a concurrent code of silence as police officers understand that their job has particular privileges or privacies built in, but also that it is a brotherhood that should be protected in some regards. This culture must be accounted for as these informal and formal practices, if left unchecked or unchallenged, can become part of a broader repertoire of ideologies and actions with real-life impacts on racialized people and specifically people of colour. In Canada, racialized policing plays out in a particular way within the broader context(s) of colonialism, and specifically within the broader framework of settler colonialism.

SETTLER COLONIALISM

The release of the Truth and Reconciliation Commission's (TRC) Calls to Action (2015) drew direct attention to the ongoing impact of colonial practices and structural inequality in Canada. The need for reform in the justice system is most striking as the TRC dedicates seventeen of its Calls to Action to this area alone (the largest number of items in any subsection). Rather than framing these impacts to be the result of colonialism, understood to be something from the past, we need to understand how racialized practices in the justice system are emblematic of something called settler colonialism. Eric Wolfe (2006: 388) notes that with settler colonialism, the "invasion is a structure not an event" — the structure is part of a larger project to displace people. This is distinct from the notion of colonialism that is often characterized by one country invading another territory with the goal of extracting resources (people and materials), but not occupying that territory. As Woroniak and Camfield (2013: para. 8) explain:

> The main goal of settler colonialism … was to displace Indigenous peoples from their lands, break and bury the cultures that grew out of relationships with those lands, and, ultimately, eliminate Indigenous societies so that settlers could establish themselves.

The concept of settler colonialism focuses on the ongoing occupation and dispossession of Indigenous peoples and is distinct from colonialism as an invasion from an outside group. As Wolfe (1999) indicates, traditional notions of colonialism understand it as an event. The invasion occurs by an outside group with a homeland, and much of the attention is on the extraction of resources and labour. This is distinct from settler colonialism, in which the goal is to actively settle and displace. As Wolfe (1999) further indicates: settler colonialism is *not* an event but rather a structure — it is a structure for new relationships to be forged, relationships that are predicated on dispossession.

Dispossession is a central characteristic of settler colonialism because the occupying force actively displaces structures and organizations to have settlers take over these roles. In this way, the settling of Canada is a clear example, such that the lands were cleared (through violent dispossession) to make way for settlers to arrive. The lands were cleared through a range of state and non-state practices, including disease, warfare, residential schools and reserves. One could argue the land continues to be cleared by placing Indigenous children in foster care and Indigenous peoples in the justice system. In the Prairie provinces, for example, Indigenous peoples make up less than 6 percent of the overall population, but constitute upwards of 80 percent of the overall prison population as adults, and as children can comprise nearly 90 percent of the children in state "care." There are currently more children in state care than during the residential school program — and that cluster of children are understood to populate a pipeline that leads directly the justice system, as each experience of systemic violence and contact with agencies is a compounding risk factor for the justice system. The ultimate goal is for settlers to establish themselves — and continue to clear the plains.

Understood this way, racialized policing is part and parcel of settler colonialism as it reinforces and naturalizes structural inequalities. Sherene Razack (2015) argues that at the base of this inequality is an ideology that understands Indigenous bodies as "remnants" — as leftover people that are otherwise broken, diseased or withering and this serves to justify forms of physical, sexual and structural violence. Whereas physical and sexual violence might be more familiar terms, structural violence can appear more abstract. Structural violence refers to the forms of violence created and executed at the broader level — these are practices that are often systemic and, while they might not be formally coordinated, can result in practices that actively exclude, marginalize or punish particular groups of individuals (often based on race, class, gender/sexual orientation or religion). In his book, *Clearing the Plains,* James Daschuk (2013) demonstrates in stark terms the brutal and purposeful starvation, infection with disease and removal of Indigenous children and adults. However, it is a mistake is to think that colonialism ended with the closing of the residential schools. The TRC Calls to Action point to particular interventions that might remedy the situation (addressing structural inequality in a range of sectors including health, child welfare, justice and education), but in the absence of addressing the structural factors that underlie settler colonialism we are left with the calls for reform (changing sentencing practices versus changing the conditions that find Indigenous peoples over-represented in the CJS) to a system that is fundamentally flawed. Moreover, it is this system of structural inequality that served as the backdrop that allowed for there to be a political appetite to engage in the structural violence that is the Starlight Tours; it was not a matter of a few bad apples in the Saskatoon Police Service, as similar reports have been uncovered in other parts of Canada.

FREEZING DEATHS AND THE STONECHILD INQUIRY

On November 24, 1990 Neil Stonechild and Jason Roy were out playing cards and having a few drinks. The pair then left to visit Stonechild's exgirlfriend. They stopped at a local 7-Eleven on the way and were told to leave because they were causing a disturbance. Roy and Stonechild would soon part ways for the night when Stonechild struggled to recall the correct apartment number to visit his ex-girlfriend. When he correctly identified her apartment number, she wouldn't let him in. Saskatoon Police Service Officers Hartwig and Senger were dispatched to the scene just before midnight. The call indicated a drunk was to be removed; dispatch named Neil Stonechild and his age. At 12:17 a.m. the officers typed "GOA" in their mobile terminal to indicate the individual was gone on arrival. What happened that night would become the cause for an Inquiry as Jason Roy would later report that the police stopped him with Neil in the back of the car, bloodied and screaming that the police were going to kill him. That was the last that Jason saw of his friend Neil, who died of hypothermia before the night was over (Comack 2012; Lugosi 2011).

In the days that followed, Neil's family reported him missing to the police but their concerns were rejected. The family was told that Neil was likely hiding because he was unlawfully at large and in breach of his probation conditions (Lugosi 2011). Five days later, a city worker would find Neil lying face-down, frozen, in a field on the outskirts of the city wearing only one shoe (Comack 2012). He had strange marks on his face and wrists, which the family raised concerns about prior to the funeral (and after). Had Neil been beat up as it looked like he had a broken nose? Neil's brother thought the marks on his wrists looked like handcuff marks (Razack 2015). The police investigation into Neil's death was completed in three shifts and not rigorously; the responding coroner and investigating officer didn't secure the scene, including walking over the tracks in the snow, compromising the investigation (Lugosi 2011). It was concluded that Neil died walking from the convenience store on the way back to the youth facility from which he was at large (CBC 2005). The marks on his body were reported to be from his body settling into the frozen grass and impressions made by the frozen grass, snow and twigs.

It would be over a decade before the questions raised by Neil's family and friends would be formally addressed. The combination of many factors would result in an inquiry. The ongoing community pressure from individuals including: friend and witness Jason Roy; advocates and journalists that continued to raise questions about the circumstances of Neil's death and the injuries he appeared to sustain; and the revelation of the deaths of two more Indigenous men and the survival of another that would finally bring the Starlight Tours into full public view (Comack 2012). By 2000 it was clear that Neil was not the first or last person subjected to a Starlight Tour.

On January 29, 2000 the body of Rodney Naistus was found on the outskirts of Saskatoon. He was not wearing a t-shirt and had been seen earlier that day in downtown Saskatoon. On January 30, Darrell Night told a police officer that he had survived a similar incident, having been dropped off outside of town in only a light jacket and summer shoes on January 28. On February 3, 2000, Lawrence Wegner was found frozen outside town, in close proximity to where Naistus was found. Wegner was not wearing shoes. He had been seen just one day after Rodney was found and the same day that Darrell reported surviving such an incident. All of the men were Indigenous. The news of these and other stories quickly spread, leading to vigils, marches, news stories and public and political pressure to look into these suspicious deaths. Indigenous organizations reported receiving hundreds of calls about similar incidents (Comack 2012). In addition to these deaths of individuals outside of town, the bodies of Lloyd Dustyhorn and Darcy Dean Ironchild were also found in early 2000, shortly after they had been released from police custody (Green 2006).

In February 2000, two police officers (Dan Hatchen and Ken Munson) were suspended with pay after admitting they had picked up Night and dropped him outside town. An RCMP task force investigation was launched into Night's allegations; it concluded in March 2000. During this same time period the Federation of Sovereign Indigenous Nations (representing First Nations in Saskatchewan) launched its own investigation and started a Special Investigations Unit to address the volume of reports they had received (Razack 2015). In April, Hatchen and Munson were charged with unlawful confinement and assault (later convicted of unlawful confinement and sentenced to eight months, for which they served four). In May 2001, an inquiry into the death of Lloyd Dustyhorn was held, which concluded that he died of hypothermia and focused on the need for an emergency detox centre in the city. An inquiry that same year was held into the death of Naistus and the circumstances surrounding his death were left undetermined with recommendations focused on police policy and relations with the Indigenous community.

In early 2002, an inquiry was held into the death of Lawrence Wegner and was similarly unable to establish the circumstances surrounding his death. The following year, in February 2003, Justice Minister Eric Cline called for a public inquiry into Neil Stonechild's death. In 2004, then Deputy Chief of Police Dan Wiks was put on leave and eventually charged under the Police Act (which governs police actions in the province) for telling the media that he didn't believe police were involved in Stonechild's death, despite having seen the summary of the RCMP investigation that explicitly indicated this possibility (CBC 2005). A public inquiry would go beyond the framework of a coroner's inquest, as an inquest is focused on the factors up to the death with a goal of preventing a similar death in the future. A public inquiry, however, looks at the cause of death and investigation.

During the Stonechild Inquiry, Justice David Wright heard over sixty-three witnessed and saw 197 exhibits over the course of forty-three days, resulting in over 8,500 pages of transcripts. The *Report of the Commission of Inquiry into Matters Relating to the Death of Neil Stonechild* gave thirteen recommendations. During the course of the Inquiry, things that looked suspicious about the death of Neil Stonechild were investigated, including the gash on Neil's face, the marks on his wrist and the last individuals who were in contact with him. Experts would wrestle with the forensic evidence and the Commissioner (Wright 2004) would later release the following facts:

- Constables Larry Hartwig and Bradely Senger took Neil Stonechild into custody.
- Neil Stonechild froze to death in a field.
- Neil Stonechild's injuries were likely the result of handcuffs.
- The conditions surrounding Neil Stonechild's death were suspicious.
- The principal investigator, Morality Sergeant Keith Jarvis, did a poor job investigating the case, including not recording Jason Roy's statements.
- The Saskatoon Police Service was not responsive to questions raised about this death – including police chiefs and others in management positions.

In November 2004, within weeks of the release of the Commissioner's report, Hartwig and Senger were fired from the Saskatoon Police Service. Both professed they did not have contact with Stonechild, despite the evidence presented. In the end, the officers were removed from duty but "no criminal charges were ever laid; the gathering of factual evidence 14 years after the fact was impossible" (Poonwassie 2006: 30). Moreover, the findings of the Stonechild Inquiry did not focus explicitly on the role of systemic racism. Instead, the recommendations were largely administrative: procedures associated to complaints, additional recommendations to increase Indigenous recruitment, improvements to police-community relations and sensitivity training.

During the course of the Stonechild Inquiry, the Saskatoon Police

Service (SPS) reported that all police cruisers would be equipped with Global Positioning System (GPS) — to track movements —and the SPS also admitted to the flaws in the investigation into Stonechild's death, the police chief apologizing to Neil's mother (Radford 2015). However, the overall conditions that allowed for the Starlight Tours to occur and the ways in which the Starlight Tours are narrated continue to demonstrate the ways in which racialized policing practices permeate the landscape but are not named as such. The Starlight Tours were understood to be a specific "moment" or time period in policing, the result of a few bad apples (meaning the issue was isolated to a few people acting inappropriately), and could be addressed with administrative changes. Writing about the Stonechild Inquiry, Lugosi (2011: 311) notes, "ignoring power relations allows systemic violence to continue." These power relations, some might say, would include the fact that police have guns and the right to use force where members of the public do not. Taken further, settler states invoke particular forms of structural violence each day and police expanded that violence through a punitive practice that proved deadly. Poonwassie (2006) argues that as Neil's family had their worst fears confirmed during the Inquiry — their son was left to freeze to death in a field after likely being beaten by two police officers — they and the larger Indigenous community could not turn to the police for protection because they were actually being victimized by them:

> The wider Aboriginal community grieved not only the tragic loss of Neil's life but also the systemic hatred and racism aimed at its people, the loss of personal safety, and loss of trust in Canadian institutions and governments, again. (Poonwassie 2006: 30)

TELLING AND RETELLING THE TALE

The Starlight Tours resulted in the freezing deaths of at least three people, including Neil Stonechild. Initially, his death was quickly ruled non-suspicious. It would take fourteen years for his death to be reconsidered, leading to an inquiry. That inquiry came after the frozen bodies of two other Indigenous men were found and a third Indigenous man survived – similarly with limited clothing, on the outskirts of town. And while a number of officers faced sanction surrounding these incidents, and formal apologies were eventually offered, much effort had and continues to go into erasing this part of Canada's policing story.

In her analysis of the inquiries and the Starlight Tours, Sherene Razack (2014: 54) notes that the "Aboriginal body is a body that cannot be murdered." She means that there are systemic processes and ideologies about the lives of Indigenous peoples that imply that these are bodies that are so undervalued and disvalued that punishment surrounds their deaths — that their deaths cannot be murders. The freezing deaths and the Starlight Tours are emblematic of an ongoing process of settler colonialism: clearing the plains. During the time of the inquiries, police would often comment that they were practising PITT which stands for "Police-Initiated Transjurisdictional Transport of Troublesome Persons" (Razack 2015). PITT was rolled into a discussion about the stresses of doing police work (police stress was raised as a factor in the Stonechild Inquiry) and the need to geographically displace those things that are out of order. Meaning that the "things" that seem out of order, or out of place, in a settler state are Indigenous bodies as they are remnants or remainders of those who were first there.

Returning to understanding the role of the state — monopoly on the use of force in a territory — we are delivered a police force that is given the right to use force to maintain order. PITT is one strategy to address disorder. In so doing, people are transformed into disordered things that can simply be moved as a management strategy. In the case of the Starlight Tours, disordered things are people; in this instance and, in settler-colonial societies, one particular type of person: Indigenous. It was this logic that allowed for a group of police officers to think it acceptable to dump Indigenous people out in the dead of winter as a punishment premised on an assumption that these bodies are first and foremost disordered and therefore out of place in the city. Indigenous peoples are understood to be unruly bodies that do not fit in the city and therefore can be moved, like objects, from one place to another without consequence — their mere presence is understood to be out of order and therefore actions made against these unruly bodies are justified. For decades police did just that, they undertook these actions with impunity, without concern or worry of punishment. There were mechanisms in place that told them this was acceptable and a system in place to protect them when they undertook these actions. The fact that the Starlight Tours went on for years is evidence that it was not simply a few bad police officers, but rather there was an overarching ideology that had police officers think this activity (of punishment in the snow itself) was acceptable, with built-in protections within this culture of policing itself.

This is clear in the language that is deployed to tell of the deaths of Neil Stonechild, Rodney Naistus and Lawrence Wegner – the language of "freezing deaths" and "Starlight Tours," not the language of homicide or murder. Nicole Lugosi (2011: 302) notes the importance of how we discuss these events because "hearing and telling certain stories repeatedly, normalizes the narratives … It is important because how an issue is conceptualized directly determines policies and actions taken."

As recently as 2016, a University of British Columbia student realized that someone erased all references to the Starlight Tours from the SPS's Wikipedia page. Wikipedia is a crowd-sourced collection of information and is organized in such a way that every entry (including deletions) are registered. The IP address of the user that undertook the edit is recorded. The student looked at the IP address and realized it originated from a computer at the SPS. The SPS could not isolate who was using that particular computer during the time in question and instead noted that they implemented all of the recommendations from the Stonechild Inquiry (Zakreski 2016). The student's discovery of these Wikipedia edits became a national news story.

The Wikipedia incident served as but one of many attempts to rewrite the history of the Starlight Tours. Other examples include videos or books that seek to exonerate or uphold the virtuous nature of the officers involved (see, for example, McLean 2015). For some, there is a commitment to defend the officers as they don't believe a police officer who is endowed with that exclusive right to use force would engage in such repulsive behaviours. Others might simply wish to make the Starlight Tours part of a closed chapter in the history books, and still others might believe that these individuals deserved to be dropped off and punished for being a nuisance, for being drunk and for being Indigenous. The mixture of these reasonings makes the rewriting of this history that much more damaging because it negates the broader structural issues that surround the Starlight Tours. Accordingly, it is important to see the Starlight Tours as emblematic of broader structural issues and not simply an isolated incident involving a few police officers.

From dropping off of individuals and the lack of investigation, to the ongoing attempts to erase the story, the Starlight Tours are about systemic issues. For example, if one was to frame the deaths as a product of individual police officers who were targeting Indigenous peoples because of an alleged link between race and criminality, then one neglects to think of these acts as part of a broader story about systemic racism. Racialized policing occurs beyond the acts of specific officers as they are part of broader contexts in which police reproduce order in society (Comack 2012). In Canada, that means reproducing order in the settler state as Indigenous lives continue to be devalued and stories of violence erased. The compounding effect of these racialized policing practices and ongoing systemic violence have massive implications about who the justice system serves and which lives matter. Cao (2014: 503), drawing on Comack (2012), notes that, while various incidents of racism can appear to be unrelated, taken together, they "have broad ramifications as to how race and racism are embedded in everyday experiences and institutional practices and how they are implicated in our society's prevailing patterns of marginalization and social exclusion." These are patterns that are embedded in longer histories between Indigenous peoples and the state.

JUSTICE CANNOT BE DONE IN SETTLER COLONIALISM

There continues to be uneven access to justice in our society and that is a product of settler colonialism that will continue to displace people's stories and bodies. The case of Colten Boushie in 2016 is but the most recent case in which the police are accused of wrongdoing in handling the death of an Indigenous person. In this example, Boushie was killed on a rural property and, as the victim of a violent death (he was shot at close range), the police nevertheless left his body out in the hot August day for hours. While at his mother's home for the notification of kin, police officers are alleged to have treated the family as suspects, ransacking the home and asking the family about whether they had been drinking. This is not the "normal" expectation one should have when being notified about the death of a loved one: that this loved one will be left out in the heat all day, that when the police come to your home they will treat *you* with suspicion. This is not unique in the justice system in Canada. This is but one of many cases in Canada. While the opening chapter of this book discussed three different formulations of justice as formal, substantive and ethical practice, we are left with a larger concern: what if none of these frameworks is very satisfactory?

Formal justice is mobilized through a presumptions about just deserts and fairness: you get what you deserve. If you are doing good things, you will be rewarded. If you are doing bad things, you are punished. But in a settler state, the systems are created to actively disadvantage Indigenous peoples and the individuals that manage these systems (for example, health care, social services, justice and education) are often themselves settlers that are not aware of the structural advantages they have. These advantages can serve to mobilize the core concepts in formal justice to justify ever-increasing punitive practices that contribute the skyrocketing rates of overrepresentation in the child welfare and court systems. These rates allow workers and the general public to naturalize, not challenge this phenomena. Arguably, substantive justice gets us closer to equity if we take seriously the immediate and dire need for redistributive justice — but this demands a reckoning, not reconciliation, when thinking about the current state of affairs in Canada. This is a country with unceded territory (meaning Indigenous peoples did not sign treaties) and treaties that have not been honoured in their original spirit and intent; a country where upwards of 80 to 90 percent of children in state care are Indigenous; a country in which many reserves are living under sustained (years-long) boil-water advisories; a country in which the leading cause of death for an Indigenous youth is suicide. Redistribution would mean the tables turn and the "victor" (of colonialism) does not prevail but is actually called into account — dispossession is not permanent and there are consequences for the injustices that have been committed. In the practical sense, this means that money is exchanged explicitly and new systems are developed to address inequality. But this process, similarly to ethical practice, requires that those who hold power ultimately are in a place to "decide" if the status quo must be disrupted. We should expect that a system that asks those in power to reconsider and destabilize their power is likely a system that will not change. This is the broader structural change that is needed but is not likely in our immediate future. In the interim, we are left with the everyday acts of violence and structural inequality that do or do not directly effect us.

How any one of us understands our relationship to the police and the rights or trust you afford the police is a product of not only your own background but also the privilege (or lack of it) you have in society. It is little wonder that Indigenous peoples have low levels of confidence in the justice system. It is precisely because of practices like the Starlight Tours.

Looking at the issues surrounding the Starlight Tours raises questions about the fairness of the CJS and illustrates the limitations of expectations of fairness or of a just justice system. The ways in which the Starlight Tours are being imagined and reimagined underscores the need to re-tell and re-affirm the story. Not doing so condones the notion that these lives were disposable. The role of settler colonialism cannot be erased from these stories. The broader context within which these deaths occurred was one in which Indigenous lives were devalued. It is one in which Indigenous peoples are seen to be remnants, living lives that are both devalued and seen to be out of place, a nuisance to be removed. Settler colonialism results in Indigenous bodies continuing to be moved out of the cities and into frozen fields, out of the homes and into foster care and prisons. The death of Neil Stonechild is as an entry point to better understanding how racialized policing is part of a much larger story of settler colonialism in Canada. It is a tale about a state apparatus and police force that is understood to be delivering different forms of justice to different groups of people.

DISCUSSION QUESTIONS

1. How did the police officers justify their actions and how do these justifications relate to broader concepts about settler colonialism?
2. The Starlight Tours are emblematic of structural racism — not isolated and individual acts of racism. What are some of the ways in which broader structural issues were revealed through the course of the investigation and inquest?
3. How a story is told matters. What are some of the ways the stories of the Starlight Tours are being re-narrated and what is troubling about the retelling of history?

GLOSSARY

Racialized policing: The outcome of practices that find people of colour experiencing different forms of police scrutiny.

Settler colonialism: A conceptual framework and classification of a particular form of colonialism that is about the ongoing occupation of a territory and the dispossession of Indigenous peoples.

Starlight Tours: Both a practice and an outcome of racialized policing practices. In Saskatoon, a number of Indigenous people were left on the outskirts of the city by local police during freezing weather. The activity of dumping people in freezing weather was later formally investigated during a public inquiry into the death of Neil Stonechild.

Structural inequality: An outcome of system-wide practices (for example, across multiple forms of government) in which people of colour and other racialized people or marginalized groups experience uneven access to services or experience uneven access to making decisions and/or otherwise have their rights reduced due to biases against them that are based on perceived differences and hierarchies therein (for example, based on gender, sexuality or race).

Systemic racism: Both an outcome and active process by which racist ideas and practices move between different systems and institutions. These ideas and practices are part of broader ideologies that permeate them at both the individual and system-wide levels, which can serve to further naturalize inequalities by grounding them in individual and systemic practices.

REFERENCES

BLM (Black Lives Matter). 2017. "Black Lives Matter Guiding Principles." <http://blacklivesmatter.com/guiding-principles/>.

Cao, L. 2014. "Aboriginal People and Confidence in the Police." *Canadian Journal of Criminology and Criminal Justice*, 56, 5: 499–526.

CBC (Canadian Broadcasting Corporation). 2005. *Indepth: Neil Stonechild, Neil Stonechild: Timeline*. Nov. 3. <http://www.cbc.ca/news2/background/stonechild/timeline.html>.

Comack, E. 2012. *Racialized Policing: Aboriginal People's Encounters with the Police*. Halifax, NS: Fernwood Publishing.

Daschuk, J. 2013. *Clearing the Plains: Disease, Politics of Starvation, and the Loss of Aboriginal Life*. Regina, SK: University of Regina Press.

Foucault, M. 1977 [1975]. *Discipline and Punish* (Alan Sheridan, trans.). New York: Vintage.

___. 1991. "Governmentality." In G. Burchell, C. Gordon, P. Miller (eds.), *The Foucault Effect: Studies in Governmentality*. Chicago, IL: University of Chicago Press.

Gill, J. 2014. "Permissibility of Colour and Racial Profiling." *Western Journal of Legal Studies*, 5, 3: 1–17.

Green, J. 2006. "From Stonechild to Social Cohesion: Anti-Racist Challenges for Saskatchewan." *Canadian Journal of Political Science/Revue canadienne de science politique*, 39, 3: 507–527.

Hobbes, T. 2008. *Leviathan: Or the Matter, Forme, and Power of Common-Wealth*

Ecclesiastical and Civil. New York: Touchstone.

Lugosi, N.V. 2011. "Truth-Telling and Legal Discourse: A Critical Analysis of the Neil Stonechild Inquiry." *Canadian Journal of Political Science/Revue canadienne de science politique,* 44, 2: 299–315.

McLean, C. 2015. *When Police Become Prey: The Cold Hard Facts of Neil Stonechild's Freezing Death.* Calgary, AB: Hummingbird Press.

Poonwassie, A. 2006. "Grief and Trauma in Aboriginal Communities in Canada." *International Journal of Health Promotion and Education,* 44, 1: 29–33.

Radford, E. 2015. "Starlight Tours—A Timeline." *Saskatoon Star Phoenix,* Jan 1. <http://www.thestarphoenix.com/starlight+tours+timeline/10311264/story.html>.

Razack, S. 2014. "It Happened More Than Once: Freezing Deaths in Saskatchewan." *Canadian Journal of Women and the Law,* 26, 1: 51–80.

____. 2015. *Dying from Improvement: Inquirys and Inquiries into Indigenous Deaths in Custody.* Toronto, ON: University of Toronto Press.

Richardson, M. 2015. "Killed Outright or Left to Die: Black (Trans)Women and the Police State." <https://culanth.org/fieldsights/697-killed-outright-or-left-to-die-black-trans-women-and-the-police-state>.

Schneider, D.M. 1980. *American Kinship: A Cultural Account.* Chicago, IL: University of Chicago Press.

Truth and Reconciliation Commission of Canada. 2015. *Honouring the Truth, Reconciling for the Future: Summary of the Final Report of the Truth and Reconciliation Commission of Canada.* <http://www.trc.ca/websites/trcinstitution/ File/2015/Exec_Summary_2015_06_25_web_o. pdf>.

Weber, M. 2004. *The Vocation Lectures: Science as a Vocation, Politics as a Vocation.* Indianapolis, IN: Hackett.

Wolfe, E. 2006. "Settler Colonialism and the Elimination of the Native." *Journal of Genocide Research,* 8, 4: 387–409.

Woroniak, M., and D. Camfield. 2013. "First Nations' Rights: Confronting Colonialism in Canada." Global Research: Centre for Research on Globalization. <http://www.globalresearch.ca/first-nations-rights-confronting-colonialism-in-canada/5321197>.

Wright, D.H. 2004. *Report of the Commission of Inquiry into Matters Relating to the Death of Neil Stonechild.* Saskatoon, SK: Government of Saskatchewan.

Zakreski, D. 2016. "Saskatoon Police Removed 'Starlight Tours' Section from Wikipedia, Student Says." CBC News, March 31. <http://www.cbc.ca/news/canada/saskatoon/saskatoon-police-starlight-tours-wikipedia-delete-1.3512586>.

8

GENDER, SEXUALITY AND JUSTICE

James McNinch

OBJECTIVES

At the end of this chapter, you will be able to:

- Describe and give examples of "contested space" where a sense of justice is in dispute

- Explain what standpoint theory is

- Distinguish between trans-gender and cis-gender and between heterosexual and homosexual orientation

- Describe what pre-contact gender and sexual fluidity meant to Indigenous peoples around the world

- Describe how world religions historically entrenched "compulsory heterosexuality" and what that means

- Give an example of "co-erced conformity" as it relates to "compulsory heterosexuality"

Various definitions of social justice include assumptions about "natural" law, which is that all individuals are entitled to be treated with dignity and respect. If everyone is inherently "equal," what does this equality look like in the everyday? How do the struggles of marginalized groups in society help us to better understand the difference between injustice and justice? The struggles of the LGBTTQ2 communities and the challenges gender and sexually diverse individuals have faced and continue to face are an important part of understanding and achieving equity and justice. This is a struggle for basic human rights.

There are several terms and theories that are helpful in framing this discussion. The first is "contested space." Both public spaces, such as schools, and private spaces, such as homes, can be sites of debate about what is right and fair and for whom. Philosopher Hannah Arendt has argued that how we relate to one another in public spaces determines our humanity. She used the metaphor of the table. As individuals we can be brought together around a table and yet as we sit across from one another we are still separate, private people in a public space, both con-nected and separate at the same time (Thuma 2011). "Imagination is the prerequisite to understanding," she wrote in her teaching notes in 1955. We "should imagine how the world looks from the different points of view where these people are located. For that purpose, it is not sufficient to name these points of view in an abstract way: 'the unknown soldier', 'the revolutionary', 'the resister', 'the scientist'. It is necessary to get to know their world to be able to look at it as if one would look at it with one's own eyes" (Arendt 1955: 27).

Arendt is not just talking about empathy or walking in some else's shoes. She foresees the development of "standpoint theory," which essentially means that we each view the world from our own perspective, literally and figuratively, from where we stand. From where you stand you may see a six; but from my perspective it is a nine. Appreciating differences created by different stances also suggests just how important context is to understanding a sense of justice. As a middle-aged, white, gay, bourgeois Canadian, when I holiday in Puerto Vallarta, Mexico my sense of real-ity is quite different from the young, straight, Mexican men who trudge through the sand carrying big trays of fruity alcoholic beverages for the likes of me and other gay men from around the world. We share the same space but our standpoints — our backgrounds and upbringing — have shaped our identities in profoundly different ways. When we focus on such differences, particularly as it relates to privilege and power, we are dealing in "identity politics." When one's personal identity is built (or others build it for you) based on cultural, ethnic, gender, racial, religious or social interests, those are characteristics of a group identity. So, being a middle-aged, white, gay, middle-class Canadian guy is a construct of both an individual and a group identity.

As a result, then, an understanding of justice or fighting against injustice can be shaped by our identities. A lesbian Pakistani graduate student's identity politics might be quite different from mine given that homosexuality is against the law in her home country and our experience of our sexual orientation and our gender would be quite different. In other words, from each of our standpoints and identity we can understand "interlocking systems of domination or a matrix of oppression differently" (Collins 1990: 3). To simplify, oppression is the result of the domination of one group over another group because of their privilege and power.

The term "queer" has been re-appropriated. In 2004 I wanted to publish a book entitled *Education and Social Justice for Queer Youth*. The editor, a gay man, said that this title would confuse and alienate potential readers. We ended up using the phrase "Gay and Lesbian Youth," but this was not as satisfying because it wasn't very inclusive. Once a slur, "queer" is now reclaimed as an umbrella term under which gender and sexual minority individuals define themselves. This has included the alphabet of labels including lesbian, gay, bisexual, two-spirit, trans-gender and questioning (LGBTTQ2), but also words that explore gender and sexuality beyond binaries, such as androgynous, bi-gender, inter-sex, non-binary and polyamorous.

Gender is the construction of an identity in terms of degrees of maleness or femaleness; one's sex refers to the reproductive organs and secondary sex characteristics one has. When Shania Twain sings "I feel like a woman," she is referring to her gender. When this feeling aligns with corresponding female body parts, then we refer to that person as "cis-gender." If the feeling of being male or female doesn't align with the body parts one is born with, that person may self-identify as transgender. As you can see, gender is not linked necessarily to sexual orientation.

For gender and sexually diverse (GSD) people, there are many sites of struggle — contested spaces where the fights against injustice have been particularly intense. I have used these sites of struggle to organize this chapter to help the reader appreciate the complexity of social justice as it relates to GSD issues. The reader will find examples of formal justice, substantive justice and ethical practice across these contested spaces. Justice is not just about the law or human rights; it is about history, values, beliefs and education; it is about how and why society changes. These sites include: 1) the historical struggle for same-sex rights in Canada; 2) transgendered Canada; 3) Two-Spirit Canada; 4) sexuality and sexual health; 5) global struggles; 6) queering Christianity; 7) secular society; 8) queer educators; and 9) queer kids. This chapter will argue that social justice across this diverse terrain includes not only the right to self-expression but also the right to challenge and interrogate the status quo.

SAME-SEX RIGHTS IN CANADA

In 1965, same-sex relations were against the law in Canada and regarded as a form of criminal activity. Generally, homosexuality was seen in society as a perversion. Everett Klippert, a mechanic originally from Kindersley, Saskatchewan and a Catholic man who does not believe in lying, readily acknowledged to police that he is gay, has had sex with many men over a twenty-four-year period and is unlikely to change. In 1967, following a psychological assessment that labelled him "incurably homosexual," Klippert was sent to prison indefinitely as a "dangerous sex offender." The sentence was upheld by the Supreme Court of Canada that same year. He was the last person in Canada to be imprisoned for having consensual sex with a same-sex partner.

An MP brought Klippert's case to the attention of Parliament, calling for then Justice Minister Pierre Trudeau to amend the Criminal Code by decriminalizing homosexuality. Shortly after, Trudeau tabled his landmark omnibus bill, C-150, an act that would see the decriminalization of homosexual acts between two consenting adults over 21 years old. It would be two more years before that bill would become law and for Everett Klippert to be released from prison (Wiart 2016). Discussing the amendments, Trudeau as Prime Minister said:

> I feel that it has knocked down a lot of totems and overridden a lot in terms of taboos ... It's bringing the laws of the land up to contemporary society I think. Take this thing on homosexuality. I think the view we take here is that there's no place for the

state in the bedrooms of the nation. I think that what's done in private between adults doesn't concern the Criminal Code. When it becomes public this is a different matter, or when it relates to minors this is a different matter. (CBC News 2015)

You can hear how, in 1969, homosexuality, while decriminalized, was still regarded as a private matter, but still very much a controversial and contested subject. It would take three decades of advocacy for justice and equality for LGBTTQ2 individuals to achieve significant legislative and social milestones. These included:

1979: The Canadian Human Rights Commission recommends in its annual report that "sexual orientation" be added to the list of prohibited discriminations in the Canadian Human Rights Act.

1992: The federal court lifts the country's ban on homosexuals in the military, allowing gays and lesbians to serve in the armed forces.

1996: The federal government passes Bill C-33, which adds "sexual orientation" to the Canadian Human Rights Act following court challenges (see Egan 1995) about pension rights for same-sex couples.

1999: The Supreme Court of Canada rules same-sex couples should have the same benefits and obligations as opposite-sex common-law couples and equal access to benefits from social programs to which they contribute. (Hurley 2007)

It is important to understand that these changes did not just "happen." It took individuals and groups such as Parents and Family and Friends of Lesbians and Gays (PFLAG) and Equality for Gays and Lesbians Everywhere (EGALE) ready to stand up for their sense of justice and to challenge existing laws and practices, incrementally and persistently, often at great cost both financially and emotionally. "Gay liberation" as this social movement was then called in the 1970s took its toll on individuals and families. "Coming out of the closet" as a queer person meant learning to speak again in a new language and a new context determined by lived reality (Eribon 2004: 28). Being openly or publicly gay is quite different from hiding your sexual orientation behind a presumed veneer of heterosexuality. Gay ghettos in Montreal and Toronto and Vancouver became sites of refuge for LGBTTQ2 individuals from small towns across Canada. Over the next three decades, gay and lesbian identities were confirmed in the social world: gay sports leagues, gay choirs, gay pride parades, summer camp for queer kids, gay Olympics and, eventually in 2005, gay marriage.

For many activists in the LGBTTQ2 communities, the fight for equality culminated in provisions for same-sex marriage in Canada. In July 2005 the Liberals' controversial Bill C-38, the Law on Civil Marriage, passed a final reading in the House of Commons. It then passed the Senate and received royal assent and became the law of the land; Canada became the fourth country, after the Netherlands, Belgium and Spain, to officially recognize same-sex marriage.

A decade later, Prime Minister Justin Trudeau happily marched in gay pride parades across Canada. Carrying the pink- and blue-striped flag of the trans community in Montreal in August 2017, he was accompanied by Ireland's openly gay prime minister and his boyfriend. Meanwhile, Trudeau's government faced class-action lawsuits from members of the LGBTTQ2 community purged from military and civil service jobs in the 1960s, 70s and 80s. Activists in Canada accused the current government of dragging its heels by proposing yet another "study" of sexual minorities instead of acting on their election promises. As *Globe and Mail* columnist John Ibbitson (2017b) put it, "Exonerating those convicted of being gay needs no study." The infamous "fruit machine" was a homosexuality detection system commissioned by the Canadian government during the Cold War to cull LGBTTQ2 people out of the public service and military who were deemed to be security threats because of their "secret" sex lives. Monitoring the pupil size of candidates as they were shown same-sex pornography was designed to detect "fruits," that is, men and women attracted to individuals of the same sex (Aske and Pritchard 2016). The testimony of individuals who were forced to leave their positions, *after* and despite the decriminalization of homosexuality in 1969, vividly demonstrates that policy and practice can be two different things completely and that a just law in itself does not ensure social justice (Ibbitson and LeBlanc 2016; EGALE 2016).

Trudeau formally apologized in the House of Commons on November 28, 2017: "It is our collective shame that you were so mistreated. And it is our collective shame that this apology took so long — many who suffered are no longer alive to hear these words. And for that, we are truly sorry"

(Harris 2017). The apology was accompanied by negotiated financial compensation through a class-action suit filed on behalf of individuals who were dismissed from their jobs in the civil service or were medically discharged from the armed forces because of their orientation or were even sent to military prison when found in a same-sex relationship (Ibbitson 2017a).

In the world of identity politics, apologies for past injustices are not uncommon in Canada. Historically marginalized racial, ethnic and religious groups call, like Indigenous peoples of Canada, for "truth and reconciliation" not to change the past, but to come to terms with the consequences of that past on the present and the future. Like Canada, Germany, Britain and New Zealand are three countries that have offered apologies and pardons to those criminalized in the past for being queer. We can understand such redress as a form of social justice if we acknowledge that "criminal law has been, and continues to be, a cornerstone of oppression" (EGALE 2016: 2).

TRANSGENDER CANADA

This brief survey above has taken us quickly through fifty years of identity politics as it relates to sexual orientation and same-sex rights. The fight of feminists for women's rights and the civil rights and Black Power movements in the United States paved the way for same-sex rights, which in turn has opened the door for the transgender community to "come out." Today, the struggle focuses on the rights of gender diverse individuals, those who call themselves gender-fluid, transgender, non-gender or gender-queer. To understand the struggle for justice and equality of such individuals, one must understand the continuums for gender identities, gender expressions, sexual identity assigned at birth and physical and emotional attractions. It is estimated that for about 1 percent of the population, physical sexual characteristics do not align with gender identity. That means there are about 350,000 transgender individuals living in Canada. Transsexual celebrities such as Caitlyn Jenner, Laverne Cox, and Chaz Bono who have dramatically changed their gender and sexual identities with hormones and surgery have brought widespread publicity to transgender issues. Facebook, university application forms, and online surveys have expanded their gender nomenclature beyond male and female to include "other," "transgender," and "a-gender"; "cis-gender" is common now as a description of someone who is not transgender. In 2017 the federal government approved "gender category X" on passports for those individuals who do not identify as "M or F." As a marker of identity, it was once important to differentiate gender, since males could vote and own property when females could not. It is fair to say that the gender binary of male and female is diminishing in our society as a marker of identity and, for the transgender community, that in itself is a form of social justice.

The stand-up comedy circuit has many transgender comedians making light of their reality. In an interview, transgender comedian Ian Harvie commented:

> I remember thinking had I ever met a trans person when I was a kid, I might have known sooner who I was. It's really hard to understand who you are when you've never seen yourself in somebody else. I think so many people have been trying to scratch the surface of who they are and then when they see someone that they identify with, they're like "Oh my god! That's me!" (Hatchett 2016)

Supporting the visibility and equality of transgender individuals has become part of policy and practice of many school boards across the country. It is about more than just providing gender-neutral washrooms for those who self-identify as transgender. It is about understanding that coming out may be a choice but being transgender is not a choice. Thanks to transgender activism and education, as a society our understanding of gender is more sophisticated; we understand that gender is complex, performative and psychological as well as biological and not a simple binary of male and female (Frankel 2017). This is reflected in the replacement of the term "gender-identity disorder" with "gender dysphoria" in the fifth edition (2013) of the *Diagnostic and Statistical Manual of Mental Disorders*. A disorder implies that something isn't "right" (not in proper order and therefore wrong); dysphoria describes an individual's unease and anxiety caused, in this case, by the disjunct between gender and biology. (In comparison, homosexuality as a "disorder" was removed from the manual in 1973).

The January 2017 edition of the *National Geographic* magazine devoted its entire issue to the world-wide phenomena they dubbed "the Gender

Revolution." The magazine cover featured a 9-year-old transgender girl, Avery, who has self-identified as female since she was 5 years old and is quoted as saying, "The best thing about being a girl is now I don't have to pretend to be a boy." One of the editors takes note of "evolving notions about what it means to be a woman or a man and the meanings of transgender, cisgender, gender nonconforming, genderqueer, a-gender, or any of the more than 50 terms Facebook offers users for their profiles. At the same time, scientists are uncovering new complexities in the biological understanding of sex" (Goldberg 2017).

In May 2016, the Trudeau Government introduced Bill C-16, that would guarantee legal and human rights protection to transgender people across Canada, casting it as the latest in human rights advancements. It moved to the Senate in November 2016 where it received its second reading. Canada's poet laureate, George Elliot Clarke, wrote a short poem for the occasion: "*Male* is partly *female,* because *female*/Carries *male.* To whit, Gender's not a jail" (Gee 2016). Again, this has come after many years of advocacy and activism by members of the trans and queer communities (Mas 2016).

Of course, transgender issues are not without controversy. Many long-time subscribers to *National Geographic* cancelled their subscriptions "in a fury" after the Gender Revolution edition (Goldberg 2017). A University of Toronto psychology professor has defended his right to use only gender-specific pronouns such as "he" and "she" as a hallmark of free speech. His detractors say his refusal to use gender-neutral pronouns, like "they" or "zer" or "zi" for those who wish it, is a form of discrimination that will be outlawed by Bill C-16. In the Upper Chamber, Senator Don Plett warned that "compelling people to use terminology that violates their conscience is a hallmark of totalitarian regimes" (Gyapong 2016). Some women who run shelters for abused women argue that male-to-female transgender individuals pose a threat to women who have been traumatized by men (Tasker 2017a). Still others say protection of "gender expression" diminishes the real progress made by women in society by focusing on external appearances and not substance (Frum 2017).

In light of such changes, Catholic critics insist that gender theory is moving too fast, is ill-defined and "designed to destroy the natural family," noting that Pope Francis condemns educators who encourage children to "choose" their gender as "satanic and demonic." It should be noted that these are not the Pope's words, but the comments of anonymous

Vatican policy advisors (Sage and Kington 2016). However, it is clear that the Vatican is attempting to placate conservative forces in the Church who do not understand that children who consistently and persistently insist they are a gender different from their birth sex need support and understanding.

So, is the right to use a gender label of your choice a matter of personal taste or an issue of social justice? American President Donald Trump was disappointed to be named *Person* of the Year rather than *Man* of the Year by *Time Magazine* in January 2017. Trans artist Ivan Coyote who, with partner Rae Spoon, co-wrote *Gender Failure* (2014), says "being a girl is something that just never happened to me," but "as a trans person, this is our time, I'm living in exactly the time I was meant to be living" (*Globe and Mail* 2016).

When gender "bending" is mixed with other markers of identity such as race and class, transphobia often surfaces. Geo, a 20-year-old bi-racial trans man claims he is "fetishized for being trans and being racially ambiguous" (Cline 2005). When the prurient stare at "the other," the effect is to exoticize difference. Our gaze can turn a side show into a freak show. More subtly, on "The Fosters," an American television drama, the trans character, Aaron, explains to his girlfriend Callie, "When you come out as gay people see you as being more authentic … [but] when you come out as trans, people sometimes think you've deceived them" (Nussbaum 2018).

There is no question that transgender and trans-sexual individuals have challenged traditional understandings of gender and sex. As Jen Gilbert (2006: 32) notes, the trans phenomenon "reminds us that gender is work, and not just for those who make the transition … the challenge is to welcome what is most foreign within the self." There *is* a new normal. The gender binary of male or female has been queered, and gender as a marker of identity has blurred or been smudged and is beginning to fade. In June, the transgender flag flew on Parliament Hill when the Senate passed Bill C-16 into law. Alberta Senator and trans ally Grant Mitchell concluded, "Transgender and gender-diverse people deserve to know that they are welcome and accepted, embraced and protected, and that in Canada they are free to be their true selves" (Tasker 2017b).

TWO-SPIRIT JUSTICE

Historical records indicate that pre-contract Indigenous nations throughout the world were tolerant of what we call sexual and gender fluidity and diversity. Missionaries and explorers noted that gender roles were not rigid: there were men who attended to domestic chores around the fire while there were women who took a lead in hunting. Same-sex relationships were not uncommon and were not considered to be taboo. Individuals who were born intersex (what used to be called hermaphrodite) were regarded not as freaks of nature, but as gifts bestowed by the Creator. They often became shamans and healers and were believed to be endowed with powerful medicine. All of this changed in the sixteenth century when Europeans imposed their own views of sexuality and gender on Indigenous peoples in so many places around the world.

The narrow binaries of male and female within a Christian framework made Indigenous gender and sex appear to be the epitome of the barbarism of savages. European contact led to "the suppression of the Two-Spirit among First Nations. This view was enshrined in compulsory heterosexuality and patriarchy in Canada's Indian Act of 1876, which excluded recognition of same-sex marriage" (EGALE 2016: 15). Women who married non-Indian men lost their status and identity as Indigenous individuals (Cannon 2004). The Aboriginal body has been defiled and corrupted by the colonial experience. The physical, sexual and psychological abuse of the residential school system has been well documented (Truth and Reconciliation Commission 2015). Subjugated, individuals have felt guilt and shame. The same-sex abuse of children by clergy has been hypocritically masked by vows of celibacy and the official turning away of a purportedly heterosexual blind eye. Aboriginal women in particular have been degraded, their bodies devalued and considered disposable (McNinch 2009; Troian 2017). How can there be justice for what some have called cultural annihilation and even cultural genocide (Tuck and Yang 2012)?

Contemporary Indigenous commentators lament this history, but they also insist Aboriginal men and women must re-learn and re-claim healthy attitudes towards sexuality, including a re-claiming of pre-contact gender and sexual fluidity and diversity. Two-spirit Cree playwright Thomson Highway points out that in his language there are no "dirty" words related to body parts. You can't insult someone by calling them a pri** or a c*** like you can in English (Taylor 2008).

Jack Saddleback is Cree from the Samson First Nation. He's two-spirit; he's a transgender gay man and an inspirational speaker and a staunch advocate of queer rights. He is often quoted as saying "there are no closets in a tipi" (personal communication). Alex Wilson is a two-spirit professor in the College of Education at the University of Saskatchewan, and one of the organizers of the Idle No More Movement. She argues that "coming in" (as opposed to "coming out") is a better way to understand the need for acceptance of gender and sexual diversity and its connection to healthy living and sustainable communities (Wilson 2013).

Adrian Stimson is a gay Blackfoot man who created "Buffalo Boy," a character of performance art who embodies difference and seeks justice:

> In the Fellini-esque campsite of Burning Man, the multi-gendered Buffalo Boy — neither human, beast, boy nor girl — gives us access to the trans, to the crossing of boundaries, to metamorphosis and the hybrid. "Burning Man is about cultural fusion and appropriations," Stimson says. "But at the root of it is a notion of a kinder community in which everyone can exist. It accepts difference, though it is not always easy." ... However, Buffalo Boy returns to the Plains where he was born, and here in the once-and-still-colonial world of the Canadian West, his story is an entanglement of constraints and freedoms. (Bell 2007)

This "notion of a kinder community," as Stimson calls it, is also a notion of social justice "queered."

In the summer of 2017, Métis two-spirit elder Marjorie Beaucage from Duck Lake organized a gathering of two-spirit individuals in a camp called "Out on the Land." Exploring traditional plant medicines and living off the land, these GSD individuals engaged in personal and community health and healing. Justice in this case is to celebrate gender and sexual diversity as a gift. This kind of justice is part of truth and reconciliation — lose the shame and take pride in your body. Many believe this can be accomplished through the arts: dancing, singing and telling stories on the Pow-Wow trail (McNinch and Baliko 2014).

SEXUAL HEALTH/HEALTHY SEXUALITY

Many believe that healthy attitudes toward sexuality are a key to achieving equality and justice for the queer community (Wilson and Yoshikowa 2007). Justice is found in reclaiming sexuality as a healthy attribute of our humanity. In the same way that two-spirit and First Nations peoples in general were robbed of their bodies, GSD individuals have been labelled historically as unnatural, perverted, sick, sinful, bestial, illegal and immoral sodomites. Same-sex relations have tended to be "closeted" away from the public eye. This led to same-sex eroticism being regarded as "dirty," something illicit and furtive: sexual encounters with strangers at night in parks or in public washrooms. When what you are engaging in is illegal; there is no safe space for intimacy. The sex becomes anonymous and without emotional ties or implications. By the late 1960s, increasing resistance to police raids of bathhouses and the decriminalization of same-sex relations in Canada signaled a new era. Gay promiscuity was championed by activists as a form of liberation, even revolution, turning the tables on what was characterized as the prudish hypocrisy of heterosexuality.

The AIDS pandemic, which began in the 1980s, was interpreted by the religious right wing as a plague for the licentious behaviour of gay men. "The deadly disease, renamed acquired immune deficiency syndrome (AIDS) after the virus was identified, travelled quickly through the gay community, but fear travelled even faster in mainstream society" (Picard 2014):

> Gay men, even men suspected of being gay, lost their jobs — they were evicted from apartments and they were ostracized. Newspapers carried earnest stories about the risks of catching AIDS from a toilet seat in a public restroom. Funeral homes refused to handle bodies, and hospitals turned patients away, or placed them in isolation. There was talk of quarantining the sick in modern-day leper colonies and tattooing the infected to warn prospective sex partners of the danger. (Picard 2014)

"No one is safe from AIDS," stated *Time Magazine* at the time. Pat Buchanan, the communications director for President Ronald Reagan, called AIDS "nature's revenge on gay men." Some far-right fundamentalist preachers called for the death penalty for homosexuals and, across the Western world, there were moves to bar gays from the classroom and from health-care jobs (Lateef 2017).

But the AIDS pandemic ultimately humanized homosexuals. Celebrities, such as Princess Diana and Elizabeth Taylor, raised millions of dollars for research, and there was a growing appreciation of the important role of hospices in alleviating the suffering of the dying. The NAMES AIDS Memorial Quilt campaign, commemorating the hundreds of thousands of (mostly) gay men who died in the 1980s and 90s with quilts made by their loved ones, became the largest ongoing community arts project the world had ever seen (Lateef 2017). Being able to mourn and grieve in a public way constituted a form of natural justice.

Gradually, a disease that began by stigmatizing homosexuals ended up de-stigmatizing same-sex relations, and promoting further steps towards equality for this disenfranchised group. Social justice was framed as the right to education about safe sex and prevention of the disease. Four decades on, Western society is much more open and informed about sexually transmitted diseases, including HIV, across the entire population regardless of gender or sexual orientation. Today, sexually active individuals with multiple partners are encouraged to take medication known as "pre-exposure prophylaxis (or PrEP)" intended for people at very high risk for HIV to lower their chances of getting infected (Picard 2014). Some activists still argue that there is discrimination against gender and sexual minorities in everything from accessing health services to being denied the right to donate blood because they are sexually active. In 2016, the required period of abstinence from same-sex activity required to donate blood was dropped from five years to one year. Most activists argue that Canadian Blood Services is still being unjust and overly cautious in refusing blood from gay men, particularly those in long-term monogamous relationships (Young 2016).

Today, queer activists emphasize "healthy lifestyle choices" with posters that say "Outlasting Homophobia is the Best Revenge" and "Homophobia Makes Me Sick." Posters from PFLAG emphasize that justice for the queer community means physical, social and emotional health and that can only come when gender and sexual diversity is not just tolerated, but celebrated.

This sense of justice as a right to health is also about healthy attitudes toward sexuality and not just "safe sex"; it is about reclaiming and celebrating sexuality itself as a form of health and of justice. A 2017 campaign by

Andrew Christian, an American manufacturer of underwear targeted at young gay men, insists that "sex=power=freedom." A book of glossy photographs of nude men is promoted as "not just sexy photos ... it explains that SEX is more than SEX ... it's power, it's emotion, it's creation, it's personal expression, it's POLITICAL FREEDOM" (Andrew Christian 2017).

Perhaps there is a sense of justice in celebrating mutual desire and the mutual giving and taking of sexual pleasure. In the dangerous and repressive Trump era, this kind of promotion is a form of political push-back against oppression. Proponents would argue that this is a more just kind of sex than abusive behaviours rooted in sadomasochism and sex role playing of power domination and submission popularized, for example, by the *Fifty Shades of Grey* series of soft-porn novels and movies. The problem with an ad campaign such as Andrew Christian's is that, like fashion in general, it promotes a particular look. In this case, an idealized form of male physical attractiveness: youthful, muscular, highly toned, hairless bodies, waxed bubble-butts, big pipes and major pec decks. Little wonder critics argue that extreme bodybuilding, which produces an engorged body and popping veins, is an attempt to make the whole body into an erect penis: "'hard' all over, bodybuilders seek to transform themselves into a perpetually erect phallus, and [in] most readings of the muscled body, even with the ... turned ass-forward, Mr. America may well be soliciting a dick" (Morrison 2001: 130). Our bodies, what we do with them, and with whom, define each of us as much as our thoughts and beliefs. On a deeply personal, emotional level, natural justice means we cannot live by hiding from or ignoring the truth of our gender expressions and sexual identities.

GLOBAL SEXUAL JUSTICE

Obsessions with and critiques of what we do or don't do to and with our bodies and with whom may seem to be a decadent indulgence of Western privilege in light of huge inequities of personal freedom experienced by millions around the world. It may, however, be part of a larger understanding of justice — not merely tolerance of difference, but a healthy interrogation of meaning making. That is, gender and sexual expressions and behaviours are inherent rights because they are human rights. The luxury of this stance can be contrasted from a global perspective. What does justice look like for those individuals in the ten countries where homosexuals can be put to death and in another sixty-seven countries where homosexuality is still illegal?

In Muslim countries and sub-Saharan Africa particularly, it is common for the state to officially deny the existence of same-sex relations and at the same time enforce the most stringent punishments against them. If same-sex relations did not exist there would be no need to make same-sex acts punishable, in some cases, by death. In 2007, the President of Iran infamously insisted to the United Nations and at Columbia University that "there are no gays in Iran." Even if in translation he was misquoted and meant "not as many gays as in the US," the oppression and censure would make for misleading statistics (Reuters News Service 2007). Check out any gay website, YouTube channel or Facebook news feed, and read stories about Iranian gay men and the abuse they face if they don't remain closeted and dare to become activists seeking recognition and legitimacy (Fathi 2007).

A decade later, a Moscow newspaper cited the round-up and torture of gay men in the Russian Muslim Republic of Chechnya amid fear of reprisals for the journalists who have reported this abuse. A spokesperson for Chechnya's leader, Ramzan Kadyrov, described the report as "absolute lies and disinformation," basing his denial on the claim that there were no gay people in Chechnya. "You cannot detain and persecute people who simply do not exist in the Republic," he told Interfax news agency. "If there were such people in Chechnya, the law-enforcement organs wouldn't need to have anything to do with them because their relatives would send them somewhere from which there is no returning" (Ibbitson 2017c; Walker 2017a).

In August 2015 a video circulated on the web purportedly released by Islamic State extremists in Iraq that shows two men accused of homosexuality being thrown from a building and stoned by a crowd once they hit the ground. This happened again in May 2016 in Aleppo when a teenage boy faced the same punishment for the same alleged crime. Fundamentalists, in taking such actions, believe they are returning to the roots of Islam in the time of Mohammed when there supposedly was a purity in living by God's laws codified in the Qur'an (Al-Manteeqi 2016). Such media visuals are used as propaganda by both sides, each arguing that their aim is to seek truth and achieve justice.

Fundamentalist Christianity has played a key role in the last decade in demonizing homosexuality in Uganda "and the threat homosexuals pose to Bible-based values and the traditional African family" (Gettleman 2010). The rationalization here is that GSD individuals, and same-sex relations specifically, are insidious elements of a well-engineered plot of the decadent West to weaken traditional values and keep Africa impoverished and dependent. In one case, young men acted on this, using anti-homosexual propaganda to justify the rape of a young woman accused of being lesbian to "cure her of her attraction to girls" (Gettleman 2010). Sylvia Tamale (2014), an African human rights activist and former law school dean, noted, "It is ironic that an African dictator wearing a three-piece suit, caressing an iPhone, speaking in English and liberally quoting the Bible can dare indict anything for being un-African." Even the President had to admit that "it is legalized homophobia, not same-sex relations, that is alien to Africa." She added that African women are familiar with the "un-African" mantra when they try to assert their rights (Tamale 2014). One of the legacies of colonialism around the world is the existence of laws that have criminalized same-sex relations.

QUEERING CHRISTIANITY

The role of Christianity in stirring homophobia in Africa raises the question of its relation to gender oppression. Can we reconcile gender and sexual diversity with the stances of various Christian denominations? What does justice look like for queer Christians? There is a spectrum of attitudes and beliefs expressed by and in formal Christian organizations about gender and sexual diversity, ranging from celebrating and embracing difference to condemning and shunning it. Christian dogmas have generally not been open to non-binary sexuality. Change has occurred over time because of the concerted effort of individuals who have said that church dogma is open to interpretation and misinterpretation. Churches in the past and some today, for example, have supported the innate superiority of males and in such a patriarchy have refused to ordain women. Churches condoned slavery and many believed that Christianity had exclusive claim to God's action in the world and in so doing obliterated or damaged many Indigenous cultures and peoples around the world. Literal interpretations of Biblical passages, notably from the Old Testament book of Leviticus, have been disavowed by many theologians.

Slowly, over the past two decades, some congregations have begun to abandon the "evidence" of the creation story of Adam and Eve as proof that male and female is God's only given structure for human relations and a rationale for compulsory heterosexism. A sign (then turned chant) at an anti-gay rally in the late 1970s — "Adam and Eve not Adam and Steve!" — popularized by televangelist Gerry Fallwell, attempts to privilege the act of procreation as well as entrenching a purely heterosexual morality (Schonfeld 2017).

Within a Christian context, centuries-old systems of beliefs have been challenged and changed by listening to the voices of the oppressed. "Welcoming" or "reconciled" or "affirming" congregations of various denominations, notably of the United and Evangelical Lutheran churches across Canada, have struggled in this contested field, worked through the issues, reached consensus and concluded that, for the sake of a just society, gender and sexual diversity must be part of God's blessing and that we are all children of God (Blakley 2007).

The contested nature of this struggle is most evident today in the Catholic Church. With more than five hundred million followers worldwide, the Pope is both a spiritual and temporal leader of a large and extremely hierarchical international bureaucracy. He is regarded as "the earthly vicar of Christ" (Rostow 1968: 4). But the Catholic Church has been conflicted for centuries about homosexuality, both within its organization and within its membership at large. The current Pope's views embody this conflict. On the one hand, homosexuality itself is not regarded as a sin, but homosexual behaviour is: "Love the sinner, hate the sin" is an adage that captures this. Pope Francis has spoken about inclusion and love and said in 2013, "who I am to judge?" when asked about homosexuals (McElwee 2016).

On the other hand, the Pope has railed against the "homosexual lobby" within the Vatican itself, seeing it as part of the corruption that has shielded many priests and bishops from acknowledging their own homosexuality. There is still a connection between patriarchy and perversion, particularly in the conflation of gay priests and pedophilia. In 2016, Pope Francis reaffirmed the Church's official position condemning gay priests. He continues to oppose same-sex marriage, but has expressed some ambivalence about same-sex civil unions. He has expressed sympathy for the children of gay and lesbian couples, but has not encouraged the adoption of children by same-sex couples and, as previously noted, he condemned educators who supposedly teach gender theory, which he thinks is encouraging children to "choose" their own gender (de Jesus 2015).

Such confusion and conflict is not restricted of course to gender and sexual diversity. Issues such as masturbation, birth control and non-procreative sex in general are still officially condemned by the Catholic Church, even though millions of Catholics engage in such activities. There are many different kinds of Catholics, including those who are actively working within the Church to effect change by lobbying for women and openly gay men to become priests, while there are those on the other side of the debate who see such moves as ruinous to the Church, to the institution of the family and to society in general. Seeking a uniform understanding of justice is not easy within this institution.

SEXUAL JUSTICE IN THE SECULAR WORLD

Such confusions and contradictions are part of the larger world where an ability to live with uncertainty and ambiguity is increasingly the mark of an educated sensibility. Understandings of what constitutes justice and injustice depend on your point of view. In terms of gender and sexual difference, what is an essence and what is constructed? What is natural and what is performative? Why do people continue to insist that gender and sexual orientation are "lifestyle choices" akin to deciding what car to drive or whether to become a vegetarian or whether to smoke cigars? Ru Paul, television drag star, has written that while "we are all born naked, after that everything is drag" (1968). We certainly make choices about how we present ourselves in the world, but our gender identity and sexuality are not simply choices. However, where it is inappropriate, unsafe or even illegal, we may choose "co-erced conformity" (Yoshino 2005a) to cover and protect ourselves in order to appear to be no different from the accepted majority.

For some people, encouraging gender and sexual difference is a "slippery slope." Margaret Somerville, a Canadian ethicist and academic, has argued that same-sex marriage opens up the possibility of polygamy because it detaches marriage from the biological reality of the basic procreative relationship between one man and one woman (Somerville 2007). One should note, however, that polygamy is an extreme form of patriarchy used in many cultures to sustain status and power. Romantic notions of love in today's society privilege serial monogamy regardless of the sexual orientation of the individuals involved. Seen as an economic union, marriage often ends for many in seeking their own personal sense of justice: access to the children and an equitable division of property and pensions.

This slippery slope Somerville refers to is really about the breakdown of narrow binaries like heterosexual/homosexual and queer/straight. Youth and queer activists today reject such restrictions and talk about being gender-fluid and exploring pansexuality and polyamory. Canadian novelist Zoey Leigh Peterson in *Next Year, For Sure* (2017) troubles monogamy by "offering a robust look at positive alternatives and querying widespread cultural reluctance to expand our definitions beyond traditional narratives and typical pairings." Even when there is a legal and legislative accommodation of how people may choose to live in relation to one another, in same-sex marriage, for example, marriage still remains the privileged relationship, leaving many non-traditional relationships beyond the pale. Despite the decriminalization of homosexuality in 1969 and the legalization of same-sex marriage in 2005, there are still laws that criminalize, for example, group sex, bath houses and pornography (Salerno 2017). These are laws that were specifically designed to abuse the LGBTTQ2 community.

Sky Gilbert (2009), queer artist, academic and activist, argues that as society rushes to embrace gender and sexual diversity, being queer has lost its ability to critique heterosexuality and institutions such as traditional marriage. Gilbert has decided he's not gay, he's "ESP — an effeminate sexual person." Gilbert advocates for sexual promiscuity and gender play. However, it is certainly true that middle-class Canadian gay white men like Gilbert have enjoyed privileges as members of society that have not been accorded to racialized and economically and educationally marginalized members of gender and sexual minorities where cultural taboos reinforce the closet on "the down-low."

Kenji Yoshino (2005b), on the other hand, sees a kind of comforting justice in the "irresistible banality of same-sex marriage" as an antidote to the desperate lives of many gender and sexual minorities. "We need comedy more than tragedy and happy endings [such as marriage] like everybody else." Yoshino (2016), a legal scholar and professor of constitutional law at New York University, has written extensively about the fight for same-sex marriage in the United States. Describing himself and his husband as "ideologically progressive but temperamentally conservative," Yoshino (2016: 4) writes:

> Every time I needed a legal gate to open, it opened. When I first came out as gay in the early 1990s, the law had changed in most states to decriminalize sexual acts between men; when Ron and I wished to marry, the law in Connecticut allowed it; when we wished to have children, surrogacy and adoption laws permitted us to do so.

Changes in the law come about because of social, cultural, and political change. "Still," Yoshino concludes, "without concrete legal reform, I might have no husband, no daughter, no son. Now, it is *that* life that seems unimaginable" (2016: 4).

"What makes a family?" is a familiar refrain of early years' school curriculum, the answer to which was, simply, "Love makes a family!" accompanied by a happy face and capturing the twenty-first-century ethos of celebrating difference and diversity. How families are created these days is much different than it was even a generation ago. Yoshino praises reforms of the law that have allowed him to come out, to marry a same-sex partner, and then, through surrogacy and adoption, to have a family. Justice to gender and sexual minorities is about such rights: rights to self-definition, self-expression, self-realization, sexual choice and consent and practice, and the right to public recognition of all of the above. In this new order, same-sex parenting is now regarded as a right, a conscious decision that can involve many strangers: agency people, social workers, fertility specialists, lawyers, anonymous and known donors and insemination clinics. There are online chat rooms and blogs devoted to the trials and tribulations of lesbian mothers trying to get pregnant. There are Facebook pages where the off-spring of donors can connect with their half-brothers and sisters. Known as "diblings," these children and their parents create connections across time and space that profoundly change our understanding not just of parenthood, but of the nature of families themselves. Far from causing social upheaval, however, non-traditional families tend to be stalwart supporters of a strong sense of personal and social justice: any hint of discrimination or bullying of their children and these lesbian moms and gay dads are the first to demand that schools ensure equality and respect for all. Justice includes everyone, even diblings (Bailey 2016).

JUSTICE FOR QUEER EDUCATORS

Understanding social justice means understanding context and history. Remember that homosexuality was decriminalized in Canada in 1969. In 1975, Doug Wilson, a young gay man from Meadow Lake, Saskatchewan, was a graduate student in the College of Education at the University of Saskatchewan who had only recently "come out of the closet" when he placed an ad in the student newspaper asking for "anyone interested in participating in a campus gay organization" to contact him. The Dean of the College immediately suspended Wilson, "an avowed homosexual," from his job supervising student teachers in Saskatoon high schools. Officially, no LGBTTQ2 teachers existed at that time; no one could be "out" because homosexuality, although decriminalized, was still regarded as morally repugnant and inappropriate, particularly for anyone working in schools with children and youth (Korineck 2004). Through a vigorous campaign by a group of advocates and allies, Wilson was dubbed "the most openly gay person for at least a thousand miles" (Korineck 2003: 517). Fear of losing their jobs kept many gay and lesbian teachers firmly in the closet operating, like the American military before 2010, with an unwritten policy — "Don't Ask Don't Tell."

Didi Khayatt (1992) first identified the double-bind that LGBTTQ2 teachers find themselves in because teachers are implicitly hired as role models embodying the values that school divisions promulgate. Assumed to be heterosexual, they are seen as moral guardians living "exemplary" lives. Queer teachers still have to deal with old scripts about depravity, promiscuity, mental illness and the vulnerability of children and youth being enticed or seduced and led astray by queer teachers (as if such vulnerability didn't always exist with heterosexual teachers). Teachers are morally positioned so that their gender and sexual orientation are not supposed to have anything to do with the world of teaching and learning. Teachers are also held to "a higher standard" than others because they work with a most valuable and most vulnerable resource: the children of this country.

The lived reality of teachers in schools today is still complex and conflicted. Robert, a gay friend of mine, is a practical arts teacher in a composite high school in a small town in southern Saskatchewan. Robert is physically fit and gifted mechanically. He came out during his undergraduate years. For the third year in a row Robert is leading the annual outdoor education school canoe trip for Grade 12 students. He just came back from a white-water rafting and dirt-bike expedition in the BC mountains. In September of his first year of teaching, Robert was asked by the new principal in front of other teachers if he had a girl-friend. "No, actually, I have a boyfriend," responded Robert. "Oh." The silence was deafening. Initially Robert feels "outed." Later the principal, declares himself an ally of Robert's and an advocate for his rights as a gay teacher. With this support Robert was able to successfully complete his first year of teaching. In his second year Robert brought his live-in boyfriend to the staff Christmas party. It was one thing for there to be rumours that Robert was gay, but some staff members regarded this move as a flaunting display of his homosexuality. This is a bigger step than simply dragging your boyfriend along to prove a point. It is a public act and Robert knows that word will quickly spread in the community. He has outed himself again and this time it will be to the students in the school. The coming-out process is one that never stops. So, as a second-year shop teacher he had to contend with the same old question: "Is it true what they say?"

Robert tells a story related to his initial coming out. He pulls into the local A&W in the town where he used to live, and a high-school girl at the drive-through says to Robert, "Some people are saying you're gay! That isn't true, is it?" Like every queer person at every intersection of their complicated lives, Robert has to make a decision to be out or not. At this juncture, he replies, "Yes, it is true, but what does that have to do with me ordering an effing Teen burger?" There were also serious run-ins with the school's custodian (who is also the assistant football coach). This has included him using homophobic language within Robert's earshot, daring him to respond, as well as borrowing tools without asking and not return-ing them to the shop — in other words, not according to him the respect that he has a right to expect, not because he is gay, but because he is a professional teacher. As Robert says, "I have now developed a hyphenated identity. I am not just the shop teacher, I am the gay shop teacher whether I like it or not." And, as any member of a minority understands — like women in non-traditional roles, or First Nations and Métis peoples, or new Canadians — Robert feels he has to be twice as good as his colleagues in order to be above reproach. He is aware too that he is breaking the mold of the image of shop teachers who "aren't supposed to be gay" (in western Canada it is the male French language teacher who typically embodies the gay stereotype). Robert, in negotiating a sexual minority professional identity, embodies a form of bravery that defines masculinity beyond any stereotypes associated with being "queer" (McNinch 2012). He also has become a role model, and there are several students in the school who are "on the margins," as Robert describes them, for whom his support might be critical. A recent suicide of a young student who just came out as gay troubles the whole school, but Robert feels somehow more responsible. Seeking justice in this context is complicated.

The school's principal remains a key person he can rely on when the atmosphere is toxic, when kids are picked on by teachers or students for the slightest deviation from the norm: "Hey Dustin, what's with those white sunglasses; only fags wear those!" After two years of harassment, justice for Robert meant that the homophobic custodian was reassigned to the school division's maintenance yard away from students and teachers. Seeing beyond the particulars of Robert's situation, the school division itself implemented a series of in-services and workshops (*fYrefly in Schools*) for teachers and staff and hired a health educator consultant to organize in-school teams of allies who support gender and sexual minority children and youth and to change the culture and climate across the whole school division.

Queer teachers struggle long and hard to manage their identities in the contexts of schools where heteronormative assumptions pervade. If you look at any of the provincial "health and wellness" curricula you understand that "sexuality has always been in an uncomfortable relationship with schooling" (Youdell 2006: 251). Schools regulate sexuality and gender performances through curriculum, pedagogy, practice and policy, where heterosexuality is simply assumed. Disclosing one's sexuality is a phenomenon unique to queer people, and coming out is part of a lifelong process, which raises once again the issue of "the closet."

Bringing sexuality out of the closet in opposition to the norm means to queer or question or challenge the norm. As such, it is an eminently political act. So while Robert does not regard himself as a gay rights activist, he can be "read" or interpreted by others to be so because he came out of the closet and does not hide his sexual orientation and has insisted on fair treatment. On the other hand, not coming out can also be an act of defiance and not an admission of closeted shame, but rather an acknowledgement of an inhospitable culture.

Pat Griffin (1992), in writing about lesbians in school sports, first identified a continuum of disclosure that illustrates how teachers range from passing as heterosexual, to covering or hiding their sexuality, to being implicitly out, to being explicitly out. Along this continuum, each teacher operates at different levels and holds different motives and ideals. This is true for all queer people. Consequently, this process is more public for some than for others, and harder for some than for others. It is my observation that the coming-out process is easier for younger teachers, but it is very much dependent on the context in which they find themselves as a teacher.

Over my own forty-year career as an educator, I have witnessed various approaches to coping or thriving as a gender or sexual minority teacher (McNinch 2015). Some individuals simply leave the profession. As Jeff describes it, "the hypocrisy of the school system made me feel like a hypocrite. I felt like I lacked authenticity. I wasn't even sure what it was I was faking." Another option is to teach overseas in large cities beyond the scrutiny of small towns. Mark moved to London, England two years ago and is working in an inner-city school there and "having a blast." Research supports the idea that the more culturally, ethnically and racially diverse a community is, the more likely that the rhetoric of justice and inclusion and equality will be practised and not just preached. In a city of eight million people, Mark has the luxury of not having to hide his identity because he is already by and large anonymous and surrounded, if he chooses, by a huge "gay scene."

Another tactic involves a move away from the classroom. After graduating from the University of Regina, Jen worked as a teacher in small-town Saskatchewan but found the culture less than welcoming to her as an open lesbian. After two years she was accepted into graduate school and gleefully became a student again. She was able to study in a much more queer-positive atmosphere and to research the issue of sexual identity and schooling. The last I heard, Jan was applying to do her PhD.

It may be less than just to remain closeted. However, this strategy needs to be understood in light of the oppressiveness of staffroom heteronormativity. One female teacher, a divorced lesbian with two children of her own, was advised by her principal to have the children address her as "Mrs. Duncan." Compulsory heterosexuality was thrust upon her ("for the sake of the children," her principal insisted), for the sake of perpetuating a lie, an injustice.

Queer staff may be placed under psychological pressures that can result in stress, anxiety and depression. Some sicken and eventually go on disability. Other teachers cope by living in one place and working in another. Lots of people commute long distances, but this is also a tactic of self-preservation used to keep your personal life quite separate from your work life. This detachment can have a negative side: a lack of integration can be stressful; for some, however, "it keeps things simple."

Coming out to colleagues is a kind of middle ground — building trust at the professional level, with people who would understand and appreciate that it is not always safe or wise to share gender or sexual orientation with students. As one male teacher said to me, "I feel that I shouldn't share the fact that I live with a man and that I like having sex with men." This reflects the long shadow cast by past links of homosexuality to perversion and promiscuity. But this strategy is also an attempt to not make too big a deal, or too much, of sexuality itself. It is easier to be indirect: if you are in a relationship to simply say, "My partner and I" or, more explicitly, "my husband, Michael, and I." I do know that being an openly gay dean of education for six years has helped to change the culture of my faculty for both students and staff alike. Supportive and respectful "straight" colleagues are crucial to creating and maintaining a positive working environment. These allies also need to be supported and championed. If there are other gender and/or sexual minority individuals on staff, that, too, is a great help; "the more the merrier," as one teacher put it.

Coming out to students is a more significant move. We know there is a need to provide GSD students with much-needed public role models and to challenge processes of heterosexism and homophobia in today's schools. Not every out teacher wants to be known as the teacher that queer kids go to it they have issues, although this is a role that Robert has had thrust upon him. "Out-rageous" performances of gender or sexuality, through hair and dress and make-up, are still considered inappropriate in most school settings, even if the school is happy to fly the Pride Flag. Not acknowledging someone's "difference" can do a disservice to an out teacher and her students. A social justice approach presumes that colleagues and administrators as well as children and youth have the capacity to understand the complexities of sexual and gender diversity issues, that is, they can be educated (literally led) in that direction.

GSD educators negotiate a suite of complex discourses within their everyday school lives. The specific context in which queer teachers find themselves will play a significant role in the strategies and choices they make around the management of their personal and professional identities as they seek respect, fairness and a sense of social justice.

During the writing of this chapter I was consulted by the Saskatchewan Teachers' Federation for advice on what to do since a teacher announced that they are transitioning from one gender to another. What kind of supports are required for such an individual? Where does the human resource department stand? Are there policies and procedures in place that ensure that discretion and confidentiality are respected? These are questions that school divisions are only just beginning to understand. Again, education for understanding can lead to human justice.

JUSTICE FOR QUEER KIDS

Gender and sexual diversity have become a real "thing" in today's society and nowhere are the issues more contested than in schools. Pink Days, Days of War against discrimination, anti-bullying campaigns, Pride Days and Gay-Straight Alliances (GSAS) have given a profile to activism in schools and communities to support gender and sexual minority students. The Saskatchewan Ministry of Education has mandated *fYrefly in Schools* to help with the implementation of a guiding document entitled "Deepening the Discussion: Gender and Sexual Diversity" (2015).

Through workshops and in-services, *fYrefly in Schools* works closely with school divisions to ensure GSD children and youth feel included and feel they belong. This is a form of social justice work accomplished through building leadership and strengthening capacity to create learning environments where all students feel protected and respected. Indicators of such leadership and capacity building can be seen in active encouragement and support for GSAS, and a student and teaching population that stands up for others and can distinguish between rights, needs, privileges and responsibilities. The assumption of this kind of approach to justice is that knowledge and understanding will free us all.

EGALE Canada's national survey (2015) reveals, however, that problems of harassment and bullying are far from being solved. This means that curriculum and teaching must be purposefully inclusive and mindful. It means that administrators must have policies and procedures in place that protect a vulnerable population and for whom the determinants of mental, physical and spiritual health are more fragile. It means:

> Despite more than a decade of significant changes in Canadian law, legislation, and social institutional policies, gender and sexual minority youth ... face a stark reality: they remain a vulnerable population subjected to sustained symbolic violence (such as stereotyping, anti-GSM [gender and sexual minorities] name calling and graffiti), physical violence (such as bullying, including assault and battery), marginalization and disenfranchisement that entrench mistrust, alienation, nihilism ... and susceptibility to life-eroding or life-ending behaviours. (Grace 2015: 211)

Healthy "social education" as a form of social justice means "intelligence for power, power for self-expression and self-expression in the context of relative freedom" (Grace 2015: 53). Kris Wells refers to Camp fYrefly, a summer camp for queer kids, as a "3-H Club, focused on helping [youth] to be happy, healthy and hopeful" (Grace 2015: 93). This kind of engaged pedagogy is a form of education for citizenship. Justice comes through empowerment when individuals see themselves as agents of change. Gender and sexual minorities do not need to be placated or solaced with "It Gets Better" rhetoric. The emphasis is on making it better right now as a form of social activism. fYrefly stands for "fostering youth, resiliency, energy, fun, leadership, yeah!"

Five themes guide the development of fYrefly programs in schools and at the summer camp. They include: creating a socially just and inclusive community; fostering resilience and youth leadership capacity; empowering youth to address bullying and harassment; opening the heart and mind to other ways of knowing through art, music, writing and visual and performing arts; and building self-esteem and self-care and social development. For many, this is an example of an educational approach that will build a humane and just society for all children and youth, not only GSD individuals. Because the firefly, from which the name is derived, has the ability to light itself from within, it is a powerful symbol of the kind of personal justice that every child naturally deserves, regardless of their gender or sexual identity.

But, make no mistake, this is highly conflicted space. For example, consider the situation in which a parent demands that a teacher tell her if her son is acting "feminine" at school. The teacher knows that this Grade 6 student likes to dress as a female and even wear high heels in class, but the kid isn't ready to share this with his parents. The school counsellor, who has a son who is happily heterosexual and married but likes to dress as a woman sometimes, is worried about confidentiality and the mental health of the child. In Alberta, this argument became highly political, with the new Conservative Party leader, Jason Kenny, insisting that schools must inform parents if their children want to join a GSA because they are responsible for the well-being of their offspring. The NDP government of the day, however, opposes this because they say such a "breach of confidentiality" might endanger the safety and well-being of youth who may live in vulnerable or antagonistic circumstances. Justice here depends on which side of the debate you sit on (Bennett 2017). Justice in these circumstances is very much a "contested space." For the particular Grade 6 student, social justice is still an abstract concept. His parents decided to move him to a different school and a different community, but that only made him the object of teasing and bullying. He has finally come out to his parents, but now he doesn't want to go to school, and for this conflicted and unsupported individual child, that is one definition of injustice.

The following note addressed to me from Lee, a Grade 11 student from small-town Saskatchewan, is typical of GSD youth today and their understanding of justice and self-identity:

> Thank-you for Camp and for coming to our school tonight and presenting to parents on gender diversity. Thank-you for doing the work you do to help pave the way and ease the journey for sexual and gender diverse youth such as myself. I identify as pansexual and gender fluid. In the summer I went to Camp fYrefly in Saskatoon and it was one of the greatest experiences of my life. I met such amazing people and learned a lot. Since the second I left camp I've just been hoping I can attend in Regina this coming year. (October 17, 2017)

SEXUAL JUSTICE IS ONGOING

Gender and sex are still highly conflicted spaces, in part because of the rapid speed of social change over the past fifty years. Over this time our understanding of justice and injustice has changed and individual and social attitudes to gender and sexual diversity have changed significantly. Certainly, for someone like me who graduated from high school in 1965, when homosexuality was seen as a crime against nature and was a crime against the state, until today, profound and relatively rapid changes have occurred in our homes, in our schools and in society at large. Our sense of justice has evolved, not without controversy, not without confusion, not without concerns. In the decades of the twenty-first century we have moved more quickly away from the "continuing power of insult" to shape gender and sexual diversity and queer lives. (Eribon 2004: 17).

The history of human justice in the eighteenth century centred on the right (for white heterosexual men) to representation and to own property; this expanded in the nineteenth century to include the right to congregate and to vote. In the early twentieth century, women fought for these same rights and for other rights such as the right to work and the right to access health care. The Civil Rights movement and the Black Power movement in the US in the 1960s and 70s focused on the rights of Afro-American citizens to equality under the law, but also to human rights in their day to day lived reality.

In Canada, social justice in the twentieth century focused on the rights of minorities to cultural citizenship (Pakulski 1997). For gender and sexual minorities that has meant a struggle for the right to symbolic presence and visibility and a moving in from the margins. It has meant ending insult and stigmatization and the right to dignifying representations and the propagation of multiple identities. The social regulation of what we can and cannot do and why has been interrogated. We have insisted on the right to enjoy sexual freedom and the right to reproductive control and the right to any variety of expressions of gender.

Since the decriminalization of homosexuality, social justice has moved. "Being queer is not about wanting a right to privacy; it is about the freedom to be public" (Richardson 2000: 48). Not merely on an intellectual level, the famous French philosopher, Michel Foucault, a closeted gay man himself, understood on a deeply personal level that issues of authenticity and inauthenticity, and the right to be who we are, are at the root of social justice. His queer gaze gave us new insights into struggles both contemporary and historical against forms of domination, forms of exploitation and forms of subjection. Gender and sexual identities, constrained and bound by such forms of power, have now been released. This appreciation of justice implies that we don't see things in black and white, but grow more comfortable with nuance, innuendo, subtlety and ambiguity.

A young woman in Grade 12 e-mailed me recently to tell me that the

Harvest Christian Academy she attends has threatened her with expulsion if she dares to be seen with her girlfriend. She wants to know if the school has the right to do this. The mother of a transgender teenage boy tells me that he has been cutting himself, doesn't want to go to school and never wants to come out of his bedroom. Such human suffering simply does not seem to be just or fair. The pursuit of justice never ends. "To know how to get free is not so hard; what is arduous is to know *how* to be free" (André Gide, as qtd. in Eribon 2004: ii). For this kind of justice, it is not logic that is required, but compassion and the insistence on the right to dignity and self-expression of each and every one of us.

DISCUSSION QUESTIONS

1. We all experience some sense of difference and otherness in relation to the world around us. Can you remember a time from your childhood when you noticed that you were "different" from others or that others were different from you? Do you now regard this difference as trivial or significant? Explain.

2. What memory is invoked in you by the phrase "sex education"? What was this education comprised of? Was it formal or informal? Put into your own words the difference between your sex and your gender. Provide an example of the difference between your sexual orientation and your sexual behaviour.

3. RuPaul says, "We are born naked; after that everything is drag." What does this mean and what are some social justice implications of this stance?

4. Several other countries besides Canada are referred to in this chapter that have different attitudes and laws regarding gender and sexual diversity. Choose any country in the world and find out what the official and unofficial attitudes and sanctions are to same-sex relations and gender variance.

5. In the nature vs. nurture debate, how much do you think biology controls your destiny? How much does biology determine your sexuality? If a "gay gene" is ever discovered what might be some positive and negative consequences from a social justice perspective?

GLOSSARY

Cis-gender: This term (often abbreviated to cis) is for people whose experiences of their own gender align with the sex they were assigned at birth based on their genitalia. To be cisgender is to feel that your body parts reflect accurately who you are: "I am female and I have breasts and a vagina."

Compulsory heterosexuality: This has been assumed to be the norm in partriarchal society. The sexual and emotional attraction of the male to the female and vice-versa is viewed as the natural relationship between the sexes. A class or textbook that only discusses sex between a cis-gender man and a cis-gender woman is an example of compulsory heterosexuality. Remaining "in the closet" because of taboos against gender and sexual diversity is caused by compulsory heterosexuality.

Identity politics: This refers to social and political positions and attitudes based on the interests and perspectives of various social groups with which people identify. It includes the ways in which people's values, beliefs and politics are shaped by aspects of their identity. Some examples are: occupation ("I'm a farmer, she's a lawyer"), ethnicity ("I'm Ukrainian, he's a Japanese-Canadian"), social or economic status ("I'm a union man, she's a stay-at-home mom"), age ("I'm a boomer, she's a millennial"), pursuits ("I'm a dungeons and dragons geek, he's a techno-nerd), sexual orientation ("I'm gay, they are straight"), religion ("I'm an atheist, he's a Baptist") or race ("I'm First Nations, she's Caucasian").

Natural law: This refers to a philosophy asserting that certain rights are inherent by virtue of human nature, and can be understood universally through human reason. Variant genders and sexual orientations of some individuals are consequently considered inherently right because they are human beings and have the right to be respected.

"Natural selection" or "survival of the fittest": These are used to refer to a situation in which only the strongest people or things continue to live or be successful, while the others die or fail, which is the opposite of natural law. To say "It's a dog-eat-dog world" contradicts the natural law notion that all living things are entitled to the right to exist with dignity and respect.

Queer: Once a pejorative slur for gays, this word has now been reclaimed by the LGBTTQ2 communities as a self-affirming umbrella term. The word is powerful because it refers to the historical but continuing power of insult to shape gender and sexually diverse individuals who have been shunned, marginalized, and "othered" as not normal, as different or weird, in a word "queer."

Standpoint theory: A theory that analyzes the relations between people and the position of people in society through our group-specific understanding that the world is shaped by our lived experience of it. A slave will see the world differently than his master. A transgender person will understand and know the world differently than a cis-gender person.

Transgender: This term (often shorted to trans) refers to those who feel that their physical sexual characteristics do not align with their gender identification: "I have a penis and testicles, but I feel like am a female."

Transsexual: This term is being used to refer to a transgender person who has undergone hormonal and surgical procedures to align the sex of their body with their feelings and experiences of their gender.

Two Spirit: In some First Nations, two-spirit individuals may embody characteristics of both genders and sometimes are referred to as a third gender. Their pre-contact roles included being teachers, knowledge keepers, healers, herbalists, child caregivers, spiritual leaders, interpreters, mediators and artists. In other communities, two-spirit persons did not take on special roles but were accepted and respected as part of the community. Colonialism led to the suppression of this knowledge and gender and sexual diversity was stigmatized.

REFERENCES

Al-Manteeqi, Immanuel. 2016. "The Islamic Reasons for ISIS' Barbaric Murder of Homosexuals." June 12. <https://counterjihad.com/children-watch-isis-throws-gay-man-off-building>.

Andrew Christian website. "Sex=Power=Freedom." <https://www.andrewchristian.com/collections/sex-power-freedom.html> (accessed February 11, 2017).

Arendt, Hannah. 1955. "Political Experiences: Notes." 024160 in <http://www.wolfgang-heuer.com/wp-content/uploads/heuer_wolfgang_imagination_bari.pdf> (accessed February 16, 2017).

Aske, Sara, and Terry Pritchard. 2016. "How the Cold War 'Fruit Machine' Tried to Determine Gay from Straight." CBC News, November 3. <http://www.cbc.ca/news/canada/ottawa/archives-homosexuality-dector-fruit-machine-1.3833724> accessed November 28, 2017).

Associated Press. 2017. "Chechnya Police Arrest 100 Suspected Gay Men, Three Killed: Report." *Globe and Mail*, April 16. <http://www.theglobeandmail.com/news/world/chechnya-police-arrest-100-suspected-gay-men-three-killed-report/article34559281/> (accessed April 13, 2017).

Bailey, Elizabeth. 2016. "Desire Lines: Treading Trails and Telling Tales of Lesbian

Mothering." Unpublished MA thesis, University of Regina, Regina, SK.

Bell, Lynne. 2007. "Adrien Stimson at Burning Man." *Canadian Art.* June, pp. 44-49. <http://canadianart.ca/features/buffalo_boy/>.

Bennett, Dean. 2017. "Rachel Notley Attacks 'Super-Extreme' UCP In Campaign-Style Speech." *Edmonton Journa,* September 24. <http://edmontonjournal. com/news/local-news/rachel-notley-attacks-ucp-over-economy-gay-kids-and-fundraising> (accessed November 27, 2017).

Blakley, Carla. 2007. "Que(e)r(y)ing the Image of God: Challenging the Heterosexual Myth." Unpublished MA thesis, University of Regina, Regina, SK.

Cannon, Martin. 2004. "The Regulation of First Nations Sexuality." In James McNinch and Mary Cronin (eds.), *I Could Not Speak My Heart: Education and Social Justice for Gay and* Lesbian *Youth.* Regina: CPRC.

Cats, Ruth (producer), and Jake Witzenfield (director). 2015. *Oriented.* Norway: Conch Studios.

CBC News. 2015. "Timeline: Same Sex Rights in Canada." May 25. <http://www. cbc.ca/news/canada/timeline-same-sex-rights-in-canada-1.1147516>.

Cline, Elizabeth. 2005. "Mix-And-Match Loving: Interracial Transgender Coupling." *Village Voice,* June 14. <http://www.villagevoice.com/arts/mix-and-match-loving-interracial-transgender-coupling-7136167> (accessed April 9, 2017).

Collins, Patricia Hill. 1990. *Black Feminist Thought, Knowledge, Consciousness, and the Politics of Empowerment.* NY: Routledge.

Coyote, Ivan, and Rae Spoon. 2014. *Gender Failure.* Vancouver: Arsenal Pulp Press.

De Jesus, Ivey. 2015. "Pope Francis Embraces Gays, Lesbians, But Church Remains Divided." <http://www.pennlive.com/midstate/index.ssf/2015/08/ pope_francis_philadelphia_visi_20.html> (accessed March 8).

EGALE Canada. 2016. *Grossly Indecent: Confronting the Legacy of State Sponsored Discrimination Against Canada's LGBTQ2SI Communities.* Ottawa: EGALE Canada.

Eribon, Didier. 2004. *Insult and the Making of the Gay Self.* (Trans. Michael Lucey.) Durham, NC: Duke University Press.

Fathi, Nazila. 2007. "Despite Denials, Gays Insist They Exist, if Quietly, in Iran." *New York Times,* September 30. <http://www.nytimes.com/2007/09/30/world/ middleeast/30gays.html> (accessed April 14, 2017).

Fowles, Stacey-May. 2017. "Open Heart." *Globe and Mail,* March 4: R12.

Frankel, Laurie. 2017. *This Is How it Always Is.* New York: Flatiron Books.

Frum, Linda. 2017. "The Big Problem with Canada's Transgender Rights Bill." *Toronto Sun,* June 17. <http://torontosun.com/2017/06/17/ the-big-problem-with-canadas-transgender-rights-bill/wcm/a97ac904-e730-47ce-8804-e511309b0870> (accessed February 23, 2018).

Gee, Eric Andrew. 2016. "George Elliott Clarke's poet laureate term sparks dialogue on poetry's public value." *Globe and Mail,* December 23. <http://

www.theglobeandmail.com/news/national/george-elliott-clarkes-poet-laureate-term-sparks-dialogue-on-poetrys-public-value/article33427468/> (accessed April 10, 2017).

Gettleman, Jeffrey. 2010. "How an Anti-Gay Rally Pitted Uganda Against the West." *Globe and Mail,* January 4: A9.

Gilbert, Jen. 2006. "Let Us Say Yes to Who or What Turns Up: Education as Hospitality." *Journal of the Canadian Association of Curriculum Studies,* 4, 1: 25–34.

Gilbert, Sky. 2009. "If That's What It Means to be Gay, I Quit." *Globe and Mail,* December 1.

Goldberg, Suan. 2017. *National Geographic,* January. <http://www.nationalgeographic.com/magazine/2017/01/editors-note-gender/> (accessed April 3, 2017).

Grace, André, with Kristopher Wells. 2015. *Growing Into Resilience: Sexual and Gender Minority Youth in Canada.* Toronto: University of Toronto Press.

Griffen, Pat. 1992. "Changing the Game: Homophobia, Sexism, and Lesbians in Sport." *Quest,* 44, 2: 251–265.

Gyapong, Deborah. 2016. "Senator Urges 'Vetting' of Transgender Bill C-16." *Canadian Catholic News,* December 2. <http://www.catholicregister.org/item/23740-senator-urges-vetting-of-transgender-bill-c-16> (accessed March 25, 2017).

Harris, Anne, and Emily Gray (eds.). 2014. *Queer Teachers, Identity and Performativity.* London: Palgrave MacMillan.

Harris, Kathleen. 2017. "'Our Collective Shame': Trudeau Delivers Historic Apology to LGBT Canadians." CBC News, November 28. <http://www.cbc.ca/news/politics/homosexual-offences-exunge-records-1.4422546> (accessed Nov. 28).

Hatchett, Keisha. 2016. "Trans Male Comedian Ian Harvie on Why Representation Matters." The Mary Sue, October 20. <https://www.themarysue.com/interview-trans-male-comedian-ian-harvie/> (accessed April 25).

Homosexuality and the Catholic Church. (n.d.) Wikipedia. <https://en.wikipedia.org/wiki/Homosexuality_and_the_Catholic_Church#Francis>.

Hurley, Mary. 2007 (rev.). "Sexual Orientation and Legal Rights." Ottawa: Government of Canada. <https://lop.parl.ca/content/lop/researchpublications/921-e.htm> (accessed February 23, 2018).

Ibbitson, John. 2017a. "How Will LGBTQ Canadians Take Trudeau's Apology?" *Globe and Mail,* November 25: A10.

____. 2017b. "Trudeau Lags on LGBT Pardons." *Globe and Mail,* March 25: A18. <http://www.theglobeandmail.com/news/politics/trudeau-lags-on-lgbt-pardons/article34425506/>.

____. 2017c. "The International Community Must Respond to Attacks on Gay Men in Chechnya." *Globe and Mail,* April 16. <http://www.theglobeandmail.com/news/politics/the-international-community-must-respond-to-attacks-on-gay-men-in-chechnya/article34718214/> (accessed April 17, 2017).

Ibbitson, J., and Daniel Leblanc. 2016. "Former Military Members Who Were Discharged Over Sexuality Launch Class-Action Suits." *Globe and Mail*, November 1, rev. April 8, 2017. <https://www.theglobeandmail.com/news/politics/former-public-service-staff-launch-sexual-discrimination-lawsuits/article32609060/> (accessed February 23, 2018).

Khayatt, Didi. 1992. *Lesbian Teachers: An Invisible Presence*. NY: SUNY Press.

Korineck, Valerie. 2003. "Doug Wilson and the Politicization of a Province, 1975–83." *The Canadian Historical Review*, 84, 4: 517–550.

___. 2004. "Activism = Public Education: The History of Public Discourses of Homosexuality in Saskatchewan, 1971–93." In J. McNinch and M. Cronin (eds.), *I Could Not Speak My Heart: Education and Social Justice for Gay and Lesbian Youth*Regina: CPRC Press.

Lateef, Yasir. 2017. "The Aids Memorial Quilt." <http://www.aidsquilt.org/about/the-aids-memorial-quilt> (accessed February 9, 2017).

Mas, Suzanna. 2016. "Transgender Canadians Should 'Feel Free and Safe' to Be Themselves Under New Liberal Bill. CBC News, May 17. <http://www.cbc.ca/news/politics/transgender-bill-trudeau-government-1.3585522> (accessed April 5, 2017).

McElwee, Joshua J. 2016. "Francis Explains 'Who am I to Judge?'" *National Catholic Reporter*. <https://www.ncronline.org/news/vatican/francis-explains-who-am-i-judge> (accessed March 15, 2017).

McNinch, James. 2009. "I Thought Pocahontas Was a Movie." In Carol Schick and James McNinch (eds.), *Perspectives on Race/Culture Binaries in Education and Service Professions*. Regina: CPRC.

___. 2015. Address to the Western Canadian Teacher Federation Counsellors, Saskatoon, February 16.

McNinch, James, and Krista Baliko. 2014. "Broken Borders, Broken Binaries: Two Spirit Youth in Saskatchewan in the 21st Century." In R. Rogers and C. Ramsay (eds.), *Overlooking Saskatchewan: Minding the Gap*. Regina: University of Regina Press.

Morrison, Paul. 2001. *The Explanation of Everything: Essays on Sexual Subjectivity*. NY: New York University Press.

Nussbaum, Emily. 2018. "Fam and Cheese: Family Drama on 'Here and Now', 'This is Us' and 'The Fosters'." *The New Yorker*, February 26: 78–79.

Pakulski, Jan. 1997. "Cultural Citizenship." *Citizenship Studies*, 1, 1: 73–76.

Picard, Andre. 2014. "How the Advent of Aids Advanced Gay Rights." *Globe and Mail*, August 15. <http://www.theglobeandmail.com/life/health-and-fitness/health/how-the-advent-of-aids-advanced-gay-rights/article20083869/?page=all> (accessed February 9, 2017).

Reuters News Service. 2007. "President Misquoted over Gays in Iran: Aide." October 10. <http://www.reuters.com/article/us-iran-gays-idUSBLA05294620071010> (accessed April 19, 2017).

Richardson, Dianne. 2000. *Rethinking Sexuality*. London: Sage.

Rostow, Eugene. 1968. "The Role of the Vatican in the Modern World."

L'Oservatore Roman (English edition). May 30. <https://www.ewtn.com/library/humanity/vatmod.htm>.

RuPaul. 1996. *Letting It All Hang Out.* New York: Hyperion Books.

Sage, Adam, and To Kington. 2016. "Pope Lights Fire Under School Gender Dispute." *The Times,* October 4. <https://www.thetimes.co.uk/article/pope-lights-fire-under-school-gender-dispute-sp6v0q2fs> (accessed April 20, 2017).

Schonfeld, Zach. 2015. "The Surprising History of the Phrase 'Adam and Eve, not Adam and Steve.'" *Newsweek,* July 1. <http://www.newsweek.com/2015/07/24/surprising-history-phrase-adam-and-eve-not-adam-and-steve-348164.html> (accessed February 26, 2018).

Sedgwick, Eve. 1990. *Epistemology of the Closet.* Los Angeles: U of California Press.

Solerno, Rick. 2017. "Sorry, Justin. Your Apology to LGBTQ People Doesn't Let You Off the Hook." November 28. <http://nationalpost.com/opinion/government-oppression-of-lgbtq-community-doesnt-end-with-trudeaus-apology>.

Somerville, Margaret. 2007. "If Same-Sex Marriage, Why Not Polygamy?" *Globe and Mail,* August 11.

Tamale, Sylvia. 2014. "Homosexuality is Not Un-African." *Aljazeera America,* April 26. <http://america.aljazeera.com/opinions/2014/4/ho (homosexuality-africamuseveniugandanigeriaethiopia.html>.

Tasker, John. 2017a. "Transgender Rights Bill Threatens 'Female-Born' Women's Spaces, Activists Say." CBC News Website, May 12. <http://www.cbc.ca/news/politics/transgender-rights-bill-female-born-spaces-1.4110634> (accessed May 12, 2017).

___. 2017b. "Canada Enacts Protections for Transgender Community." CBC News, June 17. <http://www.cbc.ca/news/politics/transgender-rights-bill-senate-1.4163823> (accessed February 23, 2018).

Taylor, Drew Hayden (ed.). 2008. *Me Sexy: An Exploration of Native Sex and Sexuality.* Vancouver: Douglas and McIntyre.

Thuma, Andrea. 2011. "Hannah Arendt, Agency, and the Public Space." In M. Behrensen, L. Lee and A.S. Tekelioglu (eds.), *Modernities Revisited.* Vienna: IWM Junior Visiting Fellows. <http://www.iwm.at/iwmauthor/andrea-thuma/> (accessed February 17, 2017).

Troian, Manta. 2017. "Inquiry into Missing and Murdered Indigenous Women Has Just 122 Names Registered." CBC News Website, March 21. <http://www.cbc.ca/news/indigenous/mmiw-commission-database-just-122-names-1.4035181> (accessed April 18, 2017).

Truth and Reconciliation Commission of Canada. 2015) *Honouring the Truth, Reconciling for the Future: Summary of the Final Report of the Truth and Reconciliation Commission of Canada.* <http://www.trc.ca/websites/trcinstitution/File/2015/Honouring_the_Truth_Reconciling_for_the_Future_July_23_2015.pdf> (accessed September 27, 2015).

Tuck, Eve, and Wayne Yang. 2012. "Decolonization Is Not a Metaphor." *Decolonization: Indigeneity, Education & Society,* 1, 1. <http://decolonization.

org/index.php/des/article/view/18630> (accessed February 19, 2017).

Walker, Shaun. 2017a. "Journalists Fear Reprisals for Exposing Purge of Gay Men in Chechnya." *The Guardian International*, April 14. <https://www.theguardian.com/world/2017/apr/14/journalists-fear-reprisals-for-exposing-purge-of-gay-men-in-chechnya> (accessed April 15, 2017).

___. 2017b. "Chechen Police 'Have Rounded Up More Than 100 Suspected Gay Men." *The Guardian International*, April 2. <https://www.theguardian.com/world/2017/apr/02/chechen-police-rounded-up-100-gay-men-report-russian-newspaper-chechnya> (accessed April 15, 2017).

Wiart, Nikki. 2016. "Everett Klippert: An Unlikely Pioneer of Gay Rights in Canada." *Macleans on-line,* June 10. <http://www.macleans.ca/society/everett-klippert-an-unlikely-pioneer-of-gay-rights-in-canada/ (accessed February 13, 2017).

Wilson, Alex. 2013. "How We Find Ourselves: Identity Development and Two-Spirit People." In S. Ferguson (ed.), *Race, Gender, Sexuality and Social Class. Dimensions of Inequality*. Thousand Oaks: Sage Publications.

Wilson, P.A., and H. Yoshikowa. 2007. "Improving Access to Health Care Among the Lesbian Gay, and Bisexual Populations." In I.H. Meyer and M.E. Northridge (eds.), *The Health of Sexual Minorities*. NY: Springer Press.

York, Geoffrey. 2009. "Uganda's Anti-Gay Bill Causes Commonwealth Uproar." *Globe and Mail*, November 25. <http://www.theglobeandmail.com/news/world/ugandas-anti-gay-bill-causes-commonwealth-uproar/article1376503/> (accessed April 20, 2017).

Yoshino, Kevin. 2005a. *Covering: The Hidden Assault on Our Civil Rights*. New York: Random House.

___. 2005b. "How Opponents of Gay Marriage Will Be Bored into Submission." *Village Voice*, July 14. <http://www.villagevoice.com/arts/the-irresistible-banality-of-same-sex-marriage-7136165>.

___. 2016. *Speak Now: Marriage Equity on Trial*. New York: Broadway Books.

Youdell, Deborah. 2006. *Impossible Bodies, Impossible Selves: Exclusions and Student Subjectivities*. NY: Springer Press.

Young, Leslie. 2016. "Canada's Limitations on Gay Blood Donations 'Ridiculous': HIV Researchers." Global News, June 28. <http://globalnews.ca/news/2792150/canadas-limitations-on-gay-blood-donations-ridiculous-hiv-researchers/> (accessed March 24, 2017).

9

ENERGY, CLIMATE, THE EARTH AND JUSTICE

Margot A. Hurlbert

OBJECTIVES

At the end of this chapter, you will be able to:

- Understand environmental, energy and climate justice

- Describe different worldviews respecting the earth and environment and understand how they impact law

- Apply social justice to the environment, energy and climate change issues

- Formulate strategy to mitigate environmental, energy and climate damage and promote sustainability in the future based on principles of distributive justice and ethical practice

Environmental justice, or what some prefer to call ecological justice, expands our consideration of justice beyond the realm of inter-human relationships. Traditionally, analyses of justice issues predominantly focus on relationships between individuals or groups of people. Environmental justice, on the other hand, turns our focus towards aspects of both the physical environment in which we live, particularly how we, as humans, interact and relate to that environment and each other, and how these relations are justice issues.

Formal justice, substantive justice and ethical practice in environmental, energy and climate justice contexts depends on how one thinks about environment, energy and the impacts of climate change. This thinking relates to "cognition" and worldviews, the place of law in this relationship of cognition, distributional ecological justice issues with the distribution of earth's resources and side effects of development. The complex problem of climate change aptly demonstrates this inequitable distribution of earth's resources (fossil fuel use) and the impacts of sea level rise, drought and flood and gives rise to the third pillar of justice: ethical practice.

COGNIZING THE ENVIRONMENT, EARTH AND HUMANITY

Often when discussing the relationship between people and their environment, the notion of "cognized" environment is used. This refers to the way humans define and interpret the biophysical environment and is distinguishable from the "real environment" or the external biophysical environment independent of how people think about it. The cognized environment recognizes that people may live in natural environments but they live and act in worlds mediated and constructed by cultural symbols (Harper 2004: 38). Because a cognized environment is cultural, in a broad sense, it is helpful to understand that it is a possible component of a larger societal ideology or worldview, but yet multiple worldviews exist within a society.[1]

When humans existed in small bands of hunter-gatherers, travelling as nomads hunting small game, fishing, tracking migration and eating roots and berries, their worldview was thought of as a state of being "embedded in nature" (Harper 2004: 40). Their cognized environment was that of a living natural world of things being governed by spiritual forces or a natural living wilderness. For the Assembly of First Nations, cognized environment would be described as "Honouring Earth":

> From the realms of the human world, the sky dwellers, the water beings, forest creatures and all other forms of life, the beautiful Mother Earth gives birth to, nurtures and sustains all life. Mother

Earth provides us with our food and clean water sources. She bestows us with materials for our homes, clothes and tools. She provides all life with raw materials for our industry, ingenuity and progress. She is the basis of who we are as "real human beings" that include our languages, our cultures, our knowledge and wisdom to know how to conduct ourselves in a good way. If we listen from the place of connection to the Spirit That Lives in All Things, Mother Earth teaches what we need to know to take care of her and all her children. All are provided by our mother, the Earth. (AFN n.d.)

A recent non-Indigenous version of a cognized environment is the "New Ecological Paradigm" of Catton and Dunlap (1978). This worldview regards humans as one among many interrelated species and concerns itself with the consequences of human activity for the environment. Less faith is placed on technology and human progress solving environmental problems. The New Ecological Paradigm recognizes that humans live within a finite biophysical environment and seeks to reduce human impact on the environment through consuming less.

The dialectic opposite of the New Ecological Paradigm is the "Human Exemptionalism Paradigm" (Catton and Dunlap 1978). In this worldview, humans dominate; they are exempt from and independent of their environment as technology allows them to manipulate and control that environment to suit their needs. As such, we could understand modern industrial society without consideration of its biophysical base, and therefore environmental phenomena are irrelevant to the study of human society. The Human Exemptionalism Paradigm appears to have many parallels to the worldview present during the industrial age and belief that continuous economic growth will end poverty and sustain the planet.

Significant diversity exists in ecological worldviews. Many current environmental social movements actively challenge the idea of humans dominating nature. Organic farmers actively reject the industrialized worldview; important institutions such as the former Canadian Wheat Board have stated that their customers rejected genetically modified crops, therefore, they did not accept the remaking of nature (Canadian Wheat Board 2004). La Vía Campesina is a vocal global movement of farmers who reject the industrialized worldview (Desmarais 2007). La Vía Campesina is an example of a social group embracing a version of

CASE STUDY:
LA VÍA CAMPESINA

La Vía Campesina is was formed in 1993 as the Uruguay Round of the General Agreement on Trade and Tarriffs (GATT) negotiations were drawing to a close. Initially bringing together forty-five farm organizations, the movement now embraces 149 organizations of peasants, rural women, small- and medium-scale farmers, Indigenous agrarian communities and rural workers from sixty-nine countries in Asia, the Americas, Europe and Africa.

La Vía Campesina claims that the globalization of an industrial model of agriculture, together with increased liberalization of the food trade, is leading to the destruction of biodiversity and subsequent loss of cultural diversity, further degradation of the environment, increased disparity and greater impoverishment in the countryside everywhere. It argues that neoliberal policies are sustained by human rights abuses and increased violence in the countryside — geared specifically to intimidate peasants — while economic liberalization facilitates the corporatization of agriculture, endangers national food security and threatens the livelihood and very survival of peasant families. As a result, peasant and farm families everywhere, in the North and the South, are "disappeared" and rural communities are decimated.

Food sovereignty is at the heart of La Vía Campesina's alternative model of development and the movement sees it is the only viable solution to current global food, energy and environmental crises (Desmarais 2007). Food sovereignty entails peoples' right to define their agricultural and food policy. Most importantly, food sovereignty includes farmers' and peasants' "right to produce our own food in our own territory" and "the right of consumers to be able to decide what they consume and how and by whom it is produced" (La Vía Campesina 2000).

the New Ecological Paradigm. They acknowledge the interconnection of people with their biophysical environment but do so in the context of the rights of people to self-determination and food sovereignty.

There is no doubt that humans have an impact on the environment.

There is also a circular impact it is having on humans in the form of climate change. Science clearly establishes the New Ecological Paradigm and discounts the Human Exemptionalism Paradigm. The impacts of climate change are so certain scientists have agreed to declare that the earth is now in a new geological time scale. We now live in a time of the "anthropocene," a geological epoch that started about 11,700 years ago and was preceded by the last glacial period. Anthropocene is derived from *anthropos*, from the Ancient Greek for human (Zalasiewicz 2008). This geological time scale is so named to recognize the significant human impact on the earth's geology and ecosystems. This time scale includes but also transcends the duration of anthropogenic climate change (Castree 2015).

LAW AND ENVIRONMENTAL JUSTICE

How we cognize the environment informs how we construct environmental justice. Consider the following illustration of environmental justice when we utilize our current conception of human rights and add in the idea of plant and animal rights. Studying and creating ecological justice is more difficult than simply adding environment into the justice equation and stirring.

The addition of the environment to our consideration of justice is more complex than expanding our notion of who and what should be included in our structures of formal justice. Who and what (animals, plants, water) should be included in our justice analysis? How do we assess issues of just deserts when it comes to the environment? Does just deserts mean that only some people deserve clean air, clean drinking water and sanitation? The environment is important to Canadians, and because of this laws have been enacted to protect the environment (set out in the Case Study of the Rights of Plants and Animals). However, have these laws achieved environmental justice that might be a clean, sustainable environment available to future generations?

LEGAL ENVIRONMENTAL JUSTICE

For people who suffer environmental harm, environmental law and procedural environmental justice guarantees three rights: the right to information; the right to a hearing; and the right to compensation

CASE STUDY:
THE RIGHTS OF PLANTS AND ANIMALS

Can environmental justice be approached by simply adding the earth, plants and animals into our current considerations of justice (Wenz 1988)? Do animals (both sentient and non-sentient organisms) have rights and are they part of our justice equation? In other words, should dogs, cats, horses and cows have rights? Should all animals have rights, or only the ones humans rely on? If they do, must we become vegetarians? Must carnivorous animals, such as wolves, become vegetarians? Otherwise rabbits will never have meaningful rights unless domesticated, but, would they then be happy? What about the rights of the wolves to make an honest living (meal)?

Is the concern to protect future human generations who rely on these entities or to protect those entities because of their own right to existence?

Some prefer the term "ecological" justice when expanding the ambit of justice beyond human relationships to recognize this broader focus.

(Cutter 2006: 249). This definition is really about simple procedural or process equity, or addressing the direct causal mechanisms of inequity. This conception of environmental justice reflects a legalistic approach to environmental justice (termed "legal environmental justice") wherein the government is responsible for passing necessary legislation to protect the environment, and people affected by pollution or environmental contamination can access remedies in court. Environmental justice in this definition is akin to formal or procedural justice.

Remedies available to people through the common law for damage to their health have been supplemented with statutory remedies in environmental protection legislation to make the commencement of these lawsuits easier. These measures have had only limited success. Bringing a court action for environmental damage is always brought after the damage has been done. The process is slow, time consuming and expensive. Scientific proof is required that the defendant (or person sued) caused the environmental damage and that the damage harmed the person(s) bringing the lawsuit. Proof is required on a balance of probabilities. These factors

> ## CASE STUDY:
> ## ENVIRONMENTAL ENFORCEMENT AND MONITORING
>
> This legalistic approach to environmental justice is also reflected in the emergence of government departments or ministries of environment in the 1970s and the plethora of environmental protection legislation passed by various governments since then. This legislation includes environmental protection acts, clean air acts, endangered species acts, hazardous substances acts and pest control acts, to name a few. During the massive government cutbacks of the 1980s and 1990s, environment departments were the subject of some of the deepest cuts and, as a result, enforcement actions have reduced. For instance, the number of inspections carried out annually under the Canadian Environmental Protection Act, 1999 fell during the 1990s from two thousand to seven hundred (Benidickson 1997). Of known violations, only a handful are prosecuted. Government reports acknowledge that hundreds of companies and municipalities regularly break environmental laws without being prosecuted (Christie 2000). Now, Saskatchewan has adopted a results-based regulation that doesn't require any enforcement by environmental protection officers. Instead, permit holders track and monitor their own compliance and "qualified persons" hired by the permit holders sign and attest to the permit holder's reports of compliance.

impede access to justice and create significant barriers for the courts to play an effective role in protecting the environment.

Legal environmental justice is elusive. Courts are not generally accessible due to cost and time delay; governments are inactive due to budget constraints. Formal legal environmental justice should be expanded such that the following principles of environmental justice are guaranteed:

- protection from environmental degradation;
- prevention of adverse health impacts as a result of deteriorating environmental conditions before the harm occurs, not afterwards;
- mechanisms for assigning culpability for environmental harm and shifting the burden of proof of contamination. Polluters

should have to prove they are not polluting (or causing harm) instead of people proving that polluters are;
- redressing the impacts of environmental degradation with targeted remedial action and resources.

In some countries around the world, the important place of Mother Earth is enshrined in law. Justice looks quite different if we start with the earth, instead of with humans and their relationships as the key consideration. By way of example, in Bolivian law, The Law of the Rights of Mother Earth (Law 071 of the Plurinational State) was passed December 2010 and recognizes the rights of Mother Earth and her constituent life systems, including human communities. Rights include those of life, diversity of life (for the variety of beings that comprise Mother Earth), water, clean air, restoration and to live free from contamination (with regards to toxic and radioactive waste).

EARLY ENVIRONMENTAL JUSTICE MOVEMENTS

Some of the earliest environmental justice movements in North America were focused on a specific, local, hazardous environmental practice. They relied on the media and a legalistic approach. Often the group was of low socio-economic status and represented a racial minority. In the U.S., the environmental justice movement's genesis is thought to have begun in 1982 in Warren County, North Carolina. Here, the state selected a site to host a hazardous waste landfill containing thirty thousand cubic yards of PCB contaminated soil. Residents, rural and poor, were joined in their protests by national civil rights groups, environmental groups, clergy and the Black Congressional Caucus. A group of Black Americans of lower socio-economic status was not protected from a hazardous environmental practice (the storage of PCBs) and its resultant adverse health effects. Studies surrounding this event confirmed environmental racism. The perspective, voices and wishes of these poor, marginalized Black people were not heard; narrow procedural and legal environmental justice was non-existent because these people were Black (Cutter 2006).

Pursuing environmental justice, just like pursuing legal justice, requires us to set aside our belief that law and legal principles represent the pinnacle of justice. Regardless of the number of pieces of legislation passed or the number of lawsuits commenced, the environment continues to be degraded at an increasing rate. Contributing to this is the fact that, although voluminous, environmental legislation is an inconsistent patchwork of rules. This legislation allows excessive discretion of environmental protection officers to do nothing and is generally inadequately implemented and enforced (Boyd 2003).

ECOLOGICAL JUSTICE: THE EARTH COMMONS

Environmental justice requires us to reassess our relationship to the earth, to reconsider our material requirements from the earth, to evaluate our relative share of earth's resources with our community and worldly neighbours and to consider all of this while taking into account the interests of future generations. Today, our use of energy from the food we eat and the coal, oil and gas we consume by driving, heating our homes and producing the disposable items we rely on (our phones, clothing and comfort goods) is profoundly impacting our earth and therefore us. Environmental justice and its constituent components of energy justice and climate justice is connected to how we impact and share our earth commons.

Environmental justice highlights a fundamental dynamic: humans depend on the earth to live and we are reliant on one another's environmental practices such that we rely on each other to share it. A picture of the earth from space drives home the fact that humans share and depend on a fragile planetary ecosystem, an earthly "commons" of land, water and atmosphere. Natural resources such as the air, water and parks still exist as common property to be shared by all. If we go back only a few hundred years, far more of the earth's forests, waters and minerals existed in a state of commons than today. In England, Wales and Scotland, millions of acres of land in the seventeenth century was termed "common land" and open to common rights of grazing livestock and mowing meadows. The process of "enclosure" converted most of these open fields to private property (Callander 1987). However, some common property still exists. For example, there were eighty-seven community pastures in the Canadian Prairies in 2008 (Kulshreshtha et al. 2008). Now, global commons include the global ocean, the atmosphere and outer space. Even with private property, when viewed from space, it is clear that humans continue to share Mother Earth.

Even though all humans must share the earth's resources to live, we are very far from global equality in access to those resources, which can be depicted by the amount of emissions that countries release into the atmosphere. Research by the Intergovernmental Panel on Climate Change has shown that depicting emissions of countries from the Organisation for Economic Co-operation and Development (OECD) in North America, versus Latin America, Africa and the Middle East is skewed. The wealthier countries consume more resources, produce more energy and emit more greenhouse gasses.

Although there have been improvements in world poverty in the last decade, the World Bank Group reported in 2013 that 10.7 percent of the world's population, or 767 million people, lived on less than $1.90 USD per day. The political and economic ideologies that have created and continue this inequality is not predetermined or inevitable. Anthropologists have shown that gifting and sharing has existed as a basis for community relationships in societies around the world, contrary to the common misconceptions that people are individualistic and selfish by nature (Keltner et al. 2010). The question for environmental justice is what sharing of the earth's resources is just? Every human being is entitled to the minimum of basic goods of life that is consistent with respect for human dignity (Weil 2002).

Human access to and use of the earth's resources for economic growth and livelihoods has also led to harm to the earth and depletion and degradation of its resources. Population growth, increased consumerism, more sophisticated technology and processes of resources extraction have increased the degradation of the earth (Cronin 2009). The environment suffers from both a depletion of resources such as air, water and soil, the destruction of habitats and ecosystems and the extinction of wildlife (Johnson et al. 1997). A distributive environmental justice perspective would argue that environmental ills such as pollution have been inequitably distributed with predominantly marginalized people experiencing disadvantage through the contamination of their environments (Dobson 1998), but not having access to the benefits of development through an equitable share of resource revenues. The disproportionate effects of environmental degradation on people and places are illustrated in Nigeria where Shell pumps oil to make a considerable profit, but the local Ogoni people live without adequate roads, electricity and water in a wasteland of environmental degradation from Shell's pumping activities (Watts 2001).

Closer to home, Indigenous peoples in Ontario are poisoned from years of mercury released in their water supply as a result of industrial activities causing Minamata Disease (loss of motor control, speech, memory, vision and hearing and the development of cerebral palsy) (Harada 2005).

Justice theorist John Rawls espoused that a fair distribution of societal goods could be arrived at by pretending one is behind a veil of ignorance and one's own life chances and circumstances are not yet determined. Without the personal bias of being either wealthy (and wanting to maintain that wealth) or being poor (and wanting a better status), one would then philosophize about how a just society would allocate its goods. If one was omnipresent, or identified more closely as a "global citizen" than that of a particular country, then preferences and choices would equitably allocate the benefits of wealth and the detriments of pollution and development globally. Rawls' theory of distributive justice can be illustrated in analyses of energy justice.

ENERGY JUSTICE

Although Heffron et al. (2015) believe energy justice is separate from environmental and climate justice, I believe energy justice has many parallels to environmental justice and the study of justice framed in this book. As will be illustrated, aspects of formal justice, substantive justice and ethical practice can be found in relation to energy.

Energy justice relates to the full energy production, supply and distribution chain (Jenkins et al. 2016; McCauley et al. 2013). This includes oil and gas mining, oil refining, oil and gas distribution, electricity and its production and the consumption of these and other forms of energy. Developing energy justice also includes the negative impacts related to these activities. Energy justice can be characterized and understood according to the foundational concepts of justice: formal justice, substantive justice and ethical practice. For some authors, energy justice is envisioned as involving a framework of three key elements: distributional justice, procedural justice and justice as recognition, which coincides with certain elements of formal, substantive and ethical practice (McCauley et al. 2013). Others developed an "energy trilema"; signifying a just and equitable balance of economics (energy finance), environment (climate change mitigation) and politics (energy security or supply) (Heffron 2015).

Formal Energy Justice

Formal justice is characterized by treating equals equally, procedural justice and concepts of just deserts and fairness. Energy poverty is an important component of energy injustice as it refers to the unequal access to energy resources in relation to the social and spatial distribution of energy (Bickerstaff et al. 2013). Fuel poverty exposes the links between poverty and lack of access to clean, affordable fuel. In rural Saskatchewan, for example, many people do not have access to the electricity grid, but instead must rely on expensive, inefficient and polluting fuels such as diesel fuel. In Africa, low-income households prepare food by burning local materials that contribute to deforestation and pollute the air, thereby harming health. People do not have the same access to a warm (or cool) home, resources to cook food or cool stored food, and therefore formal equality is not achieved.

Green et al. (2016) have developed an indicator of energy poverty. Households that spend more than 10 percent of their income on energy goods (electricity, gas and the like) are deemed to be energy poor. Greater than 10 percent of expenditure is considered a burden on household resources. In Canada, in 2013, 19.4 percent of households were energy poor, while Atlantic Canada had 38.5 percent of households facing energy poverty and Alberta had 12.8 percent (Green et al. 2016). This indicator marks the point of "strained" circumstances when access to energy for heating, cooling and cooking is disproportionately burdensome and therefore inequitable for households at and above this level of expenditure.

Energy justice is also procedural. Energy justice requires equitable procedures that engage everyone in energy decisions (Walker 2009). All groups should participate in decision making and their contributions should be taken seriously. Full information disclosure and impartiality must be present when decisions surrounding energy issues are made, such as whether to build a pipeline or what type of power production should be used (like nuclear fuel or coal) (Heffron et al. 2015). For instance, in the Supreme Court of Canada case of Chippewas of the Thames (2017 SCC 41), the National Energy Board approved the expansion of a pipeline despite the objections of the Chippewas of the Thames. The case was dismissed because the pipeline was pre-existing. Therefore, its expansion was determined not relevant.

This procedural component is informed by the principle of

cosmopolitanism, the idea that we are all global citizens as our decisions and their consequences impact people all over the world.

Substantive Energy Justice

Distributional energy justice is inherent in the spatial, temporal and societal aspects surrounding energy. It includes the (un)equal allocation of environmental benefits (energy jobs, secure supply of energy for heating and powering modern homes) and the (un)even distribution of associated responsibilities and ills (polluted air from coal power generation or diesel fuel) (Heffron et al. 2015). Energy distributional justice involves basic freedoms that are advanced by access to affordable sustainable energy systems that should be maximized. Intervention and redistribution should occur when inequalities in energy goods and services disproportionately affect the least advantaged. In Saskatchewan, the 1949 Rural Electrification Act was a measure addressing energy poverty. While urban residents had access to reliable affordable power, rural residents throughout the province did not. Energy poverty in this case had a gender component, as women suffered the most hardships being responsible for hauling water and wood for basic activities of cleaning and cooking (Champ 2001).

Because environmental degradation and energy poverty disproportionally impact those who are economically and racially marginalized (Schlosberg 2004), they need to be involved in decisions on matters impacting the environment and energy for their communities. Facilitating a respectful dialogue incorporating diverse perspectives to achieve consensual decisions is a practice of participatory environmental justice (just as participatory justice and ethical practice discussed below). As such, a plurality of interests and knowledge are recognized, which allows different sorts of knowledges to be opened up and engenders different environmental decision-making processes. It is then possible to value the traditional ecological knowledge that Indigenous communities hold within a framework that appreciates plurality as elaborated in ethical practice below (McLean 2007).

ETHICAL ENERGY PRACTICE

Participation and recognition are important components of energy justice. Reconciliation of conflict in energy justice is about recognition, which is more than tolerance. It means ensuring individuals are fairly represented, free from threat and have complete and equal political rights (Schlosberg 2003). It requires participation, impartiality and full information disclosure by government and industry and use of appropriate and sympathetic engagement mechanisms (Schlosberg 2003; Todd and Zografos 2005). Real recognition in decision making ensures that the misrecognition (distorting people's views that may appear demeaning or contemptible) or under-recognition of sections of society do not occur (McCauley et al. 2016).

Participation and recognition justice are also recognized in other environmental justice areas. A common theme in struggles for social justice and ecological reform, and among social movements for environmental justice, is the call for the democratization of political institutions and processes for decision making (Schlosberg 2004; Adkin 2009; Fraser 2005). As illustrated in the Chippewas' case of pipeline objection, often peoples' voices are unheard. Many terms reflect this idea, including "deliberative democracy," "participatory justice," "green democracy" and "ecological citizenship." All envision local people and communities playing a greater role than they currently do in making decisions affecting the environment which include decisions about what economic developments occur close to them, and how environmental effects of these developments are mitigated (Anand 2004). Participatory environmental justice ensures everyone the ability to contribute to environmental decisions affecting community (both local and global) risks and benefits (Shrader-Frechette 2002).

Participation and recognition are important components of energy and environmental justice. However, reconciliation of conflicting perceptions and viewpoints requires more than procedural safeguards for the participation of marginalized peoples and recognition of their cognized environments and worldviews. In this exercise, ultimately an ethical practice is needed. Climate justice illustrates issues around ethical practice.

CLIMATE JUSTICE AND ETHICAL PRACTICE

The consideration of climate change illustrates the need for the adoption of the ethical practice of "leximin," which means prioritizing the interests of the weakest in society. Human-induced climate change has become a very real and very significant threat to the environment and sustainability. The cause of climate change is disproportionately attributable to the developed world, which includes Canada, the United States and Europe. In 2014, the largest CO_2 emitters were China (30 percent) and the United States (15 percent) (Boden et al. 2017). However, many of the most severe effects will be experienced in the developing world, and specifically in small island states where rising sea levels reduce their land mass, create storm surges, contribute to coastal erosion and compromise the water resources and fisheries on which they depend for food (Mimura et al. 2007). Because these small islands are already poor they will not have access to the necessary resources to adapt to these changes. One study concludes that, if unchecked, climate change will become a major obstacle to continued poverty reduction for these vulnerable countries such as the Maldives or Kiribati (Stern 2007). It is this state of affairs that dictates Canadians and Americans must consider our actions in contributing to this global inequity.

CLIMATE CHANGE

It is now indisputable that the earth's climate is changing due to the activities of humans. Because of human reliance on energy for our production of food, materials and transportation, we have emitted gases, including CO_2, into our environment in amounts vastly greater than would have been emitted through natural processes. This excess of CO_2 is contributing to global warming. Not only will there be increasing average temperatures, but there will also be increasing precipitation, intensity and frequency of droughts, floods and severe storms and as yet unforeseen abrupt changes and extreme climatic events (Sauchyn et al. 2007; IPCC 2014). People will have to migrate to other areas, sometimes other countries, causing potential conflict. The number of people who will live in water-stressed countries is expected to get much larger. Already food-insecure regions are expected to see radical declines in agricultural yields (IPCC 2014).

Negative impacts of climate change will not be experienced equally. Already, vulnerable people have limited capacity to adapt to climate change and consequently will suffer the most. These people in countries like Africa, Bangladesh and the Maldives are not the people who have contributed to the emissions of CO_2, yet they will suffer the worst consequences in our current global system. Stated another way, Canada, the United States and Europe have historically and currently have the largest amounts of industry and the largest populations who drive cars contributing to CO_2 emissions, but these countries will have access to resources (such as money or technology) to adapt to the changing climate.

Climate change is also bringing increased excessive precipitation and drought, and poor countries are experiencing these impacts. The number of storms and other weather-related disasters in Latin America and the Caribbean has risen to 571 in 2000–2009 from 356 in 1990–1999, 256 in 1980–1989, and 134 in 1970–1979 (Bello 2015). Floods constitute 44 percent of all disasters and droughts account for 6 percent. However, droughts result in 35 percent of disaster-related deaths, while floods account for 9 percent (Bello 2015).[2] Countries with low Human Development Index scores are more vulnerable, in that they experience far higher mortality rates (UNDP 2010).

Climate change has become a story of extinction. As global temperatures rise dramatically, with indications that it will be by as much as six degrees celsius by 2100, it is estimated that approximately one quarter or more of all species on land will be threatened with extinction by 2050 (Harvard School of Public Health 2017). Although not without uncertainty, estimates of species loss by 2100 include 12.6 percent of plants, 9.4 percent of invertebrates and 17.7 percent of vertebrates (Bellard et al. 2012). The world's coral reefs are already suffering from higher temperatures, killing coral reefs and their inhabitants. Annual severe coral bleaching is occurring in the northern Great Barrier Reef and is projected to continue to occur for 99 percent of the world's coral reefs in the twenty-first century (van Hooidonk et al. 2016). Climate change is irreversible on a multi-century to millennial timescale; ocean acidification and the rise of global mean sea levels will increase for centuries beyond 2100 if CO_2 emissions continue to strongly affect marine ecosystems (IPCC 2014). The IPCC predicts that sea levels will rise by 26–82 cm between now and 2100. The sea will continue to wash over Kiribati and the Marshall Islands, likely making them unliveable in the future (IPCC 2014).

In addition to the ethical considerations regarding developed countries like Canada changing the climate policy and carbon emissions that contribute to this global inequity, there is also an ethical practice for recognizing adaptation plans for vulnerable countries. Ethics of recognizing the autonomy of these nations is paramount. Members of the United Nations Framework Convention on Climate Change (UNFCCC) should act in the best interest of the small island state, respecting non maleficence (doing no harm) and justice (distributing resources equitably) (Mohanti 2009). But how can ideas about successful adaptation be imposed? Who judges successful adaptation? How do we finance adaptation? Who will welcome climate refugees?

At the sixtieth session of the U.N. General Assembly in 2005, Kiribati's President spoke of the need for relocation, an ultimate form of adaptation. The President hoped for increased labour migration, so family members could support their extended family remaining in Kiribati through remittances (Loughry and McAdam 2008). The Marshall Islands, in contrast to Kiribati, are considering adaptive actions that include protecting some of their island areas from erosion by landfilling to create new land for immigrants, building high-rise, multi-unit accommodations where appropriate and addressing land tenure implications from land loss and land creation (Holthus et al. 1992). Kiribati has commenced buying land on higher ground in countries such as Fiji for their relocation. The Marshall Islands has chosen not to purchase land, but rather to stay and fight. Their decision is based on their identity and culture that is tied to the land (Lewis 2015). The ethical practice of climate change and recognition would require that here, small island states be allowed to determine their future adaptation pathways.

Some countries are concerned that climate-healing CO_2 emission reductions may result in reduced economic growth. Consider the position of Saskatchewan Environment Minister Scott Moe (who became Premier in 2018):

"A $50 a tonne carbon tax would amount to $2.5 billion in Saskatchewan," he said, and that's a cost its export-based economy cannot bear. "We'll use everything in our disposal to not have that cost imposed on industries here in the province of Saskatchewan and that may include going to a court of law." (Canadian Press 2017: n.p.)

This sentiment optimizes industry and the economy over the reduction of CO_2 emissions. British Columbia, on the other hand, introduced a carbon tax in 2008 that has decreased per-capita emissions in 2008–2013 12.9 percent compared to 2000–2007, which is three-and-a-half times as pronounced as the 3.7 percent per-capita decline for the rest of Canada (Komanoff and Gordon 2015). The discussion of local economy should be replaced with a discussion of the cosmopolitan global community and our shared obligation to reduce harmful greenhouse gas emissions in order to preserve the planet for future generations and prevent harm to already marginalized people.

SOCIAL ENVIRONMENTAL JUSTICE

Environmental, energy and climate justice illustrate many of the themes, disciplines and theoretical approaches to studying justice. Laws, regulations and civil court actions are important for people seeking redress, compensation and protection from environmental degradation. However, law is not the only avenue to pursue ecological justice and often is limited in that the law reflects the cognized environment or dominant worldview of the country in which it exists. Canada's laws allow for environmental redress after damage is suffered, but often (as in the Chippewas of the Thames case) prioritizes industrial development.

Distributional environmental justice focuses on the distribution of benefits and costs (or ills) of the environment and its resources. Today, the impacts of climate change are most serious. Energy decisions and energy justice contribute to this. Participatory environmental, energy and climate justice offers the solution by calling for people to participate and decide in the distribution of costs and benefits. Having all people participating in decisions of energy choice while understanding the implications of climate change might bring awareness and imbed ethical practice into one's own energy decisions. However, the danger of participatory justice practices is that marginalized people continue to be marginalized and are not really a part of democratic decision making. The hegemonic power structures of society may continue to operate in (so-called) participatory environmental decision-making bodies. Putting into real practice a philosophy of "leximin" — making decisions that take into account the position of the least favoured or neediest person in society — could go a long way to alleviating this power imbalance when it comes to environmental decisions. Much more study, writing and thought on implementing this approach is required.

If the current climate change emission reduction debate were reconsidered incorporating principles of environmental justice (other than legal environmental justice), a very different result would occur than has to date. For example, concerns expressed that climate-healing CO_2 emission reductions may result in reduced economic growth would be replaced with a discussion of the cosmopolitan global community, social inequality (class, race, gender) and perhaps concern for future generations and the true sustainability of our future.

DISCUSSION QUESTIONS

1. What are the impediments to solving the problem of global warming?
2. How can countries like Canada do more to reduce greenhouse gas emissions?
3. What does formal justice, substantive justice and ethical practice look like in relation to the earth?
4. What is energy justice?
5. Does participatory justice involve energy and climate justice?
6. How important is ethical practice to environment, energy and climate justice?

GLOSSARY

Cognized environment: An environment defined and interpreted by humans.

Distributional environmental justice: A fair distribution of societal resources (water, clean air, pristine earth) and societal bads or ills (pollution, soil degradation, contaminated water).

Ecological justice: A conception of justice that expands the relevant players beyond humans to include animals and plants and other aspects of the environment into the justice equation.

Environmental equity: A fair adjustment of the distribution of resource development such that its benefits and costs are fairly dispersed globally, nationally and locally.

Environmental racism: Occurs when socially and economically disadvantaged communities experience a disproportionate share of environmental burdens such as pollution, poor water quality and extreme weather events.

Formal environmental justice: Attaining fairness and just deserts and employing procedural justice in relation to energy and the earth's resources.

"Leximin": The principle that a person holding the least favoured position, or the neediest person in society, should have their interests taken into account in decision making.

Participatory environmental justice: The resolution of environment issues through the meaningful participation of a representative group of people expressing a plurality of perspectives and knowledges making real impact in respect of the distribution of environmental costs and benefits.

Sustainability: Ensuring decisions surrounding our environment preserve our environment and its resources for future generations.

Worldview: The totality of a group of people's cultural beliefs about the world and reality.

NOTES

1. A worldview is a shared view by a group of people. It is the totality of a group of people's cultural beliefs and belief systems about the world and reality (Harper 2004). It is not necessarily "all" Canadians or Americans, but Canadians or Americans as a "whole." The concept of worldviews usually requires a great degree of generalization so is somewhat obscure as there is always a certain amount of diversity of opinion, and diversity of worldviews.

2. Other disasters include storms, extreme temperature, wildfires and mass movement (WMO 2014).

REFERENCES

Adkin, L.E. 2009. "Democracy from the Trenches: Environmental Conflicts and Ecological Citizenship." In L.E. Adkin (ed.), *Environmental Conflict and Democracy in Canada.* Vancouver, BC: UBC Press.

AFN (Assembly of First Nations). 2018. Honouring Earth. <http://www.afn.ca/honoring-earth/>.

Anand, R. 2004. *International Environmental Justice: A North-Nouth Dimension.* Hampshire, England: Ashgate.

Bellard, C., C. Bertelsmeier, P. Leadley, W. Thuiller, and F. Courchamp. 2012. "Impacts of Climate Change on the Future of Biodiversity." *Ecology Letters,* 15, 4: 365–377.

Bello, O.D. 2015. "Planning and disaster risk reduction in Latin America. Regional conference on strategies and tools for integrating disaster risk reduction into development planning and financing." United Nations Economic and Social Commission for Asia and the Pacific. Bangkok, Thailand. February 18.

Benidickson, J. 1997. *Environmental Law*. Toronto, ON: Irwin Law.

Bickerstaff, K., G.P. Walker and H. Bulkeley. 2013. "Introduction: Making Sense of Energy Justice." In K. Bickerstaff, G. Walker and H. Bulkeley (eds.), *Energy Justice in a Changing Climate: Social Equity and Low-Carbon Energy*. London: Zed Books.

Boden, T.A., G. Marland and R.J. Andres. 2017. "National CO_2 Emissions from Fossil-Fuel Burning, Cement Manufacture, and Gas Flaring: 1751–2014." Carbon Dioxide Information Analysis Center, Oak Ridge National Laboratory, U.S. Department of Energy, doi.10.3334/CDIAC/00001_V2017.

Boyd, D.R. 2003. *Unnatural Law*. Vancouver, BC: UBC Press.

Callander, R.F. 1987. *A Pattern of Landownership in Scotland with Particular Reference to Aberdeenshire*. Finzean: Haughend Publications.

Canadian Press. 2017. "Saskatchewan Will Not Allow A Carbon Tax Happen: Moe." PLANT: *Advancing Canadian Manufacturing*, May 5.

Canadian Wheat Board. 2004. "Customer Opposition to GM Wheat Growing." <http://www.cwb.ca/public/en/newsroom/releases/2004/031804.jsp> (accessed June 3, 2009).

Castree, N. 2015. "The Anthropocene: A Primer for Geographers." *Geography*, 100, 2: 66–75.

Catton, W.R., and R.E. Dunlap. 1978. *Environmental Sociology: A New Paradigm. American Sociologist*, 13: 41.

Champ, J. 2001. "Rural Electrification in Saskatchewan During the 1950s." Prepared for the Saskatchewan Western Development Museum, December 4.

Christie, E. 2000. *Pulping the Law: How Pulp Mills Are Ruining Canadian Waters with Impunity*. Toronto, ON: Sierra Legal Defence Fund.

Cronin, R. 2009. "Natural Resources and the Development-Environment Dilemma." Exploiting Natural Resources, The Henry L. Stimson Centre.

Cutter, S.L. 2006. "Race, Class and Environmental Justice." In S.L. Cutter, *Hazards, Vulnerability And Environmental Justice*. London: Earthscan.

Desmarais, A.A. 2007. *Globalization and the Power of Peasants: La Vía Campesina*. Halifax, NS: Fernwood & Pluto Books.

Dobson, A. 1998. *Justice and the Environment: Conceptions of Environmental Sustainability and Theories of Distributive Justice*. Oxford: Oxford University Press.

Fraser, N. 2005. "Reframing Justice in a Globalizing World." *New Left Review*, 36: 69–88.

Green, K.P., T. Jackson, I. Herzog, and M. Palacios. 2016. "Energy Costs and Canadian Households: How Much Are We Spending?" Fraser Institute, March. <https://www.fraserinstitute.org/sites/default/files/energy-costs-and-canadian-households.pdf>.

Harada, M. 2005. "The Global Lessons of Minimata Disease: An Introduction to Minamata Studies." *Advances in Bioethics*, 8: 299–335.

Harper, C.L. 2004. *Environment and Society: Human Perspectives On Environmental Issues*, third ed. New Jersey: Pearson Prentice Hall.

Harvard School of Public Health 2017. "Climate Change and Biodiversity Loss." <http://www.chgeharvard.org/topic/climate-change-and-biodiversity-loss>.

Heffron, R.J., D. McCauley and B.K. Sovacool. 2015. "Resolving Society's Energy Trilemma Through the Energy Justice Metric." *Energy Policy*, 87: 168–176.

Holthus, P., M. Crawford, C. Makroro and S. Sullivan. 1992. "Vulnerability Assessment of Accelerated Sea Level Rise. Case Study: Majuro Atoll, Marshall Islands." United States National Oceanic and Atmospheric Administration. SPREP Reports and Studies Series no. 60.

IPCC (Intergovernmental Panel on Climate Change). 2014. "Summary for Policymakers." In O. Edenhofer, R. Pichs-Madruga, Y. Sokona, E. Farahani, S. Kadner, K. Seyboth, A. Adler, I. Baum, S. Brunner, P. Eickemeier, B. Kriemann, J. Savolainen, S. Schlomer, C. von Stechow, T. Zwickel and J.C. Minx (eds.), *Climate Change 2014: Mitigation of Climate Change. Contribution of Working Group III to the Fifth Assessment Report of the Intergovernmental Panel on Climate Change.* Cambridge/New York: Cambridge University Press.

Jenkins, K.E.H., D. McCauley, R. Heffron, H. Stephan and R.W.M Rehner. 2016. "Energy Justice: A Conceptual Review." *Energy Research & Social Science*, 11: 174–182.

Johnson, D.L., S. Ambrose, T.J. Bassett, M.L. Bowen, D.E. Crummey, J.S. Isaacson, D.M. Johnson, P. Lamb, M. Saul, and A.E. Winter-Nelson. 1997. "Meanings of Environmental Terms." *Journal of Environmental Quality*, 26: 581–589.

Keltner, D., D. Adam McCauley, R.J. Heffron, H. Stephan and K. Jenkins. 2013. "Advancing Energy Justice: The Triumvirate of Tenants." *International Energy Law Review*, 32, 3: 107–110.

Komanoff, C., and M. Gordon. 2015. "British Columbia's Carbon Tax: By the Numbers." A Carbon Tax Center Report. The Carbon Tax Center, Vancouver, B.C. <carbontax.org/wpcontent/uploads/CTC_British_Columbia%27s_Carbon_Tax_By_The_Numbers.pdf>.

Kulshreshtha, S., G. Pearson, B. Kirychuk and R. Gaube. 2008. "Distribution of Public and Private Benefits on Federally Managed Community Pastures in Canada." Society for Range Management. Rangelands, 30, 1 (February): 3–11.

Lewis, R. 2015. "'Nowhere to Move': Marshall Islands Adapts Amid Climate Change Threat." Aljazeera America Environment. <http://america.aljazeera.com/articles/2015/5/19/Marshall-Islands-climate.html>.

Loughry, M., and J. McAdam. 2008. "Kiribati – Relocation and Adaptation." *Forced Migration Review*, 31, Climate Change and Displacement. <http://www.fmreview.org/climatechange/loughry-mcadam.html>.

McCauley, D.A., R.J. Heffron, H. Stephan and K. Jenkins. 2013. "Advancing Energy Justice: The Triumvirate of Tenets." *International Energy Law Review*, 32, 3.

McCauley, D., R. Heffron, M. Pavlenko, R. Rehner, R. Holmes. 2016. "Energy justice in the Artic: Implications for energy infrastructural development in the Arctic." Energy Research and Social Science 16: 141–46.

McLean, J. 2007. "Water Injustices and Potential Remedies in Indigenous Rural Contexts: A Water Justice Analysis." *Environmentalist*, 27: 25–38.

Mimura, N., L. Nurse, R.F. McLean, L.J. Agard, P.L. Briguglio, R. Payet and G. Sem. 2007. "Small Islands." Contribution of working group II to the fourth assessment report of the Intergovernmental Panel on Climate Change. In M.L. Parry, O.F Canziani, J.P. Palutikof, P.J. Van Der Linden and C.E. Hanson (eds.), *Climate Change 2007: Impacts, Adaptation and Vulnerability.* Cambridge: Cambridge University Press.

Mohanti, B.K. 2009. "Ethics in Palliative Care." *Indian Journal of Palliative Care,* 15, 2 (July to December): 89–92.

Sauchyn, D., and S. Kulshreshtha. 2007) "The Prairies." In D.S. Lemmen, F.J.Warren, J. Lacroix and E. Bush (eds.), *From Impacts to Adaptation: Canada in a Changing Climate 2007.* Ottawa, ON: Government of Canada.

Schlosberg, D. 2003. "The Justice of Environmental Justice: Reconciling Equity, Recognition, and Participation in a Political Movement." In A. Light and A De-Shalit (eds.), *Moral and Political Reasoning in Environmental Practice.* London: MIT Press.

____. 2004. "Reconceiving Environmental Justice: Global Movements and Political Theories." *Environmental Politics,* 13, 3: 517–540.

Shrader-Frechette, K. 2002. *Environmental Justice: Creating Equality, Reclaiming Democracy.* New York: Oxford University Press.

Stern, N. 2007. *The Economics of Climate Change: The Stern Review.* Cambridge: Cambridge University Press.

Todd, H., and C. Zografos. 2005. "Justice for the Environment: Developing an Indicator of Environmental Justice for Scotland." *Environmental Values,* 13: 483–501.

UNDP (United Nations Development Programme). 2010. *Human Development Report 2010, 20ᵗʰ Anniversary Edition. The Real Wealth of Nations: Pathways to Human Development.* Palgrave MacMillan, New York.

Van Hooidonk, R., J. Maynard, J. Tamelander, J. Gove, G. Ahmadia, L. Raymundo, G. Williams, S.F. Herons, and S. Planes. 2016. "Local-Scale Projections of Coral Reef Futures and Implications of the Paris Agreement." *Scientific Reports,* 6. <nature.com/articles/srep39666>.

Walker, G. 2009. "Beyond Distribution and Proximity: Exploring the Multiple Spatialities of Environmental Justice." *Antipode,* 41, 4: 614–636.

Watts, M. 2001. "Petro-Violence: Community, Extraction, and Political Ecology of a Mythic Commodity." In N.L. Peluso and M. Watts (eds.), *Violent Environments.* Ithaca, NY: Cornell University Press.

Weil, S. 2002. *The Need for Roots: Prelude to a Declaration of Duties Towards Mankind.* New York: Routledge Classics.

Wenz, P.S. 1988. *Environmental Justice.* Albany: State University of New York Press.

Zalasiewicz, J. 2008. "Are We Now Living in the Anthropocene?" GSA *Today,* 18, 2: 4–8.

10

LAW AND JUSTICE

Margot A. Hurlbert

OBJECTIVES

At the end of this chapter, you will be able to:

- Understand the jurisprudential approach to studying law and also think of the law as a social system

- Describe Canadian court structures

- Understand the difference between civil law and criminal law

- Describe the sources of law

- Understand several perspectives on studying law as a social system

It is most important to understand that law is a social system like any other (for example our system of reproduction, part of which is the family, or our system of education, part of which are schools). One way in which societies institutionalize particular views of justice is through their legal system. The critical analysis of the institution of law reveals its weaknesses, inconsistencies and inequities, which is an important first step in understanding it as a tool for social change, and not taking the justice of the legal system for granted.

Legal justice, or the justice that emerges from the legal system, and the workings of its component parts (such as courts and written laws) is regarded by some as the ultimate expression of what justice is. An issue such as whether an Indigenous person can hunt is thought to be dependent on various licensing acts and land ownership issues; whether a credit company can charge 30 percent interest for cashing a paycheque is dependent on whether a law allows or prevents such a high interest rate. If it does, then, according to this approach to justice, receiving $71.00 for a $100.00 paycheque (and paying 29 percent interest) is more just than receiving $70.00 (and paying 30 percent interest).

Wading through licensing acts, ownership issues and credit acts are all tasks of accessing the law. The definition of law and legal rules begins with the state and proceeds on the assumptions that legal decision making is rational, and legal processes are legitimate and essential to social order (Milovanovic 1988). Law schools in North America study law in this manner: in a rational, orderly, internal system much like an exact science where specific legal questions always have specific legal answers generated in the legal system. This is a "jurisprudential" approach to the study of law. Traditionally, most people think of jurisprudence as an institution that dispenses justice in an unbiased manner, without favour and ill will, akin to the blindfolded maiden of justice on the cover of this book — blind to one's exact identity, race or socio-economic circumstance. In this manner, law is presented as a formal and coherent body of rules, doctrines and principles concerned with interpretation of acts and case readings and expounding legal doctrines. Law is constituted through textual manifestations of legal decisions, judgements and opinions (Banakar 2005).

Studying legal "justice" is much broader than this. It is much more than solving a problematic situation or conflict between people by applying the set of rules encompassed in the law to the situation. Studying justice requires that the normative, moral and philosophical perspective reflected in law be debated and questioned; next it requires a critical analysis of law's influence on relationships between people, especially in light of unequal power structures in society. In the example of the Indigenous hunter, the narrow review of provincial licensing acts disregards promises of hunting rights made in the late nineteenth century when treaties were made, the fact that Indigenous hunting rights pre-existed colonization, the value of a hunting and trapping lifestyle and the history of oppression and colonization of Indigenous peoples. Making these justice arguments expands the law to recognize Indigenous rights previously unrecognized by courts of law and illustrates the importance of an expanded study of legal justice from the traditional jurisprudential approach taught at law schools. However, more than this is needed.

Because Canadian law is taught, practised and dispensed by courts of law based on this jurisprudential approach, only narrow societal change can occur within the confines of the Canadian legal system. Recognizing and empowering Indigenous peoples and their customs often occurs outside the traditional Canadian legal system. Indigenous legal scholars have documented their shock over concepts of "property law" in law school, including the premise of the "doctrine of discovery," which holds that the state considered the land vacant upon European contact (Martin 2002). This colonial principle ignores that Indigenous peoples occupied the land at this time. These scholars challenge Canadian legal assumptions (for example, Mi'gmaq people view the land at the time of contact as occupied, not vacant) and enable the governance of Indigenous peoples in Indigenous courts. Melinda Martin (2002) writes that victories for the Mi'gmaq have been rare or marginal at best in "newcomers' courts" and the Mi'gmaq are resisting the legal and social structures that were forced upon them when the first newcomers came, challenging the economic and political powers that usurped their jurisdiction and its laws of "property." By asserting Indigenous jurisdiction (now incrementally recognized in areas such as fishing rights and child welfare), the Mi'gmaq are building a nation-to-nation relationship with Canada (Martin 2002). In this way, Mi'gmaq law exists and is practised in a sphere on its own, outside of Canadian jurisprudential law. Von der Porten (2012: 10) adds another perspective about Indigenous self-determination: it "is not only contingent on Indigenous voices being heard within legal and political discourse, but on the fact that Indigenous perspectives and interests must come first in their own framework and initiative."

A solid foundation in understanding legal justice begins with an understanding of how law is made and how it is applied. To understand this, components of the legal justice system must be understood, including the sources of law: the court system where cases are heard and the process for how law is created. Also fundamental in understanding these components is being able to distinguish between civil and criminal matters. This chapter will cover the basics of the court structure, the legal distinction of civil and criminal matters and the sources of law in Canada.

In addition, the chapter will introduce several approaches to thinking of law as a social structure and critically analyzing it as such.

LAW AS A SOCIAL SYSTEM

The law is a social structure that represents the society within which it is situated. Law both reflects and informs interactions and relations between people. This is a critical insight for those studying justice and has been a focus of study for centuries by scholars including Max Weber and Emile Durkheim. This insight into law assists in explaining why laws differ between countries and different historical periods (a focus of Durkheim). The fact that divorce can be accessed after living separately for one year (without regard to fault for marriage breakdown) and that this type of divorce was not available fifty years ago reflects a change in Canadian society surrounding the norms respecting relations between couples and marriage.

Weber, a lawyer by training, focused on how law interacted with the relations between people. He outlined the characteristics of a formally rationalized legal system within the basis of a modern political authority as part of a more general theory of sociology. In theorizing order and conduct in society, Weber analyzed, contrasted and distinguished custom (a practice valid because of practical convenience), convention (a practice valid through external guarantee) and law (a practice externally guaranteed through a specialized staff expressly in charge of compliance) (Weber 1922). These concepts form a continuum, not mutually exclusive categories, where the boundaries are fluid and often imperceptible. A custom might be a person walking through a door and holding it open for another; a convention might be having only one intimate partner at a time (the breach of which is met with disapproval, but not with legal sanction); and a law might be not speeding or committing murder. Weber (1922) distinguished substantive rationalization based on certain values and conceptions of justice, whereas formal rationalization rested on general rules and procedures. Maintaining one monogamous intimate relationship at a time would qualify as substantive rationalization (people often regard their intimate partner's infidelity as unjust). This action would only qualify as formal rationalization if one were legally married (and breach of this rule entitling one to divorce). This example reflects the book's distinction between procedural justice and substantive justice: formal rationalization reflects the concept of formal or procedural justice and is enshrined in law; substantive rationalization relates to substantive justice or treating people and groups of people perhaps differently to achieve justice. This justice is sometimes, but not always reflected in law.

Durkheim (1893) conceived of law as the most important observable manifestation of the collective consciousness and its transformation. As such, it was a visible symbol of social solidarity, or social norms and culture, and he used it as a lens to study society. Durkheim concentrated on laws and behaviours of groups, as opposed to questions of how individuals interpreted specific actions. Durkheim's work informed structural functionalism's lens of analysis. Expanding on some of Durkheim's principles, Sorokin (1957) distinguished between official law (obligatory law norms protected and enforced by the authoritative power of government) and unofficial law (law norms not protected and enforced by government but enforced within some groups). Earlier, Ehrlich (1913) had referred to the "living law" as the whole of law dominating social life (even that which may not be in legal propositions and juristic law). Living law could be observed in various aspects of everyday life, whether legally recognized or not.

Although Karl Marx did not write specifically on the topic of legal justice, his ideas on law within his perspective of historical materialism have been influential in the study of justice. As outlined in Chapter 2, Marx asserted that the economic conditions of society determine what type of state will develop. In a capitalist society this implies the state will be controlled by the bourgeoisie as an instrument to secure economic rights and to moderate class conflict (Marx 1848). He similarly viewed the law and legal system as an instrument of control serving bourgeois interests. Rather than endorsing the principle of the rule of law (which holds that it is just for the law to be applied equally and fairly to all), Marx maintained that capitalist law actually enhances the conditions of inequality that exist in capitalist society. The capitalist legal system contributes to, as well as legitimates, the inequalities that exist as a result of capitalist economic conditions. Individualized rights of freedom are established to benefit those who own property (the bourgeoisie), while disfavouring those who are without property. Formal equality (granted in law by treating various parties who are in contract with one another or with the state as equal) sustains and exacerbates the economic inequalities that exist between legal subjects. Thus, the ultimate triumph is that the ideology of capitalist law becomes widely accepted, even among those members of society who are economically disadvantaged and subject to inequalities (Marx 1842). Marx laid the foundation for analyzing law and inequality based on the power imbalances in society discussed below.

The recent legalization of cannabis illustrates some of Durkheim, Weber and Marx's principles. In the years preceding the legalization, changes in custom and convention (the unofficial law) occurred. People[1] in possession of small amounts of marijuana were not charged criminally, first by custom (unofficial practice and convenience) and later by explicit policy (Bojkovsky et al. 2017). Many of these customs and conventions predated the prime minister's declaration that the law would change (Gayle 2015), and after the declaration, these customs and conventions increased dramatically. However, during this transition, vendors of marijuana were targeted for violating laws surrounding the sale of marijuana. The policing of vendors protected the economic interests of companies emerging in the manufacture, sale and dispensation of marijuana (generally larger and taking better advantage of the timing), as Marx would have predicted. At the same time, the federal and provincial governments discussed models of marijuana growth, manufacture and sale. Some people consulted argued that a model used for alcohol sales (highly restricted licensing) should be used, while others argued for a free open market (Bojkovsky et al. 2017). These changes in the laws show norms and laws changing, as well as the protection of economic interests.

The study of law as a social system is a vast topic — too vast to cover in this introductory book to pursuing the study of justice — but some basic legal justice information including the court structure, distinction between civil and criminal matters and the sources of law will be reviewed to establish a foundational understanding of Canadian law. The chapter will conclude with an overview of law as a social system using the theoretical perspectives developed in Chapter 2 of structural functionalism, symbolic interactionism, conflict theory, post-structuralism and feminism.

STRUCTURE OF THE COURT SYSTEM

If people are unable to resolve their conflicts, the ultimate forum of resolution is a court of law. At first glance, the variety and diversity of courts may appear complex, but we can identify three important characteristics: the government creating it (provincial or federal); its place in the hierarchy of courts (whether it is a court of first instance where trials occur, or an appeal court); and what types of matters it can deal with (criminal matters, family divorce matters or human rights complaints). This section will provide a brief overview of courts created by provincial governments followed by a description of courts created by the federal government.

Provincial Courts

Each province has a distinct provincial court system. Generally there are two types of courts: criminal and civil. Provinces may call these courts different names. For example, in Alberta, Saskatchewan, Manitoba and New Brunswick the civil court is called the Court of Queen's Bench and is almost identical to the Supreme Court (trial division) in Ontario and the Court Superieure in Quebec. These are the courts where trials take place in most of the matters that are not criminal (and more serious criminal matters that proceed by way of indictment). When a party to one of these trials believes the judge hearing the matter made an error, an appeal may be made to an appeal court. This higher level of court is called the Court of Appeal in British Columbia, Alberta, Saskatchewan, Manitoba, Ontario, Quebec and New Brunswick, and the Appeal (or Appellate) Division of the Supreme Court in other provinces. Most criminal trials occur in criminal courts termed Provincial Courts, District Courts or County Courts (although in Alberta, Saskatchewan and New Brunswick these have been amalgamated with the Superior Courts).

Ontario and Saskatchewan have created divisions or branches known as family courts and juvenile courts to handle a specific kind of case. Saskatchewan even has specialized criminal courts that operate in northern Saskatchewan in the Cree or Dene language, and many provinces have therapeutic drug courts for drug offenders, and courts that deal exclusively with domestic violence.

Federal Courts

The only federally constituted courts in Canada consist of the Supreme Court of Canada and the Federal Court of Canada (trial and appeal divisions). The Supreme Court of Canada hears appeals from provincial appeal courts and the Federal Court of Appeal and is the final judicial authority on the entire body of Canadian law, including the civil law of Quebec. It consists of nine judges appointed by the federal government.

The federal court hears and decides legal disputes arising in the federal domain, including claims against the Government of Canada, and matters in the federal domain such as citizenship, taxation, immigration, copyright and patent issues. Appeals from this court are taken to the Federal Court of Appeal and thereafter the Supreme Court of Canada.

Quasi-Judicial Tribunals

The federal government and provincial governments create quasi-judicial tribunals to handle specialized matters such as trade union matters, human rights complaints, occupational health and safety and workers' compensation. Although the details of structure and function may vary from province to province, these bodies are limited to the power invested or specifically delegated to them by provincial statute law, and do not have all of the powers that a court of law would have — thus they are "quasi" or "partly" judicial. These bodies, which often take the form of tribunals, are usually characterized by:

- a concern with some form of specialization of subject matter, such as human rights, collective bargaining or contract terminations;
- the need for judicial procedures in establishing facts, calling witnesses and arriving at conclusions; and
- the authority to decide the dispute.

Decisions and awards of quasi-judicial bodies are in all cases subject to some review by courts of law. Figure 10-1 shows the hierarchy of courts in Canada.

In the jurisprudential approach to the study of law and the rules regarding court hierarchy are essential. For instance, the Supreme Court of Canada is the highest court in Canada and its judgements are binding

Figure 10-1 Canadian Court System

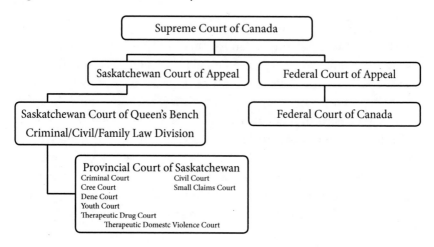

on all other courts in Canada. Similarly, within a province, quasi-judicial tribunals must follow decisions of courts of law and all courts follow decisions of Courts of Appeal. However, a broader study of justice recognizes this normative ordering of hierarchical decision making, but identifies and studies the inconsistencies, resistance and restructuring occurring between the lived experience of the people participating in the various courts, tribunals and other forums or places where disputes are resolved. This approach to studying the social system of law is termed legal pluralism (Merry 1988, 2008) and has been used to analyze norms and systems of legal ordering in relation to tuna courts in Tokyo (Feldman 2006) and various business instruments (letters of credit, export credit insurance and so forth) in the United States (Levit 2005). Its origin is the study of colonial societies in which a colonial nation, equipped with a centralized and codified legal system, imposed this system on societies with far different legal systems, often unwritten or informal structures for judging and punishing (Merry 1988). In the imperial/colonial context the law-centeredness of traditional studies of jurisprudential law are rejected; Indigenous peoples often reject the imposition of jurisprudential law and point out that not all law or legal decision making takes place in courts. It is argued that not all law takes place in courts. The symbols of law operating in unofficial forums of dispute resolution incorporating the law of the people are studied and documented in this way. In Canada, the scholarship of John Borrows (2016) and other Indigenous legal scholars explains the customs, conventions and laws (as per Weber 1922) of Indigenous peoples in Canada. As outlined by de Santis in Chapter 11 on Social Justice and Human Rights, a power imbalance exists when one nation's sovereignty must be recognized within the courts of another sovereign nation (this will be discussed further in relation to oil pipelines). Perhaps in Canada this can be a meaningful outcome of reconciliation with Indigenous peoples.

One of the most important milestones of Canadian justice is the Truth and Reconciliation Commission of Canada (TRC) and its findings, which began in 2008 and ended with the release of the culminating report in 2015. The TRC was established and mandated to reveal the history and ongoing legacy of the church-run residential schools as well as guide and inspire a process of truth and healing for Indigenous peoples in Canada. Hearings, ceremonies and events, were held from 2008–2014 across Canada with participation from many Indigenous peoples, including residential school survivors, church employees and non-Indigenous people.

Residential schools ran from the late nineteenth century continuing well into the twentieth century; they were established on the belief that only Christianity, isolation and education could "prepare Indians for a life without Indian-ness" (Neu and Therrien 2003: 102). By removing children from homes and transferring them far away from parents, families and cultural values and traditions were disrupted (TRC 2015). In 1883 Sir John A. MacDonald, then prime minister of Canada, explained in the House of Commons:

> When the school is on the reserve the child lives with its parents, who are savages; he is surrounded by savages, and though he may learn to read and write his habits, and training and mode of thought are Indian. He is simply a savage who can read and write. It has been strongly pressed on myself, as the head of the Department that Indian children should be withdrawn as much as possible from the parental influence, and the only way to do that would be to put them in central training industrial schools where they will acquire the habits and modes of thought of white men. (Canada 1883: 1107–1108)

At least 139 residential schools run by the Roman Catholic, Anglican, Presbyterian and Methodist churches were established in Canada, taking at least 150,000 students from their families (TRC 2015). Many of these schools continued to operate through the 1980s and the last one closed in 1996 (Native Web 2015).

Life in the residential schools was severe. Children were not allowed to speak in their language, siblings were separated from each other and students suffered physical punishment and often sexual abuse (TRC 2015). The TRC (2015) has documented the extensive traumas to which survivors were subjected. Poor food and living conditions contributed to high death rates and criminal health conditions. In 1907 Dr. Peter Bryce, Medical Inspector for the Department of Indian Affairs, cited an average death rate of 40 percent in residential schools; many students were deliberately infected with diseases like tuberculosis and left to die untreated (*Ottawa Citizen* 1907). The TRC's findings show that the government did not keep a record of students' deaths; at the TRC hearings, however, many people testified about family members who never returned from residential schools.

At the TRC hearings, former lieutenant-governor of British Columbia, the Honourable Steven Point said:

> And so many of you have said today, so many of the witnesses that came forward said, "I cannot forgive. I'm not ready to forgive." And I wondered why. Reconciliation is about hearing the truth. That's for sure. It's also about acknowledging that truth. Acknowledging that what you've said is true. Accepting responsibility for your pain and putting those children back in the place they would have been, had they not been taken from their homes … What are the blockages to reconciliation? The continuing poverty in our communities and the failure of our government to recognize that "Yes, we own the land." … I'm going to continue to talk about reconciliation, but just as important, I'm going to foster healing in our own people, so that our children can avoid this pain, can avoid this destruction and finally, take our rightful place in this "Our Canada." (Point 2013: 14)

A salient point being made is that reconciliation is both an internal and an external process. Point outlines clearly what he is going to do, but many of the activities including "hearing the truth," "acknowledging that truth" and "accepting responsibility" require that settlers also engage in the discussion. When this discussion happens, what might the possible outcomes and fruits of that discussion be? How can we respond to and implement the ninety-four calls to action of the TRC?

CRIMINAL LAW VIS-À-VIS CIVIL LAW

Courts deal with jurisprudential matters that are either criminal or civil. The distinction between the courts require us to understand why some actors are designated by society as "criminal" or "not criminal." Why is loitering in a public place a crime? What tends to be the socio-economic status of people who are charged with this offence? Why is it a crime to carry a concealed weapon in Canada, but not the United States? A broader study of justice concerns itself with exploring these questions and how dominant, powerful groups and interests determine what activities and actions are illegal. Consider the following examples of what our society deems criminal and not criminal.

A jurisprudential approach to determining what is "criminal" is different from a legal determination. The federal government has the official legal authority to decide what is or is not criminal, pursuant to section 91(27), of the British North America Act, 1867. Over the years, most of our criminal law has been embodied in the Criminal Code. One Canadian authority states, "Criminal law can be defined in many ways but it is essentially a prohibition coupled with a penalty" (Beckton 1982: 2). Another Canadian authority concludes that, "Criminal matters involve disputes between individuals and the state" (MacKay 1984: 204). The gist of these definitions is that society, through government, determines what is harmful or undesirable and uses the sanctions of fines and/or imprisonment to enforce its view.

In a criminal case, the Crown prosecutor must prove the guilt of an accused person beyond a reasonable doubt. "Beyond a reasonable doubt" is not easy to define. However, reference is usually made to moral or honest certainty in believing that a person is guilty. The usual caveat is that moral certainty does not mean absolute certainty. For instance, accused are often convicted on the basis of circumstantial or "surrounding" evidence. This means they have been convicted not on evidence directly proving that they committed the offence (such as the existence of a witness who saw them commit the specific offence) but based on evidence that they were in the vicinity or had the opportunity and motive to commit the offence.

CASE STUDY:
CORPORATE "DEATH"

Individuals comprise the overwhelming majority of cases proceeding through the criminal justice system. Occasionally an individual is charged for a crime committed in the course of their employment or business, such as committing fraud in a business transaction or criminal breach of trust as a result of wrongfully taking money. Examples include better known cases such as Martha Stewart and Sir Conrad Black. Although corporations are regarded as "individuals" by law, they are rarely, if ever, charged for crimes. Given that a corporation's main and primary goal is the accumulation of profit over time, and not a moral existence, this warrants further exploration.

Like any aspect of the law, determining what is or is not a crime is an exercise in social construction. Delineating something as "criminal" is based on social norms and power and effected by a combination of social actors including judges and legislatures (see Sources of Law). Thinking critically about what constitutes a "crime" requires careful consideration of what harms are done and what is morally reprehensible. Acts of killing or violence are correctly labelled (and codified) as "crimes." However, consider harm in our society a bit more expansively. How many people are harmed by cigarette smoking, workplace accidents or stress, faulty products or unsafe medication? If our definition of crime is harmful behaviour or acts that cause harm to people, why are these harms listed not considered a crime? Consider a few specific cases:

Asbestos: The health dangers of asbestos have been known since 1900 (exposure is linked with potentially fatal illness, scarring the lungs, stifling breath and impeding the flow of oxygen to the blood), and medical journals as far back as 1935 have documented links to cancer (Snider 2006). Yet, companies continued to mine asbestos, largely in Quebec, up until 2012, exposing their workers and customers to health risks, with full knowledge of these risks. Finally, after the last mine closed, the federal government announced it would ban asbestos by 2018 (Kohut 2016). Is the killing of people through exposure to asbestos any different from killing someone during a robbery?

Bhopal, India and Union Carbide: In 1984, a gas leak at the plant killed over two thousand people and maimed over half a million more. The U.S. company, Union Carbide, had chosen to set up shop in Bhopal because of the cheap costs associated with low safety standards there compared with the United States. The company violated safety regulations, failed to train employees, failed to respond to warning signs and tried to deny culpability (Rajan 2001).

In both of these cases there are no criminal charges. Why do we as a society not think of these actions by these corporations as "criminal"? A conflict theory perspective shows that our law turns a blind eye to behaviour by powerful entities in our society, including large corporations. Although we like to think that everyone is treated equally before the law, the reality is that powerful groups and interests — individuals and corporations — escape the full force of the law. In this way, law perpetuates the power structures in our society and makes it appear natural that our criminal justice system only deals with individuals killing individuals in a moment of passion.

If the judge or jury is convinced based on this evidence and believe there is no reasonable doubt as to the accused's guilt, they may convict. This occurred in the case of David Milgaard. Without any direct evidence linking him to the murder of Gail Miller, he was convicted and served twenty-two years in prison. He merely had previous interaction with the police for minor offences, a bad reputation and had been in the vicinity at the time of the murder. In the summer of 1997, DNA testing provided positive proof of his innocence (Anderson and Anderson 1998).

Civil law and civil cases are defined as everything that is not criminal. These cases are diverse and range from family matters such as divorce or child custody to trademarks, disputes about wills or inheritance and wrongful dismissals from jobs. In a civil case the plaintiff need not prove beyond a reasonable doubt that the defendant is guilty. Instead, a lesser burden of proof is required based on the balance of probabilities; the court must answer whether the allegations made by the plaintiff are probably true. An example of a civil case is a court action against a doctor for negligently performing a medical procedure. If it can be proven with greater than 50 percent probability that the doctor did not meet an

CASE STUDY:
OMAR KHADR

A legal case can have both civil and criminal implications, as in the case of Omar Khadr. Born in Canada, Khadr was taken to Afghanistan by his father. On July 27, 2002, when he was 15 years old, Omar was severely wounded in a fight between Taliban fighters and U.S. soldiers. During that fight, the U.S. alleges that Omar threw a grenade that killed a U.S. soldier, Sergeant Christopher J. Speer (Koring 2010). After being held in detention in Guantanamo Bay in Cuba where he was deprived of sleep, placed in solitary confinement and allegedly abused, Khadr pleaded guilty to "murder in violation of the laws of war" and four other charges before the United States military commission. This plea agreement was offered on condition he be returned to Canada and eventually be released. The Canadian government sent lawyers and csis agents to interrogate Khadr and turned their findings over to the United States prosecutors, which contributed to his conviction. In 2010 the Supreme Court of Canada ruled that the participation of Canadian officials in Khadr's interrogations at Guantanamo violated his Charter rights (*Canada* v. *Khadr* 2010). Finally, in 2012, Khadr was transferred to Canadian custody to serve the remainder of his sentence. In 2013, Khadr filed a $20 million civil suit against the Government of Canada, alleging it conspired with the U.S. to abuse his rights. In 2017 the government issued an official apology and paid Khadr $10.5 million in compensation for the violation of his rights as determined by the 2010 Supreme Court of Canada case (Shephard 2017). At the same time, the widow of Speer has filed a wrongful death and injury lawsuit against Khadr.

acceptable standard for a medical doctor, then the doctor will be found liable. The jurisprudential approach to law asserts that both parties (the complainant and the defendant) are more or less of equal strength. As a result, there is thought to be less need to protect the litigants and rules concerning admissibility of evidence may not be as strict as in criminal cases. The reality is that injured patients have less money, less stamina, and fewer resources (such as expert medical witnesses) than doctors who are covered by medical insurance companies.

Even though the criminal law and civil law are definitively and distinctly different from each other, one single act by one individual may constitute at the same time both a crime and a civil wrong or "tort" in legal terms. For example, a person committing assault against another might be charged with a crime under the Criminal Code and might also be sued by the victim in civil court for damages to the victim caused by the assault. The concerns, proceedings and results would be very different in each case.

In the criminal case, the issue is the accused's duty to the public to obey the law and keep peace and order in society. Khadr was charged with the crime of "murder in violation of the laws of war" in the United States. In the civil case, the concern relates to the duty of the offender not to cause injury to another individual and to pay damages when found guilty of such action. Khadr sued the Government of Canada for abusing his rights, and he was sued for wrongful death by the widow of the United States soldier he allegedly killed.

In the criminal proceedings, the behaviour of the accused may be determined, and a conviction may be decided, even though no injury was caused to the victim. In the civil case, the focus of the proceedings is on both the offender and the victim and determines whether the victim was injured, whether there was a factor that contributed to this (such as alcohol consumption) on the part of the victim and the extent of both. These considerations are all very important in determining whether the plaintiff (victim) is allowed to succeed or whether the defendant (offender) has a right to dismissal.

COMPONENTS OF CRIMINAL CASES

In general, every crime has a physical element (*actus reus*, that is, the guilty or wrongful act) and a mental element (*mens rea*, that is, the state of mind). *Actus reus* relates to the type of conduct of an accused, consequences of that conduct and surrounding circumstances of the conduct. In *mens rea* the question is whether the accused had the mental intent necessary to commit a crime; that is, whether the accused foresaw the consequences of the wrongful act, was aware of the contingent circumstances or intended to cause the consequences. For example, if a person hits another without that other person's consent, they will be guilty of assault only if they intended or meant to hit the other person. If the act of hitting was an accident, no "intent" or *mens rea* would exist and no criminal assault would have been committed. If either *actus reus* or *mens rea* are absent, then no crime is committed.

These concepts can be illustrated with the crime of sexual assault. Jian Ghomeshi was a famous Canadian Broadcasting Corporation (CBC) personality. When several women came forward with allegations of sexual misconduct and assault he was dismissed from his position and criminally charged. The situation and subsequent criminal court trial was heavily covered by the media (Grinberg 2016). In his trial not only did the act of sexual intercourse (the *actus reus*) have to be proven, but also the criminal mental state (the *mens rea*) of having sexual intercourse with another without consent. In the Ghomeshi case, the act was proven but the *mens rea* of committing the act without consent was not proven beyond a reasonable doubt. Generally there will be two witnesses to a sexual assault: the complainant, who alleges intercourse occurred without consent; and the accused, who may defend based on the position that the complainant consented. Although there is a great deal of common law surrounding what is or is not consent, the trial may end with the complainant alleging lack of consent and the accused alleging consent. Because the standard of proof is such that the accused must be proven guilty beyond a reasonable doubt, obtaining a criminal conviction in this case is difficult. Without a reason to dismiss one or the other person's testimony, the judge will be unable to convict the accused. It is impossible to dismiss one or the other's testimony and satisfy the burden of proof.

The Ghomeshi case predated the Me Too movement, in which women in the U.S., and eventually elsewhere, brought to light the sexual harassment and abuse of powerful men (Smartt 2018). By December 2017, the movement led to numerous firings or resignations of men and the hashtag of the social movement has been re-tweeted over several million times (Lapowsky 2017). An important social movement resisting sexism and sexual violence, Me Too has also been lauded for starting an important discussion about what is and is not sexual assault and the importance of freedom of speech. The Supreme Court of Canada Justice Beverley McLachlin concluded in *Grant* v. *Torstar* (2009) that freewheeling debate on matters of public interest are to be encouraged and the media serves a vital role in providing a vehicle for such debate. She stated this while recognizing that the law does not confer a license to ruin reputation and determining that journalists should be responsible in their journalism by considering the status and reliability of the source of the information, the seriousness of the allegation and the public importance of the matter. In the realm of the media, the criminal burden of proof does not exist, and *mens rea* is in the realm of determination by the public.

Mens rea can also relate to recklessness. The Supreme Court of Canada has held that a person is reckless when that person foresees the possibility of a harmful consequence and then takes the unreasonable chance that harm will not result. Stated another way, a person must be aware of the danger involved in an act or a decision, and if that person does not foresee consequences, then that person is not reckless. However, the risks must be reasonable or justifiable (*Creighton* v. *R.* 1993). Hence, there is a great deal of difference between the responsible doctor who operates on a patient who consequently dies and the irresponsible hunter who target shoots in a public park and consequently kills a child at play.

Both the intent for recklessness and the *mens rea* previously described are called "subjective *mens rea*" because it is the accused's state of mind that is important. It is for the trier of facts (judge or jury) to determine what was in the mind of the accused at the relevant time. This is contrasted from an objective intent or a determination of what a reasonable person in the accused's situation would have or might have believed. Those practising jurisprudentially resolutely assert that judges and juries are capable of hearing evidence and determining what the accused did or did not believe (Roach 2009). Approaching law in a critical manner and analyzing it as a social structure puts this assumption into question (Norrie 1998). How is a judge capable of determining exactly what was in an accused's mind at the time of the offence? Would a judge not always be "objectively" judging the accused or applying an "outside" standard, a standard of conduct influenced by the background and biases of the judge?

THE SOURCES OF LAW

According to a jurisprudential study of law, the major sources of Canadian law include the Constitution, regular statutory law (including regulations and policy) and common law. Law is developed through struggle, activism and social change. This discussion will follow a jurisprudential recounting of the three major sources of law in Canada, the Constitution, statute law and common law. The actors who create law within these sources are the Canadian parliament, the provincial legislatures and the courts. Parliament and the provincial legislatures make law by passing statutes; courts make law through judicial decision (what we term "common law").

Canada's Constitution

A constitution defines the powers and limits of powers that can be exercised by different levels and branches of government. It is the foundation of a country's political and legal system. It is contained in statute, so is part statutory law, but it is not "regular" statutory law because of its importance and the difficulty entailed in amending the constitutional statutory documents.

Through colonization, Canada became a country by an act of the parliament of Great Britain in 1867. It is noteworthy that there was no consent or participation in this by Indigenous peoples. On April 17, 1982, the Constitution of Canada was patriated (or brought home from Britain — meaning that Canada gained formal sovereignty from Britain). A number of important statutes, including the Constitution Act, 1867 (formerly called the British North America Act, 1867), continue to form an important part of our Constitution. These documents (some thirty acts and orders) declare the Constitution of Canada to be the supreme law of Canada. Canada's dual legal system is affirmed with provinces having jurisdiction in relation to some matters, such as property and civil rights, and the federal government over other matters, such as peace, order and good government and the criminal law. The Constitution also includes Indigenous rights, such as those related to the historical occupancy and use of the land by Indigenous peoples, treaty rights and agreements between the federal government, provincial governments and Indigenous nations in relation to self-government.

The Constitution Act, 1867, which established Canada as a federal state, continues to include in its preamble a statement that Canada is to have a constitution similar in principle to that of the United Kingdom. This one phrase covers an unwritten but vital part of Canada's Constitution. Consequently, British constitutional principles have been read into the 1867 Act as required and Canada is full heir to British common law principles, conventions and prerogatives. For example, Canadian laws, both civil and criminal (outside of Quebec), fall within the traditions of British jurisprudence; the pre-eminence of statute law over common law or legislative supremacy applies in Canada as it does in Britain; and the 1867 Act does not explicitly describe the roles or functions of the prime minister, cabinet, political parties or civil service. The British North America Act, 1867 is not dead and is still very much alive as the new (in name only) Constitution Act, 1867. The Canadian Constitution, therefore, continues to be partially written and partially unwritten.

In addition to a new Charter of Rights and Freedoms, the Constitution Act, 1982, added provisions to our Constitution, including a recognition and affirmation of existing Indigenous and treaty rights, the principle of equalization among provinces, and the strengthening of provincial powers over resources. The addition of the Charter of Rights and Freedoms was important because it gave the rights contained in the Charter constitutional status, protecting them from amendment and infringement by governments. The Charter protects fundamental freedoms (religion, expression, association), democratic rights (voting), mobility rights (entering, remaining or leaving the country), legal rights (life, liberty security of a person, right to a lawyer), equality rights, language rights (English and French), minority language educational rights and Indigenous rights. Significantly, the Charter of Rights and Freedoms did not include economic rights.

Some of the most innovative law making in Canada occurs when the Supreme Court of Canada applies constitutional law to new situations. One such case is *Canada* v. phs *Community Services Society*. In the early 1990s, injection drug use and associated health issues of hiv/aids and Hepatitis C reached epidemic proportions in Vancouver's Downtown Eastside (dtes). In response, in 2003, harm-reduction workers set up safe injection sites called Insite to help drug users safely inject under medical supervision. At the time, such sites were illegal, but the federal government exempted the dtes site from prosecution for criminal drug charges. Prime Minister Stephen Harper's Conservative government refused to continue the exemption. The Supreme Court of Canada found that the government's refusal to exempt Insite was a breach of the injection drug users' rights to life, liberty and security of the person, and ordered an exemption to be granted.

Statute Law

"Statutory law," known as written or enacted law, did not exist in British jurisprudence prior to the thirteenth century. It began to constitute an important part of English law with the Magna Carta and the abolition of serfdom. In the Canadian context, statute law refers to legislative enactment: a bill is passed to make a legal provision for something to be done or for something to be prohibited. Statute laws may be enacted by a government to cover new circumstances not covered in existing law, to change existing law or to make existing laws more certain and ascertainable. Statutes achieve the goals of making the law accessible and written. However, the challenge is that it is very difficult to write laws that cover every circumstance and situation. As a result, judges must interpret and apply the law to every circumstance and situation. These decisions form the basis of the common law.

Common Law

Canada, with the exception of Quebec, is a "common law" state. Common law was imported to Canada from Britain. The founding father of common law was King Henry II, who reigned in the twelfth century. He sent judges on a circuit through the country to hold court in the larger villages and trading centres. The appointed judges worked together to compare cases and make group decisions to establish a consistent law in the interests of the King; they developed one law for all of England — a law common to all, hence called "common law." This coincided with the development of a penal code and prosecution of "criminal" matters on behalf of the King or state. This concept will be revisited in Chapter 14. British common law has continued to evolve over the centuries and was brought to Commonwealth settler countries including Canada, the U.S., Australia and New Zealand.

The common law is much more complex than an accumulation of judicial decisions over time, usually referred to as "case law." Case law is not enacted by the legislature, but is a written record and evidence of how the law applies in a specific case. In another case, circumstances may be very different, and a different result may occur in the application of the law. It is this feature that makes the common law dynamic and elastic, rather than uncompromisingly rigid and unable to adapt to changing times and conditions.

The three sources of law — the Constitution, statutory law and common law — are a jurisprudential perspective on where law is derived. It assumes these three sources create a logical body of rules independent of surrounding social institutions. Philosophy has a different perspective about where the law comes from (and there are some similarities to the jurisprudential approach to the study of law). In philosophy, "legal positivism" views the law as being created and written by governments (this is similar to statute law); "legal interpretation" holds that the law is interpreted by judges (this is similar common law); and "natural law" holds that there is a relationship between law and morals, and that law is what "ought to be" — it is a universal, unchanging and everlasting set of legal principles. The Roman lawyer Cicero identified three components of natural law philosophy drawing on Stoic philosophy:

(i) true law is right reason in agreement with nature, universal application, unchanging and everlasting;
(ii) it is a sin to alter or repeal or abolish natural law;
(iii) God is the author and enforcing Judge of natural law. (Wacks 2006: 3)

Over time, the idea of natural law has waxed and waned. One example is Hitler passing the Nuremberg laws to deny Jewish people rights. This denial of rights and the popular apathy to it resulted in the eventual genocide of Jewish people by Nazi Germany in World War II. International rules and laws, which are based on "natural law" (as well as various international treaties), characterized genocide as a criminal act, and their status overrode the laws passed by Hitler in Germany. This is an illustrative example of the tension existing between the three sources of law for philosophers — common law, statute law and natural law — which is still debated by philosophy and legal scholars today (Roach 2001).

A Canadian example of the tension of these ideas of the sources of law can be seen in the famous case of *R. v. Morgentaler* (1988) (the case that legalized abortion). The Criminal Code clearly made it a criminal offence to terminate a pregnancy unless the procedural requirements of the section (which required the approval of a committee at a hospital) were followed. This section was challenged on the basis of section 7 of the *Canadian Charter of Rights and Freedoms*. It was argued that this provision of the Criminal Code denied women of their right to life, liberty and security of the person.

The Supreme Court of Canada had the herculean task of reconciling these two laws: the Charter right to security and the Criminal Code restriction of abortion. The actual dispute was over having to obtain approval of a committee for an abortion instead of a woman being empowered to make her own decisions. The latter principle and the unequal access to abortion across Canada for women resulted in the abolition of the sections of the Criminal Code requiring committee approval. The Supreme Court of Canada did invite Parliament to amend the Criminal Code and introduce a crime of having an abortion that would not infringe the Charter. This has not yet been done by Parliament. As with many justice issues, this legal decision had strong support from many women's organizations, yet strong opposition from many anti-abortion groups. The court's exercise of its power of legal interpretation doesn't preclude the government's ability to pass law and exercise its power of legal positivism.

Socio-legal scholars take a different approach to the issue of where laws originate. An American legal scholar, Oliver Wendell Holmes Jr., rejected this jurisprudential approach (he termed "legal formalism") and the proposition that judges merely find the law in legal codes that they apply in specific cases. He recognized that judges contribute to formulating law by selecting the relevant principles of law and precedents to decide the outcomes of cases. As a result, the judges' normative conceptions influenced the law. Legal scholar Rosco Pound (1942, 1959) regarded law as a form of social control and an institution which could be adapted to respond to changing societal conditions.

In summary, law comes from the legislatures or parliament — they write and pass law (the view of the legal positivist). Law is also made by judges as they perform their task of deciding cases, just as we saw with the Morgentaler case. Natural law reflects the idea that some laws arise and exist in a universal, unchanging manner based on morals. No one position is correct or incorrect. In a jurisprudential approach, law comes from all three sources.

PERSPECTIVES ON LAW AND SOCIETY

Various perspectives can inform the social study of law. The perspectives introduced here have been grouped in the same framework used in Chapter 2 on Theorizing Justice. Again, this process of grouping is for introductory purposes to the study of theory; generalizing in this manner is often strained and loses important detail that a more in-depth review of various theories would expose.

Structural Functionalist Perspective

A structural functionalist perspective of the law uses society as a group of institutions performing functions in a system. For example, key social institutions (like the family, the law, education or religion) are needed for society to operate effectively. Law, as a social institution, resolves the myriad social conflicts through the courts. Law does not function so much to impose one group's will on others, but it controls, reconciles and mediates the diverse and conflicting interests of individuals and groups within society in order to maintain harmony and social integration (Vago 1994). Both Pound and Durkheim can be categorized as structural functionalists because of their macro theories of law as an institution and its place in society.

One legal systems theorist, Luhmann (2004), envisioned the law as a closed system (meaning a system without external influences). Even new scientific methods of evidence such as DNA testing didn't exist within the law until a judge determined that the methods were credible and applicable in a particular case. Luhmann's conclusions were based on the specialized actors and institutions and utilized similar logic to the jurisprudential view of law.

There are many problems with the structural functionalist perspective of the law. First, social values are rarely uniform. Interpersonal conflict is generally rooted in differing values, priorities, power and interests. It also fails to explain social inequality in our society. By assuming a relatively uniform standard of values and interests it fails to take into account the plight of those who are poor, marginalized and oppressed. Not only can it not analyze power dynamics in society (and therefore cannot account for social inequality), but it also cannot explain social change. The use of this perspective often only "reifies" (ratifies and reproduces) current laws and practices (that is, structural functionalists take the "official version of law" for granted) or calls for harsher laws to bring dysfunctional behaviour into alignment. As well, the structural functionalist perspective assumes all people can equally access the legal system; the reality is that access to expensive lawyers and courts is really only available to the wealthy. However, the structural functionalist perspective does emphasize mediation·and reconciliation, often used in labour management disputes and negotiations and other court processes, a significant component of many Western democratic societies.

Symbolic Interactionism

Expanding on Durkheim's ideas on law as a manifestation of collective consciousness and on Ehrlich's ideas, Cotterrell regarded law as a social structure, both shaping and being shaped by the society in which it operates. Law seen this way is a "living law" or a set of rules actually followed by individuals in social life — not just a set of codified legal rules (Cotterrell 1996: 29). Stated another way, there is what is termed an "official version of the law" and another structure often called the "living law," which is not only greatly influenced by the law but also influences law reform. This approach is most akin to that of symbolic interactionism. One example is the highly technical area of water rights. Determining water right priorities can be made with a very technical, legalistic review of interests, dates of licenses, types of use and so on. However, one research study showed how legal rules around water priorities were found to be largely ignored in times of water conflict (or disagreement over who has priority to water during times of shortage when all people can't receive their water share). The researchers conducted interviews with people affected by the water shortage in Alberta and ascertained the norms and behaviours (the "living law") that resolved the specific water conflict — particularly community practices of sharing and maximizing benefits (Hurlbert 2009). This study shows that the "official" version of the law may be very different from the living law.

Although this approach illustrates discrepancies between law in practice and its official version, it fails to analyze or explain power differentials, or to provide reasons for this power difference or remedies for unequal power relations. In the water research study discussed, the water dialogue excluded the First Nation (Hurlbert 2009a). In fact, from a jurisprudential view of law, or the "official version of law," Indigenous water rights have not been recognized (Laidlaw 2010; *Tsuu T'ina First Nation* v. *Alberta*). The official version of the law that gives the Crown or federal government ownership of all water continues to marginalize and silence Indigenous peoples (Hurlbert 2009b). Thus, exploring the living experience of law, or the reality of social practices of water sharing that marginalize Indigenous peoples, and comparing these with the official version of the law, illustrates the marginalized space of Indigenous peoples. Power imbalance is more aptly addressed using the conflict perspective below.

Conflict Perspective

The conflict perspective postulates that the law can be either an instrument of the economically powerful in society to continue to exert their economic power, or it can be used by the state in support of the economically powerful (perhaps through arguments about maintaining the economy and jobs). The balancing of Indigenous rights and oil pipelines are illustrative. In the summer of 2017, the Supreme Court of Canada dismissed the challenge of the Chippewa of the Thames First Nation who wanted to stop Enbridge's Line 9 — a crude oil pipeline that travels from Sarnia, Ontario to Montreal, Quebec and through its territory — from reversing the flow of oil and expanding its capacity. The First Nation feared that the potential oil spills might harm their hunting, trapping and fishing rights, and they argued that the pipeline regulator, the National Energy Board (NEB), didn't properly consult them. Freedman and Hansen (2009) foreshadowed the defeat:

> It is difficult to see how a public interest-based approach to determining section 35 rights [which affirms existing Indigenous and treaty rights] can satisfy the important purposes behind granting those rights constitutional protection in the first place. How is the important objective of reconciliation to be achieved if projects can simply be approved because of the money they will bring in or the jobs they will create? How in such a framework will the Indigenous perspective of their rights and the need for the land, environment, and ecosystem to remain in a certain state be properly taken into account? In our view, the rights and interests of First Nations are ignored or downplayed in these public interest-based tribunals.

The Supreme Court ultimately found that the NEB adequately consulted the First Nation and made reasonable accommodations — Line 9 would be allowed to carry oil through their territory. The NEB assessed the increased risk of a spill or leak from Line 9 and the potential negative impacts, but ultimately found the risk was low and could be adequately mitigated. The NEB was "confident that Line 9 would be operated in a safe manner" (*Chippewas* v. *Enbridge* 2017: para 56). The case illustrates the justice system's continued support of corporate commercial "public" interests to the detriment of both Indigenous and environmental rights.

Post-Structuralist Perspective

Critical legal studies analyzes law from a loosely conflict tradition and post-structural perspective. It recognizes that the law is a site in society that reproduces gender, race and class inequality (Comack and Balfour 2004). This theoretical perspective sheds light on the perpetuation and reproduction of inequality in our society. Critical legal scholars view the jurisprudential version of law (and legal education) as a reflection of dominant thinking about the social world and a perpetuation of idealized liberalism and the rights of the individual. Judges are seen as perpetuating a particular kind of elitist politics in their decision making, rationalized by paltry references to precedent case law (or the common law). Jurisprudential law's preoccupation with individual rights fails to show how the individual is the very product of both the socio-economic forces and the legal authority that put them before the law to begin with (MacDonald 2002).

To illustrate, consider the issue of the over-incarceration of Indigenous peoples: in 2016, Indigenous peoples represented 5 percent of Canadian population but composed 25 percent of people incarcerated (CBC 2017). In Saskatchewan, Indigenous peoples represent 11 percent of the population but make up 80 percent of the prison population (Mason 2013). This disproportionate overrepresentation has not been remedied by decades of individual rights, including rights to lawyers, fair trials or freedom from self-incrimination. Breaking free of this "idealized liberalism" or emphasis on individual responsibility within the criminal justice system (the arrest, conviction and sentence) is near impossible. Parliament attempted to remedy the overincarceration of Indigenous peoples in 1997 by amending criminal law to direct judges to take into consideration "all available sanctions other than imprisonment that are reasonable in the circumstances … with particular attention to the circumstances of Indigenous offender" (s. 718.2(e) of the Criminal Code).

In 1999 the Supreme Court of Canada in *R.* v. *Gladue* advised lower courts that an Indigenous offender's circumstances be considered in the sentencing, including colonial and socio-economic oppression that had contributed to bringing the Indigenous person before the court (these principles were later affirmed and expanded in *R.* v. *Ipeelee*). Although this initially generated optimism over the possibility that incarceration rates among Indigenous peoples might be lowered, overincarceration has in fact worsened (Jeffries and Stenning 2015). Indigenous offenders often receive a far harsher sentence than other comparable cases (ibid.). This case study showed that the strategy of addressing the social inequality, hidden power structures and socio-economic disadvantage that brought an individual before the law, within the structures of jurisprudential law and the traditional Canadian court system (which is based on liberalism), was doomed to failure.

A post-structural perspective highlights structures of power in our society by analyzing the language of law and its practices in our society. The interconnection of legal discourses (court transcripts, statutes and written court decisions, for example, internally constructed by law) are compared and contrasted with social discourses or practices external to law. This analysis uncovers peoples' lived experiences of discrimination, violence and injustice. This analysis of law shows that the law is the social process through which inequality is perpetuated. Stated another way, the ways in which laws are both made and enforced, in the long run, protects the interests of (economically) powerful groups in society.

As an example, Sherene Razack (2002) analyzes the 1995 murder and subsequent trial of the killers of Pamela George (Ojibway), a Saulteaux Nation woman. She analyzes the language or discourse emerging at the trial. The victim, George, is referred to in the trial as the "hooker" or prostitute with just a few moments when one witness remembered her as a nice person and the mother of two children who crafted and could cook. In contrast, the two white accused, Steven Kummerfield and Alex Ternowetsky, both white, athletic college boys, had the benefit of white respectability and were referred to as "boys who did pretty darn stupid things" (Razack 2002: 148). When the Crown prosecutor asked why Kummerfield left town after killing Pamela, he replied, "I really didn't want to be arrested or anything like that just because there are so many opportunities I had to be successful" (2002: 149); it was the ultimate unremorseful expression of privilege. Ultimately, Kummerfield was sentenced to six and a half years in prison with credit for the twenty months served awaiting trial.

Feminist Perspective

The feminist perspective of law has existed formally since the nineteenth century. Like the conflict and the post-structural perspectives, it challenges the jurisprudential perspective of law as just and impartial and points out its role in perpetuating inequalities (Boyd and Sheehy 1989). One feminist scholar, Ngaire Naffine (1990), recognized that the official version of the law is not coherent, logical, internally consistent nor rational. In fact, Naffine (1990: 13) noted that law reflects the "priorities of the dominant patriarchal social order." Laws have been largely written by men and for men without taking into consideration the perspectives of women.

Although advances have been made in recent decades, especially with the advent of such things as the right to equality guaranteed by section 15 of the Charter of Rights and Freedoms, some feminists argue that many gains have been illusory. For instance, Catherine MacKinnon (1987) notes a string of defeats and declines for women including the lack of effective sex-equality provisions for pay, opposition to the right to safe abortion and a movement towards sharing custody of children after separation, all of which leave the ideal of women's equality before the law far from realized. Elizabeth Schneider (2000: 228) explores the law and domestic violence over the course of the last several decades and concludes that the assertion of domestic violence claims has advanced the "political conversation" and has made what used to be private, public. However, the fundamental vision of equality that generated the movement against domestic violence has been subverted. Women who come forward with their experiences are seen as "unreasonable" or "difficult" and there is a tendency to pathologize them (that is, to view them as "sick"). Although intimate violence has been recognized as a "public" harm, the recognition is that it is a problem between individuals, not a systemic or social problem; quick-fix explanations and solutions deny the link to gender.

The struggle continues to this day. In 2013 the Supreme Court of Canada declared the criminalization of prostitution unconstitutional as it created a dangerous situation for the vulnerable women who are sex workers. Chief Justice Beverley McLachlin ruled that Parliament could regulate against nuisances, but not at the cost of the health, safety and lives of sex workers (*Canada* v. *Bedford* 2013: para 136). In defiance, Prime Minister Stephen Harper reintroduced almost identical provisions to those declared unconstitutional.

NEO-LIBERALISM AND LEGAL JUSTICE

The jurisprudential approach to studying law has parallels with neo-liberalism, an ideology and political strategy that emphasizes the life choices of individuals and de-emphasizes social problems (discussed in Chapter 2). The jurisprudential approach to law emphasizes the application of the rational rule-based legal system to individual cases, emphasizing individual life choices that have brought a particular individual in contact with the legal system. The social problems that may have contributed to the individual's legal problems have very little if any relevance when analyzing the person's situation, which is consistent with the ideology and political strategy of neo-liberalism.

In the jurisprudential context of analyzing individual legal problems, the presumption that individuals run into legal problems because they've made poor choices drives the legal and political systems' impetus to control crime through harsh penalties and longer jail terms. The evidence shows that this disciplinary approach leads to a conflict with neo-liberal aims to reduce government involvement in private lives; after all, harsher penalties require an increase in government services via court and jail services. Conversely, when individuals' social problems are factored into their problems with the law, social programs alleviating poverty, meeting the needs of troubled youths or providing early childhood special education are understood as part of the solution to reducing crime. Investment in these social programs reduces government services in the areas of court and jail services.

Expanding the focus of legal justice to include an analysis of social oppressions increases the ambit of the study of legal justice to include social justice or substantive justice. Individuals are viewed not just as rational actors making individual choices, but as agents living and functioning in a social system, affected by the institution or social system of law, all of which informs and contributes to their life chances. Viewing legal justice in this expanded way, which includes an analysis of social justice in addition to the procedural and formal rules enshrined in the system of law, increases the chances that reform of law and policy will achieve justice.

DISCUSSION QUESTIONS

1. What is the difference between the official version of the law and the living law? Illustrate with examples.
2. Which framework for analyzing the law is most reflective of how society operates? Why?
3. How is law changed over time and why does it change? Illustrate with examples?
4. What is the difference between civil and criminal law? Can a matter have both civil and criminal consequences? Illustrate with examples.

GLOSSARY

Actus reus: A latin term denoting the objective element of a crime, or the guilty act.

Appellate court: A court that sits in appeal of another court. An example is the Court of Appeal for a province. The Superior courts and Court of Queen's Bench sit as appellate courts to the provincial courts.

British North America Act, 1867: This was an act of the British Parliament that created the Dominion of Canada. It outlined Canada's system of government, modeling it after the British parliamentary system. When Canada's constitution was patriated, or brought home to Canada in 1982, its name was changed to the Constitution Act, 1867.

Canadian Charter of Rights and Freedoms: This is a bill of rights entrenched in the Constitution of Canada. It is the first part of the Constitution Act, 1982 and it guarantees political and civil rights of people in Canada from policies and actions of all levels of government.

Civil law: Law dealing with matters and procedures that are other than of a criminal nature.

Civil suit: An action started in civil courts against others for compensation, damages or another form of relief.

Civil trials: A trial in civil court for a non-criminal matter.

Constitution: The system of fundamental principles by which a nation or a state is governed and the documents which comprise or embody these principles.

Constitution Act, 1867: This was an act of the British Parliament, originally called the British North America Act, 1867, which created the Dominion of Canada. It outlined Canada's system of government, modeling it after the British parliamentary system. When Canada's constitution was patriated, or brought home to Canada in 1982, its name was changed to the Constitution Act, 1867.

Court of Appeal: This is the appeal court for a province hearing appeals from lower Superior or Queen's Bench courts and provincial courts. Appeals from this court can be taken to the Supreme Court of Canada as long as the Supreme Court of Canada grants leave to hear the appeal.

Court of Queen's Bench: This is a superior court that hears civil and criminal law cases as well as appeals from provincial courts. There are no monetary limits for claims that it may hear, although usually if less than $20,000 matters would be heard in a Small Claims Court, which is a provincial court instead. Appeals from this court would be taken to a Court of Appeal.

Criminal law: Law dealing with matters and procedures of a criminal nature.

Crown attorney: A government lawyer who acts on behalf of the Crown or the State to prosecute criminals pursuant to criminal statutes such as the Criminal Code.

Defence: An accused person in a criminal matter will present a defence to the Crown's case setting out why they are innocent.

Defendant: In a civil suit this is the person against whom an action has been commenced.

District courts/county courts: The term for a general trial court in the United States.

Dockets: Court records setting out the names of parties, file numbers and other miscellaneous information.

Examination for Discovery: A court process prior to trial that allows the parties to a court action to attend before a court reporter and examine the opposing side under oath. The testimony is produced as a written record called a transcript.

Federal Court of Appeal: A court of the federal government hearing appeals from the Federal Court of Canada and other specific boards designated by the federal government.

Grievances: The circumstance, act or cause of a complaint or wrong against oneself or of another.

High Court of Justice: Another name for the Superior Court of Justice. Ontario uses the name "Court of Justice" for its provincial court and "Superior Court of Justice" for its Superior Court or similar court to the Court of Queen's Bench in other provinces.

Judge: A lawyer who has been appointed by the government to be a judge of a court.

Judicial decision: A decision of a particular judge in a particular court case, whether it be civil or criminal.

Jurisdiction: Authority given to a legal body (such as a court or tribunal) or to a political leader (prime minister) to deal with legal matters, and to pronounce or enforce legal matters.

Jury: People selected to sit and hear a particular court case.

Lawyer: A person who has attended law school and passed the necessary provincial exams to be admitted to the law society of a province.

Legal interpretation: The creation of law by judges through decisions in courts.

Legal positivism: The creation of law by governments by such instruments as statutes and regulations.

Mens rea: A latin term denoting one element of a crime, or the guilty mind, which usually has to be proven in addition to the *actus reus* or guilty act.

Natural law: Law that arises in human morals, that is in agreement with nature, unchanging, everlasting and of universal application.

Plaintiff: The person commencing a civil action.

Principles of law: Precedents, rules norms and procedures comprising the social institution and structure of the "law."

Provincial courts: Lower courts of the provinces that hear lesser matters of criminal, civil (small claims) matters. There may be specialized courts such as youth courts, traffic courts, therapeutic drug courts or domestic violence courts.

Quasi-judicial: This is a body, usually called a tribunal, that resembles a court of law or has some attributes of a court of law. An example is the Human Rights Tribunal.

Serfdom: A social structure that creates slaves. In British history, slaves were in a condition of servitude to a lord, attached to the lord's land and transferred with the land from one owner to another.

Small claims court: This is a provincial court with jurisdiction to hear civil claims of a small sum. Currently this is set at claims which are less than $20,000.00

Statement of claim: This is the document that is issued by a court and commences a civil claim. After being issued it is served on a defendant.

Superior courts: This is the same as a court of Queen's Bench and Supreme Court for some provinces. Ontario uses the name "Superior Court of Justice" instead of Queen's bench. This court hears civil and criminal law cases as well as appeals from provincial courts. There are no monetary limits for claims. Appeals from this court would be taken to a Court of Appeal.

Supreme Court: Several provinces use the term "Supreme Court" for their superior court instead of Court of Queen's Bench. These would include the Yukon, Prince Edward Island, and Nova Scotia.

Supreme Court Act: The federal statute which establishes and governs the Supreme Court of Canada.

NOTES

1, Mostly white people. Black people with no history of criminal convictions have been three times more likely to be arrested by Toronto police for possession of small amounts of marijuana than white people of similar backgrounds (see Rankin 2017).

REFERENCES

Anderson, B., and D. Anderson. 1998. *Manufacturing Guilt: Wrongful Convictions in Canada*. Halifax, NS: Fernwood Publishing.

Banakar, R., and M. Travers. 2005. *Theory and Method in Socio-Legal Research*. Oxford: Hart.

Beckton, C.F. 1982. *The Labour and the Media*. Toronto, ON: Carswell.

Bojkovsky, C., D. Callan, J. Childs, G. Hartner, J. Konescsni and K. McNutt. 2017. "Legalizing and Regulating Cannabis in Saskatchewan." Policy Brief. Regina: Johnson-Shoyama Graduate School of Public Policy, University of Regina.

Borrows, J. 2016. *Freedom and Indigenous Constitutionallism*. University of Toronto Press, Toronto.

Boyd, S., and E. Sheehy. 1989. "Overview: Feminism and the Law in Canada." In T. Caputo, M. Kennedy, C. Reasons and A. Brannigan (eds.), *Law and Society: A Critical Perspective*. Toronto, ON: Harcourt Brace Jovanovich.

Canada. 1883. House of Commons Debates, 9 May.

Canada (Attorney General) v. Bedford, 2013 SCC 72.

Canada (Attorney General) v. PHS Community Services Society, 2011 SCC 44.

Canada (Prime Minister) v. Khadr, 2010 SCC 3 <http://canlii.ca/t/27qn6>.

CBC news. 2017. "Gaps Between Indigenous and Non-Indigenous Inmates Growing, Latest Statics Show." September 15. <http://www.cbc.ca/news/politics/crime-corrections-indigenous-prisons-1.4291568>.

Chippewas (Chippewas of the Thames First Nation) v. Enbridge Pipelines Inc., 2017. SCC 41.

Comack, E., and G. Balfour. 2004. *The Power to Criminalize: Volence, Inequality and the Law*. Halifax, NS: Fernwood Publishing.

Cotterrell, R. 1996. *Law's Community: Legal Theory in Sociological Perspective*. Oxford: Clarendon Press.

Durkheim, E. 1964 [1893]. *The Division of Labour in Society*. New York: Free Press.

Ehrlich, E. 1962 [1913]. *Fundamental Principles of the Sociology of Law*. New

York: Russell & Russell.

Enbridge Pipelines Inc. 2014. "Reasons for Decision." Application dated 29 November 2012 for the Line 9B Reversal and Line 9 Capacity Expansion Project. National Energy Board. Canada. OH-002-2013. March. <B18%2D2%20%2D%20Response%20to%20NEB%20IR%20No%203%20 %2D%20A3I6L7.pdf>.

Feldman, E.A. 2006. "The Tuna Court: Law and Norms in the World's Premier Fish Market." *California Law Review,* 94: 313.

Freedman, Hansen 2009. "Indigenous Rights vs. The Public Interest." Prepared for Pacific Business Law Institute conference, Vancouver, BC (February 26, 2009)

Gayle, D. 2015. "Cannabis. Police Won't Target Pot Smokers and Small-Scale Growers, Say Commissioners." *The Guardian*, July 22,.

Globe and Mail. 2010. "Facts About the Khadr's Charges." October 25.

Grant v. Torstar, 2009 SCC 61.

Grinberg, E. 2016. "Jian Ghomeshi, Canadian Radio Star, Acquitted in First Sexual Assault Trial." CNN, March 25.

Hurlbert, M.A. 2009. "An Analysis of Trends Related to the Adaptation of Water Law to the Challenge of Climate Change: Experience from Canada." *International Journal of Climate Change Strategies and Management,* 1, 3: 230–40.

___. 2009a. "The Adaptation of Water Law to Climate Change." *International Journal of Climate Change Strategies and Management,* 1, 3: 230–40.

___. 2009b. "Comparative Water Governance in the Four Western Provinces." *Prairie Forum* (special edition on climate change), 34, 1: 45–77.

Jeffries, S., and P. Stenning. 2014. "Sentencing Aboriginal Offenders: Law, Policy, and Practice in Three Countries." *Canadian Journal of Criminology and Criminal Justice* 56,4: 447–494.

Juristatt. 2009. 85-002-X, July. <http://www.statcan.gc.ca/pub/85-002-x/2009003/ article/10903-eng.htm#a5>.

Kohut, T. 2016. "Canada to Ban Asbestos: What You Need to Know about the Common Carcinogen." Global News, December 15.

Koring, P. 2010. "U.S. Naval Station Guantanamo Bay, Cuba." *Globe and Mail,* October 27, updated March 26, 2017.

Laidlaw, D.K. 2010. "Water Rights and Water Stewardship: What about Aboriginal People?" *Canadian Institute of Resources Law,* 107.

Lapowsky, I. 2017. "The Year Women Reclaimed the Web." *Wired,* December 26.

Levit, J.K. 2005. "A Bottom-Up Approach to International Lawmaking: The Tale of Three Trade Finance Instruments." *Yale Journal of International Law,* 30: 125.

Luhmann, N. 2004. *Law as a Social System.* Oxford: Oxford University Press.

MacDonald, G.M. 2002. *Social Context & Social Location in the Sociology of Law.* Peterborough, ON: Broadview Press.

MacKay, A.W. 1984. *Education Law in Canada.* Toronto, ON: Emond-Montgomery.

MacKinnon, C. 1987. *Feminism Unmodified: Discourses on Life and Law.* Cambridge: Harvard University Press.

Martin, M. 2002. "The Crown Owns All the Land?" In G.M. MacDonald, *Social Context & Social Location in the Sociology of Law*. Peterborough, ON: Broadview Press.

Marx, K. 1842. "Debates on the Law on Thefts of Wood." Supplement to the *Rheinische Zeitung*, October–November. <www.marxists.org/archive/marx/works/1842/10/25.htm>.

Marx, K., and Friedrich Engels. 2004 [1848]. *Manifesto of the Communist Party*. Marxists Internet Archive. <en.wikipedia.org/wiki/Marxists_Internet_Archive>.

Mason, G. 2013. "More Jail Won't Solve Canada's Indigenous Incarceration Problem." *Globe and Mail*, April 5.

Merry, S.E. 1988. "Legal Pluralism." *Law & Society Review*, 22: 869–895.

____. 2008. "International Law and Sociologic Scholarship: Toward a Spatial Global Legal Pluralism." Special issue: Law and Society Reconsidered. *Studies in Law, Politics, and Society*, 41: 149–168.

Milovanovic, D. 1988. *A Primer in the Sociology of Law*. New York: Harrow & Heston.

Naffine, N. 1990. *Law and the Sexes: Explorations in Feminist Jurisprudence*. Sydney, Australia: Allen & Unwin.

Native Web. 2015. "Hidden from History: The Canadian Holocaust." <www.canadiangenocide.nativeweb.org/intro2.html>.

Neu, D., and R. Therrien. 2003. *Accounting for Genocide: Canada's Bureaucratic Assault on Indigenous People*. Winnipeg/Halifax: Fernwood Publishing.

Norrie, A. 1998. "The Limits of Justice: Finding Fault in the Criminal Law." In M.S. Archer (ed.), *Critical Realism, Essential Readings*. New York: Routledge.

Ottawa Citizen. 1907. "Schools Aid White Plague. Startling Death Rolls Revealed. Among Indians. Absolute Inattention To Bare Necessities of Health." November 15. <canadiangenocide.nativeweb.org/keynewsschoolsandwhiteplague.html>.

Point, Steven. 2013. TRC, AVS Steven Point, Statement to the Truth and Reconciliation Commission of Canada, Vancouver, British Columbia, 20 September 2013, Statement Number. BCNEW304 reported in TRC at page 14, footnote 38.

Pound, Roscoe. 1942. "Social Control Through Law." *Social Forces*, 21, 2.

____. 1959. *Jurisprudence* (Vols. 1–5). St. Paul, MN: West.

R. v. Creighton [1993] (3) S.C.R. 3.

R. v. Gladue [1999] 1 S.C.R. 688.

R. v. Morgentaler [1988] (1) S.C.R 30.

Rajan, S.R. 2001. "Towards a Metaphysics of Environmental Violence: The Case of the Bhopal Gas Disaster." In N.L. Peluso and M. Watts (eds.), *Violent Environments*. Ithaca, NY: Cornell University Press.

Rankin, J. 2017. "Toronto Marijuana Arrests Reveal 'Startling' Racial Divide." *Toronto Star*, July 7. <thestar.com/news/insight/2017/07/06/toronto-marijuana-arrests-reveal-startling-racial-divide.html>.

Razack, S. 2002. "Gendered Racial Violence and Spatialized Justice: The murder of Pamela George." In S. Razack (ed.), *Race Space and the Law: Unmapping a White Settler Society.* Toronto, ON: Between the Lines.

Roach, K. 2001. *The Supreme Court on Trial: Judicial Activism or Democratic Dialogue.* Toronto, ON: Irwin Law.

___. 2009. *Criminal Law.* Toronto, ON: Irwin Law.

Schneider, E.M. 2000. *Battered Women and Feminist Lawmaking.* London: Yale University Press.

Shephard, Michelle. 2017. "Khadr to Get Apology, Compensation Over $10M as Lawsuit Settled." *Toronto Star*, July 3. <https://www.thestar.com/news/canada/2017/07/03/khadr-to-get-apology-compensation-over-10m-as-lawsuit-settled.html> (accessed July 11, 2017).

Smartt, Nicole. 2018. "Sexual Harassment in the Workplace in a #MeToo World." *Forbes.* Archived from the original on January 16, 2018. Retrieved January 16, 2018.

Snider, L. 2006. "Relocating Law: Making Corporate Crime Disappear." In E. Comack (ed.), *Locating Law: Race, Class, Gender, Sexuality Connections,* second ed. Black Point, NS: Fernwood Publishing.

Sorokin, P. 1957. *Social and Cultural Dynamics: A Study of Change in Major Systems of Art, Truth, Ethics, Law, and Social Relationships* (revised and abr. ed.). New Brunswick, NJ: Transaction.

TRC (Truth and Reconciliation Commission of Canada). 2015. "Honouring the Truth, Reconciling for the Future." Summary of the Final Report of the Truth and Reconciliation Commission of Canada. <www.trc.ca>.

Vago, S. 1994. *Law and Society,* fourth ed. Upper Saddle River, NJ: Prentice Hall.

von der Porten, S. 2012. "Canadian Indigenous Governance Literature: A Review." *AlterNative: An International Journal of Indigenous Peoples*, 8, 1: 1–14.

Wacks, R. 2006. *Philosophy of Law: A Very Short Introduction.* Oxford: Oxford University Press.

Weber, M. 1978 [1922]. *Economy and Society: An Outline of Interpretive Sociology* (G. Roth and C. Wittich, eds.). Berkeley, CA: University of California Press.

11

PURSUING JUSTICE THROUGH HUMAN RIGHTS

Gloria C. DeSantis

OBJECTIVES

At the end of this chapter, you will be able to:

- Describe human rights and their central principles that inform ethical practice

- Offer highlights on the historical evolution of human rights

- Identify the main United Nations (U.N.) structures and processes

- Describe individual and collective rights including examples of treaties that best exemplify them

- Explain the contested yet optimistic nature of human rights as a mechanism to advance formal and social justice.

This chapter demonstrates that human rights have formal structures and processes for monitoring, implementing and holding sovereign nations to account for human rights violations. In this regard, formal justice is enacted through these structures and processes via a multitude of treaties and conventions that have been adopted by the United Nations. Countries that become signatories to these treaties essentially make promises to abide by the contents (for example, the Convention on the Rights of Persons with Disabilities requires that people with disabilities be treated with dignity and not institutionalized in deplorable conditions where physical and emotional abuse is rampant). However, justice is undermined by nations that abuse their power and control, and further, do not attempt to rectify the ongoing inequality among people living in their country. Indeed, some countries continue to discriminate against certain groups of people such as religious minorities (for example, the Rohingya people are a Muslim minority group not legally recognized by the Myanmar government who are fleeing that country to avoid government massacres).

Social justice is a vital lens on human rights; it is also inherently connected to ethical practice. "Social justice is about assuring the protection of equal access to liberties, rights and opportunities as well as taking care of the least advantaged members of society" (Robinson 2010: 79) such that "there are no constraints on life choices based on social group differences" (Antony et al. 2017: 19). Social justice can be conceptualized as four dimensional. The first dimension is the most well-known: it is the equitable redistribution of material (income) and non-material goods (rights, opportunities, power). The second dimension refers to the recognition and respect for the dignity of all people. The third refers to the importance of participation in decision-making processes — at all levels of one's life (where someone chooses to live as well as who to vote for) — and how obstacles to this participation can exist independent of redistribution and recognition to systematically marginalize people. The fourth embraces the notion of development of people's capacities and human potential, which Gindin (2002) insists should focus on what we can become, not what we should have fairer access to (for a detailed explanation of each of these, refer to DeSantis 2008). Integral to each of these dimensions are ethical practices regarding the pursuit of justice.

SITUATING HUMAN RIGHTS

Much like the contested nature of other justice concepts, an exploration of human rights is no different. Different people approach human rights differently. Lawyers focus on the jurisprudence of human rights and formal justice tools used to render decisions about human rights violations. Social justice scholars explore the inequitable application of human rights both locally and globally as well as the abuse of power exercised by sovereign states to create compliant citizens. People whose rights have been violated seek venues to rectify the injustice caused to them by the state, private companies and other groups. Further, human rights are defined differently by philosophers, sociologists, anthropologists and criminologists. For example, criminologists would "associate human rights with criminal justice rights such as the right to a lawyer, the right to remain silent and the freedom from unreasonable search and seizure" (Hurlbert 2011: 166). Human rights have also become commonplace in our conversations and in the media.

Human rights may best be seen as a movement with multiple sub-movements that has been shaped by numerous forces over hundreds of years (Clapham 2007; Clément 2016). Human rights movements range from the local to the international. Human rights are not simply about a clear collection of legal obligations that governments around the world are responsible for implementing. Rather, human rights movements have shifted in emphasis based on the actions of international entities such as the United Nations, the actions of individual sovereign states and the actions of groups of people who join together in solidarity to resist injustices.

The "possession paradox" is characteristic of all rights: "having a right is ... of most value precisely when one does not have the object of that right" (Donnelly 1989: 11–12). Consider homelessness in Canada. If you are homeless, you do not possess shelter nor do you possess an object of the right to a decent standard of living (an adequate home). Furthermore, depending on where you are homeless, you may be apprehended by the police because you are deemed to be trespassing and sleeping in a place illegally, even if you have no choice because all the emergency shelters are full. This possession paradox moves us from the realm of social justice to criminal justice very quickly.

The concept of human rights is multilayered, complex and shifts over time. It has a geographic scope based on individual countries, continents or regions. The jurisdiction of human rights varies from individual states to global entities such as the United Nations. Finally, human rights has a formal legal perspective regarding what issues make their way through various courts of law and what legislation is passed in parliaments. In each of these instances, shifts in content and areas of emphasis occur over time. For example, in the 1970s, reducing the prevalence of torture was prioritized, whereas today, the rights of Indigenous peoples around the world are prioritized.

The complexity of geography and timing and the role of sovereign nations is illustrated with an example that recently came to an end in 2007 when a Canadian citizen won a $10 million settlement against the Canadian Government. This was the story of Maher Arar who, in 2002, not long after 9/11, was arrested in the U.S. As Hurlburt (2011: 166) describes:

> [he] was apprehended in the USA (with the assistance of Canadian security officials) when passing through the airport in New York while travelling home from a holiday in Tunis. He was detained for two weeks in solitary confinement without accessing a lawyer or being charged on suspicion of being a member of Al-Qaeda. The USA then deported him to Syria where he was tortured. He has been found by authorities in Syria and Canada to be innocent. For advocates lobbying on his behalf, knowing the Canadian Justice system, Mr. Arar's human rights as a Canadian and his international right not to be tortured, were instrumental in securing his eventual release.

Our political and ideological context shapes our understanding and responses to human rights. Consider how the atrocities of World War II inspired the creation of the United Nations in 1945 and the subsequent drafting, release and signing of the Universal Declaration of Human Rights (UDHR) in 1948. Similarly, our current era shapes how people view, define, collaborate on and agitate for human rights. Interestingly, concerns about human rights protections have been emerging over the past few years along with questions about whether there is movement into a post-human rights era (Alston 2017). With the election of Donald Trump as the President of the United States in the fall of 2016, and the growing number of other sovereign nation leaders who share similar neo-conservative, right-wing ideologies (such as restricting civil liberties, the need for stricter post-9/11 national security protections, restricting immigrants from predominantly Muslim countries, shrinking democratic spaces as governments use states of emergency to combat terrorism and a return to interrogation methods that constitute torture), there is cause for concern (Alston 2017). However, the protection and advancement of human rights has always been based on ongoing struggle and there have always been anti-human rights movements.

Human rights are fundamentally about the relationship between nation states and their citizens. Let us consider the example of Germany when Adolf Hitler was president from 1934 to 1945. Hitler's government passed laws that labelled Jewish people as lesser human beings who should therefore be exterminated. These government policies paved the way for the Holocaust and the murder of millions of Jews. Some argue that sovereign states should have this power and control to pass their own laws and deal with their own people as they choose. But this is contrary to international agreements and too often such history repeats itself. In 1979 in Cambodia, an estimated two million people were killed by the government; by 1994 in Rwanda, an estimated 800,000 Tutsis were killed by the majority Hutu government; in 2016 in Syria, a United Nations special envoy estimated 400,000 civilians had been killed during the preceding five years — most of these deaths were by the forces of President Bashar al-Assad.

HUMAN RIGHTS AND CENTRAL PRINCIPLES

"A human right is a right one possesses simply for being human" (Reis Monteiro 2014: 456). The United Nations Office of the High Commissioner on Human Rights (OHCHR) explains that human rights are inherent to all human beings regardless of their personal characteristics. Reis Monteiro (2014: 456) states:

> It is a legal right recognized of every member of the human species, without discrimination, irrespective of ethnic, cultural, religious, political or other membership, of gender, age, handicap or of whatever circumstances.

Human rights can be broken into four main categories or generations (Hurlbert 2011; Langlois 2016). These generations of rights are not based on specific time periods, nor do they replace one another, but rather, each generation is substantively different with some overlap. For example, civil and political rights evolved at the same time as economic and cultural rights. There are tensions across generations (such as individual property versus collective development rights) and within generations (for example, religious organizations should adopt non-discriminatory hiring practices, yet this may conflict with free religious expression) (Clapham 2007; Langlois 2016).

"First-generation rights" are known as civil and political rights and encompass liberty rights. Some examples of civil and political rights are the right to security of person, equality before the law, freedom of movement within one's country, freedom of thought and conscience, freedom of opinion and expression, freedom of peaceful assembly and association and freedom to take part in the government of one's country. This generation of rights is known as "negative rights" because governments must refrain from interfering with these rights.

"Second-generation rights" focus on economic, social and cultural rights. Some examples include: the right to an adequate standard of living; the right to an education; the right to participate in the cultural life of one's communities; the right to standards of health; and the right to social security, to work in favourable conditions and to belong to unions. This generation of rights is known as "positive rights" because governments must actively provide programs and services as well as expend financial resources in order to deliver these rights to people.

"Third-generation rights" evolved after first- and second-generation rights and took on a global focus on issues such as poverty and famine. At the same time, there was growth in thinking about the role of non-state actors, such as private corporations, in human rights. This generation of rights is identified as group solidarity and collective rights. Some examples include: the right to peace; the right to humanitarian relief during natural disasters and wars; the right to sustainable development; the right to social development; and the right to cultural self-determination. This generation of rights includes a mix of negative and positive rights.

"Fourth-generation rights" are known as "new frontier" rights and concentrate on non-human life forms such as animals and plants as well as other human rights such as those surrounding bio-ethical issues. Some examples of these rights are: the rights of endangered species; the right of animals to be treated humanely during pharmaceutical testing; a fetus's right to life; and the right to choose to end one's life with the assistance of a physician. Further, some Indigenous groups explain that rivers, lakes and oceans are sacred and also have rights. Thus, when the Husky Oil pipeline leaked approximately 225,000 litres of oil into the North Saskatchewan River near Maidstone, Saskatchewan in 2016, Indigenous peoples living along that river expressed grave concerns about plants, animals and amphibians that live in or near the river (Global News 2016).

The United Nations (U.N.) is responsible for inspiring the twentieth-century evolution of human rights. The U.N. was formed in 1945 at the end of the Second World War. The Universal Declaration of Human Rights (UDHR) was passed by the United Nations General Assembly in 1948. There are thirty articles in the UDHR (United Nations 1996). Article 1 explains the philosophy of human rights. Article 2 focuses on the principle of equality and non-discrimination. Article 3 focuses on life, liberty and security and is the cornerstone for Articles 4 to 21, which delve into civil and political rights (such as the right to vote, the right to free speech and the right to peaceful assembly). Article 22 concentrates on rights that are indispensable for human dignity and the full development of one's personality and the importance of national efforts and international co-operation; it sets the stage for Articles 23 to 27, which are economic, social and cultural in nature (such as the right to education and health care). Collective/solidarity rights are more recent in nature and are not included in the 1948 UDHR, although these rights are foreshadowed in Articles 28 and 29, which refer to "social and international order," duties to community and a democratic society. Many of these articles are directly connected to the various social justice dimensions (such as redistribution, recognition, participation and capacity development). Despite the almost unanimous support for the UDHR, there has been and continues to be an uneven distribution and implementation of human rights around the world.

There are also an important series of foundational principles that accompany human rights that also inform ethical practice. The U.N. Office of the High Commissioner for Human Rights (OHCHR) presents the following essential human rights principles:

- Universal — human rights are extended to all people regardless where they live.
- Inalienable — human rights cannot be taken away except in specific situations and by due process.

- Interdependent and indivisible — the many types of human rights are interconnected in that the improvement or degradation of one right influences others (e.g., taking away one's right to an education affects one's right to self-determination).
- Equal and non-discriminatory — non-discrimination is included in all human rights treaties and international human rights law. This principle "prohibits discrimination on the basis of a list of non-exhaustive categories such as sex, race, colour and so on" (ibid.). Further, the principle of equality supplements this principle of non-discrimination as expressed in Article 1 in the UDHR: "all people are born free and equal in dignity" (United Nations General Assembly 1948).
- Rights and obligations — these exist at both the level of the individual and the state. At the individual level, we are entitled to human rights but we are also obligated to respect the human rights of others. At the level of the state, "states assume obligations and duties under international law to *respect*, to *protect* and to *fulfil* human rights" (U.N. OHCHR 2017, emphasis added).

It is noteworthy that "dignity" is both a right and a principle and applies to all people, not just those born into the upper class or a certain racial group or a certain gender group. "All human beings are born free and equal in dignity and rights" (United Nations General Assembly 1948: Art.1). "Human dignity is the core of human rights philosophy ... [even though] there is no generally agreed legal definition of human dignity, any more than of human rights" (Reis Monteiro 2014: 199). The lack of an agreed-upon universal definition is but one barrier to the implementation of human rights.

All people around the world are entitled to basic human dignity without discrimination, however, this is elusive. Think about refugees fleeing their homeland where they are forced to beg for food, live in unsanitary conditions and deal with the constant threat of violence against them and their children because of a brutal dictator. Think about child labour in countries where poverty is pervasive and parents send their childen to do dangerous work in underwater mining operations run by transnational corporations in order to earn money for their extended family. In each case, people's basic dignity is compromised and numerous human rights are violated.

Canada also does not have a clean human rights record, nor does it consistently enact the central principles. One of the most striking examples of human rights violations was declared in January 2016. It began in 2007 when Cindy Blackstock and the First Nations Child and Family Caring Society of Canada initiated legal action against the Government of Canada for what they believed was discrimination against First Nations children. After almost ten years of proceedings and deputations by a litany of individuals, chiefs, the Assembly of First Nations and numerous organizations, the Canadian Human Rights Tribunal ruled that the federal government discriminates against First Nations children living on reserves by underfunding children's services by between 22 percent and 34 percent (depending on the First Nations community) (First Nations Child and Family Caring Society of Canada 2016).

A BRIEF HISTORY OF HUMAN RIGHTS

Human rights, even though inalienable, do have a history. What follows here is an overview framed by a European perspective. There may be much writing about human rights in other non-English societies and many may a have long, deep oral traditions, like Indigenous societies. Thus, this overview, largely because of colonialism, is European in nature.

In the 1200s, freedom came through social and political status. Basically if you owned land and if you were part of the aristocracy you had rights. Few others had rights. During this time, writings were about standards of decent behaviour and the objective moral order was known as "natural law" (Clapham 2007; Langlois 2016).

> This order was conceptualized as the natural law, which, after the rise of Christianity, became associated with the Church. Under the natural law, people had duties to one another and to God; rights were derived from the duties we owed one another under God. The practice of claiming modern secular rights, rights that have as their focus the subjective freedoms and liberties of individuals, rather than *objective right* (the divinely sanctioned moral order of the day) is associated with the long development of the idea of individual liberty culminating in the Enlightenment. (Langlois 2016: 12, emphasis in original)

CASE STUDY:
A BRIEF HISTORY OF RIGHTS AND CONSTITUTIONS

1215: *Magna Carta* — linked to Canada through British common law

1689: *English Bill of Rights* (in England)

1776: American Declaration of Independence

1789: French Declaration on the Rights of Man and Citizen

An early women's rights activist, Mary Wollstonecraft, who wrote *Vindication of the Rights of Women* in 1792, demanded revisions to the French Constitution

1867: British North America Act

1917: Mexican Constitution is the first document in the world to specify social rights

1919: League of Nations and International Labour Organization formed — the first multilateral efforts to protect minorities on an international scale

1945: The establishment of the United Nations and its Charter

1947: Saskatchewan Bill of Rights (the first province in Canada to pass such an act)

1948: *Universal Declaration of Human Rights* by the United Nations

1960: *Canadian Bill of Rights*

1966: *International Covenant on Civil and Political Rights* as well as the *International Covenant on Economic, Social and Cultural Rights*

1982: Constitution Act, *Canadian Charter of Rights and Freedoms* — emphasis on civil and political rights, not economic, social and cultural rights

Source: (Clapham 2007)

In the period stretching from 1400s to the latter part of the 1700s, the emergence of "natural rights" occurred — coined by the philosopher John Locke — as both status and freedom became important (Langlois 2016). During the period running roughly between the 1650s and 1790s, known as the Age of Enlightenment, many revolutions ensued that were linked to ideas about liberalism (Langlois 2016). Liberalism was defined by ideals of individual freedom, equality, personal property and personal responsibility. During this Age of Enlightenment, rational, natural order and human reason replaced the word of God. It was during this time that the scientific method was born.

Between the latter part of the 1700s and early 1900s, a fundamental shift began to spread wherein "men" were deemed to be entitled to individual rights and freedoms that were heavily oriented toward civil and political rights — known as the "rights of man" (such as the right to vote) (Langlois 2016). Many sovereign nations wrote constitutions that enshrined these individual rights and freedoms (such as the American Declaration of Independence in 1776). The modern era, roughly 1900 to present day, ushered in "human rights" as we know them today including economic, social, cultural and collective rights. This era also saw the global spread of human rights.

Some argue that the 1948 release of the Universal Declaration of Human Rights (UDHR) was the pivotal moment in the history of human rights. Others disagree, arguing that human rights began centuries ago (Reis Monteiro 2014). In terms of the modern era of human rights, World War II and the Jewish Holocaust created by Germany drew moral shock around the world and a general commitment to not repeat these atrocities. In 1945 the United Nations was born and in 1948 the UDHR was released. The Nuremberg Tribunal saw Nazis charged and tried for their role in murdering thousands of Jewish people in death camps. Those legal proceedings saw a retreat to "natural law" from a few hundred years ago (Langlois 2016).

The United Nations

The League of Nations, which had been in existence since 1919, was replaced by the United Nations. In 1945, fifty-eight countries came together and established a Charter outlining the purpose of the United Nations (U.N.). The U.N. Charter of 1945 specifies four main purposes: to maintain international peace and security; to develop friendly relations among nations; to foster cooperation in solving social and economic problems across countries; and "to be a centre for harmonizing the actions of nations in the attainment of these common ends" (United Nations 1945). Naturally, the U.N. has evolved over time. Its current structure includes five main organs, or bodies (Smith 2012; United Nations nd):

General Assembly comprises representatives from 193 countries (of a total of approximately 198 countries, depending on how countries are defined) making it the only U.N. body with universal representation. Each country has one vote. It is the main deliberation and decision-making organ of the U.N. where treaties are adopted. Each year the Assembly meets in New York City and each country speaks at this annual general meeting session.

Economic and Social Council has 54 members elected by the General Assembly. Its main functions include coordination of U.N. work, research, policy critique and dialogue, and the formulation of recommendations. It receives the reports from subsidiary bodies, commissions and the nine committees that are each responsible for monitoring treaty implementation. The nine committees are: Committee on Economic, Social and Cultural Rights; Committee for the Rights of Persons with Disabilities; Committee on the Elimination of Racial Discrimination; Committee on the Rights of the Child; Committee on Enforced Disappearances; Migrant Workers Committee; Committee on the Elimination of Discrimination Against Women; Committee Against Torture, and; the Human Rights Committee) (Smith 2012: 53).

Security Council is made up of ten non-permanent members and five permanent members. These five permanent members were the powerful countries in 1945 at the end of World War II: France, China, former Soviet Union, the U.S. and the United Kingdom. They have veto power in all decisions — this is a major source of criticism today. Its primary function is the "maintenance of international peace and security", thus it assesses threats to peace and acts of aggression and recommends settlement options for those involved in disputes (United Nations n.d.).

International Court of Justice is the main judicial organ of the U.N. Its main role is "to settle, in accordance with international law, legal disputes submitted to it by States and to give advisory opinions on legal questions referred to it by authorized United Nations organs and specialized agencies" (United Nations n.d.).

U.N. Secretariat has the seat of the Secretary-General, who is the Chief Administrative Officer of the U.N.. He/she is appointed by the General Assembly and Security Council for a five-year term. It is at the Secretariat that all the day-to-day administrative work mandated by the General Assembly and the various organs is done by thousands of staff from around the world.

Over time, the U.N. has created numerous international human rights mechanisms and tools for the promotion of human rights around the world. In very general terms, the U.N. adopts various "treaties" — including declarations, covenants and conventions — that all have specific U.N. meanings. "Treaty" broadly means: "conventions, agreements, protocols, and exchange of letters or notes may all constitute treaties" (Reis Monteiro 2014: 481). Some examples include: the Convention on the Elimination of all Forms of Discrimination Against Women in 1979; the Convention against Torture in 1984; and the U.N. Declaration on the Rights of the Child in 1989.

However, none of the treaties — not even the UDHR — are legally binding. That is, no sovereign nation, not even those who are members of the U.N., is required to adopt and implement the rights outlined in each treaty. Instead, the U.N. human rights system actually concentrates on encouraging the creation and spread of human rights norms using non-adversarial approaches for implementation (DeLaet 2015). The creation of norms have focused on issues such as reducing the prevalence of forced child labour, torture, discrimination against women and hate speech. However, the U.N. is also known to have weak monitoring bodies; these include simply gathering information from each country regarding its progress on moving human rights forward. Nonetheless, the very nature of this information-gathering process has been known to positively influence the spread of human rights because public conversations and debates occur.

Additionally, the U.N. has both humanitarian and military intervention roles to play when atrocities such as genocide are unfolding within or between sovereign states. The "Responsibility to Protect" (Clapham 2007) "refers to military intervention for the purpose of protecting fundamental human rights" (DeLaet 2015: 150). The Security Council can invoke chapter VII of the U.N. Charter after it deliberates over and decides on non-military and military responses directed at sovereign states when there are threats to international peace and security. Multilateral interventions take place when many states come together and intervene in a country's affairs (for example, in the early 1990s the U.N. Security Council approved multi-country intervention in the Somali civil war) (DeLaet 2015). Unilateral interventions take place when one country forcibly moves into another country based on humanitarian grounds (for example, in 1978 Vietnam invaded Cambodia to end the Cambodian genocide that had begun a few years earlier). "Just war theory" posits that these kinds of humanitarian interventions are acceptable, but only when certain conditions are met: there must be just cause; a country must provide advance notice of its war objectives; war must be assessed and deemed to be the last alternative; and "harm caused by a war must be proportional to the harm it is seeking to prevent" (DeLaet 2015: 152). Thus, there are some mechanisms that can be used to advance human rights around the world.

The structure developed by the U.N., including the role of sovereign nations, is known as a "top-down" approach to human rights promotion (DeLaet 2015). Top-down refers to those who make policies, legislation and laws as well as the mechanisms to enforce them. On the other end of the spectrum are bottom-up forces that are grounded in communities and include non-governmental organizations, coalitions and social movements that promote human rights (see the next section for more details). The U.N. has subsidiary bodies such as the Human Rights Council made up of forty-seven members, treaty-monitoring bodies and the U.N. High Commissioner on Human Rights that engages in global awareness campaigns. Finally, there are sovereign nations that adopt U.N. treaties and then go on to create their own national human rights plans — these too, are known as top-down. For example, the United Nations General Assembly approved the Convention against Torture after experts researched and wrote it; it was then up to the U.N. and sovereign nations around the world to encourage all countries to adopt it. The abolishment of torture focuses on the respect for the dignity of all people, a dimension of social justice.

U.N. Processes: Monitoring, Measurement, Compliance

The U.N. is a complex structural system and its processes are similarly complex. The U.N. engages representatives from countries around the world to do its monitoring, measurement and compliance work. As described above, there are numerous organs or entities that make up the U.N. structure. However, the U.N. has adopted a non-adversarial approach, focusing on the creation and adoption of shared human rights norms globally and the collection of information on human rights. It has weak monitoring vehicles, and periodically uses a kind of global public shaming to advance human rights (DeLaet 2015).

When members of the General Assembly vote in favour of a treaty, the representatives from these countries are essentially indicating they agree in principle with the contents of a treaty, but they must take the treaty back to their own country for discussion and formal adoption at the national level. A country is known to "ratify" a U.N. treaty when it follows national, constitutional procedures and votes to adopt it (Goodhart 2016: 433). After ratification, that country is then expected to develop legislation, public policies, national action plans and processes for its own country that are aligned with the contents of that U.N. treaty. Depending on the treaty, that country must submit a report to one of the U.N. monitoring committees at specified time periods (such as every four years). For example, Canada submitted its national progress report to the U.N. Committee on Economic, Social and Cultural Rights and then presented to that Committee in February 2016 (Government of Canada 2013). This committee is composed of eighteen experts in the field of economic, social and cultural rights and is responsible for monitoring the implementation of the International Covenant on Economic, Social and Cultural Rights (ICESCR). This committee receives reports from all the countries that have adopted this treaty. The committee received Canada's report and then made numerous recommendations to Canada in order to better achieve the standards outlined in the ICESCR. One recommendation in particular is worth noting:

> The State party [Canada] should engage civil society and organizations of Indigenous Peoples in that revision, with a view to broadening the interpretation of the Canadian Charter of Rights and Freedoms, notably sections 7, 12 and 15, to include economic social and cultural rights, and thus ensure the justiciability of Covenant rights. (U.N. Economic and Social Council 2015: 2)

Essentially, the Committee noted that these sections of Canada's Charter — section 7 about "the right to life, liberty, and security of the person," section 12 wherein no one is to be "subjected to any cruel and unusual treatment or punishment" and section 15 in which everyone is considered "equal under the law ... without discrimination" — do not support economic, social and cultural rights. For example, people who live in poverty — many of whom are Indigenous peoples — are not free to live lives with a sense of security because they are often forced to live in unsafe neighbourhoods where rents are the cheapest, may have to get their food at foodbanks, which feels like cruel treatment, and may be viewed suspiciously by police who they may encounter late at night as they walk home from their minimum-wage job. All of this is a problem for Canada because we are a signatory to this treaty and our country's report shows that we do not meet U.N. standards. In Canada, the media usually reports on our visit to the U.N. Committee and it is in this way that the public becomes aware of U.N. standards and how we measure up (or not). When U.N. reports are released publicly, often these reports become a form of public shaming and peer pressure from other sovereign nations emerges, which then compels that country to remedy their problems.

The U.N. monitoring system also encourages engagement, research, dialogue, report writing and presentations from non-U.N. and non-government entities. This is often referred to as the bottom-up promotion of human rights. These independent, self-organizing entities are non-profit organizations, voluntary organizations and non-governmental organizations (NGOs), more generally known as civil society organizations. For example, Mining Watch is an NGO that tracks human rights abuses perpetrated by mining companies around the world (such as unsafe working conditions and forced disappearances of local residents who stand up against the destruction of their land). Often, these organizations band together in networks, coalitions and social movements to press for human rights implementation.

These entities work at various geographic scales to advance human rights including local, regional, provincial/territorial, national and international levels. At times, these organizations come together in coalitions to write and present their perspectives. For example, in 2016, an NGO called Canada Without Poverty engaged the BC Poverty Reduction Coalition, the Canadian Poverty Institute, the Niagara Poverty Reduction Network, the MacKillop Centre for Social Justice and the Canadian Centre for Policy Alternatives to research and write a brief to the ICESCR Committee that was critical of Canada in the following areas: poor housing standards and homelessness; food insecurity; poverty; refugee health care; low minimum wages; violence against women; and the government defunding of non-governmental organizations working with marginalized communities. Numerous other non-governmental organizations also made similar presentations, critical of the lack of action on safe water and poverty, for example, and included Amnesty International, Asubpeeschoseewagong/ Grassy Narrows First Nation and Ligue des Droits et Libertés (PSWG), to name but a few.

Social movements are another form of bottom-up human rights promotion. Social movements are collectives of non-U.N. and non-governmental organizations, as well as individuals, that come together to act and agitate for a change to the status quo based on a perceived injustice, usually centred on shared values and couched in a similar vision of a better world. A social movement is based on sustained action over a long period and may exist as tight clusters or loose networks (Clément 2008; Smith 2014). The target may be to change societal values and norms in general or state policies specifically — or both simultaneously (Clément 2008; Smith 2014). For example, anti-poverty movements in Canada have been active for many decades, challenging the poor living standards for certain groups of people in Canada (such as people with disabilities and Indigenous peoples), which is a violation of economic rights (specifically, a violation of UDHR Art. 25 and ICESCR Art. 11 regarding inadequate food, clothing and housing).

In some bottom-up cases, individuals, with non-governmental and advocacy organizations assisting them (like the National Association of Women and the Law, Rights and Democracy), have taken the government to court to hold them accountable for creating poor living conditions. Attempting to re-frame poverty as a violation of human rights through the courts in Canada has not been fruitful, though (McIsaac 2016). The case of Louise Gosselin is a clear example of this failure of the courts:

> Article 25 of the UDHR states that a person has the right to "a standard of living adequate for the health and well-being of himself [sic] and of his family, including food, clothing, housing and medical care and necessary social service." In the Supreme Court of Canada, Louise Gosselin argued that the government of Québec violated her right to life, liberty and security of the person and to equality, as stated in sections 7 and 15 of the Charter, when it reduced welfare benefits to young people and mandated program involvement as an eligibility requirements. The Charter

does not contain specific rights to such things as food, clothing and housing: the closest provision was the right to "life, liberty and security of the person" contained in section 7. The UDHR was not raised (again, because it is not a legally binding treaty). Gosselin argued that the $170 per month as social assistance allotted to her by the Government of Québec was impossible to live on ... The Supreme Court of Canada determined that section 7 of the Charter did not create a positive obligation on governments to guarantee adequate living standards ... Given the Supreme Court of Canada ruling, it seems obvious that the important step is to have the government define, life, liberty and security as including the right to a standard of adequate living. (Hurlbert 2011: 184)

Major advancements in human rights around the world have been the result of the work of NGOs and social movements. For example, in the 1960s, women's NGOs and movements in many countries around the world advocated against discriminatory practices against women, which led to the Convention on the Elimination of all Forms of Discrimination Against Women that was adopted by the U.N. in 1979. In the 1970s, Amnesty International was instrumental in bringing torture to the attention of the world and paving the way for the creation of the Convention Against Torture that was adopted by the General Assembly in 1984. In Canada, a more recent struggle continues to unfold as John Howard Societies actively campaign through evidence-based reports and public dialogue against "solitary confinement" as a state-sanctioned human rights violation — cruel and inhumane treatment. NGOs and social movements advance human rights through numerous advocacy strategies (such as street demonstrations and sit-ins) (DeSantis 2010).

The nature of the U.N. requires both bottom-up and top-down entities working together in the formulation of "national action plans" within countries. Once a country has adopted a U.N. treaty and has had it ratified through their national government, multiple levels of government within that country as well as non-governmental entities should work together on all phases of the national plan — from preparatory work to the developmental phase to implementation, to monitoring work and, finally, to the review and annual reporting phase — because the advancement of human rights is not solely the work of governments or the U.N. (U.N.

OHCHR 2002). Despite this ideal vision of how governments and non-governmental organizations should work together, research on thirty-nine countries around the globe indicates there are some serious problems with these action plans, including lack of comprehensiveness, lack of resources, the lack of political will and the lack of stakeholder awareness (such as the public, the media, academics, marginalized groups and NGOS) (Chalabi 2015). For example, in terms of ongoing support for the status quo, the Chinese government reported to the U.N. recently that there is no censorship when there is much evidence to say otherwise. Formal justice is reflected in human rights treaties but it appears that national action plans developed by numerous countries have significant problems and social injustices persist.

RIGHTS OF INDIGENOUS PEOPLE IN CANADA: A CASE STUDY

"Under international law, there is no official definition of Indigenous, although the U.N. generally identifies Indigenous groups as autonomous and self-sustaining societies that have faced discrimination, marginalization and assimilation of their cultures and peoples due to the arrival of a larger or more dominant settler populations" (First Nations and Indigenous Studies 2009).

In the context of Indigenous peoples, it is collective rights that are the most salient. Collective rights are third-generation rights described earlier in this chapter. Collective rights are attributed to groups of people who share common characteristics and social identities, often based on marginalized life circumstances with whom there should be, ethically, a "social contract" due to prevailing beliefs about mutual reciprocity and moral supports in society (Reis Monteiro 2014). There are numerous examples of collective rights that are expressed through U.N. treaties: the Declaration on the Rights of the Child; the Convention on the Rights of Persons with Disabilities; and the Declaration of the Rights of Indigenous Peoples.

The Declaration of the Rights of Indigenous Peoples (UNDRIP) was passed by the U.N. General Assembly in 2007 after twenty-five years of activism by Indigenous peoples, NGOS and social movements (Hanson 2010). UNDRIP is perceived by people all over the world to be, on the one hand, a validation of the existence of colonialism and oppression on a global scale and, on the other hand, empowerment for Indigenous peoples (Hanson 2010). There were 144 countries that became signatories to the Declaration in 2007, while eleven countries abstained and four voted against it. Canada was one of the countries that voted against it, citing incompatibility with our Constitution and the *Canadian Charter of Rights and Freedoms* (Hanson 2010). According to 101 lawyers who signed an open letter, the federal government erroneously argued that "UNDRIP affirms only the collective rights of Indigenous peoples and fails to balance individual and collective rights or the rights of Indigenous and non-Indigenous peoples" (Nation Talk 2008).

In 2010, Canada provided a conditional signature stating: "although the Declaration is a non-legally binding document that does not reflect customary international law nor change Canadian laws, our endorsement gives us the opportunity to reiterate our commitment to continue working in partnership with Aboriginal peoples in creating a better Canada" (Indigenous and Northern Affairs Canada 2010). During this time, the federal government, led by the Conservative Party, indicated that it believed it was doing a fine job on Indigenous peoples' rights. Finally, at a meeting on May 10, 2016 of the Permanent Forum on Indigenous Issues at the United Nations, led by the Liberal Government, Canada removed its objector status and became a full supporter of UNDRIP (Fontaine 2016). Canada is now required to measure, report on and comply with UNDRIP standards.

UNDRIP protects the collective rights of Indigenous peoples, but it does not override the agreements that Indigenous peoples have with their own countries (Hanson 2010). UNDRIP comprises forty-six articles including: foundational rights; self-governance and self-determination; life and security; language, culture and spiritual identity; education, information and employment; participation, development and economic and social rights; and rights to country, resources and traditional knowledge. Two UNDRIP articles create the foundation upon which all other rights rest (U.N. General Assembly 2007):

Article 3: Indigenous Peoples have the right to self-determination. By virtue of that right they freely determine their political status and freely pursue their economic, social and cultural development.

Article 4: Indigenous Peoples, in exercising their right to

self-determination, have the right to autonomy or self-government in matters relating to their internal and local affairs, as well
as ways and means for financing their autonomous functions.

The right to self-determination is a super-construct on which most
other rights rest. Self-determination embodies the principle of participation in all decision making and requires governments "to consult
Indigenous Peoples in matters that may affect them, based on the principle of free, prior and informed consent" (U.N. Expert Mechanism on
the Rights of Indigenous Peoples 2010: 3).

Yet, in Canada, consent does not seem to be operational. An example of
clear violations of numerous Indigenous peoples' human rights unfolded
in 2011 at the Lake St. Martin Anishinaabe community in Manitoba. In
May of that year, the Manitoba government chose to divert massive vol-
umes of flood water into their community in order to protect cottagers
and farm land (Ballard 2017). It was in that community — and numerous
others in the region — that the Anishinaabe people were forced to evacuate
from their communities and into hotels in Winnipeg. Even though the
Anishinaabe people had created their own community development plan
and identified an area of land for re-settlement, many were still homeless
and landless in 2015 because neither the federal government nor the
provincial government would listen to them. The incredible stress and
disintegration of the Anishinaabe people's way of life over those years
in hotels in Winnipeg (from 2011 to 2015) is not hard to imagine. In
addition to violations of UNDRIP Articles 3 and 4 noted above, there were
numerous other violations, but only two are cited here as examples: the
right to live in freedom and peace (Art. 7) and the right not to be forcibly removed from their land (Art. 10). This example illustrates that the
federal government controls the Anishinaabe people through the Indian
Act, while the provincial government controls land and lake policies —
Anishinaabe people's participation in decision making was denied, thus
social justice was denied.

In light of present-day stories such as the Lake St. Martin Anishinaabe
disaster, valid questions persist about how Indigenous rights are and
should be protected in Canada and around the world. There are three
principle U.N. bodies that conduct research, track progress, monitor
compliance and take action on Indigenous rights (U.N. OHCHR 2013):

Expert Mechanism on the Rights of Indigenous People — this body provides thematic, expert advice to the Human Rights Council annually. At this annual meeting in Geneva, Indigenous People, sovereign states, NPOS, scholars, national human rights institutions and others participate.

Special Rapporteur on the rights of Indigenous Peoples — rapporteurs visit countries to assess progress on Indigenous rights, examine obstacles to the protection of Indigenous Peoples' rights, gather information, and formulate recommendations.

Permanent Forum on Indigenous Issues — this body provides advice to the U.N. Economic and Social Council, raises awareness of issues, promotes the integration and coordination of activities on Indigenous issues within the U.N., and finally, prepares & disseminates information. It was here in 2016 that federal government representatives removed all conditions and fully endorsed UNDRIP.

Yet, enforcement is still problematic. In 2015, Mr. James Anaya, Special U.N. Rapporteur and expert on Indigenous issues, visited Canada and conducted a nine-day research project. After visiting Indigenous communities he issued a report indicating that Canada fell exceedingly short of UNDRIP standards. Mr. Anaya's report amounted to public shaming of Canada — this is but one tool used to move countries to greater compliance.

Started in 2009, the work undertaken by the Truth and Reconciliation Commission of Canada (TRC) on the residential school legacy, which culminated in a series of documents, are essential tools for the advancement of UNDRIP in Canada. In fact, in the "Calls to Action," UNDRIP is cited numerous times, but the most critical of all are: #43 "We call upon federal, provincial, territorial, and municipal governments to fully adopt and implement the UNDRIP as the framework for reconciliation" and #44 "We call upon the Government of Canada to develop a national action plan, strategies, and other concrete measures to achieve the goals of the UNDRIP" (TRC 2015: 4). Thus, the TRC makes the work to be done quite clear.

SOME PARADOXES AND DEBATES ABOUT HUMAN RIGHTS

There are numerous paradoxes in the field of human rights. DeLaet (2015) describes three main paradoxes that are inherent to the U.N. system. First, the U.N. Human Rights Council should be made up of countries that have made major progress on human rights and have near-perfect human rights records, but there are none. Second, in terms of international action on human rights, the strongest procedures exist in countries where they are needed the least. A third paradox exists when we think about countries that have perpetrated human rights abuses against their own citizens, and are told by the U.N. to cease such abuses; it is naïve to believe that these countries will then voluntarily agree to change their behaviour and protect these same citizens (for example, between 1975 and 1985, the Guatemalan government targeted and killed almost 200,000 Maya peasants, including children). These paradoxes illustrate the difficulties of operationalizing human rights and expose the reality of substantive justice — a very uneven practice around the world.

Further, there are many debates about human rights, but only four are highlighted here. First, Indigenous peoples around the world "are among the most marginalized, impoverished and frequently victimized members of society" due to racism, dispossession and colonization (Amnesty International Canada 2016). Given the formal justice nature of the human rights system, Indigenous peoples should have both their individual and collective rights, as defined in numerous treaties, met. However, Indigenous rights are complicated. For example, Amnesty International (2016) claims: "extending universalism is tantamount to assimilation: it is the precise approach that Indigenous Peoples have been fighting against for hundreds of years." As Peter Kulchyski (2013) argues, Indigenous peoples have "inherent customary rights" directly linked to their specific ways of life and longstanding ancestral occupancy of the land (such as the right to hunt, trap and fish) that cannot simply be given to them from a higher power like the United Nations. In Canada, we continue to wrestle with particularities regarding Indigenous rights because of the many peace/friendship and numbered treaties that the federal government entered into with Indigenous peoples. Our country's inability to meet our Indigenous treaty obligations is a barrier to substantive human rights justice and reflects the interests and power of settlers.

Second, "universalism," a key pillar for modern-day human rights, is regularly challenged. Human rights are intended for all people, regardless of country, religion, age and so on. There is a universal philosophical justification for human rights in that all individuals have equal moral worth, basic dignity and human capacity for autonomy and choice (Langlois 2016). This is aligned with the concept of formal justice wherein all people are to be treated equally. However, one of the most serious challenges to universalism is cultural relativism. Cultural relativism is the "conceptual rejection of rights which states that norms are only appropriate for cultures out of which they emerge" (Langlois 2016: 17). Langlois goes on to explain that cultural relativists criticize human rights for illegitimately privileging one set of values over another and that the moral code of a society should determine what is right and wrong within that society. This view implies that within the U.N. system, sovereign nations should have the ultimate power to decide how they will deal with their own citizens (DeLaet 2015). Cultural relativism lies in opposition to formal justice because people of different nations are not treated equally.

Another critique of human rights is that they are used by some sovereign nations to further political agendas outside their own boundaries. Human rights can be used as a "tool to promote and defend Western interests" and justify invading another sovereign nation (Langlois 2016: 17). Clapham (2007) states Western human rights foreign policies disguise hegemonic ambitions and creeping justification for military intervention. Foreign policy puts the spotlight on other countries, not one's own (Clapham 2007). For example, the U.S. recently pointed its finger at China for its human rights abuses, yet many U.S. states still have the death penalty — the ultimate violation of the right to life.

Finally, in this foreign policy context, transnational corporations (TNCs) benefit from open borders between countries to trade freely, set up factories, extract gas and mine minerals. In general, however, the economic interests and power of TNCs have had a negative impact on human rights and are barriers to the realization of social justice. A TNC is "an enterprise that undertakes foreign direct investment, owns or controls income-gathering assets in more than one country, produces goods or services outside its country of origin, or engages in international production" (Westaway 2012: 65). Often, this happens at much reduced costs to the corporation because they pay lower wages to workers and receive tax incentives to locate their companies' operations in foreign countries. In general, TNCs have been known to directly violate human rights by disregarding workplace/labour standards (such as using child labour) and by infringing on environmental rights (such as polluting local water sources). TNCs also indirectly support repressive governments and are complicit in host countries' police brutality, including the suppressing freedom of speech when locals try to speak out about injustices (for example, Texaco in Equador and Walmart factories in China and Honduras) (Westaway 2012). Further, Laine (2015: 641) explains that TNCs are not obligated to follow international legal principles and, in fact, it is sovereign states that have "the sole legal responsibility to protect human rights from abuse by third parties operating" in their state. This is just a few of a litany of social injustices that TNCs are known to perpetrate. Some progress is being made on modifying TNC behaviour around the world through developments such as the 2000 United Nations Global Compact and the 2008 United Nations Framework for Business and Human Rights. This movement to pressure TNCs to change their abusive conduct reflects the ongoing struggle for ethical practice.

CONCLUSION

Human rights that are coded in multiple international treaties formulated by the United Nations are the means to pursue formal justice. Even though none of these treaties are legally binding, the United Nations has created monitoring, measurement and compliance mechanisms and processes to hold sovereign nations to account for human rights abuses. However, a social justice lens reveals an uneven implementation of human rights within and between countries. This uneven distribution results from many barriers that are rooted in social injustice practices — lack of redistribution of material and non-material goods, lack of recognition of the dignity of all people, lack of participation and lack of capacity development — perpetrated by governments and TNCs, as well as citizens. These, too, are found unevenly distributed within and between countries. In particular, Canada has been called to the U.N. to explain why it continues to ignore the rights of Indigenous peoples. The evidence of serious human rights violations is pervasive; free, prior and informed consent is in UNDRIP and thus codified in formal justice, however, it is also about ethical practice.

Human rights have a very long, deep and diverse origin and history.

Some scholars have argued that the origins of human rights are a Western manifestation and thus do not embody diverse cultures, value systems and ways of life around the world. However, both original and present-day human rights are not solely couched in Western philosophies because various religious traditions are reflected in human rights treaties, including Confucian, Hindu, Buddist and Christian traditions (Clapham 2007; Reis Monteiro 2014). Reis Monteiro (2014: 399) explains that human rights have roots in Chinese wisdom and, further, that "Islam was the first to recognize basic human rights almost 14 centuries ago when it set up guarantees and safeguards." Indeed, the creation of the 1948 UDHR was a miracle created by thousands of minds from around the world (Reis Monteiro 2014) — seventy years onward, our collective challenge is to embrace similar diversity to continue to promote a just world.

DISCUSSION QUESTIONS

1. Are human rights primarily a modern-day invention?
2. What are the multiple layers in the structure of human rights from the local to the international?
3. What are some of the tensions between the international applicability of human rights, the universality of human rights and state sovereignty?
4. Who are the many actors in the U.N. system working either for or against human rights? What are differences between top-down and bottom-up approaches to promoting human rights?
5. How are human rights and social justice related to each other?

GLOSSARY

Bottom-up promotion of human rights: refers to forces that push for human rights that are grounded in communities and include non-governmental organizations, coalitions and social movements.

Generations of human rights: is a way to classify human rights by characteristics. There are four main categories: first generation rights are civil and political rights; second generation rights are economic, social and cultural rights; third generation rights focus on group solidarity and collective rights; fourth generation rights focus on the rights of non-human forms and bio-ethical issues.

Human rights: The U.N. explains that human rights are inherent to all human beings regardless of their personal characteristics.

Social justice: Focuses on ensuring no groups in society have constraints on their life choices and that all people are protected, especially the most marginalized. Social justice can be conceptualized as four-dimensional and includes: the redistribution of material and non-material goods; the recognition of the dignity of all people; one's full participation in society; and one's personal capacity development.

Top-down promotion of human rights: Top-down refers to those who make policies, legislation and laws as well as the mechanisms to enforce them.

REFERENCES

Alston, P. 2017. "The Populist Challenge to Human Rights." *Journal of Human Rights Practice,* 9, 1: 1–15.

Amnesty International Canada. 2016. "Indigenous People." <http://www.amnesty.ca/our-work/issues/indigenous-peoples>.

Antony, W., J. Antony and L. Samuelson (eds.). 2017. "Social Problems and Social Power: Individual Dysfunction or Social Injustice." In W. Antony, J. Antony and L. Samuelson *Power and Resistance: Critical Thinking about Canadian Social Issues,* sixth ed. Winnipeg: Fernwood Publishing.

Ballard, M. 2017. "Who Is Minding the First Nations during the Flood? Failing Advocacy at Every Policy Turn during a Human/Environmental Crisis." In N. Mulé and G. DeSantis (eds.), *The Shifting Terrain: Non-Profit Policy Advocacy in Canada.* Montreal, CA: McGill-Queen's University Press.

Chalabi, A. 2015. "The Problem-Oriented Approach to Improving National Human Rights Action Plans." *Journal of Human Rights Practice,* 7, 2: 272–298.

Clapham, A. 2007. *Human Rights: A Very Short Introduction.* New York: Oxford University Press.

Clément, D. 2008. *Canada's Rights Revolution: Social Movements and Social Change, 1937–82.* Vancouver: UBC Press.

____. 2016. *Human Rights in Canada.* Waterloo, ON: Wilfrid Laurier University Press.

DeLaet, D. 2015. *The Global Struggle for Human Rights: Universal Principles in World Politics,* second ed. Stamford, CT: Cengage Learning.

DeSantis, G. 2008. "A Critical Exploration of Voluntary Sector Social Policy Advocacy with Marginalized Communities Using a Population Health Lens and Social Justice." Unpublished PhD dissertation, University of Regina, Regina, SK.

____. 2010. "Voices from the Margins: Policy Advocacy and Marginalized Communities." *Canadian Journal of Nonprofit and Social Economy Research,* 1, 1: 23–45. <http://www.anserj.ca/index.php/cjnser/article/viewFile/24/28>.

Donnelly, J. 1989. *Universal Human Rights in Theory and Practice.* Ithaca, NY:

Cornell University Press.

First Nations & Indigenous Studies. 2009. "Global Actions." University of B.C. <http://indigenousfoundations.adm.arts.ubc.ca/global_actions/>.

First Nations Child and Family Caring Society of Canada. 2016. "I am a Witness." Canadian Human Rights Tribunal. <https://fncaringsociety.com/tribunal-timeline-and-documents>.

Fontaine, T. 2016. "Canada Officially Adopts U.N. Declaration on Rights of Indigenous Peoples." May 10. <http://www.cbc.ca/news/indigenous/canada-adopting-implementing-un-rights-declaration-1.3575272>.

Gindin, S. 2002. *The Terrain of Social Justice*. Toronto, ON: Centre for Social Justice, Foundation for Research and Education.

Global News. 2016. "Husky Energy Gives Saskatchewan First Nation Compensation for Oil Spill." Global News, Oct. 3. <http://globalnews.ca/news/2979752/husky-energy-gives-saskatchewan-first-nation-compensation-for-oil-spill/>.

Goodhart, M. (ed.). 2016. *Human Rights: Politics and Practice*. UK: Oxford University Press.

Government of Canada. 2013. "Consideration of reports submitted by States parties under articles 16 and 17 of the International Covenant on Economic, Social and Cultural Rights - Sixth periodic reports of States parties due in 2010, Canada." <www.refworld.org/docid/56cebbd64.html>.

Hanson, E. 2010. "U.N. Declaration on the Rights Of Indigenous People." <http://indigenousfoundations.arts.ubc.ca/un_declaration_on_the_rights_of_indigenous_peoples/>.

Hurlbert, M. 2011. "Human Rights." In M. Hurlbert ed.), *Pursuing Justice: An Introduction to Justice Studies*. Winnipeg, MB: Fernwood Publishing.

Indigenous and Northern Affairs Canada. 2010. "Canada's Statement of Support on the United Nations Declaration on the Rights of Indigenous Peoples." <http://www.aadnc-aandc.gc.ca/eng/1309374239861/1309374546142>.

Kulchyski, P. 2011. "Human Rights or Aboriginal Rights: Reflections on the U.N. Declaration on the Rights of Indigenous Peoples." *Briarpatch*, 40, 4: 33–36.

____. 2013. *Aboriginal Rights Are Not Human Rights: In Defence of Indigenous Struggles*. Winnipeg, MB: ARP Books.

Laine, A. 2015. "Integrated Reporting: Fostering Human Rights Accountability for Multinational Corporations." *The George Washington International Law Review*, 47, 3: 639–667.

Langlois, A. 2016. "Normative and Theoretical Foundations of Human Rights." In M. Goodhart (ed.), *Human Rights: Politics and Practice*. UK: Oxford University Press.

McIsaac, E. 2016. "Re-Framing Poverty as a Matter of Human Rights." *The Philanthropist*, 1–6. <http://thephilanthropist.ca/2016/04/re-framing-poverty-as-a-matter-of-rights/>.

Nation Talk. 2008. "Open Letter - U.N. Declaration on the Rights of Indigenous Peoples, Canada Needs to Implement This New Human Rights Instrument." May 3. <http://nationtalk.ca/story/

open-letter-un-declaration-on-the-rights-of-indigenous-peoples-canada-needs-to-implement-this-new-human-rights-instrument>.

Reis Monteiro, A. 2014. *Ethics of Human Rights*. Switzerland: Springer International Publishing.

Robinson, M. 2010. "Assessing Criminal Justice Practice Using Social Justice Theory." *Social Justice Research*, 23, 1: 77–97.

Smith, M. (ed.). 2014. *Group Politics and Social Movements in Canada*. North York, ON: University of Toronto Press.

Smith, R. 2012. *Textbook on International Human Rights*. New York: Oxford University Press.

TRC (Truth and Reconciliation Commission of Canada). 2015. *Truth and Reconciliation Commission of Canada: Calls to Action*. Winnipeg, MB.

U.N. Economic and Social Council, Committee on Economic, Social and Cultural Rights. 2015. "Concluding Observations on the Sixth Periodic Report of Canada." <http://docstore.ohchr.org/SelfServices/FilesHandler.ashx?enc=6 QkG1d%2FPPRiCAqhKb7yhskswUHe1nBHTSwwEsgdxQHJBoKwgsS0jm HCTV%2FFsa7OKzz9yna94OOqLeAavwpMzCD5oTanJ2C2rbU%2F0kxd os%2BXCyn4OFm3xDYg3CouE4uXS>.

U.N. Expert Mechanism on the Rights of Indigenous Peoples. 2010. "Progress Report on the Study on Indigenous Peoples and the Right to Participate in Decision-Making." Third Session, 12–16 July 2010, Item 3 of the Provisional Agenda. <http://caid.ca/UNHRCExpMec2010.pdf>.

U.N. General Assembly. 2007. "United Nations Decaration of the Rights of Indigenous Peoples." <http://www.un.org/esa/socdev/unpfii/documents/ DRIPS_en.pdf>.

U.N. OHCHR (U.N. Office of the High Commissioner for Human Rights). 2002. "Handbook on National Human Rights Plans of Action, Professional Training Series No. 10." <http://www.ohchr.org/Documents/Publications/ training10en.pdf>.

___. 2013. "Indigenous Peoples and the U.N. Human Rights System, Fact Sheet No. 9/Rev.2." <http://www.ohchr.org/Documents/Publications/fs9Rev.2.pdf>.

___. 2017. "What Are Human Rights?" <http://www.ohchr.org/EN/Issues/Pages/ WhatareHumanRights.aspx>.

United Nations. 1945. "U.N. Documents, Gathering a Body of Global Agreements. United Nations Charter: Preamble, Purposes and Principles." Signed in San Francisco, CA on June 26. <http://www.un-documents.net/ch-ppp.htm>.

___. 1996. "Fact Sheet No.2 (Rev.1), The International Bill of Human Rights." <http://www.ohchr.org/Documents/Publications/FactSheet2Rev.1en.pdf>.

___. n.d. "Main Organs." <http://www.un.org/en/sections/about-un/main-organs/index.html>.

United Nations General Assembly. 1948. *Universal Declaration of Human Rights*. Geneva, Switzerland.

Westaway, J. 2012. "Globalization, Transnational Corporations and Human Rights — A New Paradigm." *International Law Research*, 1, 1: 63–72.

12

EQUALITY RIGHTS
AND JUSTICE

Marilou McPhedran

OBJECTIVES

At the end of this chapter, you will be able to:

- Understand differing approaches to defining equality in Canada and internationally

- Discuss how equality theory and jurisprudence have influenced the justice system

- Appreciate the difference between equality rights in theory and "lived rights"

"Rights"… is still deliciously empowering to say. It is the magic wand of visibility and invisibility, of inclusion and exclusion, of power, and no power. The concept of rights, both positive and negative, is also the marker of our citizenship, our relation to others. (Williams 1991: 153)

This chapter explores the concept of equality as an essential component of justice at the provincial, national and international levels. In a Canadian context, equality rights and values are integral to building an inclusive democracy.[1] Examples are provided and topics for thought and discussion are introduced to help integrate the notion of equality with that of justice and human rights, and to assess the usefulness of the concept of equality in the pursuit of justice. Until the 1980s, the term "constitutional equality rights" was unknown in this country. The human rights we now associate with the *Canadian Charter of Rights and Freedoms*, Part 1 of the Constitution Act, 1982, and provincial/territorial human rights codes were introduced conceptually in the human rights parlance of the founding of the United Nations (U.N.), following the atrocities of World War II. But the concept of "rights" goes much further back. In 1817, the philosopher Hegel observed:

> Whether what is called ancient *right and constitution* is actually right or not cannot depend on its antiquity. For the abolition of human sacrifice, of slavery, of feudal despotism and innumerable other infamies was also the abolition of what had been an ancient right. (cited in Habermas 1973: 122)

Chapter 8 discussed the advent of human rights as articulated in the first and highest level overarching policy of the U.N. — the Universal Declaration of Human Rights (UDHR). Although the UDHR is not legally enforceable, because it is a high-level policy statement, or "declaration," it has had tremendous influence in the thinking behind legal definitions of rights considered essential to building civilized societies sustained by the Rule of Law. Dating back to the *Magna Carta* of 1215, the Rule of Law is part of the British Common Law tradition adopted in Canada and other countries — particularly those that are members of the British Commonwealth — holding that law should be written down and applied consistently rather than at the whim of monarchs or governments. For 115 years (from 1867 to 1982), Canada operated with a Common Law constitution and without a constitutionally entrenched bill of rights that defined equality.

WHAT IS EQUALITY?

In Chapter 1 we were encouraged to set aside our normative thinking and reach for a deeper understanding of justice. Similar "rules of engagement" apply in the study of equality:

- Since we generally think within the confines of our own values, norms and experiences, we must honestly acknowledge our own centrism, plus our centrism in our social context (such as ethnocentrism). For example, in a challenge to a provincially appointed marriage commissioner who refuses to officiate at same-sex marriage ceremonies, an equality analysis must approach the issue from multiple perspectives, since both freedom of religion and freedom from discrimination on the basis of sexual orientation are covered by section 15 of the Charter and provincial human rights statutes. Perspectives to consider include local human rights norms, international human rights norms and questions such as whether it is necessary to fire the marriage commissioner in order to enforce the rights of the same-sex couple.
- Since majority viewpoints do not always resemble "justice," equality analysis must reach beyond personal experience to consider the perspectives and lived experiences of members of marginalized populations — both *within* the particular population and *between* that population and society-at-large. For instance, as a woman member of the Muslim community in Regina, Saskatchewan, Canada; and as a Muslim in Regina compared to other populations in Regina, in Saskatchewan and in Canada.

A thorough study of equality cannot be limited to the law. Equality has meaning and is a concept "beyond the law," and our understanding of equality is informed by other disciplines, including philosophy, history, economics, sociology, religious studies and criminology.

Formal versus Substantive Equality Interpretations

In *Ethica Nichomacea*, Aristotle concluded that equality was achieved by treating likes alike and unlikes unalike. Aristotle's reasoning is at the root of what we today consider to be the principle of "formal equality." The Aristotelian-derived formula of "same = equal" has proven problematic

— particularly for equality seekers. Clearly, women are different from men, persons living with a disability are different from those who do not, and Aboriginal Canadians are a different people than non-Aboriginal Canadians. So, according to Aristotle, do their differences define them as "unlike" and therefore they are to be treated unequally? Does inequality mean different treatment for likes, same treatment for unlikes? Perhaps the best known application of the Aristotelian approach is found in American constitutional Fourteenth Amendment terms that require equality claimants to be "similarly situated" before they will be considered eligible to pursue their equality claim. MacKinnon (2006: 107) challenges this approach:

> But what if social life is unequal? Legal equality then becomes a formula for reinforcing, magnifying, and rigidifying the social inequalities it purports to be equalizing and might have rectified.

While "formal" equality requires that claimants must be "similarly situated," the approach in international human rights law is different and can be seen as a strong influence in the first Canadian Charter cases decided under Chief Justice Brian Dickson in the 1980s, which led to the distinction between "formal" and "substantive" equality (Young 1990: 199–200). "Substantive" equality requires recognizing the inherent value of each individual human being, and assessing the impact of alleged discrimination demands more thought and inquiry than the formulaic approach where judges apply the same formal equality analysis to all cases.

Indigenous Interpretations of Equality

To appreciate that interpretations of "equality" can differ, a close examination of the content and context of the United Nations Declaration on the Rights of Indigenous Peoples (2007) is helpful. Based at the University of Saskatchewan for many of the years when he participated in negotiations that resulted in the Declaration, Professor James (Sa'ke'j) Youngblood Henderson (2008: 10) explains:

> To place the Declaration in context, it is important to recognize four insights. First, Indigenous peoples reflect diverse humanities, independent of race, science and biological concepts, which comprise many overlapping and shifting categories in different

knowledge and legal systems. These peoples have shared concerns about the territorial appropriations of their homelands, about cultural and cognitive imperialism, and the exploitation by colonial and decolonized Eurocentric states. The U.N. system recognizes the key features of Indigenous peoples as a significant historical attachment to territory, an explicit commitment to cultural distinctiveness, and a resolve to preserve both territory and culture as a means of achieving community. Second, Indigenous nations and peoples are never just a product of state ideologies, never just a product of an educational system. They are always able to relate to traditional teachings and Indigenous knowledge, regardless of how state, religious, or educational systems attempt to assimilate them. Third, Indigenous teachings and legal traditions live on in the unconsciousness and the consciousness of the peoples who were oppressed by colonization; they were passed from one generation to another through stories, art, and ceremonies so that each people could restore them at the right time and transform them into the Declaration. Fourth, the Indigenous diplomatic network learned that it could not settle accounts with colonialism in a way that would allow the spirit of colonialism to penetrate our own consciousness, our own activities, and thus our own spirits. We learned that such remedies turn us to revenge, cruelty, and the ideologies of imported colonial strategies rather than giving us the ability to overcome these strategies.

We need to question what equality means in legal systems that have different foundations. As with the Declaration, Aboriginal rights are considered a subset of "universalist" international human rights in the U.N. system. Kulchyski (2013) disagrees, arguing that Indigenous peoples need specific rights, in part to balance against the universalist core of human rights. Canada has progressed towards adhering to the Declaration with the passage of Bill C-61, sponsored by Mi'kmaw Senator Daniel Christmas, which gave effect to the Anishinabek Nation Education Agreement. This Agreement was signed by the Government of Canada and twenty-three participating Anishinabek First Nations to recognize their control over education on reserves from Junior Kindergarten to Grade 12. The autonomous nature of this Agreement serves as a model toward decolonization by Indigenous leaders of Indigenous education in Canada.

Constitutional Equality in Canada

Constitutions are considered to be the supreme law of the land for defining the limits of governmental powers in a country. The Canadian Constitution is the source for legally defining the division of powers among federal, provincial, territorial and municipal governments in Canada — such as which level of government can tax what, which has responsibility for health care and which is responsible for the military. When defining a liberty or freedom, the constitutional question is whether there are any explicit limits on the power of governments to constrain certain liberties that are particularly important to people, such as the freedom to practise one's religion or freedom of expression.

Prior to passing the Constitution Act, 1982, with its entrenched Charter, there were few national, legally enshrined rights guarantees in Canada. The British Common Law (BCL) position on people's liberty is that individuals are free to do whatever the law does not prohibit — which may suit most people as long as their government does not pass oppressive laws. However, the BCL does not explicitly guarantee individual rights and freedoms that governments must respect. Compared to an explicit constitutional guarantee of a freedom (such as freedom of expression/ speech), the common law notion of the scope of an individual's freedom is that we have as much liberty as remains *after* we obey any laws that governments may have enacted to restrict that freedom. In the common law tradition, governments would not be acting outside their power (that is, unconstitutionally) if they took away such freedoms or rights because there are no clear rules or principles in the common law that forbid such governmental actions. Constitutional rights may be described as legally protected "spaces" in the justice system that allow people to claim freedoms that are considered essential to a democracy — in other words, to have choices and to be able to live their rights.

Rights are used to defend our liberties. Historically, rights were not guaranteed widely; civil rights and liberties were available to those privileged enough to own property. The right of American Blacks in the southern United States to vote was a major organizing focus of the social movement against racial segregation in the United States that gained momentum in the 1960s, commonly known as the "civil rights movement." This focus on civil rights raised awareness worldwide about the connections between citizenship and the basic human rights set out in

1948 in the Universal Declaration of Human Rights (UDHR). Therein, rights are defined as *equal* and *inalienable*, meaning that they are the inherent rights of *every* human, *because* they are human, and *regardless* of their immutable personal characteristics, such as race. The first lines of the Preamble to the UDHR state:

> Whereas recognition of the inherent dignity and of the equal and inalienable rights of all members of the human family is the foundation of freedom, justice and peace in the world.

Legal rights are rights recognized by law and therefore enforceable in courts. In Canada today, legal rights include equality rights. But what is the connection between constitutions, rights and liberties or freedoms? In everyday terms, liberty or freedom means the ability to do something if we want to do it, as long as it does not hurt others and is not illegal; this includes the freedom *not* to do something, not to be subjected to certain governmental requirements. Judges are tasked with trying to balance rights in the best interest of our society and they often reach different conclusions as to which governmental actions are unconstitutional.

CASE STUDY:
BALANCING INDIVIDUAL AND COLLECTIVE RIGHTS

When Alberta made photographs on drivers' licences mandatory, members of the Hutterian Brethren of Wilson Colony, who sincerely believed the Second of the Ten Commandments of the Christian/Judaic faiths prohibited them from having their photographs willingly taken, began proceedings against the Alberta government, alleging breach of their religious freedom. The Supreme Court of Canada (SCC) in *Hutterian Brethren of Wilson Colony* v. *Alberta* (2009) overruled the decisions made in the Alberta courts that had decided in favour of the Hutterian members. Balancing competing interests, the SCC concluded that Alberta's universal photo requirement did not limit freedom of religion more than was required to meet the important goal of minimizing identity theft. Using the language of section 1, the SCC held that this infringement was a "reasonable limit prescribed by law" and was "reasonably justified" in Canada as "a free and democratic society."

Does Equality Include Economic and Social Rights?

The UDHR introduced the idea of economic, social and cultural rights, such as: the freedom to work; the right to an adequate standard of living, which includes food, clothing, shelter, medical care and social services; as well as a right to education and a right to cultural life in the community (Articles 22–27).

While the Charter does guarantee equality rights, specific social and economic rights are not listed in section 15. Canadian judicial decisions where aspects of poverty have been central to the issues to be decided have not been encouraging to the notion that Canadians have social and economic rights or that "poverty" should be included as a section 15

CASE STUDY:
HUMAN RIGHTS AND POVERTY IN CANADA

Three of the more compelling examples of Canadian judicial reasoning on poverty that demonstrate a judicial "disconnect" to the reality of those who live "below the poverty line" are *Gosselin v. Quebec (Attorney General)* [2002] 4 S.C.R. 429, *Federated Anti-Poverty Groups of B.C. v. Vancouver (City)* [2002] B.C.J. No. 493, and *Masse v. Ontario (Ministry of Community and Social Services)* (1996), 134 D.L.R. (4th) 20, 35 C.R.R. (2d) 44 (Ont. Div. Ct.); leave to appeal to C.A. denied [1996] O.J. No. 1526; leave to appeal to S.C.C. denied [1996] S.C.C.A. No. 373. In the *Gosselin* and *Masse* cases, one from Quebec and the other from Ontario, poor citizens argued that their Charter rights were violated because their governments kept social assistance below subsistence levels. The judges favoured the governments — in *Masse*, government cutbacks were found to be acceptable and in *Gosselin*, the claimant lost because she was under the age of 30 and did not participate in a provincial workfare program for youth. In *Federated Anti-Poverty Groups of B.C. v. Vancouver (City)* [2002] B.C.J. No. 493, the British Columbia Supreme Court upheld a Vancouver bylaw restricting areas where panhandling was allowed, finding that it did not violate the rights of poor people who begged to their freedom of expression under section 2 of the Charter or to their access to fundamental justice under section 7.

equality right to be protected from discrimination by the Charter. The "five faces" of oppression, often mirrored in poverty, include exploitation, marginalization, powerlessness, cultural imperialism and violence (where violence against a particular group is accepted more than when directed to more advantaged groups) (Young 1990: 199–200).

Gwen Brodsky and Shelagh Day (2002: 200) have argued that it is incumbent on the Canadian government to observe and implement the rights set out in both the International Covenant on Social and Cultural Rights and the International Covenant on Civil and Political Rights because one set of rights cannot be implemented without the other. Essentially, civil and political rights for disadvantaged Canadians are not achievable unless they have the capacity to be full citizens, which comes with economic and social rights. Conservative Senator Noel Kinsella (2008: 16) has written that there is already a *de facto* "charter of social rights" in Canada, achieved through combining the 1999 federal/ provincial/territorial Social Union Framework Agreement (SUFA) goal to "ensure access for all Canadians … to essential social programs and services of reasonably comparable quality" with section 36 of the Canadian Constitution. SUFA commits to:

- promoting equal opportunities for the well-being of Canadians;
- furthering the economic development to reduce disparity in opportunities; and
- providing essential public services of reasonable quality to all Canadians.

Amartya Sen (1988: 57–68), a Nobel Laureate in economics, observed that it is often not the failure of economic production, but rather the failure of "entitlement systems" whereby the rights claimed by the most vulnerable in society to such basics as food and housing are devalued relative to the property-oriented rights claimed by more privileged people with more capacity to actualize their own rights.

In *Tanudjaja v. Canada (Attorney General)* [2014], the Court of Appeal for Ontario upheld a motion judge's decision to strike a claim under the *Canadian Charter of Rights and Freedoms* in which it was asserted that actions and inaction on the part of Canada and Ontario have resulted in homelessness and inadequate housing. The claim was brought by four individuals suffering from homelessness and inadequate housing and an organization dedicated to human rights and equality in housing called the Centre for Equality Rights in Accommodation. The application alleged that: changes to legislation, policies, programs and services instituted by Ontario and Canada have resulted in homelessness and inadequate housing; Canada and Ontario have taken either no measures or inadequate measures to address the impact of these changes on the groups that are most vulnerable to or at risk of becoming homeless; Canada and Ontario have failed to undertake appropriate strategic coordination to ensure government programs protect those who are homeless or at risk of homelessness; and, as a result, Canada and Ontario have created and sustained conditions that lead to, support and sustain homelessness and inadequate housing (*Tanudjaja* v. *Canada (Attorney General)*, [2014] 123 O.R. (3d) 161 (Ont. C.A.)).

In 2017, the Canadian federal government announced a new national housing strategy that aims to reduce homelessness and build affordable housing over the next ten years. This strategy recognizes that lack of housing affects the most vulnerable Canadians, including women, Indigenous peoples, seniors and persons with disabilities. In order to rectify the disparities between the vulnerable and the privileged, there must be a greater shift in recognizing housing as a human right (Government of Canada 2010).

EQUALITY RIGHTS MADE IN CANADA

An understanding of how equality rights came to be in the Charter begins with a discussion of the longstanding leadership of Canadian women on the issue. After decades of battles in courts and parliaments, much of what women gained in the articulation of sex equality served to extend the notion of "equality rights" to include and benefit other equality-seeking groups in Canadian society.

The examination of women's struggle for equality in the Canadian political sphere must recognize that the federation model of government was not imported to Canada. Aboriginal self-government was well developed when Europeans immigrated. For example, the Iroquois Confederacy, in which women held significant positions of authority, straddled what we now see as the American border, and served as a model for some aspects of Canadian federalism.

With the 1982 patriation of Canada's constitution and Charter, equality seekers — including advocates for women, people with disabilities, Aboriginal peoples and other racialized minorities such as Japanese-Canadians interned in World War II — successfully pressured parliamentarians to ensure that Canada's Charter committed to more than mere formal equality and individualistic rights. Alexandra Dobrowolsky (2009: 205) notes:

> Women's rights groups, in particular, were celebrated for both tightening up the wording and broadening the intent of Section 15, as well as adding an entirely new equality provision, Section 28, to Canada's *Charter of Rights and Freedoms*.

But the quest of Canadian women's rights advocates for equality began long before the constitutional negotiations of the 1970s and 1980s. In what has come to be known as the Persons Case (*Edwards* v. *Canada (Attorney General)*, [1929]), the first court battle focused on the exclusionary definition of "persons" that the scc applied to wording in the British North America Act (BNA) of 1867:

> Unlike the Iroquoian model of federal governance, women had been excluded when the "Fathers of Confederation" met in Charlottetown to craft the BNA *Act*. Litigating to secure a fairer place in the affairs of the nation, more than eighty years ago five women launched the Persons Case and what has been termed a "tradition of Canadian women using the judicial system to advance equality rights." (Falardeau-Ramsay 1998: 8)

Early Fighters for Equality: The "Famous Five" in the "Persons Case"

In 1916, Emily Murphy presided over the new Women's Police Court as the first woman police magistrate in the British Empire until a male lawyer challenged her jurisdiction to hear his case because, as a woman, she could not have been lawfully appointed. On August 27, 1927, Murphy called on four other Alberta-based women — Nellie McClung, Henrietta Muir Edwards, Louise Crummy McKinney and Irene Parlby — to sign a petition under the Supreme Court of Canada Act asking for the Supreme Court's answer to a crucial question, which eventually became worded as,

"Does the word 'person' in Section 24 of the British North AmericanAct, include female 'persons'?"

On April 24, 1928, Chief Justice Anglin, for a unanimous SCC, answered in the negative, holding that the BNA Act was limited by the period in which it had been passed, noting the exclusive use of male pronouns, and that there was no English precedent of women appointed to the British House of Lords, concluding:

> women are not eligible for appointment by the Governor General to the Senate of Canada under Section 24 of the British North America Act, 1867, because they are not 'qualified persons' within the meaning of that section. (*Reference as to the Meaning of the Word "Persons" in Section 24 of the British North America Act, 1867*, [1928] S.C.R. 276)

The only recourse open to the five women petitioners was to convince the government to legislate in their favour or, since at that time the SCC was subject to the judicial review of the Judicial Committee of the Privy Council of England, to appeal. On October 18, 1929, Lord Chancellor Sankey of the British Privy Council provided a significantly different unanimous answer, overruling the SCC:

> to those who would ask why the word 'persons' should include female, the obvious answer is, "why should it not?" (*Reference as to the Meaning of the Word "Persons in Section 24 of the British North America Act, 1867*, [1928] S.C.R.276, reversed in *Edwards v. Canada (A.G.)*, [1930] A.C.124 (P.C))

CASE STUDY:
PERSON'S CASE COMMEMORATION

October 18 is now officially celebrated in Canada as "Persons Day," commemorated by the annual awarding of a Governor General's medal to five long-time activist women (as well as an award for youth leaders) and Legal Education and Action Fund (LEAF) breakfasts across Canada.

Canadian Bill of Rights

The Canadian Bill of Rights (CBR 1960: c. 44) was a "recognition and declaration of the rights and freedoms" championed by one of the few prime ministers from western Canada: the Rt. Hon. John G. Diefenbaker of Saskatchewan. Following the Second World War, numerous women subsumed personal frustrations, having experienced considerable autonomy in the war years. Soon their economic and social grievances surfaced, creating an environment where Canadian women in the mid 1960s were asking questions about their lives and about their "status" as women. In response to pressure from women's organizations and questioning commentary in the media, Prime Minister Lester B. Pearson appointed a *Royal Commission on the Status of Women* in the early months of Canada's centennial year, 1967, asking the commissioners to:

> inquire into the status of women in Canada and to recommend what steps might by taken by the Federal Government to ensure for women equal opportunities with men in all aspects of Canadian identity. (CBC Radio and Television Archives n.d.: 14)

Expectations that "justice" included women's equality were rising, as was optimism that the CBR (which is still a law in Canada) would deliver. Section 1 of Part I of the CBR states:

> there have existed and shall continue to exist without discrimination by reason of race, national origin, colour, religion or sex, the following human rights and fundamental freedoms, namely ... the right of the individual to equality before the law and the protection of the law.

However, judicial interpretation was largely cautious and unhelpful to equality seekers who tried to claim their rights under this Bill. The following decisions under the CBR delineate differences between interpretations of "justice" and the "law."

Aboriginal Women, the Indian Act and the Bill of Rights

Aboriginal women married to non-Aboriginal men felt the unfair sting of the CBR in *Canada (Attorney General)* v. *Lavell*, when federal Indian Act provisions denying status were upheld in a 1974 SCC decision.

Counsel for Jeanette Lavell and Yvonne Bédard argued that section 12(1)
(b) discriminated on the basis of sex against women of Indian status who
lost that status upon marriage to a non-Indian, but permitted a status
man to extend status to his non-Indian wife, and in turn to their children.

This decision prompted a dramatic activist response involving a group
of Aboriginal women who left the Tobique Reserve in New Brunswick
with their small children, fathered by non-status men, to walk in protest
to Ottawa. One of their leaders, Sandra Lovelace (now Senator Lovelace-
Nichols), a Maliseet woman of the reserve, gained international attention
when she petitioned the United Nations Human Rights Committee, alleging violations by Canada under the Optional Protocol to the International
Covenant on Civil and Political Rights, to which Canada had just
acceded (G.A. Res. 2200 (XXI), 1966). Canada defended the legislation.
Embarrassed internationally by the U.N. finding that the federal law
contravened the rights of Aboriginal women (*Lovelace* v. *Canada* 1981),
Canada moved slowly, even with sustained lobbying from a wide range of
women's groups. Nearly ten years after the march from Tobique, in 1981
the government enacted partial redress, leaving Aboriginal women's rights
at the discretion of bands that could ask the government to exempt them
from section 12(1)(b) (Bayefsky 1982).

Women's "Routine" Work under the Bill of Rights

In *Murdoch* v. *Murdoch* (1975), dismissing a lifetime of more than twenty-
five years of ranching with her husband in Alberta, the scc awarded
Irene Murdoch just two hundred dollars a month, agreeing with the
trial judge that hers was the "routine" work of "any ranch wife" and was
not enough to create a legal claim to the matrimonial property. Women
across Canada identified with Murdoch, and mobilized to demand their
property rights. By 1980 every province and territory had passed family
law amendments as a result of women discovering and flexing their collective political muscle.

Gender Neutral Pregnancy?

Stella Bliss lived in British Columbia when she was fired because she was
pregnant. After her baby was born, she actively sought, but did not find,
appropriate employment and so, having determined that she met the regular
criteria, applied for unemployment insurance benefits. The Unemployment

Insurance Commission refused her application because she had been pregnant when she lost her job and she did not meet the more stringent criteria applied to pregnancy benefits in the legislation. In *Bliss v. A.G. Canada* (1979), her pro-bono lawyers argued before the Federal Court of Appeal and the scc that the higher legislative bar for pregnant women discriminated on the basis of sex. To the dismay of women's groups, both courts rejected this argument in favour of the Aristotelian formal equality notion that all pregnant women were equally denied regular benefits due to a legitimate gender neutral distinction based on nature — not between men and women, but between pregnant and non-pregnant persons.

Reacting to Losses under the CBR

When Prime Minister Trudeau announced his determination to "bring home" the Canadian Constitution and to entrench within it a charter of rights and freedoms, the platform for women's constitutional activism had already been framed by the judicial use of the CBR to deny the discrimination rampant in women's daily lives.

When the draft Charter was released, the federally appointed members of the Canadian Advisory Council on the Status of Women launched in 1980 a public education campaign on the constitution led by its president, Doris Anderson. British Columbia, Alberta, Saskatchewan, Quebec, New Brunswick, Nova Scotia, Newfoundland and the Yukon all enacted new laws or amendments to their family property regimes in 1979–80, preceded by Northwest Territories, Ontario and Manitoba. So, when a women's constitutional battle broke out in January of 1981 that prompted Doris Anderson to resign in a very public manner, many grassroots women had a sense that making politicians respond was an achievable prospect and the women's movement had both human and organizational infrastructure in place and on the alert. In her article on the impact of the "ad hoc" women's constitutional conference and lobby that sprang up in early 1981, Anne Collins (1981: 22) reported:

> The issue — whether women would have a share in the future of the nation ... As Linda Ryan-Nye says, there seemed to be a peculiar readiness to speak with one voice: "A lot of us sensed it and not just in the organized women's movement. It had been building ... this shoddy treatment of a strong and honest woman at the same time as denying us our rights as citizens ... Boom."

CANADIAN CONSTITUTIONAL TRIALOGUE ON EQUALITY

So how did Canadians end up with equality rights guaranteed in a bill of human rights entrenched in the supreme law of the land — the Constitution? To understand how constitutions are made, it is important to remember that governments make laws and governments are made up of people. Constitutions are built by people — but only certain people. To understand how equality rights came to be enshrined in our Constitution, it's helpful to understand the background and context to the introduction of the Charter, and how it took years from when the first draft Charter with "non-discrimination" provisions was introduced in 1968 at a federal-provincial first ministers' conference, until more than a decade later when "equality rights" became a topic of broad public concern and televised debates and were introduced into the proposed Charter in 1981.

Journalist Graham Fraser (2002) offered this retrospective on events leading up to the Charter:

> In April, 1968, a year after becoming justice minister, Trudeau was prime minister and the agenda he had had as justice minister acquired a new importance. Within three years, a *Charter* ["Victoria Charter"] had been written and quietly negotiated with Quebec's new Liberal premier, Robert Bourassa. Fundamental liberties would be guaranteed and language rights would be protected in every province. But the Victoria *Charter* ultimately failed when Bourassa withdrew his support.

How "Equality Rights" Entered the Charter

Prime Minister Pierre Trudeau envisioned a statement of the rights and freedoms as part of the new constitution that would provide "guarantees" for people in Canada (mostly to Canadian citizens, with some exceptions) in a stronger manner than in the 1960 Canadian Bill of Rights, which was limited to federal laws, was not applicable to provincial statutes and could be amended at any time because it was not an entrenched part of the Constitution.

However, "equality rights" was not a title or term used in any of the drafts of the Charter developed by government officials or political leaders from the 1960s through to 1981, although one of the arguments for accepting the Trudeau government's "people's package" for constitutional reform was that an entrenched Charter would apply to governments across Canada and thus rights would be equally available. Equality rights in the Charter came out of the grassroots mobilization of people and groups in Canada — mostly women's rights organizations and representatives of people living with disabilities.

Accounts of this struggle vary; perspectives differed depending on the position of the participant in the constitution-building processes. Initially, the Trudeau Government was not prepared to "open up" the constitution-building process, but public pressure convinced the Government to name a Special Joint Committee of the Senate and of the House of Commons on the Constitution of Canada ("Special Joint Committee") in 1980, with members drawn from all the parties of both houses of Parliament — co-chaired by Serge Joyal, MP from Quebec, and Senator Harry Hays from Alberta. For the first time in Canada, a parliamentary committee was televised and millions of Canadians paid attention to what was happening at the hearings. Senator Hays made news when he addressed the National Action Committee on the Status of Women (NAC) executives (with this author present) in the following manner:

> I want to thank you girls [sic] for your presentation. We're honoured to have you here. But I wonder why you don't have anything in here for babies or children. All you girls are going to be working and who's going to look after them?[2] (cited in Watson Barber 1988: 141)

After months of presentations by concerned citizens and their organizations to the Special Joint Committee, Attorney General of Canada Jean Chrétien announced major changes to section 15 in January of 1981. Mary Dawson (2006: 31) and M. David Lepofsky (1998: 156) wrote first-hand accounts of what went into these changes, including altering the title to "equality rights," creating an opening for non-enumerated or analogous grounds of discrimination, reversing the order of "age" and "sex," as well as adding another enumerated ground — "mental or physical disability." The attorney general attributed the title change to "Equality Rights" to a now defunct federal body that was called the Canadian Advisory Council on the Status of Women (CACSW), then chaired by the late Doris

Anderson, with Mary Eberts acting as her legal counsel (Senate and House of Commons 1981).

The "spark" that galvanized Canadian women's constitutional activism was when Doris Anderson abruptly resigned in January of 1981, in public protest against what she considered to be government interference in the women's constitutional conference being organized by the CACSW. Again, perspectives on what happened vary, but the aptly named Ad Hoc Committee of Canadian Women on the Constitution ("Ad Hoc Committee" or "Ad Hockers") took responsibility for organizing an alternative conference, only to be surprised when more than 1300 women found their way to Ottawa on Valentine's Day in 1981. Run by consensus, the women's constitutional conference produced resolutions that guided ensuing months of lobbying for amendments to the draft Constitution to strengthen equality rights (Kome 1983).

It was this unprecedented public engagement in the 1980s Canadian constitution-building process that gave rise to the term "trialogue" to describe and validate citizens and their organizations as key contributors. Constitutional scholars Hogg and Bushell (1997, 2007) used the term "Charter dialogue" to describe the bilateral dynamic between legislators in drafting and adopting the Charter, complemented by judges using their authority under the Charter to interpret what the words written in the Charter actually meant when applied to real-life problems and challenges to the Charter brought before the courts. In arguing for a more inclusive understanding of how the Canadian constitution was built and is sustained, McPhedran (2005: 14) introduced the "trialogue" metaphor to acknowledge the ongoing engagement and influence of social movements in the drafting of constitutional text and in securing equality rights in sections 15 and 28 of the Charter:

> Too often, judges and politicians fail to appreciate that Canadians invested in an equality based constitutional democracy — often engaging directly through interventions in Parliament and in the courts — have turned the dynamic into a *trialogue*; surely one of the most significant outcomes of the s.15 impact on Canadian society.

The *Canadian Charter of Rights and Freedoms* is a bill of rights consisting of thirty-four sections entrenched within the Constitution Act, 1982, which, in effect, reintroduced all of Canada's statutory constitutional law, including the British North America Act, 1867. Prime Minister Pierre Elliot Trudeau stated at the proclamation ceremony for the Constitution Act, 1982 on April 17, 1982:

> We now have a Charter which defines the kind of country in which we wish to live, and guarantees the basic rights and freedoms which each of us shall enjoy as a citizen of Canada. It upholds the equality of women, and the rights of disabled persons. (Library and Archives Canada n.d.)

Women's determination to strengthen Charter equality rights was honed by the harsh fact that the cases brought by women in the 1970s seeking equality protections under the Canadian Bill of Rights were all lost, as discussed previously in this chapter. In the early 1980s, when the new Constitution Act and its Charter were being drafted to effect patriation to Canada, Canadians watched as American women were losing their battle to include an "Equal Rights Amendment" (ERA) in their constitution. Canadian women saw how Canadian judges followed American judges (using the Fourteenth Amendment equal protections for race- and sex-based discrimination) in foisting notions of formal equality on women. The ultimate wording of the equality sections of the Charter was substantially different from the drafts that had caused such concern.

Efforts to ensure that the new constitutional equality rights actually made a difference in the daily lives of equality seekers took many forms after the Constitution Act, 1982 was activated. But section 32 of the Charter had imposed a three-year moratorium on people being able to use section 15. So, during the moratorium from 1982 through 1985, a number of preparations were made, including publication of the first textbook on equality rights (Bayefsky and Eberts 1985) and a new organization, LEAF (the Women's Legal Education and Action Fund) — launching what Christopher Manfredi (2004: 49) described as the women's "microconstitutional campaign for substantive equality." LEAF — founded in 1985 by some of the "Ad Hockers" — has been involved in more equality cases than any other non-governmental organization in Canada, attempting to ensure that equality is interpreted by the courts through a "gender impact lens" even when the case has not focused on women.

In *Nancy Law v. Canada (Minister of Employment and Immigration)*, the scc unanimously stated that burdensome differences in treatment on the basis of prohibited grounds are discriminatory *only if they can reasonably be said to violate "human dignity."* Although the term "dignity" is nowhere to be found in the Charter, it figures prominently in the international human rights treaties, and has become significant in many Canadian judicial interpretations of equality.

Unfortunately, many of those decisions have gone against the equality seekers who brought their claims to the courts (Petter 1987). Nancy Law was married to a man quite a bit older, and when he died, she relied on the protection in section 15(1) against discrimination on the basis of age, because the benefits allowed to her as a spouse under the age of 35 were less than for those over 35. Nancy Law lost her case. This one decision has generated hundreds of pages of commentary and speculation. Through its *Nancy Law* decision, the Court established a tougher test for claimants — requiring the additional step of proving to the Court that their human dignity has been impaired — as an addition to the *Andrews* principles summarized above. The Court still applied a comparative test, but it came down to being what the Court decided a "reasonable person" in the position of the claimant would/should feel about their dignity being impaired, not necessarily what the claimant actually did feel about the impact of the alleged discrimination.

In *Withler* v. *Canada (Attorney General)* (2011), the Court did away with comparator groups as being necessary to the equality analysis. It held that a mirror comparator group analysis may fail to capture substantive inequality. A comparator group was becoming nothing more than a search for sameness, and had the effect in some cases of shortcutting the second stage of the substantive equality analysis, making it difficult to apply (2011: para. 60).

Since *Withler*, in a section 15 analysis, the role of comparison is at the first stage is to establish a distinction, but it is unnecessary to pinpoint a particular group that precisely corresponds to the claimant group except for the personal characteristic or characteristics alleged to ground the discrimination (para 62–63). This more flexible approach is a more just approach because it "provides the flexibility required to accommodate claims based on intersecting grounds of discrimination. It also avoids the problem of eliminating claims at the outset because no precisely corresponding group can be posited" (para. 63). (*Withler* v. *Canada (Attorney General)* [2011] 1 S.C.R. 396.)

When Is a Charter Guarantee Not a Guarantee?

When section 1 of the draft Canadian Constitution was introduced, deep concern was expressed before the Special Joint Committee and in the media that it did not protect rights, allowing governments to place too many limitations on rights. Many names were given to section 1 to illustrate that it was a problem, including references to it as the "Mack Truck clause" and the "bathtub clause" because it would make it too easy for politicians to "pull the plug" on human rights. Justice Minister Chrétien introduced a number of changes to the section until it reached its current wording:

> The *Canadian Charter of Rights and Freedoms* guarantees the rights and freedoms set out in it subject only to such reasonable limits as are generally accepted in a free and democratic society with a parliamentary system of government.

Opting Out of Charter Rights: Section 33 Override

Ironically, section 33 of the Charter, introduced much later in the constitutional negotiations, gave to governments a much clearer authority to opt out of rights than the much-scrutinized section 1. The Latin term for a clause like section 33 of the Charter is *non obstante* or "notwithstanding" because this clause functions like an optional legislative "override" on the rights specified in section 33 (1) of the Charter — all of the fundamental freedoms in section 2, all of the legal rights in sections 7 through 14 and the equality rights in section 15 (but not the sex equality guarantee in section 28). Section 33 is clear that there is no tight "guarantee" in the face of this governmental power.

How did so many rights in the Charter become potentially "untrenched"? One of the earliest suggestions for such a clause came from the Harvard-based Canadian law professor, Paul Weiler (1980: 231) who urged:

> We should entrench our fundamental rights in the Canadian constitution in order to give them the legal and symbolic authority which would be conducive to their flourishing. But we should include in the constitutional Bill of Rights the kind of *non obstante* provision now contained in our statutory bill ... In

typical Canadian fashion, I propose a compromise, between the British version of full-fledged parliamentary sovereignty and the American version of full-fledged judicial authority over constitutional matters.

The fundamental difference between section 1 and section 33 is that section 1 requires balancing of the rights and freedoms identified in the Charter with the needs and values of a free and democratic society, but section 33 empowers governments to decline to respect specific rights and freedoms listed in the Charter.

However, Hogg and Bushell (1997: 75) assessed the likelihood of section 33 being used often by governments as slim, even though there is nothing in law to stop them, "because of the development of a political climate of resistance to its use." Another possible contest between *non obstante* powers in the Charter has yet to unfold — there is another override still operative: the sex equality guarantee in section 28, which is not subject to section 33 in the way that equality rights in section 15 are, but a case is yet to arise (Kome 1982).

STATUTORY

Federal, Provincial and Territorial Human Rights

In 1947, soon after the United Nations was founded in 1945 at the close of World War II, Saskatchewan became the first North American government to enact a general human rights statute. Now human rights mechanisms, which are created by statute, such as human rights commissions and tribunals, operate nationally and in every province and territory in Canada, each with its own enabling legislation. For example, the national legislation, the Canadian Human Rights Act, prohibits discrimination on eleven grounds:

- Disability
- Race
- National or ethnic origin
- Colour
- Religion
- Sex

- Sexual orientation
- Marital status
- Family status
- Conviction for which a pardon has been granted

Complaints related to the grounds in the federal/provincial/territorial legislation are initially addressed through those bodies and their quasi-judicial tribunals, while complaints related to the Charter are addressed through the courts. Thus, jurisprudence (reports on the facts and outcomes of judicial and quasi-judicial decisions on cases brought to these tribunals and courts) for statutory human rights mechanisms is different from decisions by courts in constitutional Charter cases. However, when a human rights tribunal decision is challenged, then the appeal moves into the same court system as the Charter complaints — underscoring the importance of Canadian judges at every level being well educated in human rights, including equality rights, regardless of the jurisdiction (federal, provincial or territorial).

LIVED EQUALITY RIGHTS

The complexity of the pursuit of equality rights in Canada is the topic of extensive commentary. Canada's longest-serving Chief Justice of the Supreme Court, the Right Honourable Beverley McLachlin, P.C. (2001: 17) concluded:

> The *Canadian Charter of Rights and Freedoms* guarantees a panoply of rights ... And like most modern bills of rights, it guarantees equality. Of all the rights, this is the most difficult.

How do citizens of the world turn promises on paper — in constitutions and local and international laws — into "lived rights" that make a positive difference in their daily lives? This chapter has discussed how grassroots engagement altered the *Canadian Charter of Rights and Freedoms* and Canadian constitutional jurisprudence. Real life examples of "equality lived" through active section 15 claims, based on the protected grounds specified in section 15 equality rights, as well as the analogous ground of sexual orientation that was "read in" by the scc demonstrate the complexity and imperfections in the pursuit of justice based on equality rights.

However, these setbacks should not be taken as a message to "give up" on justice or equality. Consider the alternatives. In the examples that follow, look for information that gives a practical perspective on how important it is for information and evidence — particularly from the perspective of the equality seekers — to be presented to judges in the course of hearing a case before they make their decision. Because judges are supposed to make their decisions only on the evidence presented to them, this is a challenging but crucial aspect of the strategic litigation undertaken by sophisticated equality-focused organizations like Egale, the Council of Canadians with Disabilities, the Native Women's Association of Canada and, most frequently, by LEAF, often in collaboration with other equality-seeking groups.

The importance of judges having the best available evidence on which to base their decisions is unlikely to draw debate. But the value of equality-based organizations being allowed by judges to bring information and evidence in their role as "interveners" in key cases (because they are not one of the parties to the case) is less settled. The notion that frontline expertise provided to the Court through interventions should be invalidated as that of "special interest" groups — such as constitutional rights advocates — seems to be gaining ground. Such a notion is derived from an elitist perspective. Rights are just words on paper unless they can be beneficially experienced — unless they can be lived. Interventions before the Court are a form of inclusion that is consistent with Canadian Charter values, and this produces knowledge that is essential in equality cases — if only because judges are among our most privileged and protected citizens.

The interconnection of rights guarantees in the Charter and in statutory human rights law has emerged in case after case. In the discussion of examples of "lived rights" in the following section, the relationship between equality rights and other rights and freedoms in the Charter exposes how inequality is compounded by other prohibited grounds of discrimination, such as: Aboriginal status, disability or sexual orientation.

Indigenous Women's Rights

The following excerpt from a speech by Senator Lillian Quan Dyck (February 13, 2007) one of two Aboriginal women senators in Canada at the time, captures the tension inherent in Charter promises and a different reality often experienced:

I am proud to be a Canadian. Canadians have much to be proud of; our nation believes it and passes legislation that provides for basic fundamental freedoms and equality of its citizens. On the one hand I know this to be true, yet at the same time I know for some of us it is not necessarily true. As I look at the history of federal legislation and how it affected my family and others like me, the ideals of our country and the reality of our lives do not necessarily match up. There is a political and cognitive dissonance.

Sen. Dyck went on to speak of how her mother, an Aboriginal woman, qualified as a "status Indian" under the Indian Act, but Canadian law dictated that she lost her status when she married a non-Indian. This is an illustration of how the intersection of rights and personal characteristics — in this case, gender, race and culture — necessitates a balancing with Aboriginal sovereignty.

When she was National Speaker of the Native Women's Association of Canada (NWAC), Gail Stacey-Moore (1991) noted how Aboriginal women's equality advocates often experienced significant resistance from influential leaders within a number of important bodies, such as governments, academia and the media.

Aboriginal women have been legally, politically and socially subordinated by the federal government and by Aboriginal governments (Stacey-Moore 1991).

The issue of equality was at the forefront of Parliamentary debate in 2017 when the federal government introduced Bill S-3, in response to the Superior Court of Quebec decision in *Descheneaux* v. *Canada (Attorney General)*. Justice Chantal Masse found section 6(1)(a), (c) and (f) and section 6(2) of the Indian Act contrary to the Charter on the basis that the sections discriminated against Indigenous women. When Bill S-3 was introduced in the Senate, concerns were raised because yet again a partial solution was proposed to eradicate the systemic inequalities between Indigenous women and Indigenous men in registering as an Indian under the Act.

While Bill S-3 was being considered by the Senate Standing Committee on Aboriginal Peoples, Senators McPhedran and Pate introduced an amendment to Bill S-3 — referred to as "6(1)(a) all the way" — that the Senators developed in consultation with Indigenous leaders, distinguished legal scholars and advocates, including Dr. Sharon McIvor, Dr. Pam

Palmater, Shelagh Day, Mary Eberts, Dr. Lynn Gehl and Gwen Brodsky. The amendment strived to eliminate all traces of sex-based discrimination from the Indian Act and was widely supported by Indigenous organizations and Indigenous leaders from across the country. The calls on the government to act on the inadequacies in Bill S-3 to address sex-based discrimination from the Indian Act were widespread.

Indigenous and non-Indigenous senators stood shoulder-to-shoulder for 6(1)(a) all the way. Senator Dyck rose in the Senate during Third Reading of the Bill and declared, "Colleagues, refusing to implement the '6(1)(a) all the way' amendment is not an option for us as senators, nor is it an option for members of Parliament. We are debating fundamental equality rights. We cannot continue to deny granting Indian women the same rights as Indian men" (Dyck 2017). Senator Lovelace Nicholas stated, "Honourable senators, I am asking you today, as colleagues, to support the '6(1)(a) all the way' amendment for Indigenous women and girls of the generations to come, to stop the harmful discrimination. Let us be equal. After all, it was the government who created this problem" (Lovelace Nichols 2017). On June 1, 2017, Bill S-3 passed the Senate with the 6(1)(a) all the way amendment, with no dissent, sending it back to the House of Commons for review of the Senate amendments.

On National Aboriginal Day (June 21, 2017), a majority in the House of Commons stripped the Senate amendment from Bill S-3. Months of quiet negotiations ensued and Bill S-3 went through several transformations before it came back to the Senate for a final vote and Royal Assent. The final form was a culmination of the work and effort of Indigenous leaders, officials with Minister Carolyn Bennett, senators and advocates. The new law allows for monitoring the progress of the federal government in eradicating sex-based discrimination of Indigenous women in registration under the Indian Act, but the law is weak in that it does not specify a time when such equality is to be achieved.

Disability

Significant success for equality seekers came in *Council of Canadians with Disabilities v. VIA Rail Canada Inc.* (2007), "which affirms the universal application of human rights principles and the right to equality for people with disabilities" (Manitoba Human Rights Commission 2007). However, counsel for the Council of Canadians with Disabilities (CCD), David Baker and Sarah Godwin (2008), caution that the success of the case almost bankrupted the CCD and that governmental resistance does not seem to have been reduced by the decision.

In an earlier turning point for disability rights, *Eldridge* v. *British Columbia (Attorney General)* (1997), the CCD intervened, as did LEAF, in coalition with the Disabled Women's Network of Canada, to convince the Supreme Court that the government was obligated to fund sign language as part of its promise to provide medical services to all residents of the province.

Sexual Orientation

Until 1969, the *Criminal Code of Canada* contained an offence that effectively criminalized homosexuality. Now, the human rights architecture in Canada (federal, provincial, territorial and, in some places, municipal) holds that sexual orientation is not an acceptable ground of discrimination and complaint mechanisms are provided — but nowhere in the Charter will you find an explicit protection against discrimination on the basis of sexual orientation. The answer to this constitutional puzzle lies in the open wording of section 15 and the section 24 "remedies" power given to Canadian judges in the Charter to decide on appropriate remedies, including what has come to be known as "reading in rights" that are not specifically listed in section 15.

Douglas Elliott (2006: 98), counsel in a number of sexual orientation cases, including *Hislop* v. *Canada (Attorney General)* (2007) that extended same-sex pension benefits, observed how the shift in society toward equality rights for lesbian, gay, bisexual, transgendered, queer and two-spirit (LGBTQ2) Canadians, was influenced by the Charter:

> so long as growing public support did not move the politicians, the only way to move them would be through the courts ... All of these cases accepted that sexual orientation was an analogous ground, but most of the early cases ended in failure ... The public began to conceive of the issues in terms of the human rights model, and countervailing arguments based on the "sin" or "medical" models began to be viewed as antiquated at best and bigoted at worst ... The question of sexual orientation as an analogous ground finally reached the Supreme Court of Canada in the famous Egan case ... A majority of the Court found that

discrimination against same sex couples was an infringement of section 15(1) ... However, a different majority upheld the impugned law under section 1. It would be the last time that section 1 would be relied upon to reach that result, but it was a bitter blow at the time.

In 1996, the Alberta Court of Appeal ruled against Delwin Vriend, a teacher who was fired when it was discovered that he was gay. The Alberta Individual Rights Protection Act did not include sexual orientation, so Vriend sued the Alberta government, arguing that the appropriate remedy was for sexual orientation to be read into the Alberta statute. The Supreme Court agreed, overruling the Alberta Court of Appeal:

> As a remedy, the words "sexual orientation" should be read into the prohibited grounds of discrimination in these provisions. (1996: para. 497)

Although his government fought Vriend at every stage of the case, Alberta's premier, Ralph Klein, surprised many when he announced in 1998 that he would not use his legislative majority to override the Court by activating s. 33 of the Charter and he acceded to the requirement that his province's human rights legislation should prohibit discrimination on the basis of sexual orientation. Elliott (2006: 112–113) described the importance of the wide-ranging political and legal battle over the legalization of same-sex marriage in the federal government's Bill C-38:

> Parliament relented and passed Bill C-38, but only after a long and difficult political battle ... in the process, we had moved the political goalposts ... Canadians had firmly embraced the human rights model embodied in the Charter.

Prime Minister Justin Trudeau made an historic apology on November 28, 2017, to the LGBTQ2 community in Canada, specifically for the oppressive actions of the government from 1950s to the early 1990s towards LGBTQ2 members in the public service. In part, the Prime Minister said:

> Sadly, what resulted was nothing short of a witch hunt. The public service, the military, and the RCMP spied on their own people inside and outside of workplaces. During this time, the federal government even dedicated funding to an absurd device known

as the "fruit machine," a failed technology that was supposed to measure homosexual attraction … Mr. Speaker, today we acknowledge an often-overlooked part of Canada's history. Today, we finally talk about Canada's role in the systemic oppression, criminalization, and violence against the lesbian, gay, bisexual, transgender, queer, and two-spirit communities … And it is my hope that in talking about these injustices, vowing to never repeat them, and acting to right these wrongs, we can begin to heal. (House of Commons Debates 2017)

A shift also occurred at the Supreme Court of Canada in mid-2018 when a majority of five judges and two concurring reasons (with another two dissenting) found that the Law Society of British Columbia (LSBC) was correct and reasonable in denying the application of Trinity Western University (TWU) to establish a law school. The University's code of conduct bans "sexual intimacy that violates the sacredness of marriage between a man and a woman" and all students are required by TWU to sign a covenant to uphold the code of conduct. The seven judges ruled that the University's covenant as a condition of admission to the proposed

---

CASE STUDY:
ETHICAL CONSIDERATIONS

"Two central issues for ethical analysis of equality are: Why equality? Equality of what? The two questions are distinct but thoroughly interdependent. We cannot begin to defend or criticize equality without knowing what on earth we are talking about, i.e., equality of what features (incomes, opportunities, wealths, achievements, freedoms, rights" (Amartya Sen 1980: 256).

Affirmative Action for Substantive Equality

Affirmative Action (sometimes called reverse discrimination in the USA), defined in section 15(2) of the Charter, is allowed to rebalance the effects of inequality that arise from discrimination of historically disadvantaged groups in order to provide members of these groups with substantively equal opportunities for success in education, business, politics and other realms of life.

law school effectively imposed inequitable barriers on entry to the school. The majority found, "Ultimately, the LSBC determined that the approval of TWU's proposed law school with a mandatory covenant would negatively impact equitable access to and diversity within the legal profession and would harm LGBTQ individuals, and would therefore undermine the public interest in the administration of justice" (2018: para 39).

EQUALITY RIGHTS AND JUSTICE

As in the pursuit of justice, the path to equality is not only through the courts and the Charter. Following the *Nancy Law* case, most equality-seeking claims were lost before the Supreme Court. Soon after the *Law* decision, Beverly Baines (2000) predicted that the Court's unusually unanimous decision in *Law* would create additional barriers through which equality-seeking litigants would have difficulty passing. Broad judicial latitude for subjective assessment of others' reality is exposed in the split decision in *Gosselin* v. *Quebec (Attorney General)* (2002: para. 68), where the Chief Justice for the majority applied the *Law* test in dismissing a class action on behalf of the majority of young, entrenched unemployed in Quebec: "This is not a case where the complainant group suffered from pre-existing disadvantage and stigmatization."

Despite attempts to bring in a new law that would overturn what is often known as the "spanking case" — the *Canadian Foundation for Children, Youth and the Law* v. *Canada (Attorney General)* (2004), it is still the law in Canada that assaults by parents on their children are protected under section 43 of the *Criminal Code of Canada*. In upholding section 43, the Court held that such assaults on children — that would be illegal if committed on other adults — were not a violation of children's section 15 rights. On the other hand, in *Dickie* v. *Dickie* (2007), the Supreme Court held that parents who refuse to comply with Family Court orders for support of their families (about 97 percent being men) can be held in contempt of court.

It is clear that the Charter has changed Canada — equality rights and values (sections 15, 27, 28 for example) intersect with Canadian perceptions and concerns. A 2013 Statistics Canada poll on Canadian identity found over 90 percent of Canadians collectively share values of human rights, respect for the law and gender equality. The Charter was identified as one of the highest symbols of national identity (Sinha 2013). The Charter is essentially a contract between Canadians and their governments, but a Trudeau Foundation poll (Environics 2010) revealed an intergenerational difference in viewing responsibility for justice: 70 percent of young adults believed that current Canadian governments are responsible for addressing human rights violations committed by previous governments compared with only 47 percent of Canadians aged 60 and over. In 2018, *The Economist* magazine released its Democracy Index for 2017, with Canada ranked sixth in the world for its protection of democracy within five categories: electoral process and pluralism; civil liberties; the functioning of government; political participation; and political culture. (*The Economist* Intelligence Unit n.d.)

Nevertheless, there have been successes and setbacks in the quest for equality rights. Sustaining an inclusive democracy requires "everyday" Canadians, not just those in the legal community of Canada, to remain alert when there is a negative shift in the impact of how the courts are dealing with equality rights — from constructive to damaging — from section 15 acting as a beacon to illuminate and value the struggles against inequality in ordinary lives, to section 15 becoming a laser that can burn away access to justice.

Human Rights Links

Universal Declaration of Human Rights	<http://www.un.org/en/universal-declaration-human-rights/index.html>
International Covenant on Civil and Political Rights	<http://www.ohchr.org/EN/Professional-Interest/Pages/CCPR.aspx>
International Covenant on Economic Social and Cultural Rights	<http://www.ohchr.org/EN/Professional-Interest/Pages/CESCR.aspx>
International Convention on the Elimination of all form of Racism and Racial Discrimination	<http://www.ohchr.org/EN/Professional-Interest/Pages/CERD.aspx>
Convention on the Elimination of All forms of Discrimination against Women	<http://www.un.org/womenwatch/daw/cedaw/>
Canadian Charter of Rights and Freedoms	<http://laws-lois.justice.gc.ca/eng/Const/page-15.html#h-39>
Ad Hoc Committee of Canadian Women on the Constitution	<http://www.constitute.ca/>

leaf	<http://www.leaf.ca/>
International Development Research Centre	<https://www.idrc.ca/>
National Council of Women of Canada	<http://www.ncwcanada.com/>
International Women's Rights Project	<http://www.iwrp.org>
Institute for International Women's Rights – Manitoba	<http://www.iiwrmb.ca/>

DISCUSSION QUESTIONS

1. What is it about the wording in section 15 of the *Canadian Charter of Rights and Freedoms* that allowed judges to "read in" protection for characteristics not mentioned in the Charter? Can you think of any other characteristic not specified in the Charter that should be considered an analogous ground under section 15, and why?
2. Should poverty or social status be included as a section 15 equality right protected from discrimination by the Charter, and, if so, how might that change enable certain people to "live their rights"?
3. Why is "access to justice" an issue for some people who are experiencing discrimination defined as contrary to the protections in section 15?
4. When the Constitution Act was adopted in 1982, governments agreed to a moratorium on section 15 to delay equality rights coming into force until three years after the Charter was entrenched. Discuss why you think the Women's Legal Education and Action Fund (LEAF) was launched on the first day when equality rights in section 15 became available in Canada.
5. If you needed to seek justice for discrimination in Canada, would you rely on the United Nations Universal Declaration of Human Rights? Could you use the *Canadian Charter of Rights and Freedoms* and international human rights instruments in developing your claim for protection against discrimination?
6. The Canadian Bill of Rights was enacted more than twenty years before the Charter (1982) was entrenched in the Canadian Constitution, but they are both still law in Canada and they both define rights. What is different about how equality is defined in sections 15 and 28 of the Charter compared to the Bill of Rights? Does this

matter in being able to access equality rights today?

7. Are equality rights in sections 15 and 28 of the Charter the same as the protections for the rights of Indigenous women in the Charter?

8. Did governments in Canada decide on their own how to define equality rights in the Charter? Did non-governmental (civil society) leaders influence the wording of section 15 equality rights? Provide three examples of how the drafting of the Charter protections changed as a result of input from non-governmental advocates for equality rights.

9. Who are the parties in "constitutional trialogue" theory and what role has each played in defining and interpreting equality rights in the Charter? How is this different from the "dialogue theory"?

GLOSSARY

British Common Law (BCL): BCL developed from British court decisions (beginning in 1066 with the Norman Conquest) that set precedents, which are referred to in future cases of a similar nature. Parliament can pass new laws that overrule existing precedents. All provincial law in Canada is based on the common law system, except for Québec (which is based on civil law).

Canadian Bill of Rights: A statute enacted in 1960 to guarantee that individuals in Canada enjoy certain rights.

Canadian Charter of Rights and Freedoms: Guarantees rights and freedoms of individuals in Canada and protects against infringement subjects to the limitations set out therein.

Constitution: Outline of the division of powers and authorities of the provincial and federal governments in Canada.

Constitutional equality: equality protections entrenched within the Constitution.

Cultural imperialism: The norms of the dominant group are assumed to be those of everyone.

Discrimination: Different treatment of an individual on the basis of a prohibited ground of discrimination, such as national or ethnic origin, colour, religion, age, sex, sexual orientation, marital status, family status, physical or mental disability and pardoned criminal conviction.

Entitlement systems: The rights claimed by the most vulnerable in society to such basics as food and housing are devalued relative to the property oriented rights claimed by more privileged people.

Entrench: To give legal effect by inserting within a piece of legislation.

Formal Equality: equal treatment for all (that is, likes treated alike and "una-likes" treated alike).

Negative rights: right to refrain from taking a particular action.

Positive rights: right to take a particular action; may impose a duty on governments.

Substantive equality: allowing different treatment if necessary to achieve equalizing effect resulting in fairer outcomes or lived rights.

Unconstitutional: something is deemed "unconstitutional" if it contravenes the principles set out within the Constitution.

NOTES

I dedicate this chapter to the greatest gifts in my life, my "Charter babies" Jonathan Jacob and David Kitson, with gratitude to my femtors on equality: Bev Baines, Mary Eberts, Peter Hogg, Claire L'Heureux-Dubé, Michele Landsberg, Catharine MacKinnon, Hon. Nancy Ruth and other LEAF mothers, Bruce Ryder; to my former colleagues at University of Saskatchewan College of Law: Norm Zlotkin and Mark Carter, to Dr. Margot Hurlbert for inviting and editing this chapter for both editions, and for research assistance to my Senate office from University of Ottawa law students Lee Chitty (2017) and Cathy Lin (2018) as well as to research assistance provided for the first edition from 2009–2011: Sarah E. Sharp, Adele Domenco, Aaron Swanson and Dr. Christina Szurlej.

1. The author is a human rights lawyer and an Independent Senator in the Parliament of Canada, with particular interest in strengthening access and inclusion in Canadian governance.

2. To see the special joint committee on the Canadian constitution in session and hear this statement, please visit <www.constitute.ca> and view the documentary *Constitute!*

REFERENCES

Alberta v. Hutterian Brethren of Wilson Colony [2009] 2 S.C.R. 567.

Baines, B. 2000. "Law v. Canada: Formatting Equality." *Constitutional Forum* 11(3): 65-73.

Bill C-16: *An Act to amend the Canadian Human Rights Act and the Criminal Code* 42nd Parliament, 1st session. <https://www.parl.ca/DocumentViewer/en/42-1/bill/C-16/first-reading>.

Bill C-61: *An Act to give effect to the Anishinabek Nation Education Agreement and to make consequential amendments to other Acts.* (2017). 42nd Parliament, 1st session. <http://www.parl.ca/DocumentViewer/en/42-1/bill/C-61/

royal-assent>.

Bill S-3: *An Act to amend the Indian Act in response to the Superior Court of Quebec decision in Descheneaux c. Canada (Procureur général)*. (2014). 42nd Parliament, 1st session. <http://www.parl.ca/DocumentViewer/en/42-1/bill/S-3/royal-assent>.

Canada (Attorney General) v. *Lavell* [1974] S.C.R. 1349.

Canadian Bill of Rights, S.C. 1960, c.44.

Daniels v. Canada (Indian Affairs and Northern Development) [2016] 1 S.C.R. 99.

Descheneaux v. Canada (Attorney General), 2017 Q.C.C.A. 1238.

Dyck, L.E. 2017. Senate of Canada Debates (*Hansard*), June 1, 1st Session, 42nd Parliament, Volume 150, Issue 126, Indian Act.

The Economist Intelligence Unit. n.d. <https://www.eiu.com/topic/democracy-index> (accessed February 03, 2018).

Henderson, James (Sa'ke'j). 2008. *Indigenous Diplomacy and the Rights of Peoples Achieving U.N. Recognition*. UBC Press, Purich Publishing.

House of Commons Debates. 2017. Senate of Canada Debates (*Hansard*), November 28, 1st Session, 42nd Parliament, Volume 148, Number 240.

Kulchyski, Peter Keith. 2013. *Aboriginal Rights Are Not Human Rights: In Defence of Indigenous Struggles*. Winnipeg: ARP Books.

Law Society of British Columbia v. Trinity Western University [2018] 2018 SCC 32.

Lovelace-Nicholas, S. 2017. Senate of Canada Debates (*Hansard*), June 1, 1st Session, 42nd Parliament, Volume 126, Issue 126, Indian Act.

Optional Protocol to the International Covenant on Civil and Political Rights. 1996. G.A. Res 2200 (XXI), (Dec. 16).

R. v. Powley, [2003] 2 S.C.R. 207.

Sinha, Maire. 2013. "Canadian Identity." Statistics Canada. <http://www.statcan.gc.ca/pub/89-652-x/89-652-x2015005-eng.htm#a2>.

Statement by Minister Wilson-Raybould on passage of Bill C-16 in Senate and moving one step closer to ending discrimination based on gender identity or expression. June 15, 2017. <https://www.newswire.ca/news-releases/statement-by-minister-wilson-raybould-on-passage-of-bill-c-16-in-senate-and-moving-one-step-closer-to-ending-discrimination-based-on-gender-identity-or-expression-628715183.html> (accessed February 3, 2018).

Statistics Canada. 2013. *Canadian Identity*. Ottawa, ON. Catalogue 89-652-X. <http://www.statcan.gc.ca/pub/89-652-x/89-652-x2015005-eng.htm#a2> (accessed January 28, 2018).

Tanudjaja v. *Canada (Attorney General)*, [2014] 123 O.R. (3d) 161 (Ont. C.A.).

Trinity Western University v. The Law Society of Upper Canada, [2016] 131 OR (3d) 113 (Ont. C.A.).

Trudeau, J. 2017. House of Commons Debates (*Hansard*), November 28, 1st Session, 42nd Parliament, Volume 148, Issue 240, LGBTQ2 Canadians.

Truth and Reconciliation Commission of Canada. 2015. "Truth and Reconciliation Commission: Calls to Action." <http://www.trc.ca/websites/trcinstitution/File/2015/Findings/Calls_to_Action_English2.pdf> (accessed

February 2, 2018).

United Nations. 2007. *Declaration of the Rights of Indigenous Peoples.* G.A. Res. 61/295, U.N. Doc. A/RES/61/295 7.

Watson, P., and B.R. Barber. 1988. *The Struggle For Democracy.* Boston, MA: Little, Brown and Company.

13

THE CRIMINAL JUSTICE SYSTEM

Sarah Britto, Nicholas A. Jones,
and Rick Ruddell

OBJECTIVES

At the end of this chapter, you will be able to:

- Describe the three components of Canada's criminal justice system

- Critically apply theoretical explanations to criminal justice issues

- Explain why different methods are used to describe, define and measure the prevalence and characteristics of crime

- Describe how outcomes in the criminal justice system are related to the discretion of officials at various decision-making points from investigating crimes to imprisonment

- Explain the differences between informal and formal social control

- Critically assess the components of the criminal justice system with respect to formal justice, substantive justice and ethical practice

The terms crime and justice, the root words in the phrase criminal justice, point to complex moral, philosophical, and pragmatic issues in our search for just and fair outcomes in our responses to acts we have defined as crimes.

Like many of the issues presented in this book so far, the phrase criminal justice appears to be straightforward, but once we examine the meanings, we find these words involve a complex interplay of moral, philosophical, and practical issues in our search for just and fair outcomes in our responses to acts governments have defined as crimes.

But what does a focus on criminal justice mean? Does this mean justice for criminals? Justice for society in its fight against crime? Justice for victims of crime? Or some combination of the three? To begin, let's step back and define the term "crime." In a very basic way crime is any behaviour that violates what the state has defined as unacceptable conduct that carry consequences in a given society (Linden 2016). This definition, although providing considerable practical utility, obscures the purpose of criminal law and the role of power in introducing these laws.

Criminal law and the criminal justice system (CJS) are related to the broader issue of social control. Social control includes the customs, beliefs, and laws that frame a society's norms (what are and are not considered acceptable behaviours) and are designed to control behaviours in accordance with those norms (Janowitz 1975). Social control comes in many forms, and is typically divided into two distinct categories — informal and formal. Informal social control is the words and actions of parents, peers and other members of society used to control the behaviours of others, as well as the ways in which neighbourhoods, for example, are organized to encourage normative and law-abiding behaviour (Drakulich and Crutchfield 2013). One example of exerting informal social control is when you convince a friend not to drive after drinking. When society is working well, informal social control functions to keep members of society from harming each other through actions like theft, violence and so on.

Historically, as societies became more anonymous, complex and heterogeneous (moving from small groups of hunter–gatherers where "everybody knows everybody," to most people living in large postindustrial cities), informal social controls became inadequate to manage the behaviour of individuals and groups that cause harm to individuals and society. As we are more anonymous in cities, the approval or disapproval of someone we don't know is less likely to influence our actions.

Therefore, members of society participate in a "social contract" where the state provides a formal means of protecting society in exchange for giving up some individual freedoms (Hobbes 1985; Locke 2003; Rousseau 1987). Formal social control — in the form of a criminal justice system based on the rule of law — is designed to supplement informal social control by persuading or preventing individuals from violating criminal law and punishing or correcting this behaviour when they do so (Schulenberg 2010). Formal social control is based on the legal definition of crime and relies on legislatures and international bodies to define the parameters in which the CJS can operate (such as in the *Criminal Code of Canada*, the *Canadian Charter of Rights and Freedoms* and international human rights laws). In addition to the formal controls exerted by officials in the justice system, our behaviours are also influenced and regulated by persons acting on behalf of the state, and examples include campus security personnel, conservation officers and highway traffic officials who have the power to enforce municipal, provincial or federal regulations. Last, one's employer and officials working for other government bodies, such as health, educational and social service agencies, can also use their powers to influence our behaviours. Some have called these less-than-formal controls "quasi-formal" control.

Much like intersectionality affects the relative privilege and deprivation experienced by individuals, so too does the composition of informal and formal social control influence the character of justice available within given communities. Van Ness and Strong (2015: 47) argue that "in promoting justice, government is responsible for preserving a just order, and community for establishing a just peace." These authors suggest that the relationship between informal and formal social control is an inverse one; that is, if informal social controls are effective in controlling behaviour, there is a lesser need for formal controls. In some neighbourhoods and communities, informal and formal social control operate in concert and there is a healthy collaboration between community members, the criminal justice system and other agencies of formal control. In other communities, there may be a breakdown of informal social control. In those cases, agents of formal and quasi-formal social control take on a much larger role in regulating behaviours, although their activities might be ineffective if poorly coordinated or executed. Moreover, as our industrialized societies become increasingly diverse, there may be less agreement about whether an act is really a crime. One such example is polygamy (when one has more than one marriage partner); while the practice is outlawed in Canada, it is widely accepted in some communities. There is a risk that without community input, transparency and oversight — where different external bodies are overseeing their activities — this control can become oppressive. Additionally, well-functioning social control requires mobilizing collective community will, as well as adequate resources to address individual and structural factors that may contribute to criminality.

Janowitz (1975: 82) argues that social control has been discussed as both the cooperative "capacity of a society to regulate itself according to desired principles and values" as expressed in structural functionalism, and a more coercive "social repression" described by conflict theorists, where the powerful try to impose a social order on marginalized peoples in order to maintain their positions in society. Depending on how one views the world (think back to the discussion in Chapter 1 regarding ethnocentrism), one's definition of crime and, therefore, the function of the criminal justice system may be quite different.

Traditionally, the criminal justice system is seen through the lens of formal justice where the focus is on the rule of law and providing a clear system of rules (Hurlbert 2011). When these laws are violated, consequences are imposed that are intended to symbolize public disapproval of the law-violating behaviour, deter others from repeating these offences and help wrongdoers in correcting their behaviours. Procedural justice attempts to ensure that the rules, policies and procedures involved in the criminal justice system are fair, apply to all individuals and ideally result in just outcomes (Pollock 2012). The reality of criminal behaviour is that offenders and victims are shaped by the context of their lived experiences and factors such as race, gender, power and privilege. Criminal justice policies and practices that do not consider these factors can contribute to inequality and injustice, such as the disproportionate representation of Indigenous peoples in Canada's provincial and federal correctional systems. One of the challenges of justice in the twenty-first century is integrating substantive justice, which involves treating "unequals" unequally, with formal justice. Furthermore, by examining criminal justice issues through the lens of social justice and ethical practice, criminal justice agencies can find ways to establish partnerships with communities to protect the least powerful, marginalized and vulnerable in society.

DEFINING CRIME

Each of the three major theoretical perspectives covered in this book provides a different way of understanding crime. Structural functionalists define criminal law as a system of rules developed collectively by legislatures to protect all members of society equally. The criminal justice system is empowered, through a social contract with all members of society, to enforce the law for the greater good of society and humanity. To provide a very simple example, almost all of us can agree that murder is wrong. Therefore, it makes sense that in diverse societies throughout the world, law reflects the criminal nature of murder. Criminal law and the criminal justice system serve a boundary maintenance function for society by clearly defining the behaviours that a given society finds morally wrong. Viewing crime from a structural functionalist or consensus perspective, the definition of crime may change considerably over time depending on what a given society collectively considers deviant. A dramatic example of a criminal code changing over time is the Criminal Law Amendment Act 1968–69 in Canada. This Act legalized abortion and homosexuality between consenting adults, placed restrictions on firearm ownership and criminalized the refusal to take a breathalyzer to measure blood alcohol content while operating a motor vehicle (Prober 1970).

Conflict theorists take a more critical perspective of crime and note that many laws target behaviours of the less powerful, while ignoring equally or more harmful behaviours committed by individuals with more economic power (Brown, Esbensen and Geis 2013). In their well-respected book, *The Rich Get Richer and the Poor Get Prison*, Reiman and Leighton (2017: 74) argue that the harmful behaviour of corporations and the consequences of this behaviour (environmental degradation, physical injuries including death and losses of property and finances) is "a crime by any other name." From a conflict perspective, defining crime becomes a political process meant to consolidate power among specific groups and to further disenfranchise oppressed groups and maintain existing social relationships. For example, the Indian Act represents the efforts of a settler government to control First Nations peoples. According to the Royal Commission on Aboriginal Peoples (1996), the Indian Act resulted in:

- The creation of reservations and a pass system that restricted the movement of First Nations peoples;

- Residential schools to assimilate Indigenous children;
- The creation of a permit system to regulate Indigenous peoples' participation in the economy;
- The denial of status to First Nations women and their children who married non-status individuals;
- Restrictions against forming political organizations;
- Prohibitions against participating in traditional ceremonies; and
- Prohibitions against traditional spiritual practices.

The legal system was used "to restrict the movement of Aboriginal people who were believed to represent a threat to the government and to white settlers" (Linden 2016: 20). Many of the "Justice" Calls to Action found in the Truth and Reconciliation Commission Report (2015) attempt to redress the legacy of this historical legal imbalance.

Other examples of the conflict perspective of crime include vagrancy and homelessness laws that are routinely enforced in poorer and minority communities. According to the law both rich and poor can be fined for sleeping on the street, and while the law applies equally to both, the poor person is more vulnerable to being fined. In some cases, the penalties for violating municipal regulations are harsh. For example, a homeless man riding his bike on a Montreal sidewalk was given five tickets, including four tickets for not having the proper lights and reflectors on his bicycle (Bellemare 2018). If he fails to pay these fines, he might end up in court and his violation of a municipal regulation could be criminalized. Would a middle-class university student biking on the sidewalk be treated the same?

Finally, an examination of the conflict perspective must also acknowledge the many harmful behaviours committed by powerful individuals and corporations that are routinely ignored or minimized — such as white-collar crime (Sutherland 1949), corporate deviance, human rights violations committed by governments and multinational corporations (Simon 2011) — and how these acts affect all of us. Canadian bakers and grocery stores, for example, engaged in a conspiracy from 2002 to 2014 to artificially raise the price of bread, which ended up costing each family who bought one loaf per week an extra $400 (Markusoff 2018). Loblaws has offered Canadians a $25 grocery voucher to compensate for this loss, which seems to be a small cost when compared with their profits from breaking the law. It is unlikely that any of the executives involved in this theft will ever see a day inside a jail cell, even though they made hundreds of millions of dollars of profits through price fixing. Conflict theorists also point out that legislation can reinforce the abuse of others, as laws in some countries allow men to physically discipline their wives and children (Human Rights Watch 2014).

The final definition of crime comes from the symbolic interactionist perspective, which rests on the assumption that one's sense of self is developed through regular interactions with others in society (Mead 1934). As a result, individuals are constantly adjusting their behaviours based on the reactions they perceive from others (Cooley 1902). Additionally, the reactions of others to an individual's behaviour is often filtered through stereotypes of one's position in society. Therefore, disturbing the peace by hanging out and making a lot of noise in a public place may be considered harmless if the individuals in question are white and upper class, whereas the same behaviour may be deemed deviant and dangerous when performed by less affluent minorities (Blumer 1969). Lemert (1951) argued that all individuals experiment with "deviance," but it is only when they are labelled deviant by others and accept this label as a part of their identity that they become criminals. According to this perspective, certain behaviours come to be labelled criminal through a negotiated process that is highly dependent on the actions of "moral entrepreneurs" (charismatic individuals who draw attention to a particular issue) and interest groups that successfully articulate their perspectives of which behaviours, and groups of people, are the most harmful in a given society. While moral entrepreneurs present their actions in a manner that suggests they are in the best interests of society, it is often the case that they are merely seeking to meet their own agenda and get their perspective enshrined in law.

Symbolic interactionism can be used to explain the changing nature of criminal and juvenile justice in Canada. For instance, several interest groups advocated for laws that clearly articulate the developmental differences between youth and adults and therefore argue that youth sanctions must be mitigated (reduced) when it comes to sentencing and that it must be easier for youths involved in the justice system to access rehabilitative or treatment options than their adult counterparts. Those interest groups include the Canadian Bar Association, the Elizabeth Fry Society and the John Howard Society. In the case of mitigating harsh sentences for youth, some of this change may also be due to research demonstrating that their

Table 13-1: Crime and the CJS in Theoretical Approaches

	Definition of Crime	Cause of Crime	Purpose of the CJS
Structural functionalism	"Crimes are acts which shock the common conscience, or collective morality, producing intense moral outrage in people" (Lanier, Henry and Anastasia 2015: 17).	Crime is a result of the breakdown of social controls.	The CJS serves to maintain the boundaries between unacceptable and acceptable behaviour in society. Punishment is seen as symbolic (defining what is unacceptable), as having rehabilitative potential and as a method of assimilation into the norms of society.
Conflict theory	"Crime is a political concept designed to protect the power and position of the upper classes at the expense of the poor" (Siegel and McCormick 2016: 18).	Crime is a result of the social, political and economic repression of groups with limited power.	The CJS serves to reinforce existing power relations by controlling the behaviours of those without power and legitimizing the harmful behaviour of those with power.
Symbolic interactionism	State definitions of crime are socially constructed and change over time.	"Acts become deviant only because the reactions of others label them so" (Brown, Esbensen and Geis 2013: 20). Social control agencies are particularly powerful in their ability to apply negative labels to individuals.	The CJS acts as a system of social control that reinforces deviant stereotypes about individuals in marginalized groups, and thereby increases criminality among individuals in these groups.

brains are less developed than adults, and they are less capable of making sound decisions.

Other interest groups, such as Mothers Against Drunk Driving, have successfully advocated for legal changes based on a single issue. We can also see the work of different interest groups at play with the "get tough on crime" movement that defined much of the criminal justice policy in

CASE STUDY:
A SYMBOLIC INTERACTIONIST UNDERSTANDING
OF THE MURDER OF PAMELA GEORGE

On the night of April 18, 1995 Steven Kummerfield and Alexander Ternowetsky approached Pamela George asking for oral sex in downtown Regina. Pamela declined because she was wary of the potential for things to go wrong with two clients. Later in the evening, the men returned, with Ternowetsky hidden in the trunk of the vehicle, and Kummerfield again propositioned Pamela George. This time she agreed and she was driven outside the city and performed oral sex on Kummerfield and was in the process of doing the same for Ternowetsky when they brutally beat her. This mother of two young children was later found dead in a ditch.

Although the details of this case demonstrate a brutal (although likely not premeditated) murder, the social construction of this case included several stereotypes and labels that were placed on both the victim and the perpetrators during the criminal justice process that vilified the victim and minimized the criminal behaviour of the perpetrators. The media, public and the CJS collectively dehumanized Pamela George. A community member on the Sakimay reserve and loving mother of two, she was regularly referred to as an Aboriginal prostitute rather than by her name or as the victim of a brutal crime.

In contrast, Kummerfield and Ternowetsky were presented as two white university athletes who participated in the typical, although foolish, behaviour of drinking and purchasing the services of a prostitute. Their violent behaviour was largely characterized as a mistake or tragedy that threatened to ruin their promising futures. This construction of these young men minimized the forethought involved in having one of the men hide in the trunk. Furthermore, Pamela's refusal indicates a lack of consent to provide sexual services to more than one man. Additionally, both men admitted to their friends that they had beaten and killed a prostitute (an "Indian hooker"). The friends did not report the crime nor show concern for the victim and her family, rather they continued with their lives and protected the identity of the perpetrators.

At the trial, the judge reinforced many of the same labels placed on the victim and the offenders. "Justice Malone instructed the jury to remember that George was 'indeed a prostitute' when considering whether she consented to a sexual assault" (Rowe 2001: 1). Kummerfield and Ternowetsky were found guilty of manslaughter and a six-and-a-half year sentence was imposed, although both offenders were released early on parole.

Sources: *Regina Leader-Post* (2015), Razack (2002)

Canada in the 1990s and 2000s. According to Comack, Fabre and Burgher (2015: 1), the Harper government promoted a tough-on-crime agenda "based on ideology and 'making people afraid of the boogeyman.'" That government undermined previous attempts to progress toward rehabilitation resulting in a backward move wherein "warehousing prisoners" (where inmates received less access to programs) became the norm (Comack, Fabre and Burgher 2015: 1).

By understanding that individuals and groups in society have different basic assumptions about the nature of crime, individuals who commit crime and the purpose of the CJS, we can begin to understand why some people see the CJS as primarily benevolent and contributing to the goal of social justice and others view the CJS as oppressive and a contributor to injustice in society. Our ideas about justice are often related to our place in society and most middle-class whites believe the system works fairly well, while visible minorities and Indigenous peoples are more likely to believe the CJS is unjust (Cotter 2015).

MEASURING CRIME

In addition to the challenge of defining crime, in order to understand the "crime problem" and develop ways to minimize crime in society, it is necessary to measure crime. Criminologists and other social scientists around the world have long struggled with some very basic questions: How much crime is there? Who commits crime? Why do some individuals commit crimes when others do not?

There are four basic ways to "know" about crime. These include qualitative studies, official reports, victimization data and self-reports. Each of these four ways of knowing about crime requires researchers to use different ways to collect information, including: asking people about their experiences as offenders, officials or victims; using surveys to collect information from large numbers of individuals; or analyzing data collected by police, courts and correctional agencies. All these approaches have their strengths and limitations.

Qualitative studies can inform us how it feels to be an offender, a crime victim or to work in a criminal justice agency. This information is often collected by interviewing individuals and analyzing the results. Although these experiences are extremely powerful in terms of the depth of understanding of crime and its consequences, this information is rarely generalizable to large groups of people, as researchers are often unable to interview a large number of individuals or carry out interviews with individuals across the country. One example of a very thorough national-level study is the National Inquiry into Missing and Murdered Indigenous Women, which will provide researchers with a richness of information about the impact of crime that is missed when looking only at numbers, such as only describing the number of missing Indigenous women reported to police services (see Royal Canadian Mounted Police 2015).

Official reports of crime are collected by criminal justice agencies (police, courts or corrections) and reported in the aggregate at the provincial, regional and national levels. Most countries regularly collect official crime data so that crime trends can be examined and compared over time. In Canada, one example is the police-reported crime statistics, which is collected by the Canadian Centre for Justice Statistics (a division of Statistics Canada), using the Uniform Crime Reporting Survey, and made available on a yearly basis.

Victimization data is collected through surveys of the public asking about their recent experience as victims of crime. Based on these data, we can compare the amount of crimes reported to the police in a province, region or country and the levels reported by crime victims. Many developed countries complete victimization surveys on a regular basis and Statistics Canada conducts a victimization survey every five years (the last was done in 2014). Regardless of where victimization surveys are conducted, there is a universal finding that only a proportion of crimes are ever reported to the police.

Self-report surveys ask individuals about their participation in criminal behaviour. Sometimes, these surveys are conducted in an institutionalized setting, like a prison or correctional centre, but at other times they are carried out in settings such as high schools or universities. Such studies can provide very useful information about an individual's self-reported involvement in particular offences. Moreover, the results of these surveys help us better understand how much crime really occurs. Unfortunately, few of these studies are conducted on a regular basis and in a wide enough geographic area to provide meaningful trend data. These self-report surveys of the public tell researchers that most of us engage in minor crimes as teenagers and we generally "age out" of crime as we get older, and few go on to commit serious and violent offences.

All four ways of knowing about crime have merit and are useful to understanding crime and its consequences. Yet, each of these approaches also has weaknesses.

Qualitative studies can provide us with a rich source of information about crime, offenders or victims, their circumstances and the dynamic nature of the offences and our responses. However, the primary weakness of basing research on personal experience is that it is unique to each individual and on its own does not provide meaningful generalizations for understanding the crime problem, especially when studying a very small sample.

A limitation related to official, police-reported crime are the factors impacting reporting. For example, Allen (2016) suggests that the practices of individual police services may influence how many offences are actually recorded, as these agencies differ with regard to available resources, priorities, enforcement practices and policies (like the use of municipal by-laws or provincial statutes) that can affect the statistics they report. One example is when a police service requires a victim of a minor property crime (such as a theft an item valued under $100) to go to the police headquarters to file a complaint. Because of the small loss and the unlikelihood anyone will be caught, many do not bother to file a report. Thus, a police practice may inhibit some individuals from reporting a crime.

One problem shared by official reports of crime, victimization surveys and self-report surveys is the dark figure of crime, which are crimes that are not reported. The dark figure of crime suggests that in reality there is a definitive amount of crime, only some of which can be measured with our current instrumentation. Victimization surveys allow us to capture some of the crimes that occurred and are unreported to the police and to help explain the reasons for not reporting crime to the police. Because of the secretive and deceptive nature of much criminal behaviour, many victims do not want their actions and experiences known to others, especially if they were involved in some wrongdoing when the offence occurred. One example is a person who is robbed while buying illicit drugs. Other victims are unlikely to report an offence if it is a minor matter, if they fear retaliation from an offender or if they lack trust and confidence in the police or justice system (Perreault 2015). Information from Canada's victimization surveys shows us that less than half of all crimes are reported to the police (Perreault 2015). Figure 13-1 shows the estimated percentage of different crimes being reported to the police in Canada.

Victimization surveys include many crimes that were never reported to the police (Brown, Esbensen and Geis 2013). Using the United States as an example, Berg and Lauritsen (2016) found that police-reported crime and victimization surveys consistently show similar crime trends, with victimization surveys estimating higher crime rates than those reported by the police. Although self-reported victimization rates are always higher than officially reported crime data, the reality is that some people do not wish to report their victimization experiences on a survey. Similarly, some offenders will not report their offences honestly on self-report surveys. Therefore, when interpreting crime data it is important to remember that many crimes are not reported regardless of the measurement technique utilized.

Another consideration when examining our responses to crime is the "criminal justice funnel" (Ruddell 2017). The funnel shows how crimes reported to the police effectively "disappear" as individuals work their way

Figure 13-1 Percentage of Offences Reported to the Police, 2014

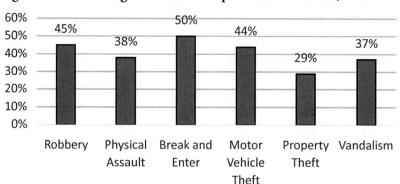

Source: Perreault 2015: table 9

through the justice system. This attrition or reduction of cases between the commission of a crime and receiving the most serious sentence in Canada — a prison sentence — is called filtering, whereby cases are lost at every decision point in the CJS. Crimes are filtered when police investigations assess that an allegation is unfounded, they cannot find enough evidence to proceed with an arrest, or prosecutors do not proceed because they do not feel they could obtain a conviction. Other individuals are diverted from the formal justice system and only a small proportion actually appear in a courtroom, many of whom receive probationary sentences and few of whom are incarcerated. Unlike the police procedurals and legal dramas that we see on television, many crimes are never addressed by the CJS, and less than 1 percent of individuals who commit an offence will set foot in a prison.

Figure 13-2 shows the "criminal justice funnel" (Public Safety Canada Portfolio Corrections Statistics Committee 2016). Of the more than two million offences reported to the police in 2014, only 4,781 persons were sentenced to serve over two years in prison, and most of these individuals will be released early on parole (Public Safety Canada Portfolio Corrections Statistics Committee 2016).

Figure 13-2 The Criminal Justice Funnel

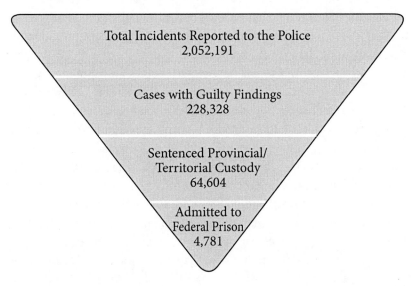

Total Incidents Reported to the Police
2,052,191

Cases with Guilty Findings
228,328

Sentenced Provincial/
Territorial Custody
64,604

Admitted to
Federal Prison
4,781

Source: Public Safety Canada Portfolio Corrections Statistics Committee (2016)

Figure 13-3 Police-Reported Crime, 1962–2016

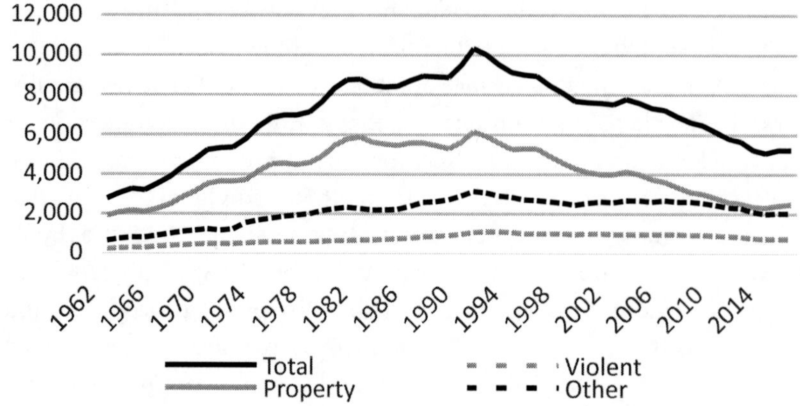

Source: Keighley (2017)

Three of the most well-known crime statistics reported in Canada by the Canadian Centre for Justice Statistics are the crime rate, the crime severity index and victimization rate.

The crime rate is usually reported as the number of offences reported to the police per 100,000 residents and is reported in the Uniform Crime Reporting Survey (UCR). This statistic allows us to make comparisons across time and between different cities, provinces or nations. Figure 13-3, for example, shows the crime rate in Canada from 1962 to 2016 (see Keighley 2017). This figure shows that, although crime increased for the thirty-year period between 1962 and 1992, crime declined steadily afterwards until 2015. It should be noted that from 2015 to 2017, some cities and provinces in Canada have experienced significant increases in crime and Canada's crime rate has shown a slight corresponding increase. Despite these increases, the crime rate in Canada is currently similar to what it was in the early 1970s. While researchers often look to local and provincial level criminal justice policy changes to explain changes in the crime rate, it is notable that Canada, the United States and England and Wales, all demonstrate similar crime trends from the 1960s to the present (Federal Bureau of Investigation 2016; Office of National Statistics 2017).

The police-reported crime rate can also be used to compare levels of crime in cities or provinces at a given time. Figure 13-4 shows the murder rate per 100,000 residents in ten large Canadian cities in 2016. Although murder receives more media coverage than any other crime (Surette

2015), it is the least frequently occurring crime in Canada (Boyce 2015). Despite its infrequency (there are about six hundred homicides a year in Canada), by looking at Figure 13-4, it is easy to see that some cities have a much larger murder problem than others.

The Crime Severity Index (CSI) is a measure of the volume (the number of offences occurring) and the seriousness of crime reported to police in a community, province or the entire nation (Keighley 2017). The seriousness of crimes is developed based on the severity of all the crimes that occurred where offences that would result in a prison sentence (and longer stays in prison) are given higher weights than offences that would result in probation. As a result, an aggravated assault is given more weight in determining a community's crime severity than a shoplifting offence when developing the CSI. This measure of crime gives researchers and the general public another way to compare crime among cities. Figure 13-5, much like the crime rate trends we examined earlier, shows that the CSI has been declining in Canada since the 1990s, with a more recent uptick that began in 2015 (Keighley 2017).

Figure 13-6 shows the same cities as were reported for murder rates. In addition to the overall CSI (which is shown in Figures 13-5), the CSI can also be reported as a violent crime severity index, a non-violent crime severity index and a youth crime severity index (Canadian Centre for Justice Statistics 2009).

Despite similar crime trends across Canada, in terms of crime increasing from the mid-1960s to the early 1990s and then declining to about 2015, the amount of crime and the severity of this crime varies

Figure 13-4 Homicide Rate, 2016

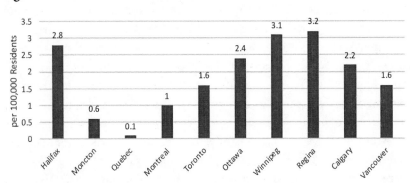

Source: Keighley (2017: table 8)

Figure 13-5 Crime Severity, 1998–2016

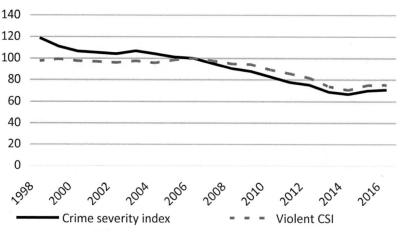

Source: Keighley (2017)

considerably from province to province and between cities. Many police services publish information about the crimes that occur on their websites. It is not uncommon to find crime maps showing areas of crime concentration or "hot spots" and areas that have relatively low crime in comparison. For example, the Regina Police Service (2018) publishes a "Community Crime Map" which is available at: <http://www.reginapolice.ca/resources/crime/crime-statistics/crime-map>.

Victimization surveys were designed to assess the validity of official crime statistics. They better capture the crimes that victims did not report to the police and provide insight into the experiences of victims that are not measured by police agencies, as well as the reasons why an individual did not report a crime (Skogan 1975). Less than one half of all crimes are reported to the police, and physical assaults and property thefts are the crimes least likely to be reported to the police. Although most murders are reported to the police due to the severity of the crime and in most cases the discovery of a body, victimization surveys do not count murders (Linden 2016). Statistics Canada reports that in 2014, less than 10 percent of sexual assaults were reported to the police, and approximately one quarter of all theft of household property was reported to the police (Perreault 2015). In a British study, Tarling and Morris (2010) suggest that there are both benefits and costs to reporting crime to the police and there are a variety of possible reasons why individuals choose not to report

Figure 13-6 Crime Severity Index, 2016

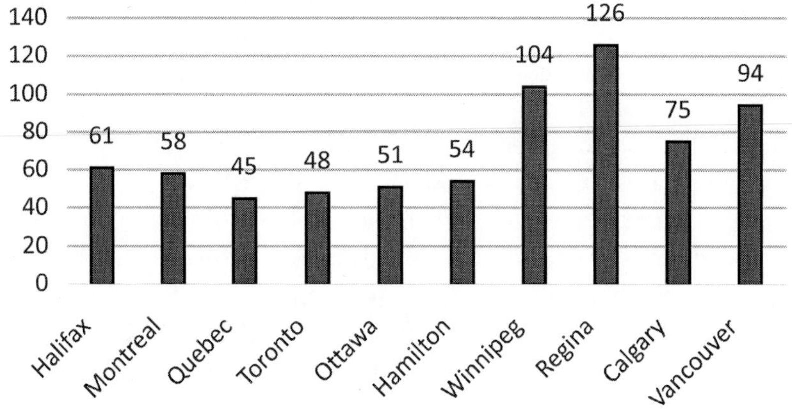

Source: Keighley (2017)

their victimization. The reasons for not reporting crimes to the police are influenced by a number of personal characteristics such as gender, age, race/ethnicity and factors such as the type of crime, the monetary value of the loss, whether the perpetrator was a friend or family member, the belief that the police will not respond positively to one's report, fear of retribution and shame and embarrassment (Perreault 2015).

CORRELATES OF CRIME

There is a common perception that victimization is a random phenomenon and all members of society have an equal risk of being crime victims. This is far from the truth. Crime is an enduring social problem and both offending and victimization are situated in complex social environments. This reality creates a challenge for policymakers because the criminal justice system is tasked with bringing individual offenders to justice, while many of the causes of crime are linked to broader problems with social, political and economic inequality in society, which are beyond the scope of the police, courts and corrections. Knowledge of the ways that context influences criminal behaviour, victimization and the responses to crime challenges CJS policy makers to move beyond formal justice and incorporate substantive justice and ethical practice into their organizations.

Individuals rarely wake up in the morning and decide, "today I am going to beat my neighbour to death." Involvement in criminality is shaped by a number of overlapping factors, many of which are shaped by conditions beyond the control of an individual. In the sixteenth century, L.A.J. (Adolphe) Quetelet and André-Michel Guerry documented the strong and consistent relationship between age, sex and crime (Siegel and McCormick 2016). Young men, throughout history and across a variety of different settings, have had consistently higher crime rates than older men and women of all ages (Brown, Esbensen and Geis 2013). There is an upside to the age-crime correlation, in that most people age out of crime. In fact, studies conducted in Canada, the United States and Sweden find that less than 10 percent of all offenders go on to be career criminals (Siegel and McCormick 2016). Other important individual correlates of crime include race/ethnicity, drug and alcohol addiction, trauma and past-victimization. These variables are all related to crime, and hold clues as to how larger social problems, such as racism, inequality and intergenerational trauma, may contribute to individual criminal behaviour.

Race/Ethnicity

Tonry (1997) observes that minority racial and ethnic groups are consistently over-represented in the CJS in all Western societies. Although Statistics Canada does not collect race-based crime data, they do collect data on Indigenous offenders. Numerous studies in Canada have found that Indigenous peoples are disproportionately represented in the Canadian CJS, especially in the prairies (Linden 2016). Figure 13-7 shows the huge gap between the percentage of Indigenous peoples in each province and territory (although data from Alberta is missing), and the percentage of Indigenous peoples admitted to correctional supervision (Statistics Canada 2011; Reitano 2017). Understanding why this occurs, and reducing this disparity, is a challenge facing all Canadians in the twenty-first century. It is the thirtieth Call to Action in the Truth and Justice Commission of Canada Report (2015: 3):

> We call upon federal, provincial, and territorial governments to commit to eliminating the overrepresentation of Aboriginal people in custody over the next decade, and to issue detailed annual reports that monitor and evaluate progress in doing so.

Often the race/ethnicity and crime relationship is a product of a number of other social inequalities in society. With respect to Indigenous peoples, for instance, Canada was colonized by England and France, and settlers from those nations imposed their ways of life and legal systems on the Indigenous residents. In their effort to assimilate this population into Western European culture, tens of thousands of Indigenous children were sent to residential schools far away from their homes, and many of these students were emotionally, physically and sexually abused (see Chapter 4, this volume). Not only did placement in these schools disrupt the traditional family life of these peoples, but the trauma from these acts disrupted families for generations, and some former residents turned to substance abuse to self-medicate. Yet, these acts did not occur in isolation and Indigenous peoples were also disadvantaged by federal government policies that resulted in poverty and sanctions for carrying out their traditional ways of life, including practising their cultural and spiritual ceremonies. Taken together, these practices contribute to a greater Indigenous contact with the justice system today than non-Indigenous peoples, and ultimately the over-representation of Indigenous peoples in correctional populations. Different ethnic and racial minorities, such as African-Canadians and Chinese immigrants, also experienced patterns of discriminatory practices and racism, and this treatment has had long-term impacts on their descendants today.

Ideally, as mentioned at the beginning of this chapter, the CJS provides

Figure 13-7 Indigenous Adults Under Correctional Supervision by Province (2015/2016)

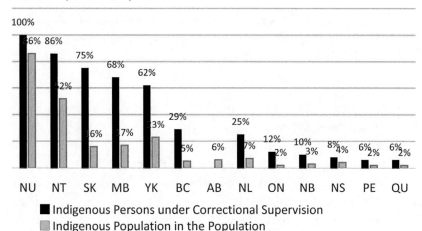

Sources: Reitano (2017) and Statistics Canada (2011)

formal social control when needed to augment informal social control, and this support helps protect everybody's safety and integrity. Unfortunately, the CJS and the laws that support it can contribute to social injustice. One commonly cited example of a discriminatory CJS practice is carding, where the police stop and interview suspicious people on the street. Certain groups, such as young African-Canadians in Toronto, were targeted in this approach and some reported being stopped and questioned dozens of times, which increased their mistrust in the police. While several restrictions have been placed on carding, it still remains a controversial practice. Examples such as carding show the need to critically evaluate and change practices, policies and laws where there is evidence of systematic racism.

Drug and Alcohol Use

Goldstein (1985) developed a model to explain the relationship between drugs and crime. Goldstein contends there are three drug-related pathways to criminal involvement:

1. The Psychopharmacological Pathway involves an individual ingesting a substance and committing crime because of the biological influence the drug has on a person's body. This can also include the psychobiological effects of withdrawing from a drug.
2. The Economic Compulsive Pathway involves an individual committing a violent or property crime in order to directly obtain drugs or to obtain money or property that can be used to purchase drugs.
3. The Systemic Pathway involves participating in the illicit economy to get drugs to clients. This category also includes participating in turf battles, which are often gang related, to secure places to distribute drugs.

A recent international meta-analysis of drug misuse studies found a strong relationship between drug use and criminality, with the probability of offending being "between 2.8 and 3.8 times greater for drug users than non-drug-users" (Bennett, Holloway and Farrington 2008: 117).

While President Trump in the United States has called for imposing the death penalty for drug trafficking (Zezima and Dawsey 2018), many countries have begun to move away from harsh punishments of drug-related criminal offences in favour of treating addictions and providing supports for individuals trying to desist from drug and alcohol abuse (Grant 2009). Problems with HIV and hepatitis transmissions between individuals who share needles, and deaths related to fentanyl, carfentanil and other synthetic opiates have led to many organizations to push for the adoption of practices related to the harm-reduction model. This model is outlined as such:

> "Harm reduction" refers to policies, programs and practices that aim primarily to reduce the adverse health, social and economic consequences of the use of legal and illegal psychoactive drugs without necessarily reducing drug consumption. Harm reduction benefits people who use drugs, their families and the community. (Harm Reduction International 2017: 1)

Some of the better known harm-reduction efforts in Canada include: safe injection sites in Vancouver and Toronto; needle-exchange programs throughout the country to reduce the transmission of communicable diseases (Ciccarone and Bourgois 2016); and the introduction of Drug Courts in larger cities, such as Toronto and Ottawa, to provide drug-involved court clients support in their efforts to reduce their drug use (Lyons 2013). Thus, while Canada and most developed nations have attempted to control the drug problem by reducing harm, the United States has harshly punished offenders and is now debating whether to execute drug dealers. This example shows how decisions about the best way to manage a social problem (drug addiction) that we have labelled as a crime can have a significant effect on all of society.

Past Victimization and Trauma

Research has long verified a relationship between victimization, particularly in the form of physical and sexual abuse, and later criminality (Widom 1989). Research suggests that witnessing violence can also contribute to socially harmful behaviour (Saunders 2003). Furthermore, criminal offending is also highly associated with victimization (Lauritsen and Laub 2007). Increasingly, there is a recognition that victimization is often a form of trauma and untreated trauma is associated with a host of negative outcomes. The American Psychological Association (2017) defines trauma "as an emotional response to a terrible event like an accident, rape, or natural disaster." Intergenerational trauma looks at how experiences of victimization and other traumas can be shared from one generation to the next. As noted above, residential schools in Canada did not just traumatize one generation; the experiences of traumatized parents and their children can continue to shape the lives of their children and grandchildren decades after the last residential school closed in 1996 (Menzies 2010).

When a crime occurs, there is not always agreement about why it happened or what to do with the offender. While some look strictly at the offender and claim that person should have known better, there are a growing number of scholars who believe that factors such as poverty and discrimination place some people at higher risk of involvement in crime. Altogether, by reviewing the correlates of crime, we find it is difficult to disentangle crime and the other social problems, and this results in some debate over the best way to manage the crime problem. Not surprisingly, these differences of opinions have resulted in the development of a number of different goals of the justice system.

GOALS OF THE CRIMINAL JUSTICE SYSTEM

The personnel in the CJS are tasked with providing formal social control to communities within their jurisdiction. The overarching goal of the CJS is reducing crime using formal social control. As such, the CJS focuses primarily on legal considerations — thereby embodying the notion of formal justice. Yet, each component of the system also remains concerned with substantive justice and ethical practice. In theory, the CJS provides an effective response to crime and disorder in society and is mandated to play a critical role in maintaining order. In practice, the operation of the CJS, while generally beneficial to society, is often problematic because the law focuses on individual criminal violations while largely ignoring poverty, inequality, racism, sexism, substance abuse and other social ills that contribute to the crime problem. Evidence of this can be seen in the recent Gerald Stanley and Robert Cormier trials where two white men were acquitted in murder trials for the deaths of Colten Boushie and Tina Fountaine, respectively. While many argue that the verdict was the end result of the application of formal justice, these cases were widely cited as lacking substantive justice.

One of the clearest articulations of the overarching goals of the

Canadian CJS can be found in the sentencing principles in section 718 of the *Criminal Code of Canada*. The preamble to this section states that public safety and maintaining a just, peaceful and safe society are the primary goals of the CJS. The use of proportionate punishment, where "punishment fits the crime," which generally relates to the severity of the offence, is argued to deter individuals (both those convicted and other members of society) from engaging in criminal behaviour. Deterrence assumes cost-benefit considerations where an individual weighs the rewards and possible costs before committing a crime. The principles further suggest that incapacitation (that is, incarceration) should only be used when necessary to ensure public safety. Programming within correctional institutions, as a means of rehabilitating offenders, should also be a consideration to provide offenders released back into the community with a greater opportunity for successful reintegration, as well as reduce the likelihood of recidivism. The principles also support the idea that harm experienced by victims (and the community in general) should be repaired. This may take the form of things such as restitution, making a payment to a person they victimized to compensate them for their losses, and/or community service, where the court requires someone to work a set number of hours to benefit the community, such as picking up trash alongside a highway. Finally, the sentence imposed by the court should make the offender aware of the harm they caused and attempts to create within them a sense of accountability so that they acknowledge what they have done and recognize that it is unacceptable behaviour.

Parts of the Criminal Justice System

To achieve these goals, the CJS is comprised of the police, the courts and corrections; each of these components are administered within a framework of laws, regulations and policies constructed by federal and provincial law-making bodies. It is described as a system because each of these parts plays an important role in responding to crime and officials very often work together. A person who has committed an offence will be subject to laws passed by a legislature or parliament that are enforced by a police officer or other official with the power to arrest or detain an individual (for example, conservation officers or a Canada Border Services Agency official). One common aspect of the officials working in the system is their use of discretion to determine which person(s) are warned

SECTION 718 OF THE *CRIMINAL CODE OF CANADA*

Purpose

718. The fundamental purpose of sentencing is to protect society and to contribute, along with crime prevention initiatives, to respect for the law and the maintenance of a just, peaceful and safe society by imposing just sanctions that have one or more of the following objectives:

(a) to denounce unlawful conduct and the harm done to victims or to the community that is caused by unlawful conduct;

(b) to deter the offender and other persons from committing offences;

(c) to separate offenders from society, where necessary;

(d) to assist in rehabilitating offenders;

(e) to provide reparations for harm done to victims or to the community; and

(f) to promote a sense of responsibility in offenders, and acknowledgement of the harm done to victims or to the community.

Fundamental Principle

718.1 A sentence must be proportionate to the gravity of the offence and the degree of responsibility of the offender.

R.S., 1985, c. 27 (1st Supp.), s. 156; 1995, c. 22, s. 6.)

or arrested, who will be charged or prosecuted and whether a prosecutor accepts a guilty plea in return for a reduced punishment. Discretion is also used by correctional officials in their determination of who will be placed in various rehabilitative programs and in higher levels of security, and those decisions may influence how long an offender stays behind bars. Altogether, the use of discretion at every decision point contributes to the filtering process of the criminal justice funnel described above.

The person may be charged and ordered to appear before a court of law. If found guilty and the crime is serious enough, they may serve time in a correctional facility or penitentiary. Correctional centers are operated by the provinces and hold persons awaiting a court date and offenders sentenced up to two years. Penitentiaries are federally run and hold offenders sentenced to two years or more. However, the descriptor "system" shouldn't assume the police, courts, and corrections are united in purpose and strategy, nor are their operations seamless and integrated. Often these bodies have different mandates, different strategies of responding to crime and different understandings of crime and priorities. Often, legislatures pass laws in the hope that people will be deterred from doing something because it has been labelled a "crime."

The Police (Law Enforcement)

The police are the most visible and regular point of contact between the criminal justice system and the public. Although members of the public often think of policing in terms of law enforcement, that only involves about one third of their workload. Police are also involved in:

- Maintaining public order and safety
- Crime prevention
- Responding to civic emergencies and events of natural and human cause
- Protecting people, especially vulnerable persons such as indigenous and trafficked females, and children vulnerable to abuse, sexual exploitation and bullying
- Supporting victims of crimes
- Communicating with the public (Canadian Association of Chiefs of Police 2016: 90)

Most calls to the police are to report acts that are not about criminal matters and are instead related to barking or loose dogs, noisy neighbours, people speeding through neighbourhoods, or drunken behaviour. Other calls have little to do with policing, such as disputes related to civil matters, such as a dispute between neighbours over who will pay repairs when one of their children damages the fence between the two yards. The police also carry out service-related duties, such as notifying the next of kin of an unexpected death. Robertson (2012: 351) describes the police as a social service agency that "responds to a variety of emergencies and all manner of personal crises, including crimes in progress, domestic disputes, disturbances, motor vehicle collisions, injuries from accidents, sudden deaths (including suicides), psychotic episodes of mental illness, and locating lost children and vulnerable adults."

CASE STUDY:
POLICE INTERACTION WITH MENTALLY ILL PERSONS

Beginning in the 1970s, the removal of persons with mental illness (PMI) from institutions as well as changes to legislation surrounding mental health led to a significant increase in the interactions between the police and PMIs, especially among homeless people (Cotton and Coleman 2010). These interactions generally fall into five categories:

1. apprehensions under the Mental Health Act;
2. arrests in and disturbances which the person turns out to appear mentally ill;
3. disturbances in which the individual appears to be mentally ill;
4. situations in which the PMI is the victim of crime;
5. social support and informal contacts by police. (Cotton and Coleman 2010: 303)

When combined, these interactions have resulted in a much greater likelihood that PMIs will interact with the police than the general population. Jim Chu — President of the Canadian Association of Chiefs of Police (CACP) — noted that "interacting with and managing people with mental illness is the 'number-one issue' facing police" (CACP and CMHC 2014: 9). Although most police — PMI interactions occur without issue, occasions have arisen where the interaction has resulted in their deaths, and Picard (2017) reports that between 2000 and 2017, Ontario police officers killed over forty PMI, including the highly publicized Sammy Yatim case. These tragic events have resulted in calls to action for something to be done to prevent future similar incidents.

In March of 2014, the CACP and the Mental Health Commission of Canada co-hosted a conference to discuss police-PMI interactions with a hope to produce better outcomes for everyone involved. Speaking on behalf of the CACP, Chief Chu stated that "police in Canada want education, training, and collaboration with community and mental health agencies to create strategies that focus on prevention and de-escalation instead of the use of force" (CACP and CMHC 2014: 9). The report published from the conference suggests that new models need to be developed that include risk assessment, the integration of information, addressing the social determinants associated with mental health, and effective crisis intervention processes collaboratively developed in processes inclusive of those with mental illness. Cotton and Coleman (2010) suggest that the most widely used model in Canada is the Mobile Crisis Team. These partnerships provide a team that includes police and a mental health professional who respond to calls involving a PMI.

A final universal issue that remains to be addressed in improving the outcomes for PMI coming into contact with police is reducing the social stigma attached to mental illness in the broader community, and thereby also within policing. Police leaders and mental health professionals have become directly engaged with each other in trying to address this pressing issue. The results of these collaborative efforts are beginning to yield positive results in jurisdictions across the country. As noted by Cotton and Coleman (2010: 312), "changes in our respective environments will in the future necessitate further changes." While much work has already been done, there is certainly more to do.

According to Statistics Canada (2017), there were 68,772 police officers in Canada or about two officers for every thousand residents. In Canada, there are federal, provincial and municipal police officers; about two thirds of them are employees of municipal governments. At the federal level, the RCMP police all provinces and territories and provide provincial and municipal services through contract in areas that do not have these services (Ruddell 2017). Ontario, Quebec and Newfoundland and Labrador have provincial police agencies. Municipal police departments, like the Regina Police Service and Service de Police de la Ville de Montréal, provide police services to most Canadian cities. In addition, there are about a dozen regional services such as the Durham Regional Police that police urban and rural areas (Burczyka 2013), and there are thirty-eight self-administered Indigenous police services (Public Safety Canada 2016).

The Courts (Adjudicating Offences)

In criminal matters, after an individual has been arrested or received a summons to appear in court the case proceeds to the judicial system. The courts provide another set of decision points where cases can be filtered from the criminal justice funnel:

> The courts main responsibility is administering justice, by ensuring that crimes are prosecuted fairly and in accordance with Canada's legal and constitutional structure. The courts are also responsible for rendering decisions regarding the culpability of those accused of committing a criminal offence, as well as determining an appropriate sentence should the accused plead or be found guilty. (Maxwell 2017: 3; Department of Justice Canada 2015a; Department of Justice Canada 2015b).

In Canada, criminal matters can be heard at four levels, including the provincial and territorial courts, the provincial and territorial superior courts, the provincial and territorial courts of appeals and the Supreme Court of Canada (Ruddell 2017). Provincial and territorial courts address most criminal matters, family law, youth justice and small claims. The provincial and territorial superior courts hear the most serious criminal matters and larger civil disputes. Once a case has been heard and decided on in either of these courts, either party may appeal the verdict and these cases are then decided on (if the court does not dismiss the appeal outright) by the provincial and territorial courts of appeals. The Supreme Court of Canada is the final judicial authority in Canada and can hear appeals from any of the lower courts. The Supreme Court of Canada usually hears less than one hundred cases a year, and these cases are hand-picked because they represent the national interest (Ruddell 2017). When the Supreme Court decides a case, all other courts must follow the precedent set by their decision.

As a case proceeds through the criminal courts, there are many decision points that may result in its removal from the criminal process, in it being moved to a diversion program or its transfer to an alternative dispute resolution process. In fact, as the criminal justice funnel implies, approximately one third of all cases are stayed or withdrawn (which means they discontinue prosecution) without a verdict being rendered (Maxwell 2017). At the preliminary inquiry, the Crown prosecutor must demonstrate there is enough evidence for a case to proceed to trial. At an arraignment, a judge reads the charges against the accused and the defendant must enter a plea of guilty or not guilty. If a defendant pleads not guilty, the defence and the Crown prosecutor may negotiate a plea bargain (for example, an agreement to plead guilty in exchange for a lesser sentence) and bring it to a judge any time before a trial concludes. Despite what we see on television, a trial is a relatively rare event and over 90 percent of criminal cases are resolved through pleas, although trials are often carried out for homicide and other serious offences. In some respects, whether a trial proceeds is related to one's ability to afford a lawyer, and those with the funds can fight relatively minor charges — such as impaired driving — that are too expensive for a minimum-wage earner.

Finally, a full criminal trial results in a verdict of either guilty (conviction) or not guilty (acquittal), at which point the defendant either proceeds to sentencing or is released. The judge, using section 718 of the *Criminal Code of Canada* as a guide, sentences a defendant for the crime. Sentences can range from an absolute discharge (which is a finding of guilt but no conviction is registered) to life in prison, depending on the seriousness of the offence. Both the Crown prosecutor and the defence can appeal the case if they believe there were procedural problems with the processing of the case, or if they believe the sentence was unjust. As legal aid offices do not typically provide counsel to represent appellants, access to these courts is limited to the rich, or individuals who represent themselves.

Corrections (Punishment and Rehabilitation)

Federal and provincial corrections have the dual task of both supervising law breakers and rehabilitating them. This can take place in the community (for example, while the offender is on probation) or in a correctional facility. This mandate is explicitly stated in the mission statement of Correctional Service Canada (CSC):

> The Correctional Service of Canada (CSC), as part of the criminal justice system and respecting the rule of law, contributes to public safety by actively encouraging and assisting offenders to become law-abiding citizens, while exercising reasonable, safe, secure, and humane control. (CSC 2012)

On any given day in 2015/2016, there were about forty thousand adults incarcerated in federal and provincial/territorial correctional facilities, and another 104,000 serving sentences in the community (Reitano 2017: 12). Provincial authorities also held about one thousand youth in custody facilities and 7,500 were supervised in the community (Malakieh 2017). There are two adult correctional systems in Canada. Adults who are arrested, are awaiting a court date, have sentences under two years or are awaiting a transfer to federal corrections are held in facilities operated by provincial governments. These facilities go by different names. In provinces with smaller populations, such as Saskatchewan, all adult facilities are called provincial correctional centres, and there are three large facilities for males in Prince Albert, Saskatoon and Regina, and two facilities for women: the Pine Grove Centre in Prince Albert and the White Birch remand unit in Regina. Offenders who have been convicted of less serious offences or who are close to the end of their sentences are sometimes placed in community training residences, which are very low-security facilities and most of the residents go to work or school during the day.

Offenders sentenced to two years or longer are held in facilities operated by the csc. In 2015/2016, the federal prison system held just under fifteen thousand offenders in fifty-seven facilities across Canada. These institutions varied in size from treatment centres, such as the Shepody Healing Centre in Dorchester, New Brunswick that has a capacity of fifty inmates, to penitentiaries that hold about five hundred prisoners. Security in these facilities ranged from minimum, which may have inmates living in dorm-like accommodations and may only have a four-foot fence around the perimeter, to maximum, where offenders live in hardened cells and their movements are strictly controlled. Several maximum-security facilities also have special handling units (shu) that hold the most difficult-to-manage or dangerous prisoners in very strict conditions (where offenders are locked in their cells for twenty-three hours a day and have little interaction with other prisoners, for example). Segregating or isolating prisoners has become a very contentious issue and in 2018 the B.C. Supreme Court found a prisoner's indefinite placement in isolation was unconstitutional because it placed them at risk of serious psychological harm (Proctor 2018).

Most federal offenders are sentenced to five years in prison or less, so there is an emphasis on preparing them, and all other prisoners, for their safe return to the community. In order to more easily reintegrate offenders from the prisons to the community, the csc operates seventeen

CASE STUDY:
THE ROLE OF THE CORRECTIONAL INVESTIGATOR

In the Canadian federal correctional system, an independent oversight body was created within the Corrections and Conditional Release Act in 1992 to ensure that federal correctional facilities are operating in a manner consistent with the principles of the *Canadian Charter of Rights and Freedoms.* The Correctional Investigator's mandate is to investigate complaints received in an impartial manner and "make recommendations to ensure safe, lawful and humane correctional practice" (Correctional Investigator 2016: 3). As a means for "pursuing justice," this office provides an annual report to the Canadian government that addresses many of the issues we are concerned with (formal, substantive and ethical practice). In the latest report, the Office of the Correctional Investigator highlighted several issues that warrant continued efforts in seeking to provide justice to those convicted of a crime in Canada. These include:

- An unabated increase in the number of Indigenous people behind bars, a rate now surpassing 25% of the total federal incarcerated population.
- The reliance on and escalating number of use of force incidents involving inflammatory agents.
- The demonstrated but unfulfilled need for more vocational skills training programs in corrections.
- Continuing decline in the quality and rigour of case management practices.
- Inadequate progress in preventing deaths in custody.
- Alternative service delivery arrangements for significantly mentally ill offenders. (Correctional Investigator 2016: 3).

The Correctional Investigator has no authority in provincial or territorial corrections. Provincial inmates can access investigators from Ombudsmen offices, who are authorized to advocate on their behalf.

Correctional centres and prisons operate behind walls and fences and few members of the public are aware of what happens inside these environments. The existence of the Correctional Investigator and the provincial Ombudsmen is important as it provides a voice to those who are otherwise powerless. Because these inmates can access people who will advocate on their behalf, they can learn how to address violations of their rights or poor treatment in a way that reduces conflict with the correctional staff. Moreover, since the Correctional Investigator or Ombudsman responds to cases from the entire federal or provincial justice systems, they may be able to identify issues and trends that are systemic, rather than the problems of one individual.

Community Correctional Centres (CCC) that allow inmates to enter the community in a structured manner. In communities not served by these centres, the CSC contracts with non-government organizations, such as the Salvation Army, to house these offenders. People living in these placements are often on day parole, which is granted by the Parole Board of Canada. Day parole allows people to attend school, treatment or work during the day and return to the CCC in the evening. A review of the parole statistics shows that women offenders often serve a shorter proportion of their sentence prior to their first parole than male offenders. By contrast, Indigenous prisoners generally serve longer sentences prior to their first parole, but two reasons for that outcome may be due to having longer criminal histories and a higher likelihood of being convicted of committing violent offences than non-Indigenous inmates (Public Safety Canada 2017).

THE BOTTOM LINE: CRIME, JUSTICE AND THE CJS IN CANADA

The CJS is comprised of three major organizations: the police, the courts and corrections. Ideally, these organizations all cooperate to protect the public by safeguarding constitutional protections, human rights and applying policies and practices in a just and fair manner for all Canadians. In providing formal social control for society, criminal justice officials routinely interact with individuals in stressful situations and negotiate conflict, aid victims and the public and provide emergency assistance to those in need of help. Long-entrenched social problems, such as poverty, inequality, sexism, racism and colonialism, form the backdrop for many of these interactions. Unfortunately, doing justice in the cjs often fails to address the social problems that form the root causes of crime, and at times may even contribute to social injustice, especially if systemic issues go unchecked. This is an enduring challenge — how can communities, including criminal justice organizations, best cooperate to create a more just society that alleviates social problems and injustices and to effectively manage outcomes after crimes occur? Education, training and dialogue are all important in realizing ethical practice in criminal justice.

DISCUSSION QUESTIONS

1. Of the goals of the cjs, which one do you feel is most important? What factors in your upbringing would make you choose that goal?
2. What are the strengths and weaknesses of asking people about their involvement in crime rather than relying on crimes reported to the police?
3. Describe the "dark figure" of crime and why this information is important in understanding the extent of crime in Canada. How can we estimate the number of crimes not reported to the police?
4. What is the importance of discretion in the operations of the police, courts and corrections, and how this does, or does not, result in the differential treatment of different ethnic or racial minority groups?
5. What are some reasons for the overrepresentation of Indigenous peoples in provincial/territorial and federal corrections?
6. Why is there so little priority placed on investigating and prosecuting cases of organizational crime, such as companies profiting by illegally pricing bread for fourteen years?
7. Civic bylaws in many communities prohibit sitting or sleeping on sidewalks, which directly target the homeless, and result in fines they can seldom pay. Why do we criminalize these acts? What are the alternatives?
8. While the United States has chosen to harshly punish drug offenders and traffickers, Canadians have adopted a harm reduction approach. What are the strengths and weaknesses of these two approaches?
9. What are the main differences between informal and formal social control? Name some examples of how you have used informal social control to regulate the behaviour of others.

GLOSSARY

Aging out: Involvement in crime tends to increase throughout the adolescent years and then decline as one ages.

Canadian Centre for Justice Statistics: An organization operated by Statistics Canada that produces reports on crime, victimization, offenders and the operations of the justice system.

Correlates of crime: Social factors such as poverty, unemployment, racism or discrimination that are often intertwined with crime.

Crime Severity Index (CSI): An indicator of the volume and seriousness of crimes reported to the police.

Criminal justice funnel: The process by which crimes reported to the police are filtered by the police and courts so that of the many crimes reported to the police, relatively few offenders are incarcerated.

Dark figure of crime: The difference between the amount of crime occurring and what is reported to the police.

Formal social control: The actions of the police and other government officials that make us follow the law.

Informal social control: The informal actions of one's family members, friends and neighbours that make us abide by social expectations.

UCR Crime Rate: The number of offences reported to the police per 100,000 residents

Uniform Crime Reporting Survey: The amount of crime reported to the police, which is published in annual reports by the Canadian Centre for Justice Statistics.

White-collar crime: Non-violent crimes committed for monetary gain and include acts of corruption, fraud and theft.

REFERENCES

Allen, M. 2016. "Police-Reported Crime Statistics in Canada, 2015." Ottawa: Canadian Centre for Justice Statistics. <http://www.statcan.gc.ca/pub/85-002-x/2016001/article/14642-eng.pdf>.

American Psychological Association. 2017. "Trauma." <American Psychological Association: http://www.apa.org/topics/trauma/>.

Bellemare, A. 2018. "Stacks of Tickets Are 'Pyschological Weight' on Marginalized Itinerants, Advocates Say." <http://www.cbc.ca/news/canada/montreal/homeless-overticketed-montreal-police-1.4556351>.

Bennett, T., K. Holloway and D. Farrington. 2008. "The Statistical Association Between Drug Misuse and Crime: A Meta-Analysis." *Aggression and Violent Behavior,* 13: 107–118.

Berg, M., and J. Lauritsen. 2016. "Telling a Similar Story Twice? NCVS/UCR Convergence in Serious Violent Crime Rates in Rural, Suburban, and Urban Places (1973–2010)." *Journal of Quantitative Criminology,* 32, 1: 61–87. doi:10.1007/s10940-015-9254-9.

Blumer, H. 1969. *Symbolic Interactionism: Genesis, Varieties, and Criticism.* Englewood Cliffs: Prentice-Hall.

Boyce, J. 2015. "Police-Reported Crime Statistics in Canada, 2014." Ottawa: Canadian Centre for Justice Statistics. <http://www.statcan.gc.ca/pub/85-002-x/2015001/article/14211-eng.pdf>.

Boyce, J., A. Cotter and S. Perreault. 2014. *Police-Reported Crime Statistics in Canada, 2013.* Ottawa: Canadian Centre for Justice Statistics.

Brown, S.E., F.-A. Esbensen and G. Geis. 2013. *Criminology: Explaining Crime and Its Context,* eighth ed. Waltham: Anderson Publishing.

Burczycka, M. 2013. *Police Resources in Canada, 2012.* Ottawa, ON: Canadian Centre for Justice Statistics.

CACP and CMHC. 2014. "Balancing Individual Safety, Community Safety, and Quality of Life: A Conference to Improve Interactions between Police and People with Mental Illness." Ottawa: Canadian Association of Chiefs of Police and Canadian Mental Health Commission.

Canadian Association of Chiefs of Police. 2016. *CACP Bulletin 2015 Annual Review.* Smith Falls, ON: iMedia Northside.

Canadian Centre for Justice Statistics. 2009. *Measuring Crime in Canada: Introducing the Crime Severity Index and Improvements to the Uniform Crime Reporting Survey.* Minister of Industry. Ottawa: Statistics Canada. <http://www.statcan.gc.ca/pub/85-004-x/85-004-x2009001-eng.htm?contentType=application%2Fpdf>.

Ciccarone, D., and P. Bourgois. 2016. "Injecting Drugs in Tight Spaces: HIV, Cocaine and Collinearity in the Downtown Eastside, Vancouver, Canada." *International Journal of Drug Policy,* 33: 36–43. doi:10.1016/j.drugpo.2016.02.028.

Comack, E., C. Fabre and S. Burgher. 2015. *The Impact of the Harper Government's "Tough on Crime Agenda."* Winnipeg, MB: Canadian Centre for Policy Alternatives.

Cooley, C. 1902. *Human Nature and the Social Order.* New York: Scribner's.

Correctional Investigator. 2016) *Annual Report of the Office of the Correctional Investigator: 2015–2016.* Ottawa: The Correctional Investigator.

Correctional Service Canada. 2012. "CSC Values Statement." <http://www.csc-scc.gc.ca/about-us/006-0026-eng.shtml>.

Cotter, A. 2015. *Public Confidence in Canadian Institutions.* Ottawa, ON: Statistics Canada.

Cotton, D., and T.G. Coleman. 2010. "Canadian Police Agencies and Their Interactions with Persons with a Mental Illness: A Systems Approach." *Police Practice and Research:* 301–314. doi:10.1080/15614261003701665.

Department of Justice Canada. 2015a. *Canada's Court System.* Ottawa:

Department of Justice Canada. <http://www.justice.gc.ca/eng/csj-sjc/ccs-ajc/pdf/courten.pdf>.

___. 2015b. *Canada's System of Justice.* Ottawa: Department of Justice Canada. <http://www.justice.gc.ca/eng/csj-sjc/just/img/courten.pdf>.

Drakulich, K.M., and R.D. Crutchfield. 2013. "The Role of Perception of the Police in Informal Social Control: Implications for the Racial Stratification of Crime and Control." *Social Problems*, 60, 3 (August): 383–407. doi:10.1525/sp.2013.60.3.383.

Federal Bureau of Investigation: Uniform Crime Reports. 2016. *2015: Crime in the United States.* Washington, DC: U.S. Department of Justice. <https://ucr.fbi.gov/crime-in-the-u.s/2015/crime-in-the-u.s.-2015/tables/table-1>.

Goldstein, P. 1985. "The Drugs/Violence Nexus: A Tripartite Conceptual Framework." *Journal of Drug Issues*, 15: 493–506.

Grant, J. 2009. "A Profile of Substance Abuse, Gender, Crime, and Drug Policy in the United States and Canada." *Journal of Offender Rehabilitation*, 48: 654–668. doi:10.1080/10509670903287667.

Harm Reduction International. 2017. *What Is Harm Reduction? A Position Statement from Harm Reduction International.* <https://www.hri.global/what-is-harm-reduction>.

Hobbes, T. 1985. *Leviathan.* (C. Macpherson, ed.) London: Penguin Books.

Howlett, K., and J. Taber. 2016. "Naloxone to Be Immediately Distributed to Released Inmates in Ontario." *Globe and Mail*, July 4. <https://www.theglobeandmail.com/news/national/naloxone-to-be-immediately-distributed-to-released-inmates-in-ontario/article30750481/>.

Human Rights Watch. 2014. *World Report 2014: United Arab Emirates.* New York: Human Rights Watch. <https://www.hrw.org/world-report/2014/country-chapters/united-arab-emirates>.

Hurlbert, M. 2011. *Pursuing Justice: An Introduction to Justice Studies.* Winnepeg: Fernwood Publishing.

Jackson, M. 1999. "Canadian Aboriginal Women and Their 'Criminality': The Cycle of Violence in the Context of Difference." *Australian and New Zealand Journal of Criminology*, 32, 2: 197–208.

Janowitz, M. 1975. "Sociological Theory and Social Control." *American Journal of Sociology*, 81, 1: 82–108. <http://www.jstor.org/stable/2777055>.

Keighley, K. 2017) *Police-Reported Crime Statistics in Canada, 2016.* Ottawa: Statistics Canada. <http://www.statcan.gc.ca/pub/85-002-x/2017001/article/54842-eng.pdf>.

Lanier, M.M., S. Henry and D.J. Anastasia. 2015. *Essential Criminology,* fourth ed. Boulder: Westview Press.

Lauritsen, J., and J.H. Laub. 2007. "Understanding the Link Between Victimization and Offending: New Reflections on an Old Idea." In M. Hough, and M. Maxfield, *Surveying Crime in the 21st Century.* Monsey, NY: Willow Tree Press.

Lemert, E. 1951. *Social Pathology.* New York: McGraw-Hill.

Linden, R. 2016. *Criminology: A Canadian Perspective.* Toronto: Nelson Education.

Locke, J. 2003. *Two Treatises of Government and A Letter Concerning Toleration.* (I. Shapiro, Ed.) New Haven: Yale University Press.

Lyons, T. 2013. "Judges as Therapists and Therapists as Judges: The Collision of the Judicial and Therapeutic Roles in Drug Treatment Courts." *Contemporary Justice Review*, 16, 4: 412–424. doi:10.1080/10282580.2013.857076.

Malakieh, J. 2017. "Youth Correctional Statistics in Canada, 2015/2016." *Juristat.* <www150.statcan.gc.ca/n1/pub/85-002-x/2017001/article/14702-eng.htm>.

Markusoff, J. 2018. "Loblaws' Price-Fixing May Have Cost You at Least $400." *Macleans.* <http://www.macleans.ca/economy/economicanalysis/14-years-of-loblaws-bread-price-fixing-may-have-cost-you-at-least-400/>.

Maxwell, A. 2017) *Adult Criminal Court Statistics in Canada, 2014/2015.* Canadian Centre for Justice Statistics. Ottawa: Statistics Canada. <http://www.statcan.gc.ca/pub/85-002-x/2017001/article/14699-eng.pdf>.

Mead, G. 1934. *Mind, Self, and Society from the Standpoint of a Social Behaviorist.* Chicago: University of Chicago Press.

Meares, T.L., and J. Fagan. 2008. "Punishment, Deterrence and Social Control: The Paradox of Punishment in Minority Communities." *Ohio State Journal of Criminal Law*, 6: 173–228.

Menzies, P. 2010. "Intergenerational Trauma from a Mental Health Perspective." *Native Social Work Journal*, 7: 63–85.

Office of National Statistics. 2017. "Crime in England and Wales: Year Ending Mar 2017." London: Office for National Statistics. <https://www.ons.gov.uk/peoplepopulationandcommunity/crimeandjustice/bulletins/crimeinenglandandwales/yearendingmar2017#what-is-happening-to-trends-in-crime>.

Perreault, S. 2015. "Criminal Victimization in Canada, 2014." Ottawa: Canadian Centre for Justice Statistics. <http://www.statcan.gc.ca/pub/85-002-x/2015001/article/14241/tbl/tbl09-eng.htm>.

Picard, A. 2017. "Mentally Ill People Need To Be Calmed Down, Not Shot." *Globe and Mail*, August 21. <https://www.theglobeandmail.com/opinion/mentally-ill-people-need-to-be-calmed-down-not-shot/article36042139/>.

Pollock, J. 2012. *Ethical Dilemmas and Decisions in Criminal Justice.* Belmont, CA: Wadsworth.

Prober, J. 1970. "The Criminal Law Amendment Act 1968–69 (Canada)." *The British Journal of Criminology*, 10, 2: 180–183. <http://www.jstor.org/stable/23636064>.

Proctor, J. 2018. "Indefinite Solitary Confinement in Canadian Prisons Ruled Unconstitutional by B.C. Court." *CBC News.* <http://www.cbc.ca/news/canada/british-columbia/charter-solitary-confinement-bc-ruling-1.4491526>.

Public Safety Canada. 2016. *Internal FNPP Summary Data from Public Safety Canada.* Ottawa: Public Safety Canada.

____. 2017. *Corrections and Conditional Release Statistical Overview.* Ottawa:

Public Safety Canada.

Public Safety Canada Portfolio Corrections Statistics Committee. 2016. *Corrections and Conditional Release Statistical Overview: 2015.* Public Safety Canada. Ottawa: Public Works and Government Services Canada. <https://www.publicsafety.gc.ca/cnt/rsrcs/pblctns/ccrso-2015/ccrso-2015-en.pdf>.

Razack, S.H. 2002. "Gendered Racial Violence and Spatialized Justice: The Murder of Pamela George." In S.H. Razack, *Race, Space, and the Law.* Toronto: Between the Lines.

Regina Leader-Post. 2015. "19 Years Ago, Pamela George's Killers Were Convicted of Manslaughter." Regina, SK, December 21. <http://leaderpost.com/storyline/19-years-ago-pamela-georges-killers-were-charged-with-manslaughter>.

Regina Police Service. 2018. "Community Crime Map." <http://reginapolice.ca/resources/crime/crime-statistics/crime-map/>.

Reiman, J. 1998. *The Rich Get Richer and the Poor Get Prison,* fifth ed. Boston: Allyn and Bacon.

Reiman, J., and P. Leighton. 2017. *The Rich Get Richer and the Poor Get Prison: Ideology, Class and Criminal Justice,* tenth ed. Oxon, UK: Routledge.

Reitano, J. 2017. *Adult Correctional Statistics in Canada, 2015/2016.* Canadian Centre for Justice Statistics, Juristat. Ottawa: Statistics Canada.

Robertson, N. 2012. "Policing: Fundamental Principles in a Canadian Context." *Canadian Public Administration,* 55, 3: 343–363.

Rousseau, J.-J. 1987. *The Basic Political Writings.* (D.A. Cress, Trans.) Cambridge: Hackett Publishing Company.

Rowe, D. 2001. "Update on the Pamela Jean George Case." *Jurisfemme Publications,* 20, 1 (Winter). <http://www.nawl.ca/en/jurisfemme/entry/update-on-the-pamela-jean-george-case>.

Royal Canadian Mounted Police. 2015. "Missing and Murdered Aboriginal Women." Ottawa, ON: Author.

Royal Commission on Aboriginal Peoples. 1996. "Chapter 9: The Indian Act, 1." *Report of the Royal Commission on Aborginal Peoples: Looking Forward, Looking Back.*

Ruddell, R. 2017. *Exploring Criminal Justice in Canada.* Don Mills, ON: Oxford University Press.

Saunders, B.E. 2003. "Understanding Children Exposed to Violence: Toward an Integration of Overlapping Fields." *Journal of Interpersonal Violence,* 18, 4: 356–376.

Schulenberg, J.L. 2010. "Patterns in Police Decision-Making with Youth: An Application of Black's Theory of Law." *Crime Law and Social Change,* 53: 109–129. doi:10.1007/s10611-009-9210-4.

Siegel, L.J., and C. McCormick. 2016. *Criminology in Canada: Theories, Patterns, and Typologies.* Toronto: Nelson Education.

Simon, D.R. 2011. *Elite Deviance.* New York: Pearson.

Skogan, W.G. 1975. "Measurement Problems in Official and Survey Crime Rates."

Journal of Criminal Justice, 3: 17–32.

Statistics Canada. 2011. "Aboriginal Peoples in Canada: First Nations People, Metis and Inuit." Ottawa. <http://www12.statcan.gc.ca/nhs-enm/2011/as-sa/99-011-x/99-011-x2011001-eng.pdf>.

___. 2017. "Police Officers, by Province and Territory." March 29. <http://www.statcan.gc.ca/tables-tableaux/sum-som/l01/cst01/legal05a-eng.htm>.

Surette, R. 2015. *Media, Crime, Criminal Justice: Images, Realities, and Policies*, fifth ed. Stamford, CT: Cengage-Learning.

Sutherland, E. 1949. *White Collar Crime*. New York: Dryden.

Tarling, R., and K. Morris. 2010. "Reporting Crime to the Police." *British Journal of Criminology*: 474–490.

Tonry, M. 1997. "Ethnicity, Crime, and Immigration." *Crime and Justice*, 21: 1–29.

Truth and Reconciliation Commission of Canada. 2015. *Truth and Reconciliation Commission of Canada: Calls to Action*. Winnipeg. <http://nctr.ca/assets/reports/Calls_to_Action_English2.pdf>.

Van Ness, D., and K.H. Strong. 2015. *Restoring Justice: An Introduction to Restorative Justice*. New York: Routledge.

Widom, C. 1989. "Child Abuse, Neglect, and Violent Criminal Behavior." *Criminology*, 27, 2: 251–271.

Zezima, K., and J. Dawsey. 2018. "Trump Administration Studies Seeking the Death Penalty for Drug Dealers." *Washington Post*. <https://www.washingtonpost.com/national/trump-administration-studying-possibility-of-seeking-death-penalty-for-drug-dealers/2018/03/09/4d9cc994-23c3-11e8-94da-ebf9d112159c_story.html?utm_term=.397f93847eeb>.

14

RESTORATIVE JUSTICE

Margot A. Hurlbert,
Hirsch Greenberg
and Nicholas A. Jones

OBJECTIVES

At the end of this chapter, you will be able to:

- Define restorative justice

- Understand the basic restorative justice skills for resolving conflict constructively

- Understand the application of restorative justice in the various contexts including the environment, school system, criminal justice system, and Indigenous communities

- Theorize about restorative justice in society

- Explore the limitations and strengths of restorative justice

CONFLICT

It's natural that conflict occurs when people live together — their different viewpoints, needs, stresses, and challenges can clash, resulting in disagreements or problematic situations (Hulsman 1986: 66; Pali and Pelikan 2014). Solving problematic situations or conflicts — restoring justice — has been practised in some form by different societies in different eras; societal interventions included blood revenge, retribution, ritual satisfaction or restoration (Weitekamp and Kerner 2002). With the emergence of penal law in the thirteenth century, the state took over the resolution of conflicts. It was during this time that a professional class of conflict resolvers — lawyers, police and judges — emerged (Christie 1977; Weitekamp and Kerner 2002).

Conflict and the Professional Class

People have come to rely on conflict-resolution professionals to solve their conflicts. Worse yet, the professional conflict resolvers have developed areas of exclusivity that prevent people from solving their own conflicts and ensure that conflict resolvers get highly paid for their specialized expertise; only lawyers certified by a law society can practice law, and rules around certification are strict, generally excluding many trained in law in other countries. For instance, an agreement to solve a conflict between two spouses is ineffective unless lawyers sign off on it. The profession excludes others from resolving family conflict and even limits people from formally resolving their own conflict. In light of the fact that people seem to have given up conflict rights to lawyers, courts, correctional institutions and police (Christie 1977), conflict itself can be considered an asset, or something off of which to make money. Instead of solving conflicts directly themselves, people delegate their conflict to these institutions. This chapter explores the line distinguishing when people should resolve their own conflict, and when it is more appropriately handled by state institutions.

Restorative justice is about reclaiming conflict, not sitting on the sidelines and delegating its resolution to professional conflict resolvers. Many conflicts are resolved every day without the use of professional conflict resolvers, so in reality people are restorative-justice practitioners; increasing the number and scope of these personal conflict resolution processes is promoting and practising a framework of restorative justice.

DEFINING RESTORATIVE JUSTICE

This chapter defines restorative justice and provides contemporary illustrations of it. First, we review a narrow definition of restorative justice emerging from the criminal justice system and then we introduce a broader definition of restorative justice encompassing social justice. Restorative justice will be illustrated in the environmental context of water, within the elementary school system and within the criminal justice system (CJS). Indigenous communities in Canada have solved conflict well before the arrival of European settlers' legal approach; several contemporary Indigenous justice practices are discussed.

The practices and approaches of this chapter are the culmination of the pursuit of justice. Restorative justice brings many aspects of justice together. In fact, if practised and implemented correctly, restorative justice responds to the central question: what is justice? It is the restoration of relationships during and after conflict, keeping in mind that conflict relationships are never brought back to an "original" position, rather relationships are re-established. Restorative justice embraces all three thematic frames of justice. It has aspects of procedural justice, using process or formal justice in its application (for example, victim-offender mediations); it has aspects of distributive or substantive justice whereby participants, including victims, have an opportunity to express themselves and their needs; and lastly, if practised properly, it is informed and constituted by an ethical practice.

The term "restorative justice" emerged in Canada in the 1980s to describe the type of justice achieved by a new criminal justice practice of victim and offender mediations. In 1974 the Mennonite Central Committee of Kitchener-Waterloo introduced victim and offender mediation in the early stages of the court process (Weitekamp and Kerner 2002) and was embraced Canada-wide in 1988 (Daubney 1988). Because of this initial criminal justice application, restorative justice is often defined within a narrow criminal context as:

> a process whereby all the parties with a stake in a particular offence come together to resolve collectively how to deal with the aftermath of the offence and its implications for the future. (Marshall 1999)

The weakness of this definition lies in the use of the word "offence," which limits the scope and practice of restorative justice to those acts that have been determined in a society to be a criminal offence — regardless of whether they create interpersonal conflict or even not (for example, loitering in a park is criminalized, even though it doesn't cause conflict). This definition does not critically examine what is an "offence." It leaves the practice of restorative justice as an appendage of the CJS, failing to address structural issues and recognizing social problems, and problems of wealth distribution noted in preceding chapters.

Restorative justice is related to a broader application of justice than simply what happens in the CJS. Sometimes the term is used interchangeably with community justice, transformative justice, peacemaking or collaborative problem solving. But even within its broader context, some, like George Pavlich (2005), have pointed out that restorative justice simply replaces a distant government or judge deciding the outcome of a conflict with a local community response. In other words, instead of a judge ordering a convicted person to perform community service, a local group of people orders that community service. Pavlich argues that restorative justice operates as corrective justice within the local criminal context rather than on the national or global political scale.

In this chapter, we propose a broader definition of restorative justice that encompasses aspects of achieving social justice and ensures that the outcome of restorative justice isn't simply replacing a judge with a community group. In this broader definition, restorative justice has four pillars and requires each to be present:

1. The Embrace of Conflict: Restorative justice entails embracing conflict or problematic situations and solving conflict without delegating the task to professionals: lawyers, government and the police.
2. The Recognition of Social Problems: Restorative justice requires the recognition of social problems inherent in individual conflicts. Conflict is viewed both as an interpersonal problem and as an outcome of broader social dynamics.
3. The Experience of Agency: Restorative justice requires individuals in conflict to actively participate in its resolution.
4. The Ethical Practice of Leximin: Restorative justice incorporates an ethic of doing no harm and protecting the most powerless

and vulnerable in the community in order to create strong and supporting relationships with the least intrusive intervention available.

These pillars of restorative justice centre an approach in which conflicts do not simply devolve into a fragmented, limiting, individualized blaming approach to dealing with conflict. They are informed by an ethical practice, and they are grounded in a critical social analysis that recognizes the role of social problems in interpersonal conflicts. How this definition is applied and practised is illustrated in this chapter's section on restorative justice applications.

In Canada, Pavlich's criticism often doesn't apply. Practised in a local context, restorative justice can support Indigenous communities from being subsumed within the larger Canadian legal-political context. In this way, restorative justice can promote and protect self-determination for Indigenous communities (this example will be discussed in more detail later).

THE BASICS OF RESTORATIVE JUSTICE PRACTICE

Most relationships inevitably face conflict. The core principle of restorative justice is about developing and supporting relationships that are open and honest, communicative and empathetic. The basics of restorative justice practice center on constructive conflict resolution.

It is important to recognize that often conflict can have some positive results. For instance, handled effectively, conflict can improve communication when people express their feelings and wishes as a result of a disagreement or a harmful action. Conflict can also yield positive social change on a societal level. Think of the civil rights movement. In the 1950s and 1960s, African Americans and their supporters organized on a massive scale to resist the racism they faced from white Americans and the state. This societal conflict resulted in the changing of societal norms and the Jim Crow laws that had prohibited Black people from eating in certain establishments, sitting in certain areas of the bus and swimming in certain public swimming pools. Since the 1960s, many of the laws that formally discriminated against Black people in the U.S. have been rectified as people sought to resolve these civil rights conflict. Today, activists

. seek to address present, urgent, but subtle practices of discrimination.

If practised and applied as a social justice project, utilizing all pillars of the broad definition of restorative justice embracing social justice, social problems can be addressed, and positive social change effected.

ADVERSARIAL VERSUS COLLABORATIVE PROBLEM SOLVING

While the adversarial legal system sets people against each other so that there is always a winner and a loser in a conflict, conflicts can also be resolved collaboratively or non-confrontationally. In an adversarial structure, it is almost inevitable that winning will be seen as the most important thing, regardless of the future impact. Those who embrace this approach believe that a conflict is over when they have doled out the punishment. In many disagreements we have with people (ranging from why a project wasn't completed on time to who was responsible for a fight) we point a finger at those at fault, and conversely those we have labelled at fault are pointing a finger at us, or another.

Collaborative problem solvers, on the other hand, espouse the view that a dispute is not won if one party believes they have lost. People and their relationships are critical and even when one doesn't agree with the other party, understanding the interests and views of others is required. Power and coercion are not substitutions for thought and understanding; this model pays careful attention to the dynamics of power in a relationship. Through this comprehensive understanding, often a dispute can be resolved constructively by achieving a solution that meets the needs and interests of the parties involved. Here, the explanation driving the conflict or the resolution of a fight is viewed by everyone in relation to their shared involvement.

People have differing needs and interests depending on their values, material conditions and personal experiences of oppression or privilege. These needs and interests can be thought of as substantive (money, quantity of time and resources), procedural (timeline of meetings and discussions) and emotional and/or psychological. The most powerful psychological needs include security, economic well-being, a sense of belonging, recognition and control over one's life (Raiffa 1982: 126–132; Strang 2002; Waller 2011). Often, adversarial problem solvers focus on substantive needs such as money; collaborative problem solvers are cognizant of all three types of needs. Many problem-solving processes fail because they do not deal with the procedural issues (that is, appropriate timing of these discussions to correspond with a person's healing or addressing any power imbalances) or the psychological interests of parties (that is, receiving a genuine apology that recognizes the harm that was caused).

Given that relationships and conflict within the workplace are a reality, collaborative problem solving has personal implications and a potentially broad application in one's career. Many professions are directly involved in resolving conflict and apply these principles in their work every day; examples include teachers resolving disagreements amongst students, managers resolving disputes with or between employees and restaurant workers responding to dissatisfied customers. Many disciplines would benefit from knowledge of the restorative justice movement.

Conversely, many academic disciplines have much to offer to the practice of restorative justice. Exploring and explaining how people think, behave, feel and physically respond to others and the world around them are some of the subjects addressed by psychologists, sociologists, anthropologists and professionals in the medical sciences, for instance. The contributions of these disciplines are important to restorative justice practice.

VALUES

Practising restorative justice involves recognizing and acknowledging particular values in resolving conflict. The values we bring to the table include the influences of our families, friends, schools and cultural and religious affiliations on our beliefs and our moral sense of right and wrong. These values have important implications for the choices restorative practitioners make in helping others to resolve conflict constructively; the values determine how a person currently views a conflict and what the practitioner will have to address in order to help the party view the conflict differently. The practitioner must work from the value set of those involved in the conflict rather than his or her own value biases. While the practitioners' values inform a moral sense of justice, the parties involved must agree on the right path forward. Recognizing peoples' different values is a critical aspect the practitioner must be mindful of when intervening.

Consider the relationship principles on the table below, which reflect different values people may have and corresponding implications for practice.

Table 14-1 Relationship Building

Relationship Principle	Implications for Practice
Our realties are separate	By presenting their perspectives, participants begin the process of understanding each other's point of view.
Everybody has different pictures	While participants may engage with each other in a common process, the expected outcomes/pictures may be different for each.
We try to understand the other person's view of the world	Participation is not predicated on the assumption that participants must see events in the same way. It is predicated on the assumption of respect for each other's point of view and acceptance that some level of harm resulted.
All behaviour is purposeful	For example, while crime behaviour is a negative social norm, for the perpetrator involved it has purpose or reward (such as fun or money).
I can't control others	Victims, in part, want to hear the offender's point of view, why he/she committed the crime and to explain the harm that resulted. That is, why did the offender make the choices he or she did?
One can only control oneself	Relationships should not be based on the assumption, "If you do what I want, I will forgive you." Relationships must be constructed in such a way that the future of the victim-offender relationship will result in respect, dignity and acceptance of each other as a member of the human community. This may or may not entail, jail sentences, community work and so on.
Collaboration and consensus create new options	Successful relationships evolve when the participants agree that overcoming problems together can be reached through consensus rather than coercion, punishment or threats.
Unlimited resources	Outcomes are based on the creativity and resourcefulness of those involved rather than looking at external resources (such as police or lawyers) for a *saviour*.
Maximum degrees of freedom	Flexibility to create new forms of relationships are essential. Cookie-cutter approaches to restorative justice do not fit every possible circumstance.
Win-win mental model	Relationship building, at the end of the day, is about finding mutually beneficial solutions. All participants are satisfied with the outcome.

It is essential to understand the dynamics of relationships and recognize values in order to adopt an ethical restorative justice practice, and possess a few tools to use in practice of restorative justice. Consider the following example. Family group conferencing is a useful restorative justice practice for issues related to domestic violence and child abuse. A conference or meeting is held with family members, child welfare professionals, service providers and community members (perhaps police, school officials, shelter workers, health service professionals and/or cultural organizations) to discuss the harm caused by domestic violence to family members and then address how to best meet the needs of each member and the family as a whole. Without such a restorative justice practice, the approach may be fragmented, with child-welfare workers apprehending children exposed to, or suffering from, violence and women accessing shelters or interacting with police, courts and lawyers. Bringing people together in a restorative justice forum has been found to result to fewer family separations, fewer children being apprehended and fewer members fleeing the home out of fear (Pennel and Burford 2000). In addition, family group conferences address the social problem of discrimination against women. Organizations participating in the conference lend support to the woman and help carry out the plans (like safety plans, housing plans and plans around financial security); they can strengthen a woman's autonomy and control, reinforce women's leadership roles within the family and reduce or end often-hidden gender discrimination (Muylkens and Smeets 2008; Pennel and Burford 2002). Restorative justice interventions promote women's control over their lives in meaningful ways that are not usually available when criminal prosecution is the sole vehicle of delivering justice.

ELEMENTS OF RESTORATIVE JUSTICE PRACTICE

Certain ethical practices — including confidentiality and privacy — are paramount in restorative conflict resolution. For instance, a facilitator's impartiality is critical for two parties in a conflict or disagreement to accept an outcome as just. A facilitator's values and biases must be suspended to empathetically understand each person's story (Smith, Young and Anderson 1996). Similarly, a facilitator must not benefit in any way from the success or failure of the process (Smith et al. 1996). A teacher resolving a dispute between students, one of whom is his or her child, has a conflict of interest (Smith et al. 1996).

Dave Gustafson, an eminent restorative justice practitioner and author, refers to "Margaret," a trauma survivor, who had addressed the June 2003 International Restorative Justice Conference in Vancouver, B.C. in answer to the question, "What is practitioner competence in restorative justice?":

> Restorative Justice needs to be rooted in values like: creating no further harms, [creating] safety, listening, validating, and empowering people to seek healing and restoration in their own way and timing. It needs to flow out of developing relationships between the clients and the practitioners. People respond to being honoured and loved and you can't fake this … RJ done well requires a huge time commitment and consistent care. When doing RJ in cases of serious crime it can be life risking and consequently life changing. So full of risks and rewards. The hardest pain imaginable faced and the biggest relief! ("Margaret," an adult survivor of violent sexual assaults in her mid-teens as recounted in Gustafson 2007: 1)

Competence is an integral part of professional practice in restorative justice. Competence goes beyond being good at relationships with friends and family. It is the capacity to empathize in ways that facilitate connecting individuals with themselves (self-reflection) and with others (changing behaviours). It means showing a capacity for compassion and courage (speaking from the heart). It is the capacity to go beyond technical or recipe interventions or personal opinion by evolving adaptive practices to fit the unique lived experience of the individuals involved in restorative justice.

When people tell their story — for example, a victim explaining how a robbery or an assault affected them — they may experience an important aspect of repairing the harm. Herman (1997: 3) calls this fundamental aspect of recovery from the harm people "reconstructing the trauma story." Additional aspects of helping a person recover include: establishing a safe environment; restoring connections to family, friends and community; providing practical and material help; and providing moral and spiritual guidance and care (Herman 1997; Van Ness and Strong 2006). Victims often recount their story among families and friends, in their homes or at the office. Not only can a knowledgeable, sensitive and trained practitioner truly hear someone's story, they can often also provide perspectives and information that families and friends are unable to objectively offer. For example, a family member of an offender may excuse an individual's behaviour, rather than help to resolve the underlying factors that led to the crime.

In many contexts, including the cjs, storytelling is an effective intervention that permits offenders, victims and their families and/or communities to express their perspectives in non-threatening ways. Storytelling may be defined as presenting information, clarifying a point, supporting someone's perspective and/or crystallizing and shaping ideas. Storytelling promotes understanding, appreciation and respect for the feelings (for example, anger) and physiological symptoms (for example, insomnia) in response to the conflict.

In the practice of restorative justice, it is critical that a practitioner can assess an individual's ability to both function autonomously on a day-to-day level and to make healthy life decisions (Herman 1997). Some practitioners who work with women experiencing domestic violence, define autonomy as "a sense of separateness, flexibility, and self-possession sufficient to define one's interest" (Herman 1997: 134). They define empowerment as "the convergence of individual support and autonomy" (Herman 1997: 134). Empowerment occurs when others, including the offender, acknowledge an individual's harm and inspire change.

Another perspective on empowerment in restorative justice is explained by Elder Phil Gatensby (2007), Raven Clan, Inland Tlinget Nation in his training circles:

> Gathering Power is a transformational experience designed to create the opportunity for participants to come to a greater understanding of themselves and the world around them. Gathering Power uncovers the treasure chest of resources that lies within each of us. It will bring an awareness of the dynamics of power and how to harness our power in order to address the ongoing struggles and the imbalances human beings are challenged with each day.

Gathering power refers to the relationship each of us has to nature, including to each other. This power or life force is ever changing, sometimes allowing one to gain direction over one's life; and sometimes the opposite, losing control over one's life events for a period of time, such as when a traumatic event — such as a physical assault — occurs.

RESTORATIVE JUSTICE AND INDIGENOUS PEOPLES

The above discussion looks at restorative justice practice, competencies and skills as they relate to individual circumstances. What if individuals experience the trauma of racism? McCaslin (2005) discusses how Indigenous peoples respond to trauma at a community level. She describes a single criminal act as a sign of "imbalance within the community as a whole — imbalances that affect everyone" (2005: 89). She explains that the criminal actions of an individual are more a warning sign that "the essential fabric of the community is starting to unwind" (2005: 89). She proposes that healing — repair the harm done by generations of colonizers — requires us to "confront multigenerational internalized trauma, oppression, colonized attitudes and habits, racism, pressures to assimilate and the ongoing degeneration of people and culture" (2005: 89). She uses the Hollow Water First Nation on Lake Winnipeg as an example of healing the harm beyond individual circumstances:

> Whatever aspects of harm we face, our communities are central to how we respond. For us, healing is about bringing the community back into the picture. It is about communities finding their own solutions. Communities can view problems as opportunities for seeing more clearly how we have drifted out of balance. The challenges give us a chance to work toward a balance that grows from our traditions and is not imposed from without. When others use our challenges as an excuse to impose their ways, we are weakened. (2005: 89–90)

Restorative justice practices are applicable to conflicts at both individual and societal levels. The approach recognizes the harm caused, recognizes the dignity, strength and spirit of the individual or community harmed and re-establishes autonomy (or in the case of Indigenous peoples, self-determination). In this way, restorative justice encompasses the third frame of justice, the ethical practice. The ethical practice of restorative justice involves taking into account the needs of the marginalized and oppressed, whether they be individuals or groups.

RESTORATIVE JUSTICE APPLICATIONS

To illustrate some the various and diverse applications of restorative justice, consider the following examples.

Restorative Water Justice

Conflict occurs in relation to our environment and our water source on a daily basis. Although we often see it on the news through examples such as an environmental group protesting the destruction of forests, or a First Nation demonstration against the building of a pipeline, the common dynamic involves the interests of economic development against concern for the preservation and sustainability of our environment. For example, tar sands in Northern Alberta pollute nearby waters and impact communities downstream (Smandych and Kueneman 2010). In times of water scarcity or drought in Alberta, not all licensed water users have enough water to use. Conflict over water scarcity is becoming increasingly common (Rojas et al. 2009; Environment Canada 2002). These conflicts have resulted in criminal consequences when protestors are charged criminally due to physical altercations (assault) or as in the Walkerton example.

In 2000, two people were charged and criminally sentenced in Walkerton, Ontario when several people died and 2,500 fell ill due to an outbreak of a highly dangerous O157:H7 strain of E. coli bacteria. Shortly thereafter in North Battleford, Saskatchewan, more than seven thousand people fell ill and fifty were hospitalized when the town's water supply became tainted with cryptosporidium bacteria. The outbreaks were traced to the city's water treatment plants and failure to treat solids in the water from livestock grazing upstream. These drinking-water incidents illustrate that the government safeguards people's health through a host of regulatory mechanisms that are backed by a threat of criminal consequences. This approach reflects our neo-liberal fragmented society, which fails to recognize the social problem in the situation: development (in this circumstance, agriculture) and impacts on the environment.

Inquiries in both North Battleford and Walkerton concluded that the municipalities needed to make changes in the way water was managed and water sources protected (O'Connor 2002; Laing 2003; GWP 2000; Conference Board of Canada 2005; Pollution Probe 2007). Historically, water management has been heavily regulated and employees and municipalities have faced criminal charges for grave mistakes they made; the changes proposed in the inquiries ushered in the principles and mechanisms of restorative justice. Across Canada, provinces have created local watershed advisory groups that establish source water protection plans (Hurlbert 2009). In Alberta, these watershed groups placed a moratorium on the issuance of any further water licenses in the South Saskatchewan River Basin, effectively halting further development in order to protect the water (Alberta Environment 2005). In Manitoba, where flooding is a great concern, watershed planning officials understand that the growing economy exerts pressures on a watershed; there, the plan ensures the resources in the watershed are managed sustainably and the plan reflects what is important to the community (Turtle Mountain 2006). Local knowledge is also informing Turtle Mountain Conservation District's process for commenting on and reviewing applications for drainage licensing requirements for the Manitoba Watershed Stewardship, thereby restoring relationships and building community (central aspects of restorative justice) (Government of Manitoba 2009). In the future, the district will likely have even greater ability to comment on licensing conditions once a surface water management plan is completed by the community (Government of Manitoba 2009). In this way, local groups in Alberta are responding to the conflict of water shortage, and in Manitoba, the local group is responding to the conflict of water excess or potential flooding.

The creation of local watershed groups (also called "integrated water resource management") to manage local water resources is happening worldwide (UNWWDR 2006; GWP 2000). This form of governance seeks to develop a consensus-based vision and decision-making process of water governance. It is defined as "a process, which promotes the coordinated development and management of water, land and related resources in order to maximize the resultant economic and social welfare in an equitable manner without compromising the sustainability of vital ecosystems" (GWP 2000). The benefits are clear: local communities are involved in making and implementing decisions, their practices, values, and knowledge are foregrounded and emerging issues or problems are quickly and flexibly attended to (Brooks 2002; Hickey and Mohan 2004).

This form of governance is reframing justice with respect to water. It is allowing people to identify and solve water-related problems where they live rather than leaving this matter to the government and professional people or private companies. Local watershed groups allow local people to actively participate in the resolution of problematic situations surrounding water and the environment and protect the environment while balancing development (jobs and wealth).

Further research is needed into the watershed advisory groups and whether their restorative justice work is achieving desired outcomes. Perhaps there needs to be more work to ensure that the community is properly represented by the membership. Perhaps the groups need to incorporate the ethic of doing no harm or protecting the least powerful and vulnerable in society. If there is a lack of knowledge about the actual process of watershed governance, there may be challenges in achieving restorative justice approaches. Further study of this emerging restorative justice practice is warranted.

Restorative Justice in Schools

Restorative justice has an important application in schools. Punishments, such as detention and suspensions, only aggravate issues such as bullying, violence, poor academic performance and parental apathy (Porter 2007). As a result, educators are increasingly exploring restorative justice practices to create safe, supportive learning environments (Porter 2007). Restorative justice practices have also been adopted by teachers and administrators to facilitate relations between students, between teachers, and relations between the school and parents. As the examples will show, some believe these practices have changed the very nature or "soul" of the school.

Restorative justice practice has been incorporated by educators into the school setting since the 1990s. While the term "restorative justice" was not commonly used at this time, the resistance to punishment (especially corporal punishment) and suspension is well documented (Redekop 2008). Educators realized that traditional punishment detracts from the central goal of developing a well-centered, balanced young person with self-discipline to do things such as show up on time and adopt patterns of behaviour to work in large groups outside the family. Punishment creates anger, damages self-esteem and is counter-productive to the development of the child (Smith 2006; Ginott 1972). Some advocates, such as Glasser (1969), have moved beyond all of these consequence-oriented approaches to a complete rejection of all methods used to control student behaviour (Redekkop 2008). Glasser (1969), for example, rejects facilitated mediation as another form of external control and relies instead on facilitated personal reflection and personal choice. The debate between whether mediation is a form of external control (with decisions influenced by others) versus personal choice remains unresolved.

One Grade 8 teacher, Elizabeth McCollum, uses an approach called "resolution circles" in anti-bullying initiatives, which "has provided an open line of communication, allowing students to feel safe" (Mirsky 2004: 1) These measures can change the entire school culture. At the Holy Innocents school in Philadelphia, a student proclaimed, "There's someone in the eighth grade who's being mistreated, who will not speak up for him or herself, and I won't tolerate it" (Mirsky 2004: 1), illustrating that the process can facilitate ethical practices of assisting the less powerful.

One study found using "punishment" had the following impacts on the school, not least the teachers:

> Staff were determined to carry out the punishment and physical confrontation ensued … The sense of community was eroding. Staff-pupil relationships changed to an "us and them" situation, vandalism and antisocial behaviour increased dramatically. Staff suffered rising levels of stress, and absenteeism and turnover increased. (Boulton and Mirsky 2006: 1)

Faculty meetings and relations also benefited from the use of circles and restorative justice (Mirsky 2004).

Restorative justice principles have not only helped change teaching practices in relation to dispensing punishment with undesirable student behaviour and teacher-to-teacher relations, but have also been applied in inter-student contexts and to encourage positive parental participation. Jenni Lyenna, a counsellor at Princess Margaret Secondary School in Surrey, B.C., explained how at one time "bullying was common and news of fights … were a given" (Huge and Lyenna 2004: 2). Then the school adopted a restorative justice intervention: "We preferred to work with students and their families rather than suspend them or kick them out" (2004: 3).

Evidence of improvements after implementing restorative justice practices is well documented in schools. A report from the International Institute for Restorative Practices called "Schools Implementing Restorative Practices," which covers six U.S. schools, two Canadian schools and two British schools over a two- to four-year period in which restorative justice practices were implemented, documents the number of students suspended, incidents/infractions (such as bullying) occurred and school-initiated sanctions reported. The findings uncovered a significant decline in the number of incidents/infractions by students, the number of students involved in disruptive behaviours and the number of result-ant suspensions. For example, in 2007–2008 in West Philadelphia High School, violent incidents were down 52 percent from the year before (Mirsky 2009).

Boulton and Mirsky (2006), Hugh and Lynnea (2004), Adams (2008) and others argue that Canadian, British, Australian and American schools could support the central tenet that "restorative practice can become a way of sensing the soul of a school" (Welden 2008: 1). Restorative justice allows a school's academic and social culture to emerge (McCold, cited in Porter 2007). Restorative justice practice in schools is not a panacea for disruptive behaviour, poor academic performance or families' non-participation in school activities. Rather, it is a model that offers a coherent multidimensional approach to problem-solving the complex nature of negative school environments and traditional reward and punishment responses.

Restorative Justice in the Criminal Justice System

A traditional criminal justice perspective sees crime as an "offence" committed by someone in violation of societal norms that are enforced by police, prosecutors, the courts and corrections; only punishing the offender can redress the situation. On the other hand, restorative justice in the criminal justice context views crime as a violation of people and relationships. The restorative justice context is concerned with how the action that constituted the "crime" (defined by the Criminal Code) harmed the people involved, including how it breached their trust and sense of well-being and security. Such violation creates an obligation to make things right. Restorative justice involves the victim, the offender and the community in a search for solutions that promote repair, reconciliation and reassurance. Restorative justice is defined as:

> A process whereby all the parties with a stake in a particular offence come together to resolve collectively how to deal with the aftermath of the offence and its implications for the future....

> Restorative justice is every action that is primarily oriented toward
> doing justice by repairing the harm that has been caused by a
> crime. (Latimer, Dowden and Muise 2005: 127)

This is similar to the narrow definition of restorative justice (Marshall
1999) provided in the first section of this chapter.

Instead of approaching crime as a matter of breaking the law or
offending against the state (the traditional criminal justice approach), it
is regarded as an injury to a person. As a result, restorative justice entails
not only the response to criminal behaviour, but also the repair of the
damage the crime has caused. The victim and offender and those col-
laterally effected (such as families) are encouraged to play active parts in
this process, not simply watch the players of the criminal justice system
(lawyers, police, prosecutors and defence counsel) handle their situation.

Legislative amendments have formally implemented restorative justice
within the criminal justice system. The *Criminal Code of Canada* (ccc)
refers to "alternative measures" as, "measures other than judicial proceedings under this Act used to deal with a person who is eighteen years of
age or over and alleged to have committed an offence." With regard to
young offenders, the Youth Criminal Justice Act (ycja) provides for the
use of "extrajudicial measures" for youth between the ages of 12 and 17
years old. Both these alternative measures and extrajudicial measures
are forms of restorative justice interventions. Within the cjs, restorative
justice interventions include non-punitive intervention strategies such
as: peacekeeping; community and family justice forums; transformative
justice; and mediation or mediation diversion. The term restorative justice
will be used interchangeably with other similar conceptual frameworks
as just listed.

In understanding restorative justice in the cjs, it is often helpful to
contrast it with the traditional retributive approach and the flaws of the
mainstream criminal justice system in respect of its treatment of victims.

The retributive approach is largely justified by the assumptions that
punishment — sentencing and incarcerating offenders — can deter
criminal behaviour. The Canadian public assesses the criminal justice
system by whether it convicts and adequately punishes those are found
guilty (Paciocco 1999). The 1987 Canadian Sentencing Commission
concluded deterrence was not working; this included both "specific deterrence" of individuals, which refers to punishment that prevents offenders

Table 14-2 Traditional Criminal Justice Approaches (Retributive) vs. Restorative Justice Approaches

Retributive	Restorative
• Crime is act against state	• Crime is act against person
• Criminal justice system controls crime	• Crime control lies primarily in the community
• Offender accountability defined as taking punishment	• Accountability defined as assuming responsibility and taking action to repair harm
• Crime is an individual act with individual responsibility	• Crime has individual and social dimensions of responsibility
• Punishment is effective as threat because it deters crime and punishment changes behaviour	• Punishment alone is not effective in changing behaviour and is disruptive to community harmony and good relationships
• Offender is defined by deficits	• Offender is defined by capacity to make reparation
• Focus on blame/guilt	• Victims are central to the process of resolving a crime
• Adversarial	• Focus on problem solving, on future
• Imposition of pain to punish and deter/prevent	• Emphasis on dialogue and negotiation
• Community on sideline, represented abstractly by state	• Community is facilitator
• Response focused on offender's past behaviour	• Response focused on harmful consequences of offender's behaviour and emphasis on future
• Dependence upon proxy professionals	• Direct involvement by participants

Source: Winterdyk and King 1999: 298

from re-offending (based on research and rates of recidivism or repeat offending), and also "general deterrence," or the intimidation of other people from offending. The Canadian Sentencing Commission findings are confirmed by other research (Redekop 2008; Roberts and Grossman 2004; Andrews et al. 1990). As most crimes are not results of a rational decision-making process with an informed weighing of the pros and cons of an action, it seems evident that deterrence constitutes a small effect of sentencing to prison.

Lastly, in some circumstances, incarceration can incapacitate or

CASE STUDY:
VICTIMS

Think about what victims in the CJS must experience. First, they have to contact the police and have a person charged with a criminal offence. Then, they have a lengthy wait for a prosecutor to proceed with the charge. Their first notice is often when they are served with a subpoena to appear at criminal court. For some crimes (serious crimes of violence and sexual assault) a victim service worker may help the victim through the criminal court process. For all crimes the victim is unrepresented. The prosecutor may have dozens of matters to deal with on that particular day so may only spend a few minutes with the victim. The victim may be questioned by the prosecutor and then cross-examined by defence counsel. If there is a conviction, the sentencing will usually be adjourned to another date. Although the victim may have completed a victim impact statement, which is read by the judge, sentencing is solely at the discretion of the judge.

Jane's partner was charged with assaulting her. She was not sure whether she wanted assistance from Victim Services. Jane said she didn't have any safety concerns and that indeed she wanted to have the "no contact" removed from the court-ordered conditions that the accused agreed to in order to be released from jail.

The Victim Services worker met with Jane the next day. The day afterward, Jane was assaulted again by her partner (court conditions were unchanged at this time). The Victim Services worker re-contacted Jane and she was now prepared to accept services. As the worker and the victim built up a positive working relationship, Jane revealed more information about the two assaults and her partner's drinking.

Jane's partner entered a guilty plea on one of the charges and the Crown prosecutor did not proceed with the second assault charge because Jane's partner was willing to enter a twenty-four-week domestic violence program. During the program he appeared to be doing quite well. During this time the Victim Services worker would check in with Jane. She did not want any conditions removed at this time, especially the no-contact provision. She said "things were going well and I am not with him."

A few weeks before the end of program, Jane's partner assaulted her again. It turned out that they had had regular contact during the program period. Jane now stated that she had genuine safety concerns and wanted the court conditions to remain in place.

The Victim Services worker informed the Crown prosecutor of the new concerns, which led to Jane's partner being remanded. He was later released.

Twelve days after the report of the last assault, Jane told the Victim Services worker she was pregnant with her partner's baby and that she no longer wanted the court conditions to remain. In addition, she said she was planning on recanting her statement to the police because "the baby needs a father that is not in jail."

With all the best of intentions, often processes facilitated through the CJS don't meet the lived experience of real people.

remove offenders from harming others in society for a limited period of time, but the financial cost is significant, at approximately \$116,000 per annum (Correctional Service Canada 2017). As a result of the Canadian Sentencing Commission findings concerning the absence of deterrence and the large cost taxpayers pay to incarcerate an individual, it can be concluded that the Canadian CJS and its criminal-sanction approach has made a false promise to Canadians. This false promise is that the criminal sanction of incarceration protects the public or reduces the amount of crime. It is not surprising that in terms of crime rates and their pattern in Canada, traditional criminal justice responses have had limited utility.

It has been apparent since the 1970s that rehabilitation programs in prisons have been largely unsuccessful, they have been underfunded, understaffed and inadequate (Paciocco 1999). In 1997, a report of the Solicitor General of Canada acknowledged Canadian prisons were most effective at educating less experienced, less hardened offenders to be more difficult and professional criminals (Spergel 1993). As the Le Dain Commission observed in 1973, these patterns in imprisonment result "from confining offenders together in a closed society in which a criminal subculture develops" (Le Dain 1973: 59); prisons are also often a recruitment center for organized gangs (Correctional Service Canada 2004).

CASE STUDY:
RESTORATIVE JUSTICE CASES

Darren Huenemann was a wealthy student at a Victoria, B.C. high school. Fellow students considered him to be a nice kid. He was doted on by his mother and grandmother, who instilled in him a sense of middle-class, materialistic values. But Darren talked with friends about killing his grandmother and mother to get a very large inheritance. They thought he was joking, but he was not. Eventually he convinced two friends dazzled by his lifestyle to kill the two women in return for money and status as his "special friends." He told the boys when the women would be together at his grandmother's home and how to get into the house. On October 5, 1990, the boys entered the grandmother's Vancouver home, beat and stabbed the women to death and took the money from the house. They disposed of the weapons on the ferry ride back to Victoria. The trail leading to Darren's conviction is complex but resulted mainly from his early boasting about the plan to a friend. Darren was found guilty of first-degree murder (Silverman and Kennedy 1993).

Josh is 12-year-old student. One day he came to school with a leg of a chair wrapped with tape at one end. The principal involved the police resource officer at the school. Upon interviewing Josh, the police resource officer learned that he had the weapon to protect himself from another student named George, who wanted to beat him up in retribution for getting beaten up by Josh's brother, Brian, for stealing his bike.

From a restorative justice perspective were there any winners and losers in the above situations? If you were to develop a restorative justice intervention in these two cases, who would you involve and why? What steps might you envision taking?

Victims of crime do not themselves participate centrally in the criminal justice process. Their participation is mediated by crown prosecutors, police and the lawyers who represent them. Restorative justice seeks to restore the victim's right to participate (Christie 1977) and to solve the problems in harmful relationships caused by criminal and other negative behaviours. "The principle of repair … justice requires that we work to heal victims, offenders, and communities that have been injured by crime" (Van Ness and Strong 1997, cited in Bazemore and Schiff 2005: 152). Therefore, the purpose or goal of a restorative justice intervention is to redress the harm perpetrated and to create new, positive relationships among the participants.

INDIGENOUS RESTORATIVE JUSTICE INSTITUTIONS

The restorative justice organization Regina Alternative Measure Program was created in 1993 with the provincial government's support to achieve the federal Indigenous Justice Strategy goal of reducing the representation of Indigenous peoples in the justice system, increasing the proportion of Indigenous peoples employed in the justice system and enhancing cultural sensitivity of the justice system for Indigenous offenders. The organization is open to all and used by both Indigenous and non-Indigenous peoples. People and resources are brought together in victim and offender mediations, community justice forums and circles after a referral from the criminal courts as an alternative to criminal prosecution. Once offenders complete the program, their charges are dropped.

Indigenous peoples have spearheaded restorative justice models and institutions. Restorative justice initiatives emerging in the 1970s within the traditional CJS supported the reformation of Indigenous justice institutions including:

(i) the recognition that the CJS was failing Indigenous peoples as evidenced by the high incarceration rate and systemic discrimination against Indigenous peoples (Hurlbert and MacKenzie 2008);

(ii) The assertion of the inherent right to self-determination or self-government by Indigenous peoples, which for some Indigenous peoples means separate justice systems founded on traditional justice practised in Indigenous communities (Ross 2006);

(iii) The recognition of Indigenous rights, first with statements made by Supreme Court of Canada judges in the *Calder* v. *A.G. of British Columbia* case and later section 35 of the Constitution Act, 1982.

Some principles of Indigenous justice inform mainstream restorative justice as a system of social control through consensus and decision making based upon customs (Boldt and Long 1984). Traditions centering on the Creator and the teachings of the Elders, oral traditions and storytelling informed many of the various and diverse Indigenous justice practices in North America (Guemple 1980; Vanderburgh 1988). Despite the differences among Indigenous communities, the underlying premise regards an individual as an integral part of the community; a dispersal of decision-making influence among many people; a reliance on consensus; and a belief people can neither be assisted nor understood as long as they are isolated from their community and family (Hurlbert 2009). These principles are congruent with restorative justice, yet very specific to the Indigenous community practising them: Indigenous restorative justice is a local institution, based on the community within which it is practised; there is no universal blueprint (Zellerer and Cunneen 2001).

Self-government, Indigenous policing, Indigenous courts and sentencing circles have each developed and contributed some changes in justice practices for Indigenous peoples. In some cases, this began with policing and community-justice programs. Police are important actors in the practice of restorative justice because they decide whether a matter is presented to a restorative justice program. Often they can resolve a matter without involving criminal charges and courts. First Nations policing occurs either through Indigenous communities establishing a self-administered police service or through partnership agreements between an Indigenous community and the federal and provincial governments (Government of Saskatchewan n.d.). The establishment of Indigenous policing has the potential to redress traditional Canadian criminal justice practices for Indigenous peoples. Some of the benefits of Indigenous policing programs include:

- decreased number of arrests;
- decreased tension when an Indigenous police officer is involved; and
- better police response because of the combination of an officer's knowledge of and commitment to the community with his/her police training. (Griffiths and Cunningham 2003: 75)

Circles of justice initially emerged within First Nations communities in Canada and are now widely practised throughout the criminal justice system globally (Zehr 2002). There are four possible uses of the circles of justice concept modeled on Indigenous traditions to resolve individual, family and community issues. The first is for the parties or community to use or access a circle of justice (that is, community members) to resolve a dispute or issue prior to the involvement of the police or courts. The second possible use is diverting and withdrawing the charge through the use of successful mediation. This is also termed "alternative measures" or "victim-offender mediation." In the third use, once a guilty plea is entered, the circle (a sentence advisory committee, an elders' or community sentencing panel or a sentencing circle) is available to determine sentencing. The fourth main use of a circle is the reintegration and assistance of an individual reestablishing themselves in the community once their period of incarceration ends (Hurlbert and MacKenzie 2008).

The criteria for a sentencing circle largely accepted in court cases (see *R. v. Joseyounen* 1995; *R. v. Alaku* 1993; *R. v. Moses* 1992) include:

- voluntary agreement by accused to have recommendations as part of the judge's consideration;
- willingness of victim to participate;
- resolution of disputed facts;
- acceptance of responsibility by offender for his or her actions;
- guilty plea;
- community support for the offender and willingness to be involved in the process on behalf of the accused;
- victim has had meaningful input;
- demonstrated sincere intention of accused to be rehabilitated and to participate meaningfully in rehabilitation.

In Saskatchewan, for example, the sentencing circle is generally opened by a prayer, and the defense and crown agree on the facts. The crown prosecutor, defence counsel, judge, accused, victim and their families (and sometimes the police) speak, going around the circle until the problem is identified, the accused takes responsibility and a proposal is agreed upon. If this isn't achieved, the matter goes back into the CJS. The end of the sentencing circle discussion is typically declared by the circle and not the judge (Peterson 2000). Practice over the years has found pre-charge diversion useful, but post-charge sentencing circles to be very time consuming and less embraced by the community (Hurlbert and McKenzie 2008).

In 2000, the Tsuu T'ina First Nation near Calgary created a peacemaking court that sits on reserve lands. The Tsuu T'ina elders established the court and advised that the traditional approach to dealing with conflict was to heal offenders and their relationship with the victim (Mandaman 2003). The court is the result of a successful investigation by the First Nation into alternative criminal justice solutions followed by successful lobbying and negotiations with both provincial and federal governments. The court is staffed by Indigenous peoples.

The peacemaking court has the equivalent jurisdiction of an Alberta provincial court. The protocols of the court, however, reflect Tsuu T'ina tradition. A smudging ceremony (a sacred pledge of truth to the Creator) commences the court, which is held in a chamber representing the circle of a teepee. In some diversions, rather than paying fines, offenders participate in healing ceremonies. In one, peacemaking was ended with a pipe ceremony, a vow by the participant to the Creator. All peacemaking ends with an elders' panel for the Tsuu T'ina people, who regard their directions as mandatory. Many checks and balances exist within the peacemaking process. The accused must choose peacemaking, and the peacemaker must be agreeable along with the crown who refers the matter and the judge who adjourns the case to allow for peacemaking. Tsuu T'ina Nation members can elect not to utilize the court; however the Tsuu T'ina Nation members are using the peacemaking court and practising restorative justice.

When the peacemaking court was originally established, the elders determined that it would not handle sexual assault, homicide, prostitution and domestic violence, though in recent years, it has begun to handle domestic violence, an approach that includes professional counselors, peacemaking and healing.

The Tsuu T'ina court is an important success for Indigenous community justice. Some argue that only through initiatives like these, in combination with a fully recognized inherent Indigenous right to self-determination and an independent Indigenous justice system, can systemic racism and inequality be eliminated (Ross 2006).

In Hollow Water, Manitoba, in the mid-1980s, a healing system known as the Hollow Water First Nation Community Holistic Circle Healing (often referred to only as Hollow Water) was developed by four First Nation communities to address sexual abuse resulting from colonial and residential school legacies. The community decided to tackle the issue head on instead of using the traditional criminal justice process of sentencing and incarceration. First Nation members guilty of abuse are still charged with an offence, and to access the Hollow Water program they must plead guilty. Hollow Water's process combines the sentencing circle with reintegration of the offender back into the community — the third and fourth types of circles outlined earlier. The accused's sentencing is delayed if they choose to participate in the Hollow Water First Nation Community Holistic Circle Healing. If they fail to remain in the program, they return to the regular court system and most likely incarceration. When the accused has finished the healing program, they will appear in court for sentencing and the team from the community will present a report to the judge about the accused's sincerity and effort and how much work, if any, still needs to be done (Goff 2004).

The healing process is a thirteen-step program based on the seven Midewin teachings of the Anishinaabe people. The process holistically involves victims, offenders and their families and creates spiritual, physical, emotional and intellectual benefits throughout the community. The process involves disclosure by the victimizer and ensuring safety and support for the victim, followed by circles with the victim and victimizer and preparatory meetings with their families leading to a special gathering/sentencing circle and ending with a cleansing ceremony. Hollow Water has saved federal and provincial governments millions of dollars, created community capacity to help people heal through the process, reduced the recidivism rate of sex offenders at Hollow Water, improved child health, allowed for higher educational attainment by community members, improved parenting skills, empowered individuals, broadened community resources, increased community responsibility, returned the community to traditional ceremony and decreased overall violence and intergenerational pain resulting from colonization (Hansen 2001; Goff 2004).

DOES RESTORATIVE JUSTICE WORK?

Restorative justice is not a panacea for all of the current shortcomings of the CJS. Some argue that restorative justice may be just another form of punishment (Woolford 2009). This criticism may be well founded if restorative justice is practised narrowly only in cases of minor, first offences.

Some others, meanwhile, criticize restorative justice because they support more severe penalties for people who commit crime (Coolican 2009), or because they believe there are certain categories of harms, like domestic violence, that should not be addressed by restorative justice (Cameron 2006). Some Indigenous women's groups have been very vocal opponents of restorative justice. Teressa Nahanee, a member of the Squamish Indian Nation and adviser to the Native Women Association of Canada, states, "The use of elders' circles has not been effective in deterring violent crimes against women" (Nahanee 1995: 362). The Manitoba Justice Inquiry confirmed this:

> The unwillingness of chiefs and council to address the plight of women and children suffering abuse at the hands of husbands and fathers is quite alarming. The failure of Indigenous government leaders to deal at all with the problem of domestic abuse is unconscionable. Their silence and failure to act actually contribute to the problem. (Smith 1993: 34–35)

Studies reported that some victims felt worse after, or because of, the conference. However, these victims were in a minority of those who felt justice was served as a result of the conference (Braithwaite 2002). There is a high approval rate among victims who participate in restorative justice, but approval is lower than among other participants in the process, such as offenders and community members (Braithwaite 2002; Latimer, Dowden and Muise 2005). It should be noted that the degree to which victims participate in restorative justice programs varies. In some cases, victims are very involved, and in others, victim surrogates might participate instead (questioning if restorative justice is truly being achieved). Yet, victims in restorative justice programs were more satisfied than victims whose cases went to court; they also experienced lower levels of fear and higher positive emotional outcomes (Braithwaite 2002; Beven et al. 2005).

Offenders were also more likely to be satisfied with engaging in a restorative justice process or program compared to those proceeding through the traditional CJS. Studies show that offenders participating in a restorative justice program had a much higher completion rate for following through with restitution obligations to victims and making reparations than was ordered through the traditional CJS (Braithwaite 2002; Latimer, Dowden and Muise 2005).

To determine whether restorative justice is effective, we should evaluate it in light of its goals. The goals of restorative justice are to reduce crime and to restore the relationships among the victim, offender and community. There are two factors that determine whether restorative justice is working. First, the conflict in the relationships among the parties involved should be positively resolved. Second, recidivism (the rate of re-offending) should be reduced. Evaluations of restorative justice initiatives have shown some promise to reduce re-offending by anywhere from three to eight percent compared to traditional criminal justice system responses (Hoffinger 2014; Latimer, Dowden and Muise 2005; Bonta, Wallace-Capretta and Rooney 2002; Bonta, Wallace-Capretta and Rooney 1998; and Roberts 1995). Specifically addressing youth, Wong et al. (2016) reported positive results in the reduction of recidivism for youth participating in restorative approaches. Results further improve when restorative justice is combined with rehabilitation programs for offenders and even more so when culturally appropriate approaches are integrated with restorative justice practices (for example, Indigenous cultural practices such as the participation of elders). Further support should be given to holistic restorative justice programs as well as culturally specific restorative justice programs. From this review, restorative justice initiatives have an important place in the Canadian CJS for both Indigenous and non-Indigenous peoples.

RESTORATIVE JUSTICE IN THEORETICAL CONTEXT

Just as defining restorative justice is challenging, so too is theorizing a context for restorative justice. It is challenging because restorative justice is not a social phenomenon to be investigated and models developed to understand and explain its nature; restorative justice is a practice or process for constructively resolving conflict. It is not a phenomenon we would analyze in the same manner as, say, the problem of crime or health in society. However, when we analyze crime in society using theoretical models we can position restorative justice in these models with respect to the resolution of crime.

As Margot Hurlburt theorizes in Chapter 2, from a structural functionalist perspective, if someone commits a crime he or she is not abiding by the standard norms of society and may be in a state of anomie or strain between his or her ideal world and realistic achievements. This state of normlessness or conflict is a dysfunction within society and the CJS in theory works to bring offenders back into the norms of society. Restorative justice is another method of bringing offenders out of the state of anomie or strain through resolving tensions (conflict) with victims. Keeping in mind the four pillars of restorative justice, social problems that created the state of anomie should be addressed. Recognizing the lived experience of the victim(s), the offender(s) and the community(ies) is a first step towards resolving the harm caused by the crime (conflict).

Because conflict theory deals with crime on a high level (statistics by community or nation), and restorative justice is an individualized practice of restoring victims and offenders into balance with one another, the actual process of healing the two parties might first appear to have little relation to the conflict theory. However, when social problems are recognized and addressed through an ethical practice of doing no harm and protecting the most vulnerable and powerless, interpersonal problems that come to light can be redressed. From this perspective, restorative justice is a process for the community to restore positive and healthy relationships among its citizens (as described by Christie 1977) and reduce the involvement for conflict professionals (such as lawyers and police). In this way, restorative justice is a process that shifts conflict resolution from professionals to communities and thus reflects the broader context of social justice advocacy and practice. According to Christie (as discussed at the beginning of this chapter), in highly industrialized societies, conflicts have been given the status of "property" and appropriated from lay people by lawyers and professionals who in turn earn a living from resolving conflict in society. People are seen as ill-prepared to resolve their own conflicts because the law is too complex, and instead defer to the police, lawyers, judges, psychologists and other expert professionals to resolve what is really a community problem.

Where traditional criminal justice responses generally conceive of crime through a lens of deviance through sanctions such as probation or incarceration, a restorative justice approach attempts to respond to relationships in conflict, foster understanding and avoid further labelling or blaming. Restorative justice is not about avoiding accountability, but about re-inclusion into the community (Joyce 2006). The problem is the behaviour, not the individual and the individual's experience such that the person should be written off.

RESTORATIVE JUSTICE AND SOCIAL JUSTICE

This chapter introduced the principles and practices of restorative justice. Restorative justice is used in a variety of contexts, in everyday personal life decisions, in different professions and in various contexts, such as schools and workplaces. It is predominantly used in the CJS as an alternative to retributive justice (the norm in the traditional CJS). Often, restorative justice is conceived in narrow terms, which limits the potential for a fulsome restorative justice practice. This chapter argues for a restorative justice definition and practice (see the four pillars on p. 407) employing themes and concepts akin to social justice.

This fulsome definition of restorative justice has been illustrated with the practices of local water advisory groups in the environmental context, within the school context and in circles of justice in the criminal context. However, to prevent a fragmented, limiting, individualized approach, these practices must also be informed by an ethical practice and grounded in a critical social analysis that recognizes social problems. Members of the community should actively participate and conflict should be seen as a learning opportunity. If all four pillars are fully employed, shortcomings of restorative justice can be reduced and the benefits of restorative justice made accessible to all.

DISCUSSION QUESTIONS

1. Can restorative justice be used in all crimes, no matter how serious or how minor?
2. What would practising restorative justice in all aspects of our daily life look like?
3. Is there evidence that restorative justice works?
4. Could restorative justice address colonialism?

GLOSSARY

Circles of Justice: Circles of justice are used in Indigenous tradition to resolve a community issue. There are four possibilities for the utilization of the circles of justice: 1) for the parties or community to utilize or access a circle of justice for the resolution of a dispute or issue prior to the involvement of the police or courts; 2) after the criminal justice system is accessed, a criminal charge may be diverted and the charge withdrawn through the use of mediation diversion; 3) once a guilty plea is entered, the circle accessed for sentencing purposes; 4) for the reintegration and assistance of an individual reestablishing themselves in the community once their period of incarceration is at an end.

Competence: This refers to having suitable or sufficient skill, knowledge and experience for some purpose. Here, specifically for the practice of restorative justice.

Confidentiality: Confidentiality refers to speaking, writing, acting on and so forth in strict privacy or secrecy.

Conflict of interest: The professional's primary commitment is to the individual participants, the process and the purpose or goal of the intervention (Smith, Young, Ish and Anderson 1996). If the professional is in conflict with an individual participant(s), the process or purpose he or she should withdraw.

Deterrence: To discourage or restrain from acting or proceeding.

Extrajudicial measures: Ways that young persons can be diverted or kept out of the youth cjs. Unlike going to court where the judge makes or guides (in the case of jury trials) all the decisions, some extrajudicial measures allow the youth and people who have been affected by the youth's actions to participate in the decision making.

Impartiality: While we all live with our own biases, or values and knowledge of the world around us, the impartial professional is self-aware of these biases and is able to avoid prejudicial interventions favoring individual participants (victims, offenders, families, communities) (Smith, Young, Ish and Anderson 1996).

Knowledge-based practice: The understanding many disciplines might offer to explain crime behaviours based on scientific, evidence-based practices and theories.

Mediation: The act of bringing about (an agreement, accord, truce, peace) as an intermediary between parties by compromise, reconciliation, removal of misunderstanding and so forth.

Peacemaking court: The peacemaking court has been created by the Tsuu T'ina First Nation outside of Calgary, Alberta. The Tsuu T'ina elders initiated the establishment of the court and advised that the traditional approach to dealing with conflict was to heal offenders to behave properly and restore offender and victim relationships (Mandaman 2003). The court is staffed by Indigenous peoples, and Indigenous traditions have been incorporated and merged into the traditional provincial court practices.

Procedural interests: Needs relating to the process by which the dispute is resolved

Psychological interests: Needs regarding how one feels about the problem and solution.

Recidivism: The instance of a person reoffending.

Rehabilitation: To restore to a good condition, operation or management or to re-establish the good reputation of (a person, one's character or name).

Restorative approach: Restorative justice views crime as an act against a person and has individual and social dimensions of responsibility. It views punishment alone as not effective in changing behaviour and as disruptive to community harmony and good relationships. Victims are central to the process of resolving a crime.

Retributive approach: Retributive justice views crime as an individual act against the state. The punishment is effective as threat of it deters crime and punishment changes behaviour. The focus of retributive justice is on blame and guilt.

Self-administered police services: Under the First Nations Policing Policy (FNPP), the federal and provincial governments work with First Nations to negotiate agreements for police services that meet the specific needs of each community. Police services must be responsive, accessible, effective, regulated and accountable through bodies that are representative of the communities they serve.

Self-determinism: Self-determinism describes participation as voluntary (Smith, Young, Ish and Anderson 1996). Practitioners will ensure all agreements in resolving the conflict are voluntary.

Storytelling: An effective intervention that permits offenders, victims and their families and/or communities to express their perspectives in non-threatening ways. Storytelling may be defined as presenting information, clarifying a point, supporting someone's perspective and/or crystallizing and shaping ideas. Storytelling promotes an understanding, appreciation and a respect for the thoughts and behaviours of victims and offenders.

Substantive interests: Needs such as money, time and resources.

Value-based practice: The influence of our families, friends, schools and cultural and religious affiliations in developing our beliefs and our moral sense of right and wrong.

REFERENCES

Adams, C. 2008. "The Talk-it-out Solution: How We Promote Safety? Try getting rid of the metal detectors." *Scholastic Administrator* Nov/Dec.

Alberta Environment. 2005. "Approved Water Management Plan for the South Saskatchewan River Basin in Alberta." October 18 draft. <www3.gov.ab.ca/env/water/regions/ssrb/pdf/Draft_SSRB_Plan.pdf>.

Andrews, D.A., I. Zinger, R. Hoge, J. Bonta, P. Gendreau and F. Cullen. 1990. "Does Correctional Treatment Work? A Clinically Relevant and Psychologically Informed Meta-analysis." *Criminology* 28: 393–404.

Beven, J.P., Hall, G., Froyland, I., Steels, B., and Goulding, D. 2005. Restoration or Renovation? Evaluating Restorative Justice Outcomes. *Psychiatry, Psychology, and Law*, 12(1): 194 - 206.

Boldt, M., and J.A. Long. 1984. "Tribal Traditions and European-Western Political Ideologies: The Dilemma of Canada's Native Indians." *Canadian Journal of Political Science* 17(3): 537–53.

Bonta, J., S. Wallace-Capretta and J. Rooney. 1998. *Restorative Justice: An Evaluation of the Restorative Resolutions Project*. Ottawa: Solicitor General Canada.

Bonta, J., S. Wallace-Capretta, J. Rooney and K. McAnoy. 2002. "An Outcome Evaluation of a Restorative Justice Alternative to Incarceration." *Contemporary Justice Review* 5, 4: 319–38. <www.psepc0sppcc.gc.ca/res/cor/sum/cprs200301_1-en.asp>.

Boulton, J., and L. Mirsky. 2006. *Restorative Practices as a Tool for Organizational Change: The Bessels Leigh School*. International Institute for Restorative Practices. <www.iirp.edu/article_detail.php?article_id=NTMx>.

Braithwaite, J. 2002. *Restorative Justice and Responsive Regulation*. New Yor: Oxford University Press.

Brooks, D.B. 2002. *Water, Local-level Management*. Ottawa: International Development Research Centre.

Cameron, A. 2006. "Stopping the Violence: Canadian Feminist Debates on Restorative Justice and Intimate Violence." *Theoretical Criminology* 10 (1): 49–66.

Christie, N. 1977. "Conflicts as Property." *British Journal of Criminology* 17 (1): 1.

Conference Board of Canada. 2005. "Water Pressure is Building in Canada." *InsideEdge* Winter: 16.

Coolican, L. 2009. "Pauchay Gets 3 Years: Drunk Father Left House In -50 Wind Chill with Two Toddlers Dressed Only in Shirts And Diapers. Both Froze to Death in the Cold." *Leader Post*. March 7. <www.leaderpost.com/news/Pauchay+gets+years/1363937/story.html>.

Correctional Service Canada 2017. "Quick Facts." June. < www.csc-scc.gc.ca/publications/092/005007-3024-eng.pdf>.

___. 2004. *A Profile and Examination of Gang Affiliation Within the Federally Sentenced Offender Population*. Ottawa: Correctional Service Canada.

Daubney, D. 1988. "Taking Responsibility." Report of The Standing Committee on Justice and Solicitor General on Its Review of Sentencing, Conditional Release and Related Aspects of Correction." Ottawa: Solicitor General of Canada.

Environment Canada. 2002. "Urban Water Indicators: Municipal Water Use and Wastewater Treatment." <www.ec.gc.ca/soer-ree/English/ Indicators?issues?Urb_H2O>.

Ginott, H. 1972. *Between Teacher and Child*. New York: MacMillan. In P. Redekop, 2008, *Changing Paradigms, Punishment and Restorative Discipline*. Scottdale, PA: Herald Press.

Griffiths C.T., and A.H. Cunningham. 2003. *Canadian Criminal Justice* (second ed.). Toronto: Harcourt Brace.

Goff, C. 2004. *Criminal Justice in Canada* (3rd ed.). Toronto: Thomson Nelson.

Government of Manitoba. 2009. *Conservation Districts of Manitoba 2008–2009 Annual Report*. Manitoba. <www.gov.mb.ca/waterstewardship/agencies/cd/ cd_annual_report2008-2009.pdf>.

Government of Saskatchewan. n.d.. "Creating Healthy, Just, Prosperous and Safe Saskatchewan: A Response to the Commission on First Nation and Metis Peoples and Justice Reference." <www.publictions.gov.sk.ca/ detailscfm?p=9870>.

Global Water Partnership (GWP). 2000. *GWP Annual Report*. <www.gwpforum. org/servlet/PSP?:NodeID=263&iFronNode/D=102>.

Guemple, L. 1980. "Growing Old in Inuit society." In V.W. Marshall (ed.), *Aging in Canada, Social Perspectives*. Don Mills, ON: Fitzhenry & Whiteside.

Gustafson, D. 2007. "Facing the Question." A workshop on a palaver on praxis. The marriage of restorative justice theory and practice following the June 2003 International Restorative Justice Conference in Vancouver. Retrieved <www.csc-scc.gc.ca/text/rj/rj2007/pdf/7_e.pdf>.

Hanson, R.K. 2001. *Age and Sexual Recidivism: A Comparison of Rapists and Child Molesters*. Ottawa: Solicitor General.

Herman, J. 1997. *Trauma and Recovery: The Aftermath of Violence: From Domestic Violence to Political Terror*. New York: Basic Books.

Hickey, S., and G. Mohan. 2004. "Towards Participation as Transformation: Critical Themes and Challenges." In S. Hickey and G. Mohan (eds.), *Participation: From Tyranny to Transformation?* London: Zed Books.

Hurlbert, M.A. 2009. "An Analysis of Trends Related to the Adaptation of Water Law to the Challenge of Climate Change: Experience from Canada." *International Journal of Climate Change Strategies and Management* 1 (3): 230–40.

Hurlbert, M.A., and J. MacKenzie. 2008. "Making Structural Changes in Criminal Justice." In J. Whyte (ed.), *Moving Toward Justice: Legal Traditions and Aboriginal Justice*. Saskatoon: Purich Publishing.

Hulsman, L.H.C. 1986. "Critical Criminology and the Concept of Crime." *Contemporary Crisis* 10: 63–80.

Hofinger, V. 2014. "Konfliktregelung statt Strafe: Zwei Studien zur spezialpräventiven Wirkung des Tatausgleichs." *Richterzeitung* 2/ S: 91-93.

Laing, R. 2003. Report of the Commission of Inquiry Into Matters Related to the Safety of the Public Drinking Water in The City of North Battleford, Saskatchewan. Regina: Queen's Printer.

Latimer, J., Dowden, C., and Muise, D. 2005. The Effectiveness of Restorative Justice Practices: A Meta-Analysis. *The Prison Journal*, 85: 127-144.

Le Dain Commission. 1973. *Final Report of The Commission of Inquiry Into the Non-Medical Use of Drugs*. Ottawa: Information Canada.

Mandamin, T.L.S. 2003. "Peacemaking and the Tsuu T'ina Court." *Justice as Healing Newsletter* 8(1): 1.

Marshall, T.F. 1999. *Restorative Justice: An Overview*. London: Home Office, Research Development and Statistics Directorate. <www.homeoffice.gov.uk/rds/pdfs/occ-resjus.pdf>.

McCaslin, W. 2005. "Introduction: Reweaving the Fabrics of Life." In W. McCalsin (ed.), *Justice as Healing: Indigenous Ways*. St. Paul, MN. Living Justice Press.

Mirsky, L. 2009. "Restorative practices and the Transformation at West Philadelphia High School." International Institute for Restorative Practices. June 22. <www.safersanerschools.org/articles.html?articleId=609>.

___. 2004. "Transforming School Culture: An Update." International Institute for Restorative Practices. December 7. <www.safersanerschools.org/articles.html?articleId=395>.

Muylkens, L. and Smeets, K. 2008. "Beyond the Offender: Group Counselling for Victims of Crime." European Forum for Restorative Justice Newsletter 9 (2).

Nahanee, T. 1995. "Dancing With a Gorilla: Aboriginal Women, Justice and the *Charter*." In Royal Commission on Aboriginal Peoples, *Aboriginal Peoples and the Justice System*. Ottawa: Canada Communications Group.

O'Connor, D. 2002. "Report of the Walkerton Commission of Inquiry." <www.attorneygeneral.jus.gov.on.ca/english/about/pubs/walkerton/part1/>.

Paciocco, D.M. 1999. *Getting Away with Murder: The Canadian Criminal Justice System*. Toronto: Irwin Law.

Pali, B., and C. Pelikan. 2014. "Con-texting Restorative Justice and Abolitionism: Exploring the Potential and Limits of Restorative Justice as an Alternative Discourse to Criminal Justice." *Restorative Justice, An International Journal* 2(2): 142-164.

Pavlich, G. 2005. *Governing Paradoxes of Restorative Justice*. London: Glass House Press.

Pennell, J., and G. Burford. 2002. "Feminist Praxis: Making Family Group Conferencing Work." In H. Strang and J. Braithwaite (eds.), *Restorative Justice and Family Violence*. Cambridge: Cambridge University Press.

___. 2000. "Family Group Decision Making: Protecting Children and Women." *Child Welfare* Mar Apr 79 (2): 131–59.

Peterson, M.R. 2000. "Developing a Restorative Justice Programme." *Justice as Healing* 5(4), Part II. Native Law Centre of Canada.

Pollution Probe. 2007. "Towards a Vision and Strategy for Water Management in Canada." Final report of the water policy in Canada national workshop series. Victoria: Polis Project on Ecological Governance.

Porter, A.J. 2007. "Restorative Practices in Schools: Research Reveals Power of Restorative Approach, Part I." April 27. *Restorative Practices eForum*. <www. safersanerschools.org/library/schoolresearch1.html>.

R. v. Joseyounen. 1995. 6 Western Weekly Reports 38, (Saskatchewan Provincial Court).

R. v. Alaku. 1993. 112 Dominion Law Reports (4th) 732 (Court of Quebec).

R. v. Moses. 1992. 3 Canadian National Law Reports 116 (Yukon Territorial Court).

Raiffa, H. 1982. *The Art and Science of Negotiation*. Cambridge, MA: Belknap Press of Harvard University Press.

Redekop, P. 2008. *Changing Paradigms: Punishment and Restorative Discipline*. Waterloo, ON: Herald Press.

Roberts, J.V., and M.G. Grossman (eds.). 2004. *Criminal Justice in Canada*. Scarborough, ON: Thomson Nelson.

Roberts, T. 1995. *Evaluation of the Victim-Offender Mediation Project: Langley, B.C.* Ottawa: Solicitor General Canada.

Rose, F. 2012. *The Art of Immersion: How the Digital Generation is Remaking Hollywood, Madison Avenue, and The Way We Tell Stories*. New YorkW. W. Norton and Company.

Ross, R. 2006. *Returning to the Teachings: Exploring Aboriginal justice*. Toronto: Penguin Books.

Rojas, A., L. Magzul, G.P. Marchildon and B. Reyes. 2009. "The Oldman River Dam Conflict: Adaptation and Institutional Learning." *Prairie Forum* (34)1: 235–60.

Silverman, R., and L. Kennedy. 1993. *Deadly Murder in Canada*. Toronto: Nelson.

Smandych, R., and R. Kueneman. 2010. "The Canadian Alberta Tar Sands: A Case Study of State-Corporate Environmental Crime." In R. White (ed.), *Global Environmental Harm: Criminological Perspectives*. Portland: Willan.

Smith, A.B. 2006. "The State of Research on the Effects of Physical Punishment." *Social Policy Journal of New Zealand* 27.

Smith, A., J. Young, B. Ish and J. Anderson. 1996. "Common ground mediation trainers." (Unpublished). Saskatoon, SK.

Smith, D. 1993. *The Seventh Fire*. Toronto: Key Porter Books.

Strang, H. 2013. "Victims and Restorative Justice: What do we Know From International Research Evidence?" Presentation at the Conference "Restoring the Balance," St Catherine's College, Oxford. November 28.

Waller, I. 2011. *Rights for Victims of Crime. Rebalancing Justice*. Plymouth: Rowman and Littlefield Publishers Inc.

Turtle M. 2006. *Taking Care Of Our Watershed: A Watershed Plan for the East Souris River Watershed*. Winnipeg: Department of Water Stewardship.

United Nations World Water Development Report (UNWWDR). 2006. *Water, A Shared Responsibility Report 2*. New York: United Nations Educational

Scientific and Cultural Organization.

Van Ness, D., and K.H. Strong. 2006. *Restoring Justice: An Introduction to Restorative Justice.* Cincinnati: LexisNexis/Anderson.

Vanderburgh, R.M. 1988. "The Impact of Government Support for Indian Culture on Canada's Aged Indians." In E. Rathbone-McCuan and B. Havens (eds.), *North American Elders: United States and Canadian Perspectives.* New York: Greenwood Press.

Weitekamp, E. and H-J. Werner (eds.). 2002. Restorative Justice: Theoretical Foundations. Cullompton, UK: Willan.

Welden, L.M. 2008. *Restorative Practices in Australia's Schools: Stronger Relationships and Multi-School Summits Help Schools "Be and Learn" Together.* International Institute for Restorative Practices. <www.iirp.edu/eforum-archive/restorative-practices-in-australia-s-schools-strong-relationships-and-multi-school-summits-help-schools-ldquo-be-and-learn-rdquo-together >.

Woolford, A. 2009. *The Politics of Restorative Justice.* Halifax/Winnipeg: Fernwood Publishing.

Wong, J.S., Bouchard, J., Gravel, J., Bouchard, M., and Morselli, C. 2016. "Can at-risk Youth be Diverted from Crime? A Meta-Analysis of Restorative Diversion Programs." *Criminal Justice and Behavior* 43(10): 1310 - 1329.

Zehr, H. 2002. *The Little Book of Restorative Justice.* Intercourse, PA: Good Books.

Zellerer, E., and C. Cunneen. 2001. *Restorative Justice, Indigenous Justice, and Human Rights Restorative Community Justice.* Cincinnati: Anderson.

FINAL REMARKS

Margot A. Hurlbert

This book closed with a chapter that is both a culmination of justice and a starting point. The ethical practice of justice is pursued every day in the relations we have with other people, no matter in what occupation or in what personal, impersonal or formal relationship. Simple practices set the stage for pursuing and achieving justice. These practices include listening, communicating and understanding. Often, we can't achieve the depth and intensity required of these practices when relying on instant messaging, emails and the phone for our human-to-human interactions. Practices of selective hearing and self-confirmation bias (where we selectively pick out information that supports our prior beliefs and thoughts) also detract from our ability to truly practise these skills. I suspect that those practices also maintain our ethnocentrisms and support our belief that our way of viewing the world, a justice issue, a personal issue even, is the only way of viewing it and that our view represents reality or the "truth."

Our truth and our reality are important and no one can take that away from us. However, by interacting with others, we can begin to understand how our truth and our reality may be viewed differently by other people. If we are brave, it is here that we can explore opinions, thoughts and beliefs. Are we a victim or a survivor? Or a warrior? We can try on the beliefs and descriptions that we hold and that others hold. When and if we are ready, we can consider how we see ourselves and if we can accept how others see us.

Personal labelling is constructive; labelling others is not and is to be avoided. In doing personal reflection, descriptors, identifiers and labels are important. We heal our minds, and we acknowledge and build our identity. When relating to others, our ethical practice requires us to recognize their self-descriptors and to set aside any labels and descriptors we have in order to allow others to self-identify, re-identify and possibly transform. As a victim of physical violence in my past, I was a victim of my antagonist; in time I preferred to call myself a survivor. Now with the passage of more time and perspective, I'm glad to call myself "friend" to that person. I find being a friend a more peaceful and fulfilling relationship, achieved after forgiveness through a personal journey of restorative justice. In my personal pursuit of justice, I reflect on, consider and reconsider how I can prevent harm, engender healing and advance myself and others along this journey.

After practising law for almost two decades, I have learned that law is not the same as justice. This is partly due to the inability of the legal system to align with each of our personal labels. To illustrate, in many matrimonial disputes, each spouse identifies as the "victim" and views the other spouse as the "abuser." Both can't be correct, or can they? Canadian divorce and separation laws render these labels irrelevant (although many people experiencing divorce still argue about them). Similarly, in the criminal justice system, a victim isn't recognized as a "victim" until a successful conviction of the accused. Because the penalty of a criminal conviction is so severe — the loss of one's liberty — the criminal trial requires proof beyond a reasonable doubt of the guilt of the accused. Whether the "alleged" victim is a victim, survivor or warrior is not the concern of the criminal justice system, which is only concerned about a conviction or not. The issue with the legal system is that the act and timing of labelling are exercised by the system, not by the people whose lives are affected by it.

The gender and the equality chapters (8 and 12) provide examples of changes in the law and practices of law and are examples of justice. However, in the gender chapter, we see that practices that negatively affect gender-diverse youth still occur. Further, the women and injustice chapter (6) illustrates that our criminal justice system still negatively impacts women. Sometimes, it is easier to see what is fair by considering what is unfair and how to address it. Clearly, the individual acts advancing social justice documented in these chapters have had an important impact, but further work is yet to be done.

It is my hope as editor of this book that readers will be inspired to advance justice in our world. I'm not certain which exact practices, issues or activities are the most appropriate or urgent. However, I believe these chapters provide an accounting of where we have come from and where we need to go. Clearly, reconciliation with Indigenous peoples in Canada is a top priority. The practices and avenues of advancing justice will be as diverse as the readership of this book. My advice is to start with oneself, what one is passionate about and what most needs to be addressed in our world. We should only stop when we can answer the following questions in the affirmative: Have we achieved equality with our neighbours both locally and globally? Are marginalized peoples treated appropriately so that all people may flourish? Do our personal, city, provincial, state and international relations embody the ethical practices of restoring justice?

INDEX